MICHIGAN STATE UNIVERSITY

acg in ur
1966-67

Anxiety and Behavior

Edited by CHARLES D. SPIELBERGER

DEPARTMENT OF PSYCHOLOGY
VANDERBILT UNIVERSITY
NASHVILLE, TENNESSEE

1966

ACADEMIC PRESS New York and London

BF
575
. A6
S65

COPYRIGHT © 1966, BY ACADEMIC PRESS INC.
ALL RIGHTS RESERVED.
NO PART OF THIS BOOK MAY BE REPRODUCED IN ANY FORM,
BY PHOTOSTAT, MICROFILM, OR ANY OTHER MEANS, WITHOUT
WRITTEN PERMISSION FROM THE PUBLISHERS.

ACADEMIC PRESS INC.
111 Fifth Avenue, New York, New York 10003

United Kingdom Edition published by
ACADEMIC PRESS INC. (LONDON) LTD.
Berkeley Square House, London W.1

LIBRARY OF CONGRESS CATALOG CARD NUMBER: 66-14893

PRINTED IN THE UNITED STATES OF AMERICA

Anxiety and Behavior

CONTRIBUTORS TO THIS VOLUME

RAYMOND B. CATTELL
CHARLES W. ERIKSEN
ROY R. GRINKER, SR.
CARROLL E. IZARD
RICHARD S. LAZARUS
ROBERT B. MALMO
GEORGE MANDLER
O. HOBART MOWRER
EDWARD M. OPTON, JR.
SEYMOUR B. SARASON
STANLEY SCHACHTER
JANET TAYLOR SPENCE
KENNETH W. SPENCE
CHARLES D. SPIELBERGER
SILVAN S. TOMKINS
DAVID L. WATSON
JOSEPH WOLPE

institutional resources and their assistance in working out a mutually beneficial colloquium schedule. I am also grateful for the support and encouragement of Professors Jum C. Nunnally and Donald L. Thistle-thwaite who served, respectively, as Chairman of the Vanderbilt Department of Psychology during the planning of the colloquium series and at the time it was carried out. Thanks are also due to Professors Julius Seeman and Carroll E. Izard, Directors of the Clinical Training Programs at Peabody College and Vanderbilt University, and to the National Institute of Mental Health whose support of these programs provided funds which helped to defray the costs of the colloquium series.

For their invaluable assistance in arranging and coordinating the colloquium series, I express my gratitude to William F. Hodges, Larry D. Southard, and Mrs. Patricia Harris. I am also indebted to the graduate students and members of the faculties of Vanderbilt University and Peabody College who attended the colloquia and the informal sessions with our speakers for making them exciting learning experiences for all who participated. Finally, I am especially grateful to my wife, Adele, for her encouragement, generous assistance, and forbearance throughout this endeavor.

Permission to reprint materials from books or journals was kindly granted by the following publishers: American Association for the Advancement of Science; American Psychological Association; American Psychosomatic Society; Duke University Press; Harcourt, Brace & World, Inc.; Harper & Row, Publishers; Liverwright Publishing Corporation; McGraw-Hill, Inc.; Ronald Press; and Springer Publishing Company.

Bethesda, Maryland   CHARLES D. SPIELBERGER
March, 1966

Contents

LIST OF CONTRIBUTORS v

PREFACE vii

Part I.   INTRODUCTION

Chapter 1.   **Theory and Research on Anxiety** 3
      Charles D. Spielberger

Current Trends in Anxiety Research 5
Objective Anxiety (Fear) and Neurotic Anxiety 9
State Anxiety and Trait Anxiety 12
A Trait-State Conception of Anxiety 16
References 19

Part II.   THE NATURE AND MEASUREMENT OF ANXIETY

Chapter 2.   **Anxiety and Motivation: Theory and Crucial
            Experiments** 23
      Raymond B. Cattell

The Definition of Anxiety 23
Laws of Anxiety Change in Pathological and Other Fields 38
Anxiety and Personality Dynamics 46
Summary 58
References 59

Chapter 3. **The Measurement of Anxiety in Children:
Some Questions and Problems** 63

Seymour B. Sarason

Reservations About Anxiety Scales 64
The Concept of Defense 69
Some Suggestions Concerning the Interpretation of Anxiety Scales 74
References 79

Chapter 4. **Affect and Behavior: Anxiety as a Negative
Affect** 81

Carroll E. Izard and Silvan S. Tomkins

Affect and Personality 82
The Affect System as the Primary Motivational System.................... 87
Fear-Terror: Anxiety as an Affect 99
Summary 123
References 124

Part III. ANXIETY AND PSYCHOPATHOLOGY

Chapter 5. **The Psychosomatic Aspects of Anxiety** 129

Roy R. Grinker, Sr.

Observations of Anxiety in Men under Stress 129
Early Investigations of Anxiety 130
Anxiety and Stress 131
The Nature of Anxiety 133
Producing and Measuring Anxiety 134
Anxiety and Defense 138
The Etiology of Psychosomatic Disorders 139
References 140

Chapter 6. **The Basis of Psychopathology:
Malconditioning or Misbehavior?** 143

O. Hobart Mowrer

A New Conception of Emotional Disturbance 144
Choice, Responsibility, and Identity Crisis 147
Psychological Science, Ancient Wisdom—and Folly 152
References 155

Chapter 7. **Studies of Anxiety: Some Clinical Origins of the Activation Concept** 157

  Robert B. Malmo

Activation 158
Experiments with Psychiatric Patients Showing High Anxiety 162
Summary 176
References 176

Chapter 8. **The Conditioning and Deconditioning of Neurotic Anxiety** 179

  Joseph Wolpe

Experimental Neuroses .... 179 –
Human Neuroses as Learned Behavior .... 182 –
The Deconditioning of Neurotic Anxiety .... 182 –
Controlling Factors in the Conditioning and Deconditioning of Neurotic Anxiety
  Reactions .... 186 –
Results of Therapy of Neurosis on a Conditioning Theory 188
References 189

Part IV. THE DETERMINANTS OF ANXIETY

Chapter 9. **The Interaction of Cognitive and Physiological Determinants of Emotional State** 193

  Stanley Schachter

Introduction 193
Cognitive, Social and Physiological Determinants 197
Physiological Arousal and Emotionality 208
Sympathetic Activity and Emotionality in Rats 212
Discussion and Implications 213
Some Effects of Cognitive Factors on the Appraisal of Bodily States 220
References 223

Chapter 10. **The Study of Psychological Stress: A Summary of Theoretical Formulations and Experimental Findings** 225

  Richard S. Lazarus and Edward M. Opton, Jr.

The Theory of Psychological Stress 228
Methodological Advances 231
Psychodynamics of Stress 240
Concluding Statement 258
References 261

Chapter 11.   **Anxiety and the Interruption of Behavior**   263
         George Mandler and David L. Watson

Interruption Theory   264
Previous Studies on the Effects of Interruption   266
An Experiment on Substitute Behavior during Extinction   268
An Experiment on Choice and Anxiety   271
The Two Determinants of Anxiety   280
References   286

Part V.   THE EFFECTS OF ANXIETY ON BEHAVIOR

Chapter 12.   **The Motivational Components of Manifest
                Anxiety: Drive and Drive Stimuli**   291
         Janet Taylor Spence and Kenneth W. Spence

A Theory of Emotionally Based Drive (*D*) and Its Relation to Performance
   in Classical Aversive Conditioning   293
Extensions of the Theory of Emotionally Based Drive to Complex Learning
   Phenomena   299
Manifest Anxiety and the Response Interference Hypothesis   308
Conclusions   321
References   323

Chapter 13.   **Cognitive Responses to Internally Cued
                Anxiety**   327
         Charles W. Eriksen

Explanatory Accounts of Defensive Behavior   347
Unresolved Issues   355
References   357

Chapter 14.   **The Effects of Anxiety on Complex
                Learning and Academic Achievement**   361
         Charles D. Spielberger

Anxiety and Drive Theory   362
The Effects of Anxiety on Performance in Complex Learning Tasks   367
Implications for Drive Theory and Clinical Practice   392
Summary   395
References   396

AUTHOR INDEX   399

SUBJECT INDEX   406

Anxiety and Behavior

Part I
INTRODUCTION

CHAPTER 1

Theory and Research on Anxiety[1]

Charles D. Spielberger

DEPARTMENT OF PSYCHOLOGY,
VANDERBILT UNIVERSITY,
NASHVILLE, TENNESSEE

The importance of anxiety as a powerful influence in contemporary life is increasingly recognized, and manifestations of current concern with anxiety phenomena are ubiquitously reflected in literature, the arts, science, and religion as well as in many other facets of our culture. Consider, for example, the following passage from a popular periodical[2]: "Anxiety seems to be the dominant fact—and is threatening to become the dominant cliché—of modern life. It shouts in the headlines, laughs nervously at cocktail parties, nags from advertisements, speaks suavely in the board room, whines from the stage, clatters from the Wall Street ticker, jokes with fake youthfulness on the golf course and whispers in privacy each day before the shaving mirror and the dressing table. Not merely the black statistics of murder, suicide, alcoholism and divorce betray anxiety (or that special form of anxiety which is guilt), but almost any innocent, everyday act:

---

[1] Work on this chapter was facilitated by a grant (HD 947) from the National Institute of Child Health and Human Development, United States Public Health Service. I am indebted to students and colleagues at Duke University and Vanderbilt University for their critical comments and helpful suggestions concerning a number of the ideas that are expressed herein, and particularly to Drs. L. Douglas DeNike, J. Peter Denny, Richard L. Gorsuch, Dale T. Johnson, and Edward S. Katkin, and to William F. Hodges, Kay Howard, Opal Purdue, Lou Hicks Smith, and Larry D. Southard.

[2] *Time,* March 31, 1961, p. 44.

the limp or overhearty handshake, the second pack of cigarettes or the third martini, the forgotten appointment, the stammer in mid-sentence, the wasted hour before the TV set, the spanked child, the new car unpaid for."

In the behavioral and medical sciences, theoretical and empirical interest in anxiety parallels the popular concern. Anxiety is found as a central explanatory concept in almost all contemporary theories of personality, and it is regarded as a principal causative agent for such diverse behavioral consequences as insomnia, immoral and sinful acts, instances of creative self-expression, debilitating psychological and psychosomatic symptoms, and idiosyncratic mannerisms of endless variety. Empirical research on anxiety has increased dramatically in the past 2 decades, as will be documented below. Much of this research has centered around investigations of learning and perception, indicating that anxiety phenomena have become more than just the concern of the clinician and the personality theorist.

While fear and covert anxiety have perhaps always been a part of man's lot, apparently not until the twentieth century did anxiety emerge as an explicit and pervasive problem. May (1950), in his book *The Meaning of Anxiety,* presents a penetrating analysis of basic historical and cultural trends in Western civilization that have contributed to making *overt* anxiety a salient characteristic of our times. The cold war with its persistent threat of total destruction in an atomic age, the pressure for social change attendant upon rapid scientific and technological advances, the social estrangement and alienation of individuals in an urban, competitive society are but a few examples of the sorts of stresses that serve to induce feelings of helplessness and impotence in modern man. To the extent that social and cultural factors undermine personal security and create problems for the individual in establishing his psychological identity, there will be heightened vulnerability to and increased manifestations of— anxiety.

In 1950, Hoch and Zubin introduced a symposium sponsored by the American Psychopathological Association with the following statement: "Although it is widely recognized that anxiety is the most pervasive psychological phenomenon of our time and that it is the chief symptom in the neuroses and in the functional psychoses, there has been little or no agreement on its definition, and very little, if any, progress in its measurement" (1950, p. v). In the past 15 years, theory and research on anxiety have proliferated but this has not led to a consistent body of empirical findings, or to convergence among theoretical interpretations. The present volume seeks to facilitate a more comprehensive understanding of the nature of anxiety and its effects on behavior by bringing together the current views of psychologists and psychiatrists whose previous work and thought in this area are already well known.

The professional training and experience of the contributors to *Anxiety and Behavior* vary widely, and each approaches the problem of anxiety with his own unique theoretical perspective and research objectives. While a meaningful synthesis of these diverse views is not yet possible, we will attempt in this introductory chapter to provide some background on relevant dimensions of the problem. First, publication trends in the anxiety literature will be surveyed and important contributions to this literature will be noted. Next, the concepts of objective anxiety (fear) and neurotic anxiety as these are used in psychoanalytic theory will be reviewed, and the concepts of trait and state anxiety as explicated in psychological research will be examined. A trait-state conception of anxiety will then be proposed as a conceptual frame of reference for viewing research and theory on anxiey.

Current Trends in Anxiety Research

Since Freud's conceptualization of anxiety-neurosis in 1894 as a discrete clinical syndrome to be distinguished from neurasthenia, clinical studies of anxiety have appeared in the psychiatric literature with increasing regularity. Similarly, following Pavlov's (1927) discovery of experimental neurosis over a half-century ago, there have been numerous experimental investigations of fear, frustration, and conflict in animals of which Liddell's sheep (1944), Gantt's dogs (1942), Masserman's cats (1943), and the rat studies of Miller (1948) and Mowrer (1940) are perhaps best known. But, prior to 1950, there was relatively little experimental work on human anxiety. Indeed, according to May (1950), anxiety was not even listed in the indexes of psychological books written before the late 1930's, except in the work of psychoanalytic writers.

Real dangers and ethical problems associated with inducing anxiety in the laboratory led May to conclude that intensive case studies of individuals in crisis situations would provide the most likely path toward a better understanding of human anxiety, and he quotes Mowrer as remarking, ". . . there is at present no experimental psychology of anxiety, and one may even doubt whether there will ever be" (May, 1950, p. 99). This prophecy proved false, however, at least in so far as the appearance of the term "anxiety" in the research literature was concerned. Since 1950 more than 1500 studies have been indexed under the heading "anxiety" in

Psychological Abstracts.[3] The mean number of anxiety entries per year for each 4-year period between 1928 and 1963 is indicated in the left-hand portion of Fig. 1, along with comparable data for the combined entries indexed under the categories "fear" and "phobia." The percentages of anxiety and fear-and-phobia entries per year relative to the total number of annual entries in *Psychological Abstracts* are given in the right-hand portion of Fig. 1. The latter categories represent content areas closely re-

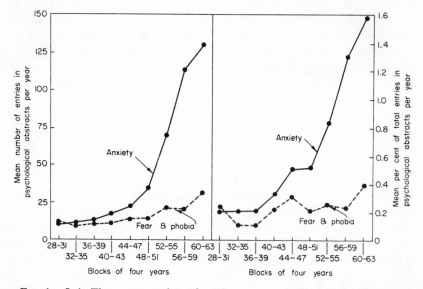

FIG. 1. *Left.* The mean number of entries per year indexed under the heading "anxiety" in *Psychological Abstracts* during the years 1928–1963. *Right.* The corresponding mean percent of "anxiety" entries to total entries during this time, compared with similar data obtained for the combined entries for the categories "fear" and "phobia."

lated to anxiety and were selected for comparison purposes in order to evaluate general trends in psychological research on clinical phenomena.

In 1928–1931 the output of research on anxiety was approximately equal to that on fear and phobia combined, as may be noted in Fig. 1, and

---

[3] During this same period, over 2500 studies were indexed under "anxiety" or "anxiety neurosis" in *Index Medicus* and *Excerpta Medica*. Of these, only 700 studies were also included in the *Psychological Abstracts*. Thus, since 1950, there have been over 3500 articles or books related to anxiety. I am indebted to Julia M. Johnson, Susan Meredith, Mary Carden, and Leonard Oberlander for their assistance in obtaining this information.

each of these categories constituted only about .2% of the abstracted psychological literature. By the late 1930's the publication rate for research on anxiety began to exceed that for fear and phobia and, by mid-century, the curves were diverging rapidly. In 1960–1963 the number of anxiety studies reported in *Psychological Abstracts* was ten times what it had been in 1930, and the ratio of anxiety entries to those for fear and phobia was greater than four to one. The percentage of anxiety studies in 1960–1963 had increased eightfold over what it had been 30 years earlier.

How can we account for this prodigious upsurge in research on anxiety? Since the percentage curves in Fig. 1 show the same relative relationships as the raw data curves, the increased output in number of anxiety studies cannot be interpreted as merely reflecting a larger total number of psychological publications. Nor can the observed research trends be explained simply by the fact that the proportion of psychologists with clinical training and interests has grown significantly since World War II. Presumably fear and phobia are areas of concern for clinical psychologists, and the number of studies on these topics, although somewhat higher than in the past, has clearly not kept pace with the marked rise in research on anxiety. Furthermore, since 1950, investigations bearing the term "anxiety" in their titles appeared in the *Journal of Experimental Psychology* almost as frequently as in the *Journal of Consulting Psychology*.

Perhaps, as suggested by Levy (1961), the research trends depicted in Fig. 1 reflect the availability of instruments and techniques for measuring anxiety rather than psychologists' interests in the problem of anxiety. With tongue in cheek, Levy makes his case by pointing to the initial appearance of the Manifest Anxiety Scale (Taylor, 1951) in the psychological literature and the corresponding rise the following year in number of entries indexed under "anxiety" in *Psychological Abstracts*. As further evidence that the research behavior of the behavior scientist was technique controlled rather than problem oriented, Levy notes that the number of entries indexed under "anxiety" in *Child Development Abstracts* showed a substantial increase the year following the appearance of the Children's Manifest Anxiety Scale (Castaneda, McCandless, & Palermo, 1956).

But Levy's argument ignores the fact that the development of instruments and techniques for measuring anxiety has mirrored the enlarged output of research on anxiety phenomena. In reviewing the anxiety literature, Cattell and Scheier report that they "counted more than 120 personality-type tests which have been claimed to measure anxiety" (1958, p. 352). And these investigators have used as many as 325 *different* variables presumed to relate to some aspect of anxiety in their own factor analytic studies. Thus, it would seem that the research activity of behavior scientists, as reflected in both the techniques they use and the problems they study, represents yet another manifestation of the *Zeitgeist* of interest in anxiety described by May (1950). Palpable and significant early landmarks in this *Zeitgeist* that have influenced empirical work on human anxiety include the recasting of Freud's theoretical views into stimulus-response terminology by Mowrer (1939) and the classic studies of *Men Under Stress* by Grinker and Spiegel (1945).

The publication in 1950 of four important books—May's *The Meaning of Anxiety,* Mowrer's *Learning Theory and Personality Dynamics,* the multi-authored volume, *Anxiety,* edited by Hoch and Zubin, and Dollard & Miller's *Personality and Psychotherapy*—undoubtedly served to stimulate experimental work on anxiety. These books provided clear explications of anxiety theory in terminology that was familiar to psychologists and made available concise evaluative summaries of the relevant research literature. Other important book-length contributions that have had significant impact on anxiety research include: *Anxiety and Stress* (Basowitz, Persky, Korchin, & Grinker, 1955); *The Dynamics of Anxiety and Hysteria* (Eysenck, 1957); *Psychological Stress* (Janis, 1958); *Anxiety in Elementary School Children* (S. B. Sarason, Davidson, Lighthall, Waite, & Ruebush, 1960); and *The Meaning and Measurement of Neuroticism and Anxiety* (Cattell & Scheier, 1961).

The sheer volume of empirical research on anxiety precludes any attempt to summarize it here, but selective reviews of important segments of this literature are available. The 1950 evaluation by Hanfmann of psychological methods used in the study of anxiety is still timely and meaningful. Critical reviews of research on psychological stress (Haggard, 1949; Lazarus, Deese, & Osler, 1952) contain much that is relevant to the investigation of anxiety since anxiety is generally regarded as a product of stress and a mediator of its influence on behavior. Articles by Spence (1958) and Taylor (1956) provide comprehensive statements of a theory of emotionally based drive that has guided a large percentage of the investigations of the effects of anxiety on learning, and the latter contains an excellent summary of early research in this area. Malmo (1957) has analyzed the relation between anxiety and physiological activation or arousal, and problems associated with the measurement of transitory anxiety have been discussed by Krause (1961). I. G. Sarason (1960) has examined theoretical issues and empirical findings emanating from the use of anxiety scales, and the research literature on the assessment of anxiety with physiological and behavioral measures has been critically reviewed by Martin (1961).

Objective Anxiety (Fear) and Neurotic Anxiety

Although contemporary interest in anxiety phenomena has historical roots in the philosophical and theological views of Pascal and Kierkegaard (May, 1950), it was Freud who first attempted to explicate the meaning of anxiety within the context of psychological theory. He regarded anxiety as "something felt," an unpleasant affective *state* or condition. This state, as observed in patients with anxiety-neurosis, was characterized by "all that is covered by the word 'nervousness'," apprehension or anxious expectation, and efferent discharge phenomena (Freud, 1924). Specific symptoms of the latter included heart palpitation (transitory arythmia, tachycardia), disturbances of respiration ("nervous dyspnoea"), sweating, tremor and shuddering, vertigo, and numerous other physiological and behavioral manifestations.

Anxiety was distinguishable from other unpleasant affective (emotional) states such as anger, grief, or sorrow by its unique combination of phenomenological and physiological qualities. These gave to anxiety a special "character of unpleasure" which, although difficult to describe, seemed "to possess a particular note of its own" (Freud, 1936, p. 69). The subjective, phenomenological qualities of anxiety—the feelings of apprehensive expectation or dread—were emphasized by Freud, especially in his later formulations, while the physiological-behavioral (efferent) discharge phenomena, although considered an essential part of the anxiety state and an important contributor to its unpleasantness, were of little theoretical interest to him. Freud was mainly concerned with identifying the sources of stimulation which precipitated anxiety rather than with analyzing the properties of such states; he hoped to discover, in prior experience, "the historical element . . . which binds the afferent and efferent elements of anxiety firmly together" (1936, p. 70).

In his early theoretical formulations, Freud believed that anxiety resulted from the discharge of repressed, unrelieved somatic sexual tensions (libido). He held that when libidinal excitation produced mental images (lustful ideas) that were perceived as dangerous, these ideas were repressed. The libidinal energy, thus blocked from normal expression, accumulated and was automatically transformed into anxiety, or into symptoms that were anxiety equivalents. Freud later modified this view in favor of a more general conceptualization of anxiety in which its functional utility to the ego was emphasized. He conceived of anxiety as a signal indicating the presence of a danger situation and differentiated between objective anxiety and neurotic anxiety largely on the basis of whether the source of the danger was from the external world or from internal impulses.

Objective anxiety, which was regarded by Freud as synonymous with fear, involved a complex internal reaction to anticipated injury or harm from some external danger. A real danger situation existed in the external world, was consciously perceived as threatening, and this perception of danger evoked an anxiety reaction. Thus:

$$\text{external danger} \longrightarrow \text{perception of danger} \longrightarrow \text{objective anxiety}$$

With objective anxiety, the intensity of the anxiety reaction was proportional to the magnitude of the external danger that evoked it: the greater the external danger, the stronger the perceived threat, the more intense the resulting reaction. The unpleasantness of the anxiety reaction, coupled with cues provided by the perception of its source, was generally sufficient to mobilize an individual either to flee the danger situation or in some way to protect himself from it.

Neurotic anxiety, like objective anxiety, was characterized by feelings of apprehension and physiological arousal. But neurotic anxiety differed from objective anxiety in that the source of the danger that evoked this reaction was internal rather than external, and this source was not consciously perceived because it had been repressed. In essence, neurotic anxiety was the historical product of an aversive conditioning process (Mowrer, 1939) involving instinctual impulses and repression, and commonly occurring in childhood. The etiology of neurotic anxiety entailed: (1) the expression of aggressive or sexual impulses for which the child was strongly and consistently punished (external danger); (2) the evocation of objective anxiety, i.e., the apprehensive expectation of punishment, by cues associated with the forbidden impulses when these were later experienced; (3) an attempt to alleviate or reduce objective anxiety by repressing (banishing from awareness) those stimuli associated with the punished impulses that elicited this unpleasant reaction; and (4) the evocation of neurotic anxiety when a partial breakdown in repression results in "derivatives" of repressed impulses (internal stimuli) erupting into awareness. Thus:

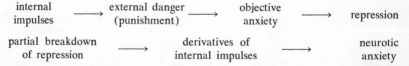

Since most of the cues associated with the punished impulses remained repressed, neurotic anxiety was experienced as "objectless," or, as in the case of phobias, the relationship between the object that was feared and the original danger situation was not recognized.

Neurotic anxiety, according to Freud, was experienced by everyone to some extent, from time to time, but when manifested in pathological amounts, it defined the clinical syndrome, anxiety-neurosis. Anxiety was the "fundamental phenomenon and the central problem of neurosis" (1936, p. 85), and understanding anxiety was considered "the most difficult task that has been set us," a task whose solution required "the introduction of the right abstract ideas, and of their application to the raw material of observation so as to bring order and lucidity into it" (1933, p. 113). Both the complexity of this task and Freud's personal commitment to it were reflected in the fact that his theoretical views on the subject of anxiety evolved over a period of nearly 50 years, were continually modified, and were never regarded as complete.

Other personality theorists have since joined the search for the "right abstract ideas" with which to illuminate and clarify anxiety phenomena, but order and lucidity have not resulted. Lack of agreement regarding the nature of anxiety, the particular stimulus conditions that arouse it, and the sorts of past experiences that make individuals more or less vulnerable to it, is the rule rather than the exception. Consider, for example, the differences among the concepts of anxiety advanced by Mowrer (1950), Sullivan (1953), and May (1950):

1. As an alternative to Freud's "impulse theory" of anxiety, Mowrer has proposed a "guilt theory" in which it is contended that ". . . anxiety comes, not from acts which the individual would commit but dares not, but from acts which he has committed but wishes that he had not" (1950, p. 537). Thus, neurotic anxiety results from the repudiation of the demands of the conscience, not the instincts, from repression that has been turned toward the superego rather than the id.[4] If one behaves irresponsibly, with too much self-indulgence and too little self-restraint, then anxiety is experienced (see Mowrer, this volume, Ch. 6).

2. For Sullivan, anxiety was an intensely unpleasant state of tension arising from experiencing disapproval in interpersonal relations. Through an empathic linkage between an infant and its mother, "The tension of anxiety, when present in the mothering one, induces anxiety in the infant" (Sullivan, 1953, p. 41). Once aroused, anxiety distorts the individual's perception of reality, limits the range of stimuli that are perceived, and causes those aspects of the personality that are disapproved to be dissociated.

3. According to May, anxiety was "the apprehension cued off by a

---

[4] Freud, too, identified a form of "moral anxiety," experienced as shame or guilt, as arising from the superego, but he differentiated moral anxiety from neurotic anxiety.

threat to some value which the individual holds essential to his existence as a personality" (1950, p. 191). While the capacity to experience anxiety was innate, the particular events or stimulus conditions which evoked it were largely determined by learning. An anxiety reaction was *normal* if it was proportionate to the objective danger and did not involve repression or other defense mechanisms. Neurotic anxiety reactions were disproportionate to the objective danger (but not the subjective danger) and involved repression and neurotic defenses. Fear was a learned response to a localized danger which did not constitute a threat to the basic values of the individual.

What is the nature of anxiety? Is anxiety innate or learned? What basis is there for differentiating between anxiety and fear? Between anxiety and guilt? How many different kinds of anxiety can be identified, and by what operational criteria may these be distinguished? What sorts of stimulus conditions elicit anxiety, and do these differ for different kinds of anxiety? Is it meaningful to speak of *conscious* and *unconscious* anxiety? Of *bound* and *free-floating* anxiety? The answers to such questions will differ depending upon one's theoretical conception of anxiety, and this, in turn, will determine the inferences and the operations which give anxiety empirical meaning in the clinic and the laboratory. Given the conceptual ambiguities in anxiety theory, it is perhaps not surprising that anxiety research is characterized by semantic confusion and contradictory findings.

State Anxiety and Trait Anxiety

Ambiguity in the conceptual status of anxiety arises from the more or less indiscriminate use of the term to refer to two very different types of concepts. Anxiety is perhaps most commonly used in an empirical sense to denote a complex reaction or response—a transitory state or condition of the organism that varies in intensity and fluctuates over time. But the term anxiety is also used to refer to a personality trait—to individual differences in the extent to which different people are characterized by anxiety states and by prominent defenses against such states. For example, consider the statement: "Mr. Smith is anxious." This may be interpreted as meaning either that Smith is anxious *now* or that Smith is an *anxious person*. If the statement is meant to imply that Smith is anxious now, at this very moment, then the validity of the statement may be ascertained by making appropriate measurements to determine whether or not Smith is manifesting (experiencing) a particular state with specifiable properties. On the other hand, if the statement is intended to signify that Smith is an anxious person, the same measurements should reveal that Smith's level of state anxiety is *chronically* higher than that of most other people, as would be the case if he were suffering from anxiety-neurosis.

Empirical evidence of different types of anxiety concepts has emerged from the factor analytic studies of Cattell and Scheier (1958; 1961). These investigators identified two distinct anxiety factors which they labeled *trait anxiety* and *state anxiety* on the basis of the procedures by which these factors were isolated and the variables which loaded on them (see Cattell, this volume, Ch. 2). The trait anxiety factor was interpreted as measuring stable individual differences in a unitary, relatively permanent personality characteristic. The state anxiety factor was based on a pattern of variables that covaried over occasions of measurement, defining a transitory state or condition of the organism which fluctuated over time. Component characterological variables that loaded the trait anxiety factor included: "ergic tension," "ego weakness," "guilt proneness," "suspiciousness," and "tendency to embarrassment" (1961, pp. 57 and 182); anxiety neurotics obtained high scores on this factor. Physiological variables such as respiration rate and systolic blood pressure markedly loaded the state anxiety factor, but had only slight loadings on trait anxiety (1961, p. 82). Thus, if Smith were anxious *now,* he would presumably score high on Cattell and Scheier's state anxiety factor, and if he were characterologically or chronically anxious, it is probable that his trait anxiety score would also be elevated.

ANXIETY AS A TRANSITORY STATE

Most empirical work on transitory anxiety has been concerned with delineating the properties of the anxiety state and identifying the stimulus conditions which evoke it. After reviewing the psychological and psychiatric literature, Krause (1961) concluded that transitory anxiety is conventionally inferred from six different types of evidence: introspective reports, physiological signs, "molar" behavior (e.g., body posture, gesturing, speech characteristics), task performance, clinical intuition, and the response to stress. Of these, according to conventional usage, introspective reports provide the most widely accepted basis for inferring transitory anxiety. For example, Basowitz et al. (1955, p. 3) define anxiety as "the conscious and reportable experience of intense dread and foreboding, conceptualized as internally derived and unrelated to external threat" (see Grinker, this volume, Ch. 5). In other words, to report that one feels "anxious" is to be anxious, provided of course that the subject is capable of distinguishing between different feeling states and is motivated to report accurately and honestly.

As a check upon the honesty of introspective reporting, Krause recommends measuring physiological signs or, to use his terminology, adrenosympathetic (a-s) activation. He questions, however, the evidential sufficiency of physiological measures, molar behavior, task performance, or clinical intuition as independent criteria for defining (inferring) transitory anxiety unless used in conjunction with introspective reports. Thus, some combination of introspective reports and physiological-behavioral signs would seem to be required in order to define unambiguously the presence of anxiety states in humans (see Lazarus & Opton, this volume, Ch. 10). Schachter and Singer (1962) provide impressive evidence that emotional states consist of two factors: physiological arousal and socially determined cognitions. The latter lead the individual to describe his feelings with particular emotional labels and provide the basis for his introspective reports about them (see Schachter, this volume, Ch. 9).

With regard to the convention of defining transitory anxiety in terms of response to stress, Krause (1961) reasons that, in the absence of introspective or physical criteria, this logically requires the identification of stressor stimuli on grounds other than the anxiety response itself. But responses of individual subjects to various stressors are known to be highly idiosyncratic, due in part to the fact that the anxiety response is readily conditioned to stimuli with which it is associated (see Wolpe, this volume, Ch. 8). Consequently, the response to a particular stressor stimulus will depend on an individual's previous experience, and any stimulus can have anxiety-producing effects if it is interpreted as threatening or dangerous, irrespective of the real danger involved. Nevertheless, it is important to determine classes of stimuli or situations (stressors) that are likely to induce anxiety states (see Mandler & Watson, this volume, Ch. 11), and to distinguish these from stimuli that are unlikely to evoke anxiety (Basowitz et al., 1955, pp. 7-9). Both types of stimuli are required in anxiety research (Krause, 1961).

Martin (1961) proposes that anxiety should be defined as a complex pattern of response and should be distinguished conceptually and operationally from the external or internal stimuli which elicit it. This approach dispenses with the traditional, stimulus-defined difference between fear as a response to a real external danger and anxiety as a reaction to some unknown threat, and emphasizes the importance of identifying and measuring the observable physiological and behavioral response patterns which distinguish anxiety (fear) from other emotional states. (For a theoretical discussion of differences between anxiety and other negative affects, see Izard & Tomkins, this volume, Ch. 4.) Martin also maintains that anxiety reactions should not be confused with "defenses" against anxiety, i.e., the reactions that have been learned in order to eliminate or mitigate anxiety states (see Eriksen, this volume, Ch. 13). This would seem to be especially important in research on older children and adults since persons characterized by chronic anxiety tend to develop a host of mechanisms or symptoms which help them to avoid unpleasant anxiety states (see S. B. Sarason, this volume, Ch. 3).

In sum, research on anxiety phenomena would seem to require that anxiety reactions or states be operationally and conceptually distinguished from the stimulus conditions that arouse them and the cognitive and behavioral maneuvers that are learned because they lead to anxiety reduction. It would appear that research on anxiety also requires that a distinction be made between anxiety as a transitory state that fluctuates over time and as a personality trait that remains relatively stable over time.

ANXIETY AS A PERSONALITY TRAIT

Experimental work relevant to the concept of trait anxiety has been concerned primarily with investigating differences between groups of subjects who are presumed to differ in anxiety level. One research strategy involves the selection of patient groups characterized by high levels of chronic anxiety and comparing them with normal control groups under stressful and nonstressful conditions. Using this approach, Malmo (1950; 1957) and his colleagues have concluded that patient groups characterized by high levels of chronic anxiety show greater reactivity and wider variability than normals on many different physiological and behavioral measures, irrespective of the stress situation (see Malmo, this volume, Ch. 7).

Trait anxiety has also been investigated in studies in which subjects who are presumed to differ in anxiety level are selected from normal populations (Spence, 1958; Taylor, 1956), typically on the basis of extreme scores on a personality questionnaire such as the Taylor (1953) Manifest Anxiety Scale (MAS).[5] The performance of high anxious and low anxious subjects are then compared on a variety of learning tasks (see Spence & Spence, this volume, Ch. 12; Spielberger, this volume, Ch. 14). It was at first generally assumed that subjects with high scores on the MAS were chronically more anxious or emotionally responsive than those with low MAS scores. Recent findings have suggested, however, that subjects with high MAS scores react with higher anxiety levels in situations that contain some degree of stress, but not in the absence of stress (e.g., Spence, 1964; Spielberger & Smith, 1966).

Such findings suggest that trait anxiety measures reflect anxiety-proneness—differences between individuals in the probability that anxiety states will be manifested under circumstances involving varying degrees of stress.

---

[5] The MAS, a self-report inventory which inquires about anxiety symptoms, has been found to correlate .85 with Cattell and Scheier's trait-anxiety factor (1961).

Thus, if Smith has an elevated trait-anxiety score, he is generally more disposed than the average person to respond with state anxiety, and, unless Smith lives in a very sheltered environment, he is likely to experience anxiety states more often than other people. It should be noted, however, that although Smith may be more disposed to react with anxiety states than other people, he may or may not be anxious *now,* and this will largely depend on whether or not he interprets his present circumstances as dangerous or threatening. While persons with extreme trait anxiety, such as acute, incipient schizophrenics and anxiety neurotics, are characterized by state anxiety much of the time, even they have defenses against anxiety that occasionally leave them relatively free of it. We have observed clinically that when such persons are occupied with a nonthreatening task as, for example, a noncompetitive but absorbing game, they may be diverted for a time from the internal stimuli that otherwise constantly cue state anxiety responses.

As a concept, trait anxiety appears to have the characteristics of a class of constructs which Campbell (1963) has called *acquired behavioral dispositions,* and which Atkinson (1964) labels *motives.* According to Campbell, acquired dispositional concepts, e.g., social attitudes, involve residues of past experience that predispose an individual *both* to view the world in a particular way and to manifest "object-consistent" response tendencies. Atkinson regards motives such as need-achievement as dispositional tendencies acquired in childhood which are latent until the cues of a situation arouse them. As an acquired behavioral disposition or motive, trait anxiety would seem to imply, on the one hand, a view of the world in which a wide range of stimulus situations are perceived as dangerous or threatening and, on the other hand, a tendency to respond to such threats with state anxiety reactions. The relation between state and trait anxiety may be conceived of as analogous in certain respects to the relation between the physical concepts of kinetic and potential energy. State anxiety, like kinetic energy, refers to an empirical process or reaction which is taking place *now* at a given level of intensity. Trait anxiety, like potential energy, indicates a latent disposition for a reaction of a certain type to occur if it is triggered by appropriate (sufficiently stressful) stimuli.

A Trait-State Conception of Anxiety

Research findings suggest that it is meaningful to distinguish between anxiety as a transitory state and as a relatively stable personality trait, and to differentiate between anxiety states, the stimulus conditions that evoke them, and the defenses that serve to avoid them. There is considerable general agreement that anxiety states (A-states) are characterized by subjective, consciously perceived feelings of apprehension and tension, accompanied by or associated with activation or arousal of the autonomic nervous sytem. Anxiety as a personality trait (A-trait) would seem to imply a motive or acquired behavioral disposition that predisposes an individual to perceive a wide range of objectively nondangerous circumstances as threatening, and to respond to these with A-state reactions disproportionate in intensity to the magnitude of the objective danger.

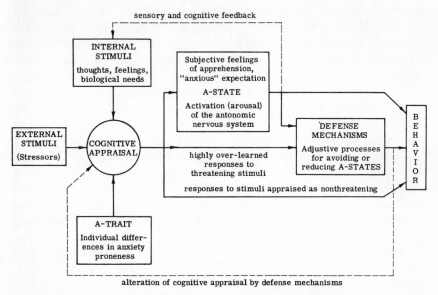

FIG. 2. A trait-state conception of anxiety in which two anxiety concepts, A-trait and A-state, are posited and conceptually distinguished from the stimulus conditions which evoke A-state reactions and the defenses against A-states. It is hypothesized that the arousal of A-states involves a sequence of temporally ordered events in which a stimulus that is cognitively appraised as dangerous evokes an A-state reaction. This A-state reaction may then initiate a behavior sequence designed to avoid the danger situation, or it may evoke defensive maneuvers which alter the cognitive appraisal of the situation. Individual differences in A-trait determine the particular stimuli that are cognitively appraised as threatening.

In Fig. 2, a trait-state conception of anxiety is proposed which postulates two anxiety concepts, A-trait and A-state. This conception is not presented as a theory of anxiety, but rather as a means of clarifying the concepts of A-trait and A-state and as a conceptual framework for viewing theory and research on anxiety phenomena. Factors believed to be important in anxiety research are schematically represented and possible interrelationships among them are indicated. As may be noted in Fig. 2,

A-trait and A-state are conceived of as independent of the threatening stimuli which evoke A-states and the defensive processes which are used to avoid them.

In essence, it is proposed that the arousal of A-states involves a process or sequence of temporally ordered events. This process may be initiated by an external stimulus, such as, for example, the threat of an electric shock in a laboratory experiment, or an internal cue—a thought or sensory representation of muscular or visceral activity associated with "feeling angry." If the stimulus situation is cognitively appraised as dangerous or threatening (see Lazarus & Opton, this volume, Ch. 10), then an A-state reaction is evoked. Through sensory and cognitive feedback mechanisms, the A-state reaction may serve as a signal that initiates a behavior sequence designed to avoid or otherwise deal directly with the danger situation. The A-state may also activate cognitive or motoric defensive processes that have been effective in the past in reducing A-states by altering the cognitive appraisal of the danger situation (see Eriksen, this volume, Ch. 13). For example, an undergraduate subject in a psychology experiment may "deny" that the experimenter is really going to shock him, or "intellectualize" ("rationalize") that if he is shocked it won't hurt him because college officials would not permit this. The subject, in effect, reappraises the danger situation and finds it less threatening, resulting in a reduction in level of A-state.

A-trait is assumed to reflect residues of past experience that in some way determine individual differences in anxiety-proneness, i.e., in the disposition to see certain types of situations as dangerous and to respond to them with A-states. Those experiences that have most influence on level of A-trait probably date back to childhood, involving parent-child relationships centering around punishment situations. Level of A-trait is not expected to influence A-state response to all stimuli, only to particular classes of stimuli. Stimuli that have little or no threat value obviously would not be expected to elicit an A-state response. On the other hand, the threat of an objectively painful stimulus, like an electric shock, may be sufficiently general so that most subjects will respond with higher levels of A-state, irrespective of their level of A-trait. For such stimuli, however, individual differences in A-state reaction may vary as a function of other acquired behavioral dispositions. It has been observed, for example, that threat of electric shock produces significant increments in A-state that are unrelated to level of A-trait (Katkin, 1965), but which are markedly correlated with fear of shock (Hodges & Spielberger, 1966).

From the standpoint of a trait-state conception of anxiety, the most important stimuli are those which produce differential changes in A-state in individuals who differ in A-trait. There is as yet little experimental evidence that bears directly on the identification of such stimuli, since most experimental investigations of anxiety have been concerned either with A-trait or with A-state, but rarely with both. However, differences in the task performance of high and low A-trait individuals are most often found under conditions of failure or ego-involvement (see Spence & Spence, this volume, Ch. 13), or under circumstances which involve risk of failure such as that found in academic achievement situations (Mandler & Sarason, 1952; Spielberger, 1962). It may be speculated that A-trait involves a "fear of failure" motive as has been suggested by Atkinson (1964).

REFERENCES

Atkinson, J. W. *An introduction to motivation.* Princeton, N. J.: Van Nostrand, 1964.

Basowitz, H., Persky, H., Korchin, S. J., & Grinker, R. R. *Anxiety and stress.* New York: McGraw-Hill, 1955.

Campbell, D. T. Social attitudes and other acquired behavioral dispositions. In S. Koch (Ed.), *Psychology: a study of a science.* New York: McGraw-Hill, 1963. Vol. 6.

Castaneda, A., McCandless, B. R., & Palermo, D. S. The children's form of the manifest anxiety scale. *Child Develpm.,* 1956, **27**, 317-326.

Cattell, R. B., & Scheier, I. H. The nature of anxiety: a review of thirteen multivariate analyses comprising 814 variables. *Psychol. Rep.* 1958, **4**, 351-388.

Cattell, R. B., & Scheier, I. H. *The meaning and measurement of neuroticism and anxiety.* New York: Ronald Press, 1961.

Dollard, J., & Miller, N. E. *Personality and psychotherapy.* New York: McGraw-Hill, 1950.

Eysenck, H. J. *The dynamics of anxiety and hysteria.* London: Routledge & Kegan, 1957.

Freud, S. *Collected papers.* London: Hogarth Press, 1924. Vol. 1.

Freud, S. *New introductory lectures in psychoanalysis.* New York: Norton, 1933.

Freud, S. *The problem of anxiety.* New York: Norton, 1936.

Gantt, W. H. The origin and development of nervous disturbances experimentally produced. *Amer. J. Psychiat.,* 1942, **98**, 475-481.

Grinker, R. R., & Spiegel, J. P. *Men under stress.* Philadelphia: Blakiston, 1945.

Haggard, E. A. Psychological causes and results of stress. In *A survey report on human factors in undersea warfare.* Washington, D. C.: National Research Council, 1949.

Hanfmann, Eugenia. Psychological approaches to the study of anxiety. In P. H. Hoch & J. Zubin (Eds.), *Anxiety.* New York: Grune & Stratton, 1950. Pp. 51-69.

Hoch, P. H., & Zubin, J. (Eds.). *Anxiety.* New York: Grune & Stratton, 1950.

Hodges, W. F., & Spielberger, C. D. The effects of shock on heart rate for subjects who differ in manifest anxiety and fear of shock. *Psychophysiol.,* 1966, in press.

Janis, I. L. *Psychological stress.* New York: Wiley, 1958.

Katkin, E. S. Relationship between manifest anxiety and two indices of autonomic response to stress. *J. Pers. soc. Psychol.,* 1965, **2**, 324-333.

Krause, M. S. The measurement of transitory anxiety. *Psychol. Rev.,* 1961, **68**, 178-189.

Lazarus, R. S., Deese, J., & Osler, Sonia F. The effects of psychological stress upon performance. *Psychol. Bull.*, 1952, **49**, 293-317.

Levy, L. H. Anxiety and behavior scientist's behavior. *Amer. Psychologist*, 1961, **16**, 66-68.

Liddell, H. S. Conditioned reflex method and experimental neurosis. In J. McV. Hunt (Ed.), *Personality and the behavior disorders.* New York: Ronald Press, 1944. Pp. 389-412.

Malmo, R. B. Experimental studies of mental patients under stress. In M. Reymert (Ed.), *Feelings and emotions.* New York: McGraw-Hill, 1950. Pp. 169-180.

Malmo, R. B. Anxiety and behavioral arousal. *Psychol. Rev.*, 1957, **64**, 276-287.

Mandler, G., & Sarason, S. B. A study of anxiety and learning. *J. abnorm. soc. Psychol.*, 1952, **47**, 166-173.

Martin, B. The assessment of anxiety by physiological behavioral measures. *Psychol. Bull.*, 1961, **58**, 234-255.

Masserman, J. H. *Behavior and neurosis: an experimental psychoanalytic approach to psychobiological principles.* Chicago, Ill.: Univer. of Chicago Press, 1943.

May, R. *The meaning of anxiety.* New York: Ronald Press, 1950.

Miller, N. E. Studies of fear as an acquirable drive. I. Fear as motivation and fear-reduction as reinforcement in the learning of a new response. *J. exp. Psychol.*, 1948, **38**, 89-101.

Mowrer, O. H. A stimulus-response analysis of anxiety and its role as a reinforcing agent. *Psychol. Rev.*, 1939, **46**, 553-565.

Mowrer, O. H. Preparatory set (expectancy): some methods of measurement. *Psychol. Monogr.*, 1940, **52**, No. 2, 43.

Mowrer, O. H. *Learning theory and personality dynamics.* New York: Ronald Press, 1950.

Pavlov, I. P. *Conditioned reflexes.* London and New York: Oxford Univer. Press, 1927.

Sarason, I. G. Empirical findings and theoretical problems in the use of anxiety scales. *Psychol. Bull.*, 1960, **57**, 403-415.

Sarason, S. B., Davidson, K. S., Lighthall, F. F., Waite, R. R., & Ruebush, B. K. *Anxiety in elementary school children.* New York: Wiley, 1960.

Schachter, S., & Singer, J. E. Congitive, social, and physiological determinants of emotional state. *Psychol. Rev.*, 1962, **69**, 379-399.

Spence, K. W. A theory of emotionally based drive (D) and its relation to performance in simple learning situations. *Amer. Psychologist*, 1958, **13**, 131-141.

Spence, K. W. Anxiety (drive) level and performance in eyelid conditioning. *Psychol. Bull.*, 1964, **61**, 129-139.

Spielberger, C. D. The effects of manifest anxiety on the academic achievement of college students. *Ment. Hyg., N.Y.* 1962, **46**, 420-426.

Spielberger, C. D., & Smith, L. H. Anxiety (drive), stress, and serial-position effects in serial-verbal learning. *J. exp. Psychol.*, 1966, in press.

Sullivan, H. S. *The interpersonal theory of psychiatry.* New York: Norton, 1953.

Taylor, Janet A. The relationship of anxiety to the conditioned eyelid response. *J. exp. Psychol.*, 1951, **41**, 81-92.

Taylor, Janet A. A personality scale of manifest anxiety. *J. abnorm. soc. Psychol.*, 1953, **48**, 285-290.

Taylor, Janet A. Drive theory and manifest anxiety. *Psychol. Bull.*, 1956, **53**, 303-320.

Part II
THE NATURE AND MEASUREMENT OF ANXIETY

CHAPTER 2

Anxiety and Motivation: Theory and Crucial Experiments[1]

Raymond B. Cattell

LABORATORY OF PERSONALITY ANALYSIS,
UNIVERSITY OF ILLINOIS,
URBANA, ILLINOIS

The Definition of Anxiety

DETERMINATION OF ANXIETY AS A UNIQUELY ROTATED SOURCE TRAIT

Anxiety in the Rating Questionnaire Media of Observation

At the stage now reached in anxiety research, the new vista of perhaps greatest interest and promise is that which relates it to the equally new objective measurement of human motivation and the theories of motivation and conflict which can now be put to the test by such measurement. The purpose of this chapter is to review our present knowledge of anxiety as a determinate factor and to propound such theories of its relation to dynamic structure as will enable experimenters with flair to attack the issues with crucial experiments. But before a bridge can be built from anxiety experiments to the objective measurement of dynamic structure, each of the pillars must be examined separately. The first two sections of this chapter will therefore deal with anxiety, and the third will discuss dynamic structure before entering on the relationship of anxiety to motivation and dynamic structure.

No apology is needed in science for time given to definition, short of

[1] The investigations reported in this chapter were supported in part by Public Health Research Grant No. MN 10274-01 from the National Institute of Mental Health.

pedantry. Considering the morass of complete terminological and conceptual confusion in which the discussion of anxiety has wallowed for 50 years, an experimenter may be forgiven some rejoicing in the sheer advance in definition, made operationally in factor analysis in the last decade. Since this work has been set out in articles and books it will surely suffice to avoid redundancy by summarizing the absolute essentials here, leaving the reader to go to the original sources if the condensation presents any technical difficulties to him.

Obviously, decades of anxiety research have generated their own futility and confusion by failing to face the theoretical taxonomic and practical instrumental problems properly belonging to the first phase of research, namely that of discovering, defining, and measuring the unitary anxiety or anxieties which may exist. In this latter task of defining anxiety positively, it became necessary also to define it by exclusion, discovering in what ways it is distinguished from such frequently confounded entities as neuroticism, stress, depression, the tension level on the escape erg (fear), and excitation level (activation), to name a few. There has certainly been no lack of definitions of anxiety at the verbal, nonoperational level, beginning with Freud's distinction of Angst and Furcht (Freud, 1936). This literature, however, at its rare best, produces definitions as unstable as our turbulent language, and susceptible later to all the whims of exegesis.

When an area of behavior is structured by factor analysis, the proper procedure is to begin with a very catholic array of responses in the area popularly designated, e.g., in the case of measuring intelligence as "intellectual" or of anxiety as "anxious." One may or may not find a single entity corresponding to the popular notion, but this gives the discoverer the semantic prerogative to use the word for his factors. Primarily he will depend on an exact symbol for his factors, as we have used QII and U.I. 24 below, and whoever chooses to call something else anxiety can do so. But if decidedly more than 50% of the variance on variables in the agreed, designated area—in this case anxiety—can be accounted for by the discoverer's factors, it would be more reasonable, to say the least, to attach "anxiety" to these measurable factors rather than to the thousands of different and ineffable concepts subjectively hatched from an armchair. To anticipate, we find a single general anxiety factor, U.I. 24, and we shall apply "anxiety" to this as Spearman applied "intelligence" to his g, though it must be recognized that the semantic usage of the butcher, the baker, Aunt Mary, and some psychiatrists will not always be the same as this— or as their own usage on other occasions.

The original massive attack by the present writer and Scheier (1958) covered some 800 kinds of response which semantics and serious psychologists had at some time called "anxious." Recognizing that there are probably instrument factors (Cattell & Digman, 1964) in each of the three possible media of personality observation—*L-data* (life behavior, rated), *Q-data* (questionnaire and consulting room introspections) and *T-data* (objective, laboratory test performance)—these investigators set out to cover the *personality sphere* (Cattell, 1946) separately in each.

The Q-data personality sphere had already been subjected to well replicated R-technique, simple-structure factorings, resulting in some 25 factors (Cattell, 1957, Ch. 4) of which the most stable and largest 16 had been made available as standardized scales in the 16 P.F. test. To psychiatric observation and analyses some 7 of these—C(−), H(−), I, L, O, Q_3(−), and Q_4 (with M as a possible eighth)—might be considered manifestations of one or another conceivable form of anxiety. It was therefore psychologically more convincing when a second order factoring of the 16 P.F., with blind rotation, revealed 6 of these 7 to belong to a single second-stratum factor, as shown in Table I (Cattell & Scheier, 1961). (Incidentally, *exvia-versus-invia,* the core of the popular conception "extraversion-versus-introversion," shown in Table I for comparison, and 5 other second-strata factors, also owe their definition to this original factor research [Cattell, 1956; Cattell & Scheier, 1961; Mitchell, 1963; Gorsuch & Cattell, 1966] and the several studies, one on a sample over 1000, which have since confirmed it.)

The present status of the definition of anxiety by this factor—indexed as QII, roman numerals indicating second-stratum factors—is as follows. It has been found independently at four different age levels (by R-technique, individual difference relationships), namely, at 13–14 years, using the same factors as the 16 P.F. but in the High School Personality Questionnaire (Cattell, Nuttall, Karson, & Freud, 1966; Cattell & Warburton, 1961; Karson, 1961; Karson & Pool, 1958); at 9–10 years, using the Child Personality Questionnaire primaries (Cattell & Meredith, 1966a,b; Porter, Cattell, & Schaie, 1966); and at the 6–7-year level by the ESPQ (Baker, Cattell, & Coan, 1966).

There are some slight but steady changes in the pattern with age which are instructive regarding the genesis of anxiety, but the main contribution of these cross sections at other ages is the addition of factor D, excitability, to the QII pattern (D being absent from the 16 P.F.). Incidentally, the reader must bear in mind that these questionnaires (16 P.F., HSPQ, etc.) cover only 18 of the presumed 25 primary factors in Q-data, so that discoveries remain to be made of possible additional primaries truly belonging in anxiety. The Welch anxiety scale in the MMPI, however, has recently been shown to cover essentially the present factors (Cattell, 1965b). It

TABLE I
FOUR MAJOR SECOND-ORDER FACTORS FOUND IN THE QUESTIONNAIRE MEDIUM

First-order factor	Second-order factor I (introversion-extraversion or invia-exvia)			First-order factor	Second-order factor II (anxiety)[c]		
	Adult trait	Adult state[a]	Child trait[b]		Adult trait	Adult state[a]	Child trait[b]
A−	−42	−38	−49	Q₄+	+67	+44	+44
F−	−40	−22	−44	O+	+60	+20	+50
H−	−35	−12	−43	Q₃−	−53	−51	−33
Q₂+	+32	+39	+06	C−	−49	−53	−40
M+	+26	+36	—	L+	+45	+08	—
Q₁+	+19	+20	—	H−	−32	−06	−57
L+	+14	+12	—	M+	+30	+18	—
				Q₂+	—	+30	—
				D+	—	—	+43

TABLE I (cont.)

First-order factor	Second-order factor III [pathemia (affectivity) vs. cortertia]		
	Adult trait	Adult state[a]	Child trait[b]
I+	+44	+50	+19
N−	−37	−50	—
A+	+28	+18	+60
Q₃−	−21	−04	−02
C−	−17	−08	−05
O+	+17	(−13)[d]	+07

First-order factor	Second-order factor IV (independence vs. subduedness)		
	Adult trait	Adult state[a]	Child trait[b]
N+	+32	+21	—
E+	+28	+52	+28
Q₁+	+27	+12	—
J−	—	—	−37
F+	+14	+17	+20
Q₃−	−01	−07	−24
D+	+43	—	+09
C−	−15	(+02)[d]	−01

[a] The state is a pattern of change-through-time for a given individual or set of individuals, while the trait is a pattern referring to interindividual differences at any given occasion of measurement.

[b] From 6 to 15 years of age.

[c] The definition of the anxiety factor initially hinges on the unique simple structure position in this and the L-data medium (Cattell, 1957). For perspective the anxiety factor (bold type) is given among others. The state factor is from d-R-technique, the others from R-technique. The child pattern lacks L, M, etc., because they are not in the HSPQ primaries.

[d] Parentheses emphasize reversals from expected, consistent direction of association.

has also been shown that the 8 Q-data depression factors do not belong in QII.

This second-stratum, QII, general anxiety factor has also been shown to retain its form and definition across cultures as well as across age levels. Simple structure, objectively pursued to a maximum, has been carried out with American, Australian (Cattell, 1965a), British (Cattell & Warburton, 1961), French (Cattell, Pichot and Rennes, 1961b), and Japanese (Tsujioka & Cattell, 1965) samples with no significant difference of pattern emerging. In accordance with the generally agreed alignment of Q- and L-data factors (Norman, 1962; Schaie, 1964), it is noteworthy that both with adults (Cattell, 1957) and with children (Digman, 1963) the same second-order factor appears in the life behavior rating data as appears in the questionnaire data.

Anxiety in the Objective Test and Physiological Medium of Observation

Personality factors are in general more easily interpreted in L- and Q-media than the T-medium, and it can readily be seen, even before we come to the clinical evidence, that QII is entitled to be called anxiety. Some striking support is given by the nature of the primaries, incidentally to the Freudian theory of anxiety. But we will only note, in passing, this evidence that anxiety is tied to ego weakness, C(—), guilt proneness, O, and ergic tension ("frustrated libido"). We shall defer discussion of the primary factor content until later in the chapter.

In regard to theoretical completeness two principal gaps remain in the above work: (a), as stated, additional L- and Q-primaries probably exist which have not had their possible affiliations to QII explored; and (b), as usual at the second order, the sample of variables is so small that uncertainties remain in simple structure, in the case notably about the loading of M, autism. One practical shortcoming also exists, namely, that questionnaires are subject to motivational distortion with uncooperative subjects. Though time and expansion of research will remedy most of these problems in the Q- and L-data region, all three are remedied when the move into objective ("performance," "laboratory") tests is taken.

When Scheier and the present writer turned to look for the equivalent of QII in objective T-data, they quickly found, on looking over 10 years' factoring of the personality sphere in the T-medium, that a clear anxiety factor, indexed as U.I. 24 in the universal index series, already existed in the literature. (This has happened in several specialized investigations, when they turned to the basic research, as a result of the comprehensiveness inherent in experiments using the basic personality sphere concept.) However, a considerable number of further objective and physiological tests were added when this was pursued specifically in the anxiety research in order to cover a variety of anxiety concepts. In the subsequent factor experiments these theoretically well-chosen variables loaded on U.I. 24. No other factor appeared which might have any claim to be called anxiety, except possibly U.I. 23, which we have called *regression* and Eysenck (1957) has called *neuroticism*. To enable the reader to judge possibilities,

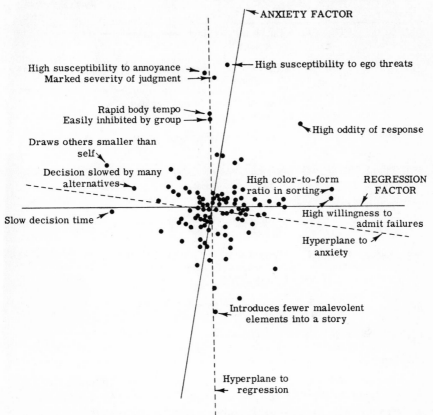

FIG. 1.   Simple structure plot of anxiety and regression.

the regression and anxiety patterns are presented side by side in Table II. Perhaps some claim to a far-out conception of anxiety could be found in the U.I.-17 pattern (see Table 7-2, Cattell, 1957; Table 7-3, Hundleby, Pawlik, & Cattell, 1965) which we have called *timid inhibition* and which has some resemblance to psychiatric concepts of "bound anxiety." U.I. 23 and 24 are virtually orthogonal in the general population, though neurotics are deviant on both (see Fig. 1).

TABLE II
ANXIETY AND REGRESSION[a]

Test battery for Factor U.I. 23: MOBILIZATION-VS.-REGRESSION

Variable	Test	G or I	Variable title	Test administration time (minutes)	Average factor loading
M.I. 2a, f	T1	G	Backward Writing: less motor rigidity	12	−.28
M.I. 42	T127	I	Body Sway Suggestibility: less swaying	3	−.16
M.I. 120	T4	G	Cancellation of Letters: greater accuracy relative to speed	4	+.31
M.I. 609	T112	G	Spatial Judgment: greater accuracy	8	+.45
M.I. 516	T299	G	Reading Speed: faster rate of reading to oneself	4	+.45
M.I. 227a	T116	G	Picture Preferences: fewer color choices relative to form choices	4	−.25
M.I. 162b	T120	G	Cancellation: less impairment in correct performances by noise distraction	5	−.32
M.I. 604	T200	G	Complex Task: higher number of correct responses	4	+.55
M.I. 41	T126	I	Two-Hand Coordination: more correct movements	2	+.13

The question which the experimentalist will now naturally be eager to answer is: is the QII factor in Q-(and L-) data the same functional unity as U.I. 24 in T-data? In other words, does anxiety, as a unitary entity, dress itself with indifference in verbal and in other behavioral manifestations so that we can use either set of indicators or instruments to measure the same thing? It was some time before an adequate sample of more than 250 subjects could be found for the 5–6 hours of testing necessary to cover both domains simultaneously; but when this crucial experiment was done (Cattell, 1955) the answer was beautifully clear: the QII and U.I.-24 axes aligned to within a few degrees. [This will happen only in nondistortive conditions for the questionnaire: with tough criminals in Joliet the agreement was quite poor, and in other instances we have had

TABLE II (*cont.*)

			Test battery for Factor U.I. 24: ANXIETY		
Variable	Test	G or I	Variable title	Test administration time (minutes)	Average factor loading
M.I. 219	T41	G	Confession of Frailties: more common frailties admitted	4	+.29
M.I. 211a	T38	G	Annoyances: more overall susceptibility to annoyance	3 .	+.52
M.I. 108	T22	G	Skills: less confident assumption of skill in untried performance	5	—.18
M.I. 116a	T9[b]	G	Opinion Inventory X: higher critical severity	6	+.22
M.I. 205	T36	G	Emotionality of Comment: more emotionality of comment	4	+.24
M.I. 473	T64	G	Friends and Acquaintances: fewer friends recalled	4	—.21
M.I. 481	T272	G	Embarrassing Situations: higher susceptibility to embarrassment	3	+.34
M.I. 55	T14	G	Association to Emotional Words: greater fluency of association to emotional relative to nonemotional stimuli	4	+.37
M.I. 144	T31	G	Aphorisms: more acceptance of aphorisms	3	+.19
M.I. 330	T47	G	Ethical Choices: better ethical choices in story completion	6	+.24

[a] Reproduced together for comparison from the O-A Battery.
[b] Only one section of test T9 has to be given.

first to separate Q- and T-data instrument factors before the alignment became clear (Cattell & Digman, 1964).]

While touching on motivational distortion and instrument factors in questionnaires, a clarification should be given to the assertions of certain workers in the itemetric tradition that QII is nothing more than a "social desirability" factor (Cattell, 1957). Before the more popular wave of interest in "response sets" arose, all kinds of sets had already (1940–1950) been investigated and incorporated into objective tests in exploring their relation to personality dimensions. The conclusions (Cattell, 1948; Cattell, 1951; Cattell, 1957) had been that *tendency to agree* (acquiescence) is an expression of four personality factors, U.I. 24 (anxiety), U.I. 21 (exuberance), U.I. 28 (asthenia), and U.I. 20 (comention); that tendency to extremity of response expresses U.I. 28, and other factors; and so on through the response styles. Most of the tendency to self-derogation ("social undesirability") is an inherent part of the expression of anxiety and only a fraction of the variance seems due to situational roles producing motivational distortion effects. That this pattern cannot be due to a role is shown by the very high correlations of QII with objective and even physiological measures of anxiety. Parenthetically, although the Institute for Personality and Ability Testing (IPAT) 40-item Anxiety Scale (Cattell & Scheier, 1963) for QII has been divided into a 20-item *overt* ("self conscious") and 20-item *covert* (not obviously anxiety-bound) set of responses, the two correlate equally well with the objective test U.I.-24 measurement.

At this point the pure clinician will want to be assured that the QII, U.I.-24 factor not only correlates with anxiety ratings in normals but also in pathological cases. Most of the (nonfactorial) evidence on this is given in the section on clinical findings, below. But the basic check, through having two noted psychiatric diagnosticians rate anxiety in the same 80 patients, was made by Cattell and Scheier (1961). The agreement between psychiatrists (reliability) was poor, but the factor analysis (of their ratings along with Q- and T-data) showed that most of their agreement was due to both loading on U.I. 24, i.e., they agreed that U.I. 24 was anxiety and after that their "personal equations" led them to add other factors, idiosyncratically and to a smaller degree. The recent study on seven psychiatrists by Cattell and Rickels (1966a) shows that clinically rated anxiety symptoms, e.g., irritability, phobias, insomnia, have most of their variance taken care of by measured U.I. 24, and that U.I. 23 (regression) is unrelated to anxiety ratings. But it also shows an interesting absorption of some rating variance in a physician-patient role factor of "sympathy," which causes the physician to overrate the anxiety of those with whom this role development has occurred more strongly.

A considerable range of physiological measures has been included with objective tests in various studies. The best summary of purely physiological and somatic associations that one can offer to theory at this point—from Grinker and Spiegel (1945), from our collaborative study with Grinker (Cattell & Scheier, 1961), from Persky, Grinker, and Mirsky (1950), and from our simple structure rotations of the work of Mefferd, Moran, and Kimble (1960),—is given in Table III.

It would be premature, even had we space, to theorize on the nature of these connections (see, however, *states* below). There is obviously general autonomic activity, and one may speculate that ACTH, through the liver, upsets amino acid (protein) metabolism, incidentally accounting for some of the loss of weight observed by Grinker and Spiegel (1945) and others in anxious subjects. One of the most interesting findings, as yet from one P-technique research only, is the high correlation of anxiety with serum cholinesterase (Cattell, 1957). The findings of Bennett, Dia-

TABLE III
LIST OF PHYSIOLOGICAL VARIABLES FOUND SIGNIFICANTLY ASSOCIATED
WITH THE PURE ANXIETY FACTOR[a]

Increase in systolic pulse pressure
Increase in heart rate
Increase in respiration rate
Increase in basal and current metabolic rate
Increase in phenylhydracrylic acid in urine
Decrease in electrical skin resistance
Increase in hippuric acid in the urine
Increase in 17-OH ketosteroid excretion
Decrease in alkalinity of saliva
Decrease in cholinesterase in serum
Decrease in neutrophils and, less clearly, eosinophils
Increase in phenylalanine, leucine, glycine, and serine
Increase in   histidine in urine
Decrease in urea concentration
Decrease in glucuronidase in urine and in serum

[a] Physiological associations are listed in approximate order of degree of association and degree of confidence in confirmation. (See Cattell & Scheier, 1961, Ch. 10, pp. 183–242, and especially Table 10-4 on p. 208.)

mond, Krech, and Rosenzweig (1964) would fit into this picture if we assume that the serum cholinesterase rise found here is "adjustive" to an acetylcholine rise in the central nervous system in anxiety. It is probable that the findings of Hoagland (1944), and those of others since, on raised 17-OH ketosteroids in endurance-stress situations fit the *effort-stress* concept here. The rise in 17-OH ketosteroids according to our loadings is steeper in effort-stress than in anxiety, but is a reaction shared by both of these states.

This concludes the demonstration that anxiety can be defined as a unitary factor in R-technique, such that different investigators will find the same unique rotation position. The further theoretical developments will take as their foundation this operational definition, and the measures, of known concept validity, in either Q- or T-media, which it makes possible.

Such measures have been developed and standardized in the IPAT Verbal (Scheier) and O-A (Objective Analytic) Battery, with which the Taylor Scale and the Welsh Scale from the MMPI correlate substantially.

THE DISTINCTION OF ANXIETY AS A STATE FROM ANXIETY AS A TRAIT, EFFORT-STRESS, EXCITATION (AROUSAL), AND GENERAL AUTONOMIC RESPONSE

Trait and State Concepts and the Measurement of States

States and moods have been relatively vague concepts in psychology. They can be given operational meaning and revealed in their rich variety by correlating behavior and introspection *across time* by the methods which have been called *P-technique* and *differential R-technique* (d-R-technique for short; Harris, 1963). The former, showing how manifestations covary in any particular individual, yields patterns reaching a generic resemblance *across* different individuals which justifies using such state terms (for all people) as anxiety, fatigue, anger, etc., provided we recognize and measure certain individualities of expression. As might be expected, d-R-technique, factoring difference scores between two occasions, for a number of people, produces a common factor pattern roughly averaging the somewhat idiosyncratic patterns found for individuals in P-technique. The technical problems of P- and d-R-techniques, which center on scaling *difference scores,* on arranging lead-and-lag correlations on the factor, etc., must be considered elsewhere (Cattell, 1963).

The findings of these methods suggest that a state is *a broad unitary response pattern,* which, because of human psychological and physiological structure, recurs in much the same form regardless of the variations in the kind and range of stimuli which have come to provoke it. However, what is the relation of such a *state* factor pattern of anxiety likely to be to that found above by R-technique for a trait? General statistical considerations show that the variance and covariance found when N people are measured and correlated for variables on one fixed occasion (R-technique) is likely to confound individual difference patterns (traits) with the fluctuant condition of the individual as caught at the moment (states). Consequently, if the psychologist had done individual difference experiments *only,* he would have no knowledge whether the patterns found were traits or states—or patterns from superimposition of the two.

Bringing these methodological considerations to bear on anxiety, how do we know whether the unitary patterns shown in Tables I–III represent a trait, i.e., what the clinician would call "characterological anxiety," or alternatively, portray the pattern of a person's temporary level on an emotional state? The answer, to the extent of telling us whether the state has any resemblance to the R-technique result, comes from P- and d-R-technique studies and is summarized in Table IV. It demonstrates that the state pattern of "what things change together" has a close, twinlike resem-

TABLE IV
ANXIETY AS A STATE

Change studies (P-technique) contributing to identification of anxiety as a state dimension: (P.U.I. 9) general anxiety[a]

Total anxiety factor score (composite score from all previously known anxiety trail markers in this battery)	.72[b]
High willingness to admit common faults	.58
High susceptibility to annoyance	.46
Fast rate of respiration	.45
High plasma 17-OH ketosteroids in blood	.43
Q_4 higher ergic tension	.42
C— lower ego strength	.41
High level of anxiety (questionnaire responses only)	.37
Q_3— lower self-sentiment	—.29
Faster heart rate	.30
Much lack of confidence in skill in untried performances	.22
High level of psychiatrically evaluated anxiety	.20

Anxiety factor from change study[c]	
High score on IPAT anxiety scale	.56
Greater tendency to agree	.54
High susceptibility to annoyance	.46
High willingness to admit common faults	.34
Less time estimated to attain life goals	—.29
Fast rate of alternating perspective	.26
Greater number of life goals	.14
Fast speed of Gestalt closure	.13

General anxiety with physiological variables (P-technique)[d]	
Low cholinesterase in serum	—.78
High pulse pressure	.71
High basal metabolic (estimated)	.59
High pH (acid) saliva	.42
Low ratio emotional/nonemotional recall	.37
Low pH (alkaline) urine	—.32
Few staff neutrophils	—.30
Low initial PGR resistance	—.25
Fast reversible perspective[e]	(.19)

[a] Cattel and Scheier (1961).
[b] Questionnaire factor loadings are the means for two studies.
[c] Nesselroade and Cattell (1963).
[d] Cattell (1957).
[e] Low-loading, but highest in matrix; hence included but in parentheses.

blance to what we have hitherto considered the trait (R-technique) pattern. As we now look at these patterns in a more sophisticated manner, the suspicion naturally arises that this resemblance could be due to the R-technique pattern itself being due to nothing but a snapshot of a state. There *could* be no real trait; the apparent interindividual covariance could be nothing but intraindividual covariance frozen in the arrest of "measurement at a given moment."

A firm rejection of this extreme doubt becomes possible, however, from the results of retesting people with the trait pattern IPAT scale and battery, after various time intervals. Both show stability coefficients, over 2 weeks to a month, close to the test dependability coefficients (.8), whereas a state should surely change in a few days. Even over a 2- or 3-year interval (Scheier & Cattell, 1962) the stability coefficients are approximately .4 and .5. Clearly a trait, though with some capacity for trait-change, is involved.

However, in this region of state and trait differentiation some very important experiments remain to be done. To define the trait pattern more precisely, R-technique studies are now needed using the means of, say, 5- or 10-times repeated measures of variables over a couple of months, to minimize intraindividual variance. Similarly the d-R-technique study should be on differences over repeated intervals, on the same kind of population. From such studies one should be able to get relatively pure trait and state batteries, avoiding the appreciable present contamination of state and trait patterns as well as the resultant correlation of whatever state and trait estimates are made from scores on present test batteries.

Meanwhile we can note what seem to be fairly emphatic differences in these patterns, through, (a) most autonomic variables, e.g., systolic blood pressure, loading the state more than the trait, presumably due to homeostatic reduction of deviations on these on the trait, and (b) the greater role in the questionnaire, d-R-technique factor pattern for QII of C—, O, and Q_4 (ergic tension could well vary daily) and the lesser role of the structural trait, Q_3 (self-sentiment strength) and of parmia-versus-threctia, H, which genetics research has shown to be highly constitutional (Cattell, Blewett, & Beloff, 1955).

The Distinction of Anxiety States from Effort-Stress, Excitation (Arousal), and Autonomic Activity

Some 9 or 10 state factors have been revealed by P-technique in objective tests, introspections, and physiological measures combined (Cattell, 1957; Cattell, 1966), and a tentative battery for researchers wishing to use the largest 7 of these has been constructed by Nesselroade and Cattell (1963) and made available by IPAT. It has been suggested that the 10-dimensional space fixed by the coordinates corresponding to these independent measures provides an exact means of representing and analyzing the action of pharmacological agents by vectors (Uhr & Miller, 1960). Since "anxiety and stress" have been so vaguely or obscurely linked in so many article titles, it is helpful at last to get definite evidence that anxiety and effort-stress are distinct response patterns. Indeed, in the second-order state structure (Uhr & Miller, 1960, p. 451) they even change oppositely, suggesting that the psychosomatic meets his problems and goes into stress while the ordinary neurotic evades them and suffers anxiety.

Space precludes discussion of the stress pattern, which the reader may study elsewhere (Cattell & Scheier, 1961), but its fairly frequent confusion in measurement and conceptualization with anxiety accounts for several false leads. For example, there is substantial evidence that stress relates to serum cholesterol and heart disease, but our studies show zero correlation of serum cholesterol with measured anxiety (Cattell & Scheier, 1961). Stress has been indexed as P.U.I. 4 in the state patterns.

A second important state dimension which has been confused, less frequently, with anxiety is that of excitation-versus-torpor. This, as its index number P.U.I. 1 indicates, is roughly the largest of state factors in terms of mean contribution to the variance of a wide array of variables. Its pattern is shown in Table V, and one can see that, insofar as one can bridge from human to animal concepts, it may be identical with the concept of arousal or activation. It is defined here only to ensure its separation from anxiety when assembling laboratory tests, and in connection with motivation theory below.

Finally, since electrical skin resistance and sweat-gland action are often rashly said to be anxiety measures, one must relate the anxiety-factor concept to autonomic action. From reanalyses of the extensive autonomic data of Wenger (1948), Royce (1966), Mefferd et al. (1960), and others, the present writer suggested (1950; 1965c; 1966) that most variance in autonomic responses can be accounted for by three factors: a general autonomic factor, covering most variables; an adrenergic pattern; and a parasympathetic pattern. P-technique data, gathered since, supports this, showing that the general autonomic activity factor may well be identical with the anxiety state response pattern, but that the adrenergic pattern is quite distinct from anxiety and that the parasympathetic may prove the same as torpor in the P.U.I.-1 pattern.

The relation to the fear response, as measured by ergic tension on the escape erg, is discussed below, but there is every evidence of its independence of anxiety. A decade of strategically planned multivariate experiment

TABLE V
EXCITEMENT (AROUSAL) VERSUS PARASYMPATHETIC PREDOMINANCE: FOUR
P-TECHNIQUE EXPERIMENTS REPLICATING THE "EXCITEMENT"
STATE DIMENSION PATTERN[a]

	Size of sample (occasions)			
	55	54	110	75
Variables	Loadings			
Small percent PGR deflections	—73	—68	—50	—84
Low initial PGR resistance	—	—40	—45	—67
High glucose concentration in blood	—	53	40	—
Low PGR upward drift in relaxation	—39	—	—38	—60
Long dark adaptation (or negative after image)	—	38	49	—
Low ataxic sway suggestibility	—75	—	—15	—
Low ratio emotional/nonemotional recall	—65	—	—12	—
Dreams described briefly	—	—70	—	—
Low volume of urine per day	—	—	—60	—
High cholinesterase in blood serum	—	—	56	—
Large lag of flicker fusion thresholds	—	—	50	—
High pulse rate[b]	—	—	29	—
High estimated basal metabolic rate	—	—	—21	—

[a] These studies are reproduced from Cattell (1957, p. 648), side by side, for comparison. A dash does not mean a failure of loading, but the absence of the variable from that particular experiment.

[b] Borderline significance.

in this region of state recognition and measurement would be immensely profitable to anxiety research at this juncture.

Laws of Anxiety Change in Pathological and Other Fields

ANXIETY AND PATHOLOGY: EVIDENCE IN THE DIAGNOSTIC FIELD

When anxiety becomes measurable with a concept validity of .8 or better, it becomes possible profitably to pursue laws of change, incidence, etc., without that swamping by error which makes a farce of any nicety of inference. Thus, it is possible to show highly significant differences·between neurotics, especially anxiety hysterics, and normals, but at the same time to demonstrate that neurotics do not deviate on anxiety, U.I. 24, as markedly as they do on other personality factors. Some comparisons both on questionnaire and objective-test measures are shown in Fig. 2. Naturally, neurotics are defined here psychiatrically, but it is noteworthy that the 16 P.F. profiles of groups of neurotics, so diagnosed in mutually remote parts of the world, show high consistency in having a characteristic profile (Cattell & Scheier, 1961).

These results at once throw doubt on the dictum of Freud that "anxiety

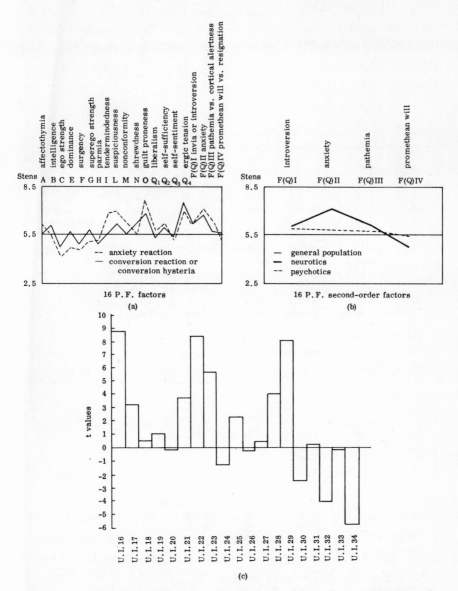

FIG. 2.   Differences of neurotics and normals: the full profile versus anxiety only. (a) primaries by questionnaire measurement; (b) secondaries by questionnaire measurement, average values; and (c) by objective (O-A) batteries (anxiety in U.I. 24 and regression is U.I. 23).

is the central problem in the neuroses" and support those who have criticized such anxiety scales as those of Taylor (1953) and perhaps Sarason (Sarason & Mandler, 1952) for defining good anxiety items as those which maximally distinguish neurotics from normals. As to the latter issue, Scheier has constructed a Neuroticism Scale Questionnaire, (Scheier &

TABLE VI

SELF-RATINGS OF PSYCHIATRIC SYMPTOMS EXPRESSIVE OF ANXIETY

Table number	Average	Research indexed as:		Symptom
		R4	R5	
1	+40	+32	+48	Jumpy, nervous
2	+39	+32	+45	Feel lonely
3	+38	+36	+39	Want to get away from it all
4	+36	+29	+43	Worry
5	+36	+32	+40	Do foolish or clumsy things, say the wrong thing
6	+36	+27	+45	Nervous movements (tap with fingers)
7	+36	+31	+41	Feel depressed or despondent
8	+34	+36	+31	Excitable
9	+34	+32	+35	Have silly, groundless fears
10	+33	+30	+36	Have a fatalistic attitude
11	+31	+36	+26	Lack self-confidence
12	+31	+32	+29	Irritable
13	+31	+22	+39	Heart pounds when excited
14	+31	+29	+32	Easily distracted
15	+30	+28	+32	Daydream
16	+30	+21	+39	Get confused for certain lengths of time
17	+30	+26	+33	Feel tense
18	+29	+33	+24	Feel like crying
19	+28	+30	+25	Pulse rapid
20	+27	+21	+32	Easily embarrassed
21	+26	+23	+29	Get cold shivers
22	+26	+46	+05	Moody
23	+25	+33	+17	Have rapid emotional changes (i.e., hate to liking)
24	+25	+28	+22	Cannot concentrate
25	+25	+24	+26	Get tired easily

Cattell, 1961) with a proper weighting of anxiety *and other* factors maximally to separate neurotics. It correlates only about .4 to .5 with his IPAT Anxiety Scale, and if it correlated more we should rightly suspect the anxiety scale of being contaminated with the other factors. As to the former issue, Freud's followers have perhaps been more impressed by what the patient complains about—his anxiety—than by his total behavior and the etiology resident in the earlier structure of his personality. A theory of *adjustment-process-analysis* coordinating hypotheses about the interaction of anxiety and the other personality factors of Table VI, in the neurotic process, has been given elsewhere (Cattell & Scheier, 1961). An order of determination of particular reported symptoms by the pure anxiety factor (though not yet for other factors) has been prepared by Scheier, Cattell, and Sullivan (1961) as shown in Table VI.

By contrast to neurotics (Cattell & Rickels, 1966a), most psychotics (except possibly schizophrenics in an earlier stage) show an anxiety-factor score insignificantly higher than normals (Cattell, Tatro, & Komlos, 1965; Cattell & Tatro, 1966). Young delinquents (Pierson & Kelly, 1963) and

	O	Q₄	C	Q₃	L	M	F	H	I	E	G	N	A	B	Q₁	Q₂
Neurosis (Grid 1-5)	+	+	−	−	+	+	−	−	+	−	...					
Character disorders (6-14) Variant 1	+	+	−	...	+	+	−	■	∴	...	...		∴	...		
Delinquent (14-18) Variant 2	∴	∴	...	−	∴	∴	■		+	−			∴	∴		
Psychosomatic and physical disability (19-26)	∴	∴	■		−		−	■		+	+	...	...			
Psychosis	∴	∴	...		...	∴	−	−	∴			...	...			

	O	Q₄	C	Q₃	L	M	F	H	I	E	G	N	A	B	Q₁	Q₂
Second-order anxiety factor pattern	+	+	−	−	+	■			−							

+ = significant positive deviation ··· = slight negative deviation
− = significant negative deviation ■ = no noteworthy deviation
∴ = slight positive deviation

FIG. 3. Deviations on primaries in second-order anxiety factor on various clinical group types.

psychopaths (Cattell & Scheier, 1961) show subnormal anxiety. Alcoholics and addicts are well above normal. The meaning of the U.I. 24 factor, as anxiety, is therefore confirmed by the nature and extent of its significant relations in clinical diagnosis, a graphic summary of which is given in Fig. 3.

ANXIETY AND PATHOLOGY: EVIDENCE FROM TREATMENT

Since Eysenck (1952) and others have rightly punctured the complacent assumption that therapy produces improvement merely because it conforms to psychoanalytic and other clinical "theories," the substitution for this assumption of a demonstration, on a foundation of experimental measurements, that significant personality change occurs has been suspiciously slow in coming. However, what was probably the first demonstration of a reduction of anxiety, as a pure factor (QII estimated from

TABLE VII

SHIFTS ON ANXIETY, REGRESSION, AND ASTHENIA UNDER THERAPY

Test	(1) Initial score	(2) Final score	(3) Change magnitude (2) − (1)	(4) Patient–control difference [(2) − (1)] − [(2) − (1)]	(5) t value of (4)	(6) P significance of (5)
IPAT Verbal Anxiety						
(N = 46) Patients	46.09	43.02	−3.07[a]	−3.71	2.07	.03
(N = 53) Controls	26.13	26.77	.64			
U.I. 24						
O-A Regression Battery						
Patients	.440	.114	−.326[b]	−.173	2.42	.01
Controls	−.458	−.611	−.153[a]			
U.I. 23						
O-A Asthenia Battery						
(94 neurotics)	2.7903	2.7212	.0691 sigma of difference = .0900	—	.76	Not significant

Difference of normals and neurotics on U.I. 28

Test	(1) Mean score of neurotics	(2) Mean score of normals	(3) Difference (1) − (2)	(4) t value of (3)	(5) P significance of (4)
O-A Asthenia Battery					
(94 neurotics)	2.7903	1.8961	.8942	9.35	.001
(53 normals)					

[a] Significant at P < .05.
[b] Significant at P < .001.

the 16 P.F.) measure was made by Hunt, Ewing, Laforge, and Gilbert (1959) on students undergoing intensive therapy in counselling. A confirmation, on private patients undergoing psychotherapy and also chemotherapy (with meprobamate), was recently given by Rickels and Cattell (1965) as shown in Table VII.

Still more illuminating insights on the role of therapy could be provided by measures with the eight-parallel-form anxiety battery (Scheier & Cattell, 1962) applied at short intervals, relating the shifts to specific treatment events, overcoming of resistances, etc., in the therapeutic process.

ANXIETY INCIDENCE AND CHANGE IN RELATION TO AGE AND CULTURE

Age changes in anxiety-need studying in three ways: in form (factor pattern), level of score, and environmental attachments. As to the first, the most prominent change—but still requiring checking for significance—is a higher $H(-)$ loading and the presence of a $G(-)$ loading in the childhood as contrasted with the adult period. The first suggests that anxiety is to a greater extent a product of timidity of temperament (threctia, i.e., threat susceptibility, $H(-)$ as an autonomic reactivity) in childhood, but of the dynamic structure [ego defect $C(-)$, self sentiment weakness $Q_3(-)$, and raised ergic tension, Q_4] in the adult. The loading on $G(-)$ suggests that good super-ego formation and expression is anxiety-reducing in the child (cf. Mowrer, 1960).

Little evidence is available on environmental attachments. In regard to specific stimuli we must note that any anxiety response, as represented for example by an item in the IPAT Verbal Scale, has a score implicitly on both strength and frequency (apparently, substantially correlated). Either of these is a function of both the situation and the individual's general anxiety level. The theory of source trait measurement by factors is that a general trait must average situations which are (a) substantially loaded, i.e., produce a good range of response over people in relation to anxiety, and (b) widely sampled, so that individual differences in area of attachment and expression of anxiety will cancel. This should not preclude use of the present tests meeting condition (a) and the grouping of items according to areas of (b) to obtain laws on change *in any particular area of fixation*. However, such areas have so far been arbitrary, and consequently no confirmed and convergent findings yet exist.

As to age change, levels of anxiety have now been explored, with verbal but not with objective T-data measures of the factor, over a considerable age range (Byrd, 1959; Cattell & Scheier, 1961; Cattell & Sealy, in press), but the curves (Fig. 4) still badly need strengthening by larger samples at the extremes.

Although the steady decline of anxiety from adolescence to early maturity fits general conceptions of the maladjustments current at adolescence, the upward trend again after age 65 needs investigation, notably as to the relative extent of cultural (job-loss) and biological causation.

Socioeconomically and occupationally, appreciable differences are demonstrable. Among occupations (Cattell & Scheier, 1961) some very significant differences exist and there appears to be an as yet insufficiently

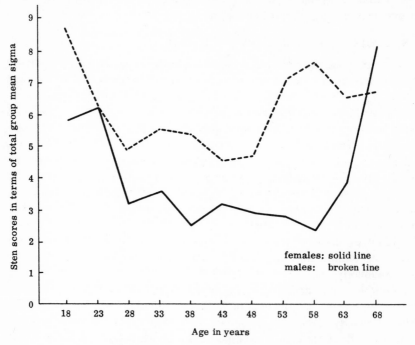

Fig. 4.   Normal life-course changes in anxiety with age.

checked slight increase with lower status. Despite the difficulties of matching for such socioeconomic status differences, several important cross-cultural differences of anxiety level have been brought to light across nations and "civilizations" in Toynbee's sense (summarized in Cattell & Scheier, 1961, p. 274). As far as one can generalize from (now) ten countries, it would seem that higher anxiety occurs with lower general economic level and the incidence of many disruptive cultural cleavages within a nation. These findings suggest that misunderstandings of cultural associations have arisen because of the confusion of the anxiety factor and the stress factor, as pointed out above. "Modern" life, as in America, may stimulate the stress factor, but it does not normally produce "the age of anxiety," which some literary folk suppose. (It is unfortunate that we do not have a sample of anxiety scale measures from the Middle Ages!)

Anxiety, Learning, and School Achievement

With several tests and batteries now available from construction based on research defining the pure anxiety factor—some, like Scheier's Eight Parallel Form O-A Battery (1962) being ideally adapted to repeated measurements—the door is opened to many simple, classical, bivariate, manipulative experimental designs which would be and have been erratic in conclusions when based on *ad hoc* tests lacking prior factor analytic experiment. Consequently, manipulative experiments yielding more consistent results have multiplied rapidly in the last 5 years. The work of Scheier (1961), considered in relation to that of Hunt, brings out that among students facing important exams, anxiety is highest *before* the exam period, and falls at the exam itself, while the stress factor then rises.

The conflicting, almost equally balanced in sign, "results" on anxiety and school achievement, can be partly explained by use of prefactorial, contaminated anxiety measurements. Sarason and Mandler (1952) have produced results suggesting that the explanation of the contradictions is that the anxiety-achievement relation is curvilinear and that lack of regard for different absolute levels in the various groups is therefore to blame for the confusion. Curvilinearity may well be involved, but a still more fundamental and overlooked explanation of the conflicting correlations—apart also from contaminated scales—is that the correlations arise partly from anxiety affecting achievement and partly from achievement affecting anxiety. Tsushima (1957) showed that announcement of supposed class failure raised anxiety in the "failures" (randomly chosen). This fits the predominantly, consistently negative relation of school achievement to anxiety when measured by factor-pure scales (Cattell, Butcher, Connor, Sweney, & Tsujioka, 1961a; Cattell & Sealy, 1965), but is still not the whole story.

For the agreement of Cattell and Scheier (1961), Spence and Taylor (1953), and others that conditioning occurs more rapidly with higher anxiety is not at all in conflict with the notion that action in the opposite direction—of anxiety upon achievement—is negative. One must recognize that school learning is not simply conditioning, but a far more complex process. There is a widespread tendency to ignore this, or, at the least, to argue that the rote learning parts of schooling are substantially conditioning and to slip in the additional assumption that anxiety is substantially motivation. These assumptions we can examine more systematically in the next section, but at the simple empirical level at least we must recognize that anxiety is more frequently a cognitive disorganizer than an aid to learning, as shown by the loadings of the anxiety factor on reduced capacity for immediate memory, poorer simple calculation performance, etc. From these considerations of two-way causal action, the difference of the total educational process from conditioning, the disorganizing action of anxiety, etc., it is easy to see why the verdict of experiment on anxiety and school achievement is very different from that deduced from the conditioning relationship or the erroneous equating of anxiety to simple motivation strength.

Anxiety and Personality Dynamics

DYNAMIC STRUCTURE IN OBJECTIVE MOTIVATION COMPONENT
MEASUREMENTS AND THE ERGIC TENSION-ANXIETY RELATION

To study anxiety and motivation it is necessary, as stated at the beginning, to offer a very brief recapitulation of dynamic calculus concepts (Cattell, 1959), based on objective motivation measurements and analysis, before bridging to anxiety.

The Dynamic Calculus in a Nutshell

Among nearly a hundred objective, widely different devices suggested by psychologists for measuring strength of motivation or interest, seven or eight *motivation-component* primary factors (labeled α through ζ) have been located. These hold their form no matter what the subject matter of the attitude-interest involved. Although promising theories exist regarding these primaries, and although the components can be exactly replicated, their conceptual nature remains a challenge to theorists. However, they do consistently yield two broad second-order motivation components which are pretty clearly interpretable as one having an *integrated,* actualized quality, labeled I, and one with an *unintegrated,* wishful, partly unconscious character, labeled U (Cattell, 1957).

When the experimenter takes a very wide array of attitude-interests (such as would constitute a "dynamic interest sphere" for our culture), measures each by a battery using the same most valid half a dozen or so devices, i.e., yielding one U and one I motivation strength measure, and then finds the simple structure among these stimulus-response (attitude) units, a dozen or more *dynamic structure factors* appear. These turn out to be such ergs as sex, fear, self assertion (achievement), pugnacity, curiosity, etc., and such sentiments (acquired structures) as those to occupation, religion, hobbies, home, and the self-concept. Since the batteries always yield both U and I motivation component factors, each dynamic structure factor appears as a pattern in U motivation measures and a pattern in I motivation strength manifestations. Thus, both a U and an I score can be assigned to an individual for each of his ergic tensions (fear, sex, assertion, etc.) and sentiment developments (to home, religion, job, hobby, etc.).

The principal claims for the *dynamic calculus*, as these constructs and the system of calculations among them have come to be called (Cattell, 1965c), are that: (1) the objective measures themselves are of an altogether higher order of validity than are obtainable from any single projective test device (as in the TAT) and have higher construct validity than the familiar opinionnaires which ask subjects in what they are interested; (2) the categories of dynamic structure—the ergs and sentiments—are not subjective, as in McDougall's, Murray's, or Edwards' lists of "propensities" and "needs," but constitute naturally existing structures definitely verifiable in experiment; (3) the resulting measures of ergic tensions have been shown to relate to real-life criteria, e.g., total clinically judged conflict (Williams, 1959) and school achievement (Cattell *et al.,* 1961a; Cattell & Sealy, 1965), in ways which would be expected from the hypothesized nature of these structures; and (4) with the aid of these concepts, calculations of summation of interests, the use of a "quantitative psychoanalysis" to discover the dynamic roots of attitudes and symptoms, estimation of the magnitudes and outcomes of conflicts, etc., can be carried out on an explicit model and with experimentally checkable results.

Two Basic Postulates on the Relation of Anxiety to Motivation

The plan now is to state basic postulates about the relation of anxiety to motivation and to work out experimental consequences. The choice of postulates is made to give a best fit to present experience and to lead to (a) theorems which are consistent with experimental findings we already possess, and (b) the design of certain new crucial experiments likely maximally to clarify the field.

The basic postulate is that *anxiety arises from a threatened deprivation of an anticipated satisfaction when the threat does not carry complete cognitive certainty.*[2] Clearly there are certatin phylogenetic and ontogenetic conditions implied by this as to the kind of organism in which anxiety can develop. Primarily, the development of the species and the maturity of the individual organism must be such that (a) deprivation can be con-

---

[2] Parenthetically, the introspected generic resemblance of anxiety to fear may be considered due to its being fear-mediated by complex, remote, and cognitively uncertain symbolic signals. This dilution of affect by attenuated cues is not peculiar to the escape erg; vaguely signaled amorous forepleasure, for example, is, correspondingly, a feeling introspectively attenuated from lust.

cretely symbolized, conceived, and anticipated, so that "fear" of *it,* rather than of the actual pain, hunger pangs, etc., can be experienced, and (b) cognitive signals of loss shall not have just a coarse, all-or-nothing quality, but be graded for uncertainty. Anxiety is therefore something more characteristic of relatively complex and highly "educable" organisms.

Even in a complex organism a present or future signaled frustration or deprivation can produce effects other than anxiety. Frustration may produce pugnacity (sometimes loosely called "aggression") and, if demonstrated to be irremediable, it leaves (a) undischarged drive tension, and (b) depression. This may be the element of reality in Dr. Johnson's assertion that "if a man knows he is going to be hanged tomorrow it clears his mind marvellously." But such pure cases of absolutely certain future deprivation without anxiety are rare, probably because absolute certainty is rare. The pure depression with simple undischarged ergic tension is rare, first, because anything in the future obviously cannot be absolutely certain, and, second, because the human cognitive apparatus even functioning at its best, and with clear cues, never entirely accepts an unpleasant certainty.

The first implication of this postulate is that some component of anxiety, A_1, will be proportional to the strength of the ergic tension, E, and to the doubt, D, concerning its satisfaction, as in Eq. (1):

$$A_1 = f (ED) \tag{1}$$

This expression D, for doubt, is a *subjective cognitive-perception value* in the individual. As such, it must be regarded as a function of two terms, V_o, the objective uncertainty (V for variability of evidence), and F, the degree of failure of the ability (i.e., ability measured negatively as an inability) of the organism cognitively to focus the real signs and narrow the uncertainty. (A person who has never been to a dentist is less able to focus, from the given preparation of instruments, how much he may be hurt and is consequently more anxious than an experienced patient. The objective uncertainty is written V_o because most of the value which a realist would commute would be derived from the calculated variance of this reward in similar situations in the past, though there would also be inferences from present signs which might modify that value.)

However, it must be remembered that we are talking about uncertainty regarding the amount of satisfaction at some future moment, not now, and that the discrepancy (even if considered only in one direction) could just as easily derive from a change in the ergic tension, E, as from a change in the external rewarding situation. The small boy may anxiously wonder whether he will be only moderately hungry or terribly hungry by the time the fixed and known quantity of picnic sandwiches is shared. The final term for anxiety, A, must therefore contain expressions both for objective variability, V_o, and subjective, ergic variability, V_e. Like the former, the latter would be predominately derived from the standard deviation (or variance) in experience over time in the past. The total uncertainty is thus the sum of the uncertainty of the rewarding mechanisms in the objective world and the uncertainty of the individual's own impulses, while the total doubt arises both from these probalities and the individual's cognitive difficulty in appraising them. These modifications of Eq. (1) may be generally stated in Eq. (2), thus, where V_o is the objective environmental uncertainty and V_e the uncertainty of ergic tension level

$$A_1 = f(E)(V_e)(V_oF) \tag{2}$$

The parentheses in these equations do not imply specifically a product function, but are used to separate the three postulated main sources of contribution to anxiety. (Parenthetically, "probability-learning" experiments seem to have ignored the important anxiety phenomena which according to our theory should be peculiarly connected with them.)

Now the term E, which represents the ergic tension of any 1 erg (according to specific subscript) of some 10 known ergs (drives), objectively measurable by such tests as MAT (Cattell, Horn, Radcliffe, & Sweney, 1964a), can, according to present dynamic calculus theory, be itself represented as in Eq. (3):

$$E = (s + k)[C + H + (P - aG)] - bG \tag{3}$$

where s is stimulus strength, k a constant, G is degree of mean prevailing gratification, and a and b the constants for reduction by gratification, respectively, of the physiological and psychological components in drive strength. (C and H are irrelevant to present arguments, being constitutional and historical components in *need strength*—the value in square brackets.) *Drive strength* is need multiplied by (s + k). The ergic tension, E, at a given moment, is drive strength minus current gratification. In the later formulas here we must distinguish between the actual current level of gratification, G, in Eq. (3), which affects the ergic tension level, E, and the anticipated gratification-versus-loss level, L, which we postulate affects anxiety.

It is possible that in Eq. (1) D will not be uncorrelated, in most life situations, with E, in that circumstances may generally be such that a large ergic tension has less chance of being satisfied than a small one, and, insofar as D represents a real estimate, a larger D has associations with greater (extreme not average) actual deprivation of tension reduction.

But at any rate for a given doubt ratio, D [or $V_e(V_oF)$], we postulate that a more powerful need will generate more anxiety than a small one.

The second postulate is one in which we have much less confidence, and we propose essentially to introduce it as a second term in the equation which may vanish to zero if it proves not to be needed. In the first term we have supposed no specific relation of anxiety to the fear erg. Instead, in spite of some introspectible similarity, we have supposed that anxiety is an experience *sui generis*, which is generated directly by experience of motivational uncertainty, and which is no more motivational or teleologically purposive than, say, the pain in a healing wound.

However, if we are to pay some heed to introspective evidence and the possible experimental evidence of a tendency to avoid anxiety-creating situations, then we must also consider the possibility that anxiety is a derivative in some sense of the fear erg—the erg of danger avoidance or security seeking which has been clearly demonstrated and delimited in man by the dynamic calculus researches (Cattell, 1957). How much weight should be given to the introspectible generic resemblance of anxiety to fear? Most of the primary emotions, one of which characterizes each erg, seem to exist also in some diluted form, with a slightly different taste, e.g., the amorous forepleasure of lust and the irritability before rage (see footnote 2). In these, as in anxiety, it is reasonable to theorize that we have a derivative of the primary emotion, attenuated by the substitution of symbolic signals for the full concrete reality of the stimulus, and by the remoteness of the stimulus. If, further, we may suppose that in a highly developed organism fear may arise not only to the primary stimuli of danger but to the concept of *deprivation* of any ergic satisfaction, then we have seriously to consider a second postulate, namely, that anxiety is an expression of the erg of escape in response to threatened future ergic deprivation of *any* kind.

A second term must therefore be added to Eq. (2) above which will have the general form

$$A_2 = f(E/R) \tag{4}$$

Here we have retained E, the existing ergic tension level in the formula and expressed $1/R$ as a fraction—the ratio which the anticipated actual level of reward bears to the ergic tension level. Thus, A_2 is a function (inverse) of the anticipated *absolute* level of gratification, R, whereas A_1 in Eq. (2) is a function of the anticipated *variability* (uncertainty) of the reward, R.

But now, if we are to consider experiments with individual differences, we must recognize that the strength of the fear erg [considered as need strength, drive strength, or ergic tension level; see Eq. (3)] will vary from person to person and its strength should magnify this effect of loss on any other erg, thus

$$A_2 = f(E_f)(E/R) \qquad (5a)$$

or

$$A_2 = f(E/R)(1/H) \qquad (5b)$$

where E_f is the individual's sensitivity to threat of any kind. An alternative to this formulation in terms of the fear erg is that the proper magnifying term is really a temperamental rather than a dynamic term, namely, the threctia factor [$H(-)$ in the 16 P.F.] expressing general autonomic reactivity to threat. At any rate, it will later become evident from the data that the connection with H [not to be confused with H in Eq. (3) incidentally] can be experimentally supported, whereas that with E_f is significant but, as we shall see, paradoxical.

The final formulation thus gives anxiety the possibility of two roots, as follows

$$A = A_1 + A_2 = f(E)(V_e)(V_oF) + f(1/H)(E/R) \qquad (6)$$

with substitution of E_f for $1/H$ as an alternative.

THEOREMS FROM THE BASIC POSTULATES REQUIRED BY CONSIDERATION OF DYNAMIC STRUCTURE

Only a fraction of the inferences from the above postulates can be discussed in this space, but they will be the more important ones. In the first place, since E enters into both terms in Eq. (4), it should in general be true that the higher the individual's ergic tension and the more enterprises in which he is engaged (assuming chance interferes equally with all such enterprises), the higher his anxiety should be. (Some such assumption seems to be invoked, for example, in Buddhism.) This may be true, but in most human activities, instead of dealing with a simple ergic satisfaction situation as set out in the formulas up to this point, we have to recognize the modifying effects of a definite dynamic structure involving internal checks and conflicts, and this greatly multiplies the derivatives from these formulas.

In the dynamic lattice (Cattell, 1957) an erg may find expression through many channels and the chances of satisfaction are peculiar to each. An anxiety value could be worked out for an erg as such only by averaging across these. And what we measure as the general anxiety level of an individual is again an average (or total) across all ergs. The possibility of calculating the ergic tension level in specific attitude-interests, ergs, or the total system exists, however, in the various estimates which can be made from the basic dynamic specification equation (Cattell, 1957), as follows:

$$I_{ji} = b_{j1}E_{1i} + \ldots + b_{jk}E_{ki} + b_{j1m}M_{1i} + \ldots + b_{jxm}M_{xi} \qquad (7)$$

The b's are *behavioral indexes* obtained as factor loadings, for the k ergs and the x sentiments, the E's are ergs, the M's sentiments, and the I_{ji} is the strength of interest of individual i in the course of action j.

Propositions and Evidence from Q-Data Measurement

Furthermore, we must recognize that the degree of integration of the various interests, as expressed in the strength of the self-sentiment (Q_3 in the 16 P.F., or S.S. in the MAT test), will enter into the evaluation. For higher integration implies a reduction of that fraction of the doubt, D, which arises from uncertainty in the impulses of the organism itself, i.e., from V_e in Eq. (2). Indeed, as far as the relations of *total* personal anxiety level to dynamic structure is concerned [provided we first make a proposition which amounts to saying that objective (V_o) and cognitive (F) terms are momentarily held constant], several clear propositions can be made and tested against existing measurement evidence as follows.

(1) A person will tend to[3] experience more anxiety in an environment with unpredictable rewards and greater deprivations than in a steady-rate, predictable environment with a higher satisfaction rate [terms V_o and R in Eq. (6)]. Our only present evidence in support of this is the higher anxiety level in cultures at a lower level of economic security and a higher level of cultural conflict (Cattell & Scheier, 1961).

(2) A higher total ergic tension score (E_i) in a person, i, will tend to result in higher anxiety. Evidence on this is difficult to obtain because the scoring of total ergic tension in objective motivation measures presents some difficulties of measurement. By reason of ipsative scoring (Horn & Cattell, 1965) in the MAT, a person's total tension score cannot be meaningfully used for this purpose. But if we take Q_4 in the 16 P.F., in a different instrumental approach to the same concept, we *do* find that Q_4 is consistently positively correlated with anxiety, to about $+.7$.

(3) The second term in Eq. (4) requires that anxiety be associated with higher score on the ergic tension score for fear, or with higher H score on the 16 P.F. The latter is highly significant ($r = .5$); the former requires more discussion below.

(4) The V_e term in Eq. (6), introducing variability in ergic need level, or impulsiveness, is represented in known personality source traits by factor C, ego strength (negatively, as ego weakness) and by $Q_3(—)$, low self-sentiment strength (which also appears as S.S. in the MAT). The connection of $C(—)$ with variability of attitudes and interests is witnessed by the research

---

[3] "Tend to" is used or implied in all of these as an alternative expression consistent with "other things being held equal," since we are in each proposition referring to only one term in isolation, among several which determine anxiety.

of Das (1955), and that of Q_3 by ratings. Since C has long been identified with the psychoanalytic concept of ego strength, the question arises whether its mere variability is the whole story or whether the specific psychoanalytic theory that low C contributes to anxiety through "fear of loss of impulse control" needs also to be invoked. (The latter follows, of course, from early life experiences of punishment following lack of impulse control per se.) From an improved perception of the nature of C factor, in recent questionnaire and rating factorings, the present writer would now agree that low C actually operates in three ways: (a) as previously stated, through the introduction of an *internal uncertainty* of impulse level, V_e, having essentially the same effect as external uncertainty due to the environmental instability; (b) through low C leading to more frequent experience of "loss-of-control" punishment; and (c) through the lack of skill in ensuring steady satisfaction for needs, associated with low C, raising the $1/R$ term, for loss of satisfaction, in Eq. (6). The role of unrealism, in $C(-)$ in increasing the inaccuracy of estimates of satisfaction, F, could also be considered.

The single concept of dynamic integration—of different need systems achieving the most ideal mutual compromises to maximize total satisfaction —seems empirically to require two factors: ego strength, C, discussed above, and Q_3, the self-sentiment. Just as we have reasoned with regard to C that poor integration should increase anxiety partly by an *internal uncertainty* reducing adjustment, even to a fixed and predictable environmental reward system, so it seems one must infer that poor integration through a defective development of habits around the self-concept would increase anxiety.

One would logically expect that poor integration would also reduce the total satisfaction and increase undischarged ergic tension. This connection is supported in the well-established significant negative correlation of Q_3 and Q_4 (Gorsuch & Cattell, 1966; Karson & Pool, 1958). But increase of anxiety would here be *directly* due to theorem (1) above. A third hypothetical action of the strength of development of Q_3 should, on the other hand, *increase* anxiety. In humans, though not in animals, any frustration (and ultimately unavoidable deprivation) is a twofold blow, (a) to the erg or ergs as such, and (b) to the self-regard of the self-sentiment. The threat to the self-sentiment might thus be expected to increase the total anxiety when the self-sentiment is strongly developed. That this effect does not eliminate the negative correlation of Q_3 with Q_4 and with total anxiety can be explained partly by the existence of the other mechanisms and partly by the structure of a really well-developed self-sentiment including pride in a self-concept able to "take" ergic deprivation [an experiment comparing Christian and other cultures might help answer this, however,

Tsujioka and Cattell (1965) found Q_3 actually more highly loaded on anxiety on a Japanese sample].

(5) Since not all contemplated interests will be morally acceptable, and some will generate possible superego punishment, higher anxiety should be found with higher general guilt proneness, O factor, and possibly with higher G, superego, itself. Since evidence is now clear that guilt proneness is independent of the extent of development of the G factor (superego, conscientiousness) or even negatively associated with it, we are coming to a theory in which factor O must, like H, be regarded as a temperamental "magnifier" of a reaction based on other origins. In this case it will magnify the reaction of the individual to a transgression of his given G standards. Much more research and penetrating reasoning is needed on the relation of O to G before the relation of both to anxiety can be worked out. Our finding that in children higher G is accompanied significantly by lower anxiety (Cattell, 1956; Tsujioka & Cattell, 1965) points to an element of truth in Mowrer's position (1960). A strongly developed superego need not increase anxiety, as our first glance above suggested, provided its injunctions are followed, which would presumably be more often with a stronger, habitually active superego. Additionally, we may suppose that a more thoroughly learned superego means less doubt about the consequences of transgression. The reason that this negative relation of G to anxiety no longer holds in the average adult may be the common adult occurrence of what we shall call the "rationalist assault" on G, raising doubts about its injunctions. Consequently, over the later age range no very definite relation of anxiety to G would be expected. But if O magnifies whatever sense of distress occurs when the individual becomes aware that he has placed himself in a position of uncertainty on superego punishment or reward, then anxiety and O should become significantly correlated at all ages.

To summarize, the experimental evidence necessary to check the above five theorems from the primary postulates already exists. For the anxiety trait factor (Table I) correlates consistently, significantly, and in most cases substantially, with Q_4, total undischarged ergic tension, as required by theorem (2); with $H(-)$, required by theorem (3); with $C(-)$ required by theorem (4), with O, required by theorem (5), and with $Q_3(-)$ as required by theorem (4). That C and Q_4 should correlate more with state than trait, relative to H and Q_3, continues to support the interpretation, though the higher O correlation with state appears anomalous. [The absence of L, protension, i.e., defense against tension by projection mechanisms, from our generalizations, despite presence in Table I, fits its interpretation (Cattell & Eber, 1966) as a *consequence*, not a cause, of anxiety.]

Propositions and Experiments from Objective Dynamic Measurement

Up to this point our theoretical structure has been tested by experiment, and though further, independent experiments along the same lines are now strongly indicated for checks, extensions, and increases of precision, the level of confidence of conclusion is substantial. On the other hand, the relating of anxiety directly to dynamic strength measures, through the new, objective measures of motivation, is so recent that we now enter a region where evidence is fragmentary and the main task is still to design crucial experiments.

However, let us first look at the fragmentary early crop of results. The only available measuring device for psychologists, which uses objective tests validated against motivation component factors and measures factorially demonstrated dynamic structures [five ergs and five sentiments, yielding unintegrated (U) and integrated (I) scores on each], is the Motivation Analysis Test (Cattell *et al.,* 1964a). Sealy in Britain and Sweney (Sweney, Cattell, & Sealy, 1966) in the United States have, however, developed a child age-level equivalent—SMAT (the School Motivation Analysis Test)—nearing standardization, which although unpublished, has been used in several large experiments mainly on motivation and school achievement and has yielded significant results on which we can draw.

As pointed out earlier, we can turn to neither instrument for a test of theorem (2) above—that total anxiety is in part a function of total ergic tension—because in the process of getting rid of contaminating device variance we have used ipsative scoring which also gets rid of any possible differences in total ergic tension. On the other theorems, however, this objective measurement of ergic tension either throws some light already or is now capable of yielding experimental answers. Indeed, with the new "partialing" scoring proposed by Horn and Cattell (1965) even the question of the relation of total motivation to total anxiety can be put to the test.

However, the present fragmentary evidence from MAT and SMAT applies mainly to the structural generalizations in theorems (4) and (5) above, relating measures of personality structures—the self-sentiment, the fear erg, and the superego—to total anxiety. Although the motivation measurement evidence thus partly covers relations on which information through other instrumentalities already exists, it is valuable. It offers evidence from an *independent* way of measuring some of the same dimensions as have been reached through the 16 P.F., namely, here, through the very different medium of objective motivation strength measures. The important verdict is that the self-sentiment here continues to be negatively correlated with anxiety. This and a number of other relations are summarized in Table VIII.

The above relations, which are significant beyond the $P = .01$ level, have appeared in more fragmentary form in other studies, and we can add to them a consistent, substantial negative relation of anxiety to superego strength, also appearing regardless of whether the latter factor is measured as G by questionnaire or as SE (superego factor) in the objective motivation measurement medium (MAT).

Our formula suggesting that anxiety should be in part a function of (1) the ergic strength, (2) its degree of deprivation, and (3) degree of uncertainty of reward is also supported by the positive correlation of anxiety with tension levels on the ergs of sex and narcissistic sex. If cultural anthropology is correct in its general assumptions, it is these, and not the

TABLE VIII

SOME SIGNIFICANT RELATIONS OF ANXIETY TO DYNAMIC FACTORS[a]

| | Correlations of anxiety with dynamic factors | |
| | Tollefson (1961) N = 101 | Cattell (1957) N = 199 |
Dynamic factors		
With ergic tension on MAT measures of		
Fear erg	−.22	−.35
Sex erg	.20	.40
Narcissistic erg	.25	.40
Self-sentiment	−.35	−.60
With 16 P.F. questionnaire measure of		
Self-sentiment (Q_3)	−.40	−.60

[a] The correlations in the upper part of the table are estimations (approximate) from assigning weights to the primaries in the second-order anxiety factor in the 16 P.F. (except self-sentiment, Tollefson, which is direct). In the lower part, values are means (approximate) of the correlations of Q_3 from a second-order factorization. The tendency of the Tollefson values to run systematically lower is probably attributable to his working with a selected student group as contrasted with general adults in the Cattell sample.

other common ergs (which show negligible correlation), that are most frustrated in our society. By the same theory we should expect substantial positive correlation of anxiety with tension level on the pugnacity erg in the MAT, but this has not yet been examined.

Correlations with self-sentiment, in both media of measurement (see Tables I and VIII) support the subjective predictivity term, V_e, already discussed above, but those with the fear erg are startling and contrary to theory. They have been reexamined to see if the U and I components of the erg might behave differently, but the only concession in this direction is that the correlation for I is less than for U. However, this proves to hold, roughly, for *all* the ergs, so the argument that anxiety might be specifically a function of unintegrated fear response cannot be entertained. One possibility which has long been debated by those working intensively in the dynamic calculus is that the fear erg is peculiar among ergs in that in using the usual perceptual and memory effects in the objective tests we might be measuring it in the wrong direction. Here the stimulus is *avoided* instead of sought, and it might be argued that a lesser score on memory, fluency, G.S.R.-response, etc., in response to stimuli indicates a *greater* concern with the goal of safety. Another possibility discussed is that a greater investment of fear in *real* and universally recognized external dangers (such as are used as the stimuli sampled for measuring the factor) might mean that *less* anxiety is available for those more personal and imaginary problems which commonly underlie neurotic anxiety. This supposes that the phobic mechanism of "projecting" anxiety to create fear of external objects and reduce anxiety is a universal one. None of these is entirely convincing, and a riddle perhaps remains. It is not merely that the ergic tension of fear fails to show the positive relation which Eq. (5a) requires, but that it shows a significant negative relation.

So far we have sought to use the new resources of ergic-tension (objective-motivation-strength) measurement through experimental relations having to do with the *total personality,* in its steady, natural environment. The door is now also opened, however, to manipulative experiments bringing out the relations of anxiety to motivation. This can be done over any erg or dynamic factor as a whole where we can manipulate its level by stimulation and deprivation and measure it on MAT (at the same time measuring anxiety *in that area*). Or it can be done for quite narrow, specific attitude-interests, which are more easily manipulated as to motivation strength, deprivation level, variability of reward, and other terms in Eqs. (3) and (4), but which offer increased difficulties in validly measuring the associated anxiety, because it now has to be anxiety measured within that small system only, and about such measurement we know little.

In arranging experiments with stimulation and deprivation in regard to anxiety changes, the model of the dynamic crossroads or chiasmata (Cattell, 1957; Cattell, 1959; Cattell & Scheier, 1961) should prove especially useful. So also should the reference of deprivation, uncertainty, etc., to the total dynamic lattice, e.g., to simultaneous frustrations of an erg and the self-sentiment. So long as Eq. (6) is considered only in the light of the effect of frustration, etc., upon a single erg or interest system, which can never be perfectly isolated by experimental manipulation, no clean and accurate inferences can be made.

To close with a somewhat obvious if not unnecessary summary on the motivation-anxiety relationship discussed in this section, one must stress that anxiety and motivation have here definitely not been simply equated. Motivation is the sum total of what is measured in the various ergic and sentiment structures. Anxiety is a special by-product of the dynamic system, degraded by a kind of entropy, as heat is a degraded product of physical energy systems. This is a mere metaphor, but it reminds us that the fact of finding significant relations, as we have above, between motivation and anxiety measures, does not in the least justify calling anxiety motivation or regarding the reduction of ergic tension as an anxiety-reduction process. For that matter, though much bivariate research has conceived all drives equally to employ "drive," the multivariate experimental work showing *distinct drives* should warn us not to beg the question of whether even *their* tensions may not be distinct in many properties. But even if there is a general ergic tension it is only quite indirectly related to the anxiety by-product.

A particularly promising field in this general area lies in the concepts of the U and the I components in the various ergs. We know that they are differently measured, and already certain interesting differences of properties have appeared between them. By hypothesis (Cattell *et al.,* 1964a), anxiety should be partly a function of the discrepancy of U and I components in a particular dynamic system. This and other hypotheses, which space denies our discussing here, are fully susceptible to experimental examination now that concept-valid factored measures exist for dynamic structures in terms of motivational component levels.

Summary

(1) A concept of anxiety can be uniquely and objectively determined as a second-order factor (labeled QII and LII respectively) in introspective response variables (Q-data) and general life-behavior rating variables (L-data). Consequently it can be measured by tests which can be raised to known and acceptable concept validities.

(2) Simultaneously, it has been found that a simple structure factor, indexed as U.I. 24, in objective and physiological measures contains most performances and responses popularly called anxious. This factor correlates with whatever is common to psychiatric ratings of anxiety and proves to align in common factor space almost exactly with the second order QII factor of anxiety as defined by the questionnaires.

(3) As so defined and measured, anxiety scores differentiate neurotics but not psychotics from normals; but half a dozen other known personality dimensions prove to differentiate neurotics from normals as potently as anxiety. Anxiety measures cannot therefore be validated by their effectiveness in separating pathological cases from normals.

(4) The loading pattern of anxiety as a *source trait,* thus discovered by R-technique factoring (individual differences), resembles but can be dis-

tinguished from the pattern of anxiety as a *state*, established by P- and d-R-techniques. Proper distinction of anxiety as a state rests upon recognition of other discovered state dimensions, notably P.U.I. 4, effort-stress, P.U.I. 1, excitement or arousal, and P.U.I. 5, adrenergic response, with which it has often been confused.

(5) When anxiety is defined by these factors, as above, its behavior in regard to clinical and other criteria continues to fit the popular usage of the term. It is significantly and decidedly higher in anxiety neurotics than normals; its measurements are significantly reduced by therapy; it rises in normals as they encounter threats and uncertainties; it shows a set of physiological associations, notably cholinesterase, 17-OH ketosteroid excretion, and amino acid changes, consistent with other findings; it changes with age, dropping from a high in adolescence and rising again in old age; and it shows significant differences across natural cultures explicable by economic insecurity and lack of cultural integration.

(6) Two basic postulates are tried, one supposing anxiety to be a function of uncertainty of reward and one of magnitude of anticipated deprivation, on any and all ergs. Five major and some other minor theorems follow from these postulates, expressed in formulas, and they are tried against evidence from personality-factor measurement and the objective measurement of dynamic traits. The evidence strongly supports the first postulate but leaves the second in doubt.

(7) A number of crucial experiments, now possible through the advance of objective measurement of ergic tensions, and the development of the concepts in the dynamic calculus, are briefly indicated. They concern the theorems on relation of anxiety to ergic tension level, E, to objective uncertainty of reward, V_o; to uncertainty of reward through ergic variability, V_e, to cognitive failure to focus probabilities, F; and to percentage magnitude of anticipated actual deprivation or loss (I/R, or $I - R$).

REFERENCES

Baker, R., Cattell, R. B., & Coan, R. C. *The early school personality questionnaire.* (2nd ed.) Champaign, Ill.: IPAT, 1966.

Bennett, E. L., Diamond, M. C., Krech, D., & Rosenzweig, M. R. Chemical and anatomical plasticity of brain. *Science,* 1964, **146**, 610-619.

Byrd, E. Measured anxiety in old age. *Psychol. Rep.,* 1959, **5**, 439-440.

Cattell, R. B. *The description and measurement of personality.* New York: World, 1946.

Cattell, R. B. Primary personality factors in the realm of objective tests. *J. Pers.,* 1948, **16**, 459-487.

Cattell, R. B. *Personality, a systematic theoretical and factual study.* New York: McGraw-Hill, 1950.

Cattell, R. B. A factorization of tests of personality source traits. *Brit. J. Psychol., Statist. Sec.,* 1951, **4**, 165-178.

Cattell, R. B. Psychiatric screening of flying personnel. Personality structure in objective tests—a study of 1000 Air Force students in basic pilot training. USAF School of Aviation Medicine (Proj. No. 21-0202-0007), 1955, Rep. No. 9, 1-50.

Cattell, R. B. Second-order personality factors in the questionnaire realm. *J. consult. Psychol.*, 1956, 20, 411-418.

Cattell, R. B. *Personality and motivation structure and measurement.* New York: Harcourt, 1957.

Cattell, R. B. The dynamic calculus: concepts and crucial experiments. In M. R. Jones (Ed.), *The Nebraska symposium on motivation.* Lincoln, Neb.: Univer. of Nebraska Press, 1959. Pp. 84-134.

Cattell, R. B. The structuring of change of P-technique and incremental R-technique. In C. W. Harris (Ed.), *Problems in measuring change.* Madison, Wisc.: Univer. of Wisconsin Press, 1963. Pp. 167-198.

Cattell, R. B. A cross-cultural check on second stratum personality factor structure—notably of anxiety and exvia. *Australian J. Psychol.*, 1965, 17, 12-23. (a)

Cattell, R. B. Source traits, surface traits, processes and species types: the four pillars of psychodiagnostics, illustrated by MMPI and 16 P.F. data. Paper read at APA Annual Meeting, Chicago, Sept., 1965. (b)

Cattell, R. B. *The scientific analysis of personality.* Harmondsworth, England. Penguin, 1965. (c)

Cattell, R. B. (Ed.) *Handbook of multivariate experimental psychology.* Chicago, Ill.: Rand McNally, 1966.

Cattell, R. B., Blewett, D. B., & Beloff, J. R. The inheritance of personality. A multiple variance analysis determination of approximate nature-nurture ratios for primary personality factors in Q-data. *Amer. J. human genet.*, 1955, 7, 122-146.

Cattell, R. B., Butcher, J., Connor, D., Sweney, A. B., & Tsujioka, B. Prediction and understanding of the effect of children's interest upon school performance. Res. Proj. No. 701 (8383), U.S. Dept. of Health, Education and Welfare. Urbana, Ill.: Lab. of Pers. Assess. and Group Behav., 1961. (a)

Cattell, R. B., & Digman, J. M. A theory of the structure of perturbations in observer ratings and questionnaire data in personality research. *Behav. Sci.*, 1964, 9(4), 341-358.

Cattell, R. B., & Eber, H. J. *The 16 personality factor questionnaire.* (3rd ed.) Champaign, Ill.: IPAT, 1966.

Cattell, R. B., Horn, J. L., Radcliffe, J. A., & Sweney, A. B. *The motivational analysis test (MAT).* Champaign, Ill.: IPAT, 1964. (a)

Cattell, R. B., & Meredith, G. M. Second and third stratum personality factors and their estimation from the HSPQ scales. *Mult. Behav. Res.*, 1966, in press. (a)

Cattell, R. B., & Meredith, G. M. Second and third stratum personality factor structure at teen age, through the Q-data medium. Champaign, Ill.: Lab. of Pers. and Group Analysis, Adv. Rep. No. 25, 1966. (b)

Cattell, R. B., Nuttall, R., Karson, S., & Freud, S. *The high school personality factor questionnaire, HSPQ.* (2nd ed.) Champaign, Ill.: IPAT, 1966.

Cattell, R. B., Pichot, P., & Rennes, P. Constance interculturelle des facteurs de personnalité mesurés par le test 16 P.F. II. Comparaison franco-américaine. *Rev. Psychol. appl.* 1961, 11, 165-196. (b)

Cattell, R. B., & Rickels, K. Diagnostic power of IPAT objective anxiety neuroticism tests. *Arch. gen. Psychiat.*, 1964, 11, 459-465.

Cattell, R. B., & Rickels, K. Prediction of clinical symptoms and role interaction from the IPAT factored tests of anxiety, regression and asthenia. 1966, in press. (a)

Cattell, R. B., & Rickels, K. The effects of psychotherapy upon measured anxiety and regression. *Amer. J. Psychother.*, 1966, in press. (b)

Cattell, R. B., & Scheier, I. H. The nature of anxiety: A review of thirteen multivariate analyses composing 814 variables. *Psychol. Rep., Monogr. Suppl.*, 1958, **5**, 351-388.

Cattell, R. B., & Scheier, I. H. *The meaning and measurement of neuroticism and anxiety.* New York: Ronald Press, 1961.

Cattell, R. B., & Scheier, I. H. *The IPAT anxiety scale questionnaire.* Champaign, Ill.: IPAT, 1963.

Cattell, R. B., & Sealy, A. P. The general relations of changes in personality and interest to changes in school performance: an exploratory study. Coop. Res. Proj. Rep. No. 1411. Dept. Psychol., Univer. of Illinois, 1965.

Cattell, R. B., & Sealy, A. P. Standard age courses in second order personality factors in men and women. *Brit. J. Psychol.*, 1966, in press.

Cattell, R. B., and Tatro, D. The personality factors, objectively measured, which distinguish psychotics from normals. *Behav. Res. Ther.*, 1966, in press.

Cattell, R. B., Tatro, D., & Komlos, E. The diagnosis and inferred structure of paranoid and non-paranoid schizophrenia, from the 16 P.F. profile. *Indian psychol. Rev.*, 1965, **1**, 108-115. (II: Concluding instalment)

Cattell, R. B., & Warburton, F. W. A cross-cultural comparison of patterns of extraversion and anxiety. *Brit. J. Psychol.*, 1961, **52**, 3-16.

Das, R. S. An investigation of attitude structure and some hypothesized personality correlates. Unpublished doctoral thesis, Univer. of Illinois, 1955.

Digman, J. M. The principal dimensions of child personality as inferred from teachers' judgments. *Child Develpm.*, 1963, **34**, 43-60.

Eysenck, H. J. The effects of psychotherapy: an evaluation. *J. consult. Psychol.*, 1952, **16**, 319-324.

Eysenck, H. J. *The dynamics of anxiety and hysteria.* London: Routledge & Kegan, 1957.

Freud, S. *The problem of anxiety.* New York: Norton, 1936.

Gorsuch, R. L., & Cattell, R. B. Second strata personality factors defined in the questionnaire medium by the 16 P.F., 1966, unpublished study.

Grinker, R. R., & Spiegel, J. P. *Men under stress.* Philadelphia: Blakiston, 1945.

Harris, C. W. Problems in measuring change. Madison, Wisc.: Univer. of Wisconsin Press, 1963.

Hoagland, H. J. Adventures in biological engineering. *Science*, 1944, **100**, 63-67.

Horn, J. L., & Cattell, R. B. Vehicles, ipsitization and the multiple-method measurement of motivation. *Canad. J. Psychol.*, 1965, **19**, 265-279.

Hundleby, J. D., Pawlik, K., & Cattell, R. B. *Personality factors in objective test devices.* San Diego, Calif.: Knapp, 1965.

Hunt, J. McV., Ewing, T. N., Laforge, R., & Gilbert, W. M. An integrated approach to research on therapeutic counselling with samples of results. *J. counsel. Psychol.*, 1959, **6**, 46-54.

Karson, S. Second order personality factors in positive mental health. *J. clin. Psychol.*, 1961, **17**, 14-19.

Karson, S., & Pool, K. B. Second order factors in personality measurement. *J. consult. Psychol.*, 1958, **22**, 299-303.

Mefferd, R. B., Moran, L. J., & Kimble, J. P. Methodological considerations in the quest for a physical basis of schizophrenia. *J. nerv. ment. Dis.*, 1960, **131**, 354-357.

Mitchell, J. V. A comparison of first and second order dimensions of the 16 P.F. and CPI inventories. *J. soc. Psychol.,* 1963, **61**, 151-166.

Mowrer, O. H. "Sin" the lesser of two evils. *Amer. Psychologist,* 1960, **15**, 301-304.

Nesselroade, J. R., & Cattell, R. B. *The IPAT 7-state battery: A contingent instrument for research.* Champaign, Ill.: IPAT, 1963.

Norman, W. T. Validation of personality tests as measures of trait-rating factors. U.S. A. F. PRL tech. docum. Rep. No. 62-64, 1962.

Persky, H., Grinker, R. R., & Mirsky, I. A. Excretion of hippuric acid in subjects with free anxiety. *J. clin. Invest.,* 1950, **29**, 110-114.

Pierson, G. R., & Kelly, R. F. Anxiety, extraversion, and personality idiosyncracy in delinquency. *J. Psychol.,* 1963, **56**, 441-445.

Porter, R., Cattell, R. B., & Schaie, K. W. *The child personality questionnaire (CPQ).* (2nd ed.) Champaign, Ill.: IPAT, 1966.

Rickels, K., & Cattell, R. B. The clinical factor validity and trueness of the IPAT verbal and objective batteries for anxiety and regression. *J. clin. Psychol.,* 1965, **21**, 257-264.

Royce, J. R. Concepts generated in comparative and physiological psychological observations. In R. B. Cattell (Ed.), *Handbook of multivariate experimental psychology.* Chicago: Rand McNally, 1966. Ch. 21.

Sarason, S. B., & Mandler, G. Some correlates of test anxiety. *J. abnorm. soc. Psychol.,* 1952, **47**, 810-817.

Schaie, K. W. The alignment of personality factors found through behavior ratings and questionnaire responses. Paper read at Annual Meeting of Soc. Multivariate Exp. Psychol., Nov., 1964.

Scheier, I. H., & Cattell, R. B. *The neuroticism scale questionnaire.* Champaign, Ill.: IPAT, 1961.

Scheier, I. H., & Cattell, R. B. *The IPAT 8-parallel form anxiety battery.* Champaign, Ill.: IPAT, 1962.

Scheier, I. H., Cattell, R. B., & Sullivan, W. P. Predicting anxiety from clinical symptoms of anxiety. *Psychiat. quart. Suppl.,* 1961, **35**, 114-126.

Spence, K. W., & Taylor, Janet A. The relation of conditioned response strength to anxiety in normal, neurotic, and psychotic subjects. *J. exp. Psychol.,* 1953, **45**, 265-272.

Sweney, A. B., Cattell, R. B., & Sealy, A. P. *The school motivational analysis test (SMAT).* Champaign, Ill.: IPAT, Exp. Version, 1966; Final Version, 1967.

Taylor, Janet A. A personality scale of manifest anxiety. *J. abnorm. soc. Psychol.,* 1953, **48**, 285-290.

Tollefson, D. L. Differential responses to humor and their relation to personality and motivation measures. Unpublished doctoral dissertation, Univer. of Illinois, 1961.

Tsujioka, B., & Cattell, R. B. A cross-cultural comparison of second stratum questionnaire personality factor structures—anxiety and extraversion—in America and Japan. *J. soc. Psychol.,* 1965, **65**, 205-219.

Tsushima, Y. Failure stress in examinations related to anxiety inventory scores. Master's thesis, Univer. of Illinois, 1957.

Uhr, L., & Miller, J. G. *Drugs and behavior.* New York: Wiley, 1960.

Wenger, M. A. Studies of autonomic balance in Army Air Force personnel. *Comp. psychol. Monogr.,* 1948, **101**, 1-111.

Williams, R. J. A test of the validity of the P-technique in the measurement of internal conflict. *J. Pers.,* 1959, **27**, 418-437.

CHAPTER 3

The Measurement of Anxiety in Children: Some Questions and Problems

Seymour B. Sarason
DEPARTMENT OF PSYCHOLOGY,
YALE UNIVERSITY,
NEW HAVEN, CONNECTICUT

In this chapter I shall be primarily concerned with raising certain questions and presenting a point of view about anxiety. There are several reasons compelling me to take this approach. First, I have made a number of informal observations and have had some thoughts which, however important I considered them, seemed somewhat tangential to the discussion of our published findings which were directed to other and more narrow questions. This is but another way of saying that in the typical research publication there is too much of the tendency to avoid presenting ideas which appear to have little empirical justification, or which may be viewed as a wholesale attack on the significance of the thinking and work of other people, or about which one simply is not sure. The knowledge that one's thoughts will receive the light of published day is a potent inhibitor of candidness receiving strong reinforcement from editors.

A second and more important reason for the approach in this chapter is that I feel we may be near the time when the fashionableness of anxiety research will begin to diminish, less because we have learned a lot and more because the fruitfulness of current formulations has been exhausted. A third reason, and one implied in the second, stems from the conclusion that the bulk of anxiety research has suffered from a limitation reflecting the assumption, usually implicit, that anxiety is *the* important personality variable. It is one thing to say anxiety is an important personality variable and it is another to say it is the most important variable. The tendency to weight variables on a continuum of importance has the frequent consequence of unduly narrowing one's observations and conceptions so that we overlook the fact that in research a personality variable is a necessary human invention that does violence to actual relationships at the same time it is used to discover them.

Since the anxiety research in which I have engaged for the past decade (Hill and Sarason, 1966; Sarason, Davidson, Lighthall, Waite, & Ruebush, 1960; Sarason, Hill, & Zimbardo, 1964) has been concerned with children, primarily from a longitudinal point of view, I shall be drawing on these findings as well as on informal observations of a number of children as a basis for the questions to be raised and the conclusions to be drawn.

Reservations About Anxiety Scales

Let us begin by describing a not infrequent occurrence: Charles is a 3-year-old who is to be taken to his first day in nursery school. There has been some discussion of this event in the family and Charles' response has been neither extremely positive nor negative. When he arises on this first day, he announces that he does not wish to go to nursery school. There is some discussion and his mother makes clear that Charles is going to nursery school. Charles begins to whimper, mildly protests his reluctance to go, and during breakfast is clearly not his usual ebullient self. In the car on his way to nursery school Charles is initially subdued in manner but soon begins to cry and then states that he will not go into the nursery school. When the car is parked, Charles' crying is louder and stronger; he begins to plead with the mother that they should return home, clings to her pathetically, and is in all respects a child in distress. He tries to run away from the mother to return to the car but she restrains him and he then clings to her in a most tenacious way, sobbing and pleadingly saying, "Mommy, take me home." There would probably be a good deal of agreement that Charles is experiencing anxiety, i.e., it appears to be a totally absorbing experience compounded of "pain," some kind of anticipated danger, terror, and an attempt at flight.

If we could observe the overt behavior of a child like Charles from the time one of his dreams becomes a nightmare to when he finally becomes pacified in the arms of his parent, very few would be inclined to disagree with the characterization that one has witnessed a child experiencing anxiety. In the preschool years such descriptions are not hard to come by and, in fact, in subsequent years it becomes increasingly difficult to make such observations.

If there is agreement that these descriptions warrant the label of anxiety, then it becomes necessary to ask if we are justified in assuming or implying that current anxiety scales reflect the type of anxiety experience we described in the preschooler. It is my own opinion that the individual who scores high on anxiety scales rarely experiences the absorbing, incapacitating, painful distress of the preschooler. This is not to say that the high scorer is not telling us that he worries, anticipates all kinds of bad happenings, and sees himself in negative terms. The point is that we have no evidence to indicate that a high score reflects the frequent, unambiguous experience of anxiety we see in very young children. This is not, I hope, a problem in the esthetics of terminology. From a theoretical standpoint it can only be a source of confusion and an obstacle to refinement if the same term refers to experiences and overt behaviors which differ markedly, albeit they may have aspects in common.

I said earlier that after the preschool years one rarely can observe individuals experiencing the pain, helplessness, diffuseness, and blatancy of affect we see in anxious, young children. The exceptions to this generalization are both interesting and instructive. The reaction of some individuals to the sudden death of a loved one, of some soldiers in battle, and of some patients in mental hospitals are some of the unusual situations or settings where one can observe anxiety as clearly as one can in young children. These instances alone are a basis for asking if what is reflected in responses to current anxiety scales is identical or even highly similar. In very young children, or in the instances given above, the *behavioral manifestations* are easy to record and they have a compelling quality which leaves little doubt in the observer that the label of anxiety is appropriate. *Manifest* anxiety as measured by anxiety scales begs the question of what *is* manifest. It is both strange and inconsistent that a manifest anxiety scale developed in a tradition utilizing *overt* behavioral data has not been systematically evaluated from the standpoint of the overt behaviors (aside from the verbal responses to the scale) which it may be reflecting.

It is completely unsatisfactory to answer the question I am raising by saying that what anxiety scales are measuring is either developmentally or dynamically related to the "unambiguous" anxiety discussed earlier or, less defensible, that what the scales measure is sufficiently similar to unambiguous anxiety so as to make the question unimportant. The first answer concedes the argument that anxiety scales do not get at the behavioral manifestations we see in unambiguous anxiety but it does nothing to clarify their relationships—it begs the question: what is the relationship. The second answer not only confuses an assumption with a fact but, in addition, cannot be substantiated by empirical evidence that individuals who score high on anxiety scales frequently manifest unambiguous anxiety. A recent study (Barnard, Zimbardo, & Sarason, 1965) of second and third grade children, from which the following is quoted, contains some data relevant to the second answer.

All of the second and third grade school children of Hamden, Connecticut, were administered the TASC and the Lorge-Thorndike intelligence test as a part of a longitudinal study being carried out at Yale University. From this population, those children scoring in the upper and lower fifteenth percentile of the anxiety distribution (total N = 320) were selected to form the High Anxiety (HA) and Low Anxiety (LA) groups, respectively. Within each of these groups subjects (Ss) were matched on IQ score as closely as possible in order to obtain sub-groups of High IQ (HIQ) and Low IQ (LIQ). The effectiveness of this matching is evident from the group mean IQ of 115 for the HA-HIQ group and 116 for the LA-HIQ, as well as from the means of 99 for the HA-LIQ and 97 for the LA-LIQ groups. A total of 96 Ss were thus finally chosen, 24 in each of these four experimental groups.

These 96 students were rated by their classroom teachers (N = 54), all of whom had already been participating in the ongoing Yale Anxiety Project. The teachers were paid for this voluntary task which they performed privately on their own time. Specifically, the task required a teacher to make 24 judgments about each subject who was her student. The judgments consisted of numerical ratings of a child on a wide range of personality and school performance characteristics. The traits were presented in pairs of contrasting trait names, along with a brief working definition of each of the terms in a pair. First, a teacher had to decide which of the two terms most accurately described the child, then she had to determine by use of a 5-point scale the degree to which the child approached the extreme of the description given for that term.

The complete list of traits can be seen in Table I, while the general format for each of the individual items is shown in the following representative example:

Dependent 5 4 3 2 1   1 2 3 4 5 Independent

Children should be rated as "dependent" to the extent that they need, want, and try to get help, support, or guidance from others with the tasks or problems that face them. "Independent" children would seek to function or perform without that help, support, or guidance. Dependent behavior would include requests for assistance, relying on others for opinions, attitudes, and guidance for action.

For the purposes of the present discussion the most relevant finding is that high anxious, high IQ children were rated by teachers in more positive terms than any of the other anxiety-IQ groups.

... a biasing in terms of a halo effect appears to explain much of this data, since teachers evaluated anxious children who were bright differently from anxious children who were not, and did so on traits shown by previous research *not* to be characteristic of the bright, anxious child. Thus, for example, while these teachers characterized the bright, anxious child with the desirable traits of "independence" and "adaptability," it has been demonstrated that the bright but anxious child is extremely dependent upon task and instruction factors as well as upon the approval of authority figures, all of which inhibit spontaneity, independence, personal expression, and flexibility in school settings (Sarason *et al.*, 1960).

It is also interesting to note that teachers do not consistently differentiate in their ratings the bright from the nonbright children when these students have low levels of test anxiety. In some way then, the bright, anxious child is perceived as special and possessing traits of which teachers approve. In short, teachers are most positive about such children.

The explanation was advanced that the favorable attitude of teachers toward the HA-HIQ children was engendered in large part by the child's

TABLE I

STUDENT CHARACTERISTICS RATED BY TEACHERS[a]

Trait[b]	Trait[b]
1. Anxious: Unanxious	13. Withdraws: Sociable
(2). Dependent: Independent	14. Daydreams: Does not daydream
3. Shows or expresses emotions: Hides or suppresses emotions	15. Active: Inactive
	16. Overachievers: Underachievers
(4). Communicates easily: Difficulty communicating	(17). Learns slowly (new material): Learns quickly (new material)
5. Aggressive: Submissive	
6. Impulsive: Cautious	(18). Retains material: Forgets material
7. Sensitive: Not sensitive	19. Fears failure: Does not fear failure
8. Tense: Relaxed	(20). Pays attention: Does not pay attention
(9). Ambitious: Unambitious	
(10). Adapts to changes: Set in ways	(21). Strong conscience: Weak conscience
(11). Well-liked: Not well-liked	
(12). Mature psychologically or emotionally: Immature psychologically or emotionally	(22). Feminine: Masculine
	(23). Pessimistic: Optimistic
	(24). Responsible: Not responsible

[a] Barnard *et al.* (1965).

[b] Trait numbers in parentheses have highest agreement as to the desirability of that trait, while those not in parentheses have least agreement and thus are least clearly positive or negative.

dependent need for approval by the teacher and by his attempts to secure it.

However much the teachers' perceptions may reflect the effects of bias, it is extremely unlikely that these children, who by their own self-report are "high anxious" *in the classroom,* manifest unambiguous anxiety which the teacher misperceives. Whatever it is the teacher is misperceiving (or misinterpreting) it is not likely to be the behavioral manifestations of unambiguous anxiety, even in a somewhat attentuated form.

It could be argued that it is only common sense to expect a child as he grows older to become more and more adept at keeping others from being able to discern feeling states which if overtly manifest would elicit a negative reaction. That is to say, the high anxious child (according to some anxiety scale) does in fact characteristically experience the paralyzing, overwhelming, and frightening state we call anxiety, but he has learned to keep this from becoming manifest and, hence, observable by others. This possibility cannot be denied although there is no basis for assuming that it would hold for all or even a majority of children who score high anxious. It should also be noted that this possibility suggests that it would be more appropriate to talk of private rather than manifest anxiety, a distinction which brings to the fore the question of why it is important for the child to keep the experience as private as possible. This distinction also permits one to ask if the frequently found interfering effects on performance reflect not anxiety per se, but rather the processes and actions related to the need to keep the experience or feeling state private. The public nature of anxiety in very young children galvanizes the human environment into action, a reaction not possible when the child's goal is to keep the anxiety private.

What I have attempted to do thus far is to bring into question two assumptions commonly held about high scores in anxiety scales: (1) that they reflect the tendency to experience and manifest frequently the overt behavioral characteristics of what I have termed unambiguous anxiety, and (2) that in the case where "anxiety" leads to inadequate behavior it is the anxiety per se which is the causal agent (rather than some intervening processes). In questioning the first assumption I am trying to bring attention to the absence of studies directed to the overt behavioral characteristics of high scores, e.g., facial expressions, postural and muscular qualities, voice changes, and other characteristics which could reflect the experience of anxiety. It certainly should give one pause if such studies did not reveal any differences between individuals with high and low scores; at the very least it would suggest that we may have been using the term anxiety in a somewhat indiscriminate way.

In connection with the second assumption it could be argued that, since scores of studies have successfully tested predictions based on the belief that anxiety scales measure anxiety, they lend credence to the hypothesized effects of anxiety. Although this argument has a degree of plausibility, and may be true, it is also possible that success in prediction may be due to variables different from but related to anxiety—a possibility which must seriously be considered when one faces the fact that the degree of accuracy with which predictions can be made is far from the point where one is ready to bet one's own money on prediction. Published studies, as well as those that remain unpublished because of negative or confusing findings, offer little basis for the assumption that anxiety scales only reflect anxiety.

For the sake of clarity I would like to indicate what I have *not* been saying or suggesting. I certainly have not intended to say or imply that anxiety is not a tremendously important force in personality development, particularly in the earlier years of life when it is most frequently experienced, publicly displayed, and responded to by the environment. In fact, the core of my argument is that anxiety is such a compelling experience that it can give rise to a pattern of reactions which, *however painful and self-defeating in their consequences,* reduces the likelihood of experiencing the anxiety again. The fact that this pattern of reaction can have interfering effects on cognitive performance similar to those of anxiety should not obscure the different factors and processes involved.

I have not intended to deny that high scores on anxiety scales are developmentally related to earlier experiences of unambiguous anxiety. The sense of this denial, of course, is that the high scores reflect attitudes, cognitive processes, and experiences which are consequences (in a development sense) of unambiguous anxiety and the environment's response to it. They are consequences which can develop a dynamic and autonomy of their own. This is not to say that high scorers never experience unambiguous anxiety. They do, of course, but I assume that in the course of development the frequency of such experiences decreases, in part because of the patterns of response which these experiences initially set in motion. This is undoubtedly too simple an explanation of either the decrease in frequency of the experience of unambiguous anxiety or its increasingly private nature during the first decade of life. We are far from understanding why in the early years of life the child can publicly display anxiety in a way he can rarely, if ever, do again.

Finally, there is nothing in my argument which is intended as a criticism of self-report scales. My criticisms have to do with the tendency to assume uncritically that a scale is measuring what its label denotes, a tendency which results in scales which never change in scope, focus, or their relation to theory. All major theories of personality concern themselves, in part at least, with constructs for which some form of self-report is the procedure of choice. The problem lies less in the difficulties of the self-report technique than in the degree to which the technique takes seriously the constructs it is supposed to measure.

The Concept of Defense

The reader familiar with the anxiety literature may regard the previous paragraphs as a distorted picture of how others have regarded anxiety scales. For example, the fact that lie and defensiveness scales have been developed and used in conjunction with anxiety scales demonstrates that anxiety scales have not been regarded as reflecting anxiety only. Although this is true, it should not obscure several things. First, the great bulk of anxiety studies have not utilized lie or defensiveness scales. Second, the development of these scales seems to have been based on the implicit assumption that they are most relevant for those with low anxiety scores, i.e., it is with low rather than high scores that one can question what the scales are measuring—high anxiety scores reflect anxiety. Third, there has been a surprising dearth of attempts on the theoretical level to understand (a) what defensiveness scales are getting at and (b) the relation of defensiveness scales to what is reflected in anxiety scores. It seems as if the development and availability of anxiety and defensiveness scales have rather effectively reinforced the tendency to collect empirical findings far more than the tendencies to make explicit and to refine the theoretical or speculative bases of the scales (Sarason *et al.*, 1960). For example, it is not at all clear if a "lie scale" reflects the tendency the label suggests, or if the significance of a particular lie score varies depending on whether it is found in the context of a high, moderate, or low anxiety score.

The need for clarification of the relationships between anxiety and defensiveness scales was raised in our first monograph (Sarason *et al.*, 1964) in relation to findings with the Lie Scale for Children (LSC) and the Defensiveness Scale for Children (DSC).

Although it was our expectation that use of the DSC scores would increase the size of the negative correlations between anxiety and IQ scores to a greater extent than would the LSC scores, the results in the present study reveal that both scores have similar effects. One possible implication is that measures designed to reach the defensive tendency give results suggesting that the perceptual, attitudinal, and control aspects of defensiveness can effect, or be related to, performance in ways similar to that of anxiety itself. In other words, the ways in which an individual avoids either the experience or the reporting of anxiety may have consequences in performance that are similar to those found when the anxiety is readily experienced and reported.

The fact that the LSC increases the strength of the negative correlations between anxiety and IQ as effectively as the DSC, raises again certain questions on the measurement of the defensive tendency. It has been our position that the defensive tendency is not unitary but varies with the content area under study. Consequently, the significance of the defensive tendency in one content area, such as anxiety, might not be clear until one related it to the pattern of defensive tendencies in other important content areas. The finding that LSC, which is concerned only with anxiety, increases the correlation as does DSC, which is concerned with other content areas, would seem to argue against our position. Clarification of the question will have to await further studies with more refined scales. For example, the LSC is a very short scale and was not devised to give comprehensive coverage of the different areas of anxiety. In the case of the DSC, the content areas are not sampled in great depth; the test probably does not sample all of what may be termed major content areas (it clearly does not sample anxiety over sexual matters). Thus, as with the LSC, we are still left with the problem of distinguishing between responses in which the child is consciously censoring his self-report and responses that he believes to be true but which reflect unconscious distortions of his perception of self and others. It is our opinion that, until these limitations are more adequately dealt with, we are not likely to further perceptibly our understanding of the reciprocal relations between anxiety and its cognitive consequences.

This problem is of obvious significance when we attempt to understand one of our most intriguing findings, i.e., the tendency (present in both sexes but more significant for boys) for the direction of extreme change in anxiety score from grade 1 to grade 3 to be related to rate of increase in IQ score over a four year period. It will be recalled that those children who decreased the most in TASC score from grade 1 to grade 3 gained more in IQ score over the period than those children who increased the most in TASC score. For illustrative purposes, let us focus on the children who in grade 1 are LA but who increase the most in TASC score in the third grade. How do we begin to understand their initial LA status? Were these children consciously distorting their responses? If so, then their ability or willingness to continue to do so changed by the third grade when they admitted to more anxiety than previously. One could speculate either that it was made easier for the child to admit to anxiety or that his experience resulted in a greater need to admit to his feelings. In any event, both speculations imply some kind of cognitive change in relation to perceived anxiety but both may not have the same effects on subsequent cognitive development. At the present we have no way of deciding between these speculations or others that might be offered.

But what if these LA children were not consciously distorting their responses to the TASC in grade 1 and their increased score in grade 3 represented a true change in perceived anxiety? This, it could be argued, suggests as one possibility that in grade 1 the child has already developed a pattern of defenses that prevents his own recognition of his anxiety but, as a result of increased school experience, the pattern breaks down. However one attempts to handle the question, the important problem is to determine the pattern of defensive or cognitive processes in relation not only to anxiety but to other important context areas as well. Although we consider the data on the extreme changers to be important, particularly in terms of the uses to which TASC may be put, we do not pretend to understand what factors make the children extreme changers. Such understanding awaits methodological developments that will take seriously the complexity of the relation between affect and defense.

The above considerations force us to return to . . . [our earlier discussion of the] . . . significance of our longitudinal results. . . . At that point we discussed the "presumed" effects of anxiety over time on indices of intellectual and academic performance. This phraseology reflected our awareness of the possibility that even if one assumed that TASC scores in the early grades were entirely valid as measures of self-report, it still did not follow that the later indices of performance, to which these early scores are related, could be explained as due to the presence of anxiety *at that later time.* Undoubtedly there are children who struggle with anxiety over the course of years and whose performance reflects the failure to control anxiety in adaptive ways. What we are suggesting here is that other children may be equally anxious initially but they develop a pattern of defense that helps them to minimize the degree of anxiety experienced. At the same time, however, these defenses subsequently have an interfering effect on performance. It is one thing to conclude from our data that among certain children anxiety is an etiological factor restricting intellectual and academic development. It is quite another thing to conclude that anxiety is not only an etiological factor in a chain of factors over time, but one that continues to exert a direct influence on later performance. This latter conclusion over-looks the possibility that over time the cognitive consequences of anxiety can affect performance in the same way as if anxiety were present.

The findings presented in our first report were found with even greater clarity in our second monograph (Hill & Sarason, 1966) which contains data over all of the elementary school years. For example, there was not a single overall relation between first-grade TASC scores and fifth-grade indexes of academic and intellectual performance. However, marked changes in anxiety scores from first to fifth grades are significantly and predictably related to indexes of academic and intellectual performance in the later grades. Table II contains data from our lower-grade sample of

TABLE II

RELATION OF CHANGE IN TASC BETWEEN FIRST AND FIFTH GRADE TO IQ SCORES FROM FIRST THROUGH FIFTH GRADE FOR LOWER-GRADE BOYS[a]

| | Mean IQ | | | | |
| Anxiety level | General | | Verbal | | |
(Grades 1–5)	Grade 1	Grade 2	Grade 3	Grade 4	Grade 5 (Otis)
LA–LA	104.4	107.8	117.4	120.2	115.1
HA–LA	111.0	114.6	121.2	125.4	121.9
LA–HA	106.7	108.0	114.4	114.9	111.9
HA–HA	107.0	105.5	109.4	110.4	108.4
Combined	107.3	109.0	115.6	117.7	114.3

[a] $N = 20$ in all cells (Hill & Sarason, 1966).

boys (those who in 1958–1959 were in first grade). Two of the groups (LA-LA, HA-HA) changed little if at all in anxiety score over the first five grades; the other two groups (HA-LA, LA-HA) changed the most in anxiety score over the same period. These and other data clearly indicated that children of both sexes changing most from high to low levels of anxiety significantly outperform those children who change most from low to high levels of anxiety on fifth-grade measures of intelligence and achievement. It should be emphasized that this meaningful relationship between changes in anxiety scores and indexes of performance is obtained consistently. Bas-ing the analyses on changes in anxiety score for the lower-grade sample from first to third grade and for the upper-grade sample from fourth to sixth grade results in similar findings. In addition, the moderately high negative correlations between change in TASC and change in either LSC or DSC (which for lower-grade boys and girls changes from first to fifth grade and ranges from —.52 to —.65) give further evidence that marked changes in measured anxiety over the years are systematically and predictably related to indexes of academic and intellectual performance.

The preceding findings underline again the need for further investigations focusing on three classes of variables: anxiety, defensiveness, and cognitive performance. In all major theories of personality great importance is placed on the relation between anxiety and defense. What our data seem to add to the problem is the suggestion that cognitive processes and performance interact over time with the relation between anxiety and defense in ways which are as yet undetermined. This suggestion, however, underlines the complexity of the problem without introducing any theoretical clarity.

I am of the opinion that we are at the point when we can no longer accept the label of a scale (e.g., lie, defensiveness, anxiety) as a meaningful symbol for the processes or behavior it presumably reflects. If lying is a conscious process, issues can only be obscured if a lie scale reflects more than a conscious distortion in self-report. If, as in psychoanalytic theory, defense is conceived of as an unconscious process, it becomes crucial and a test of consistency in use of theory to determine whether or not a defensiveness scale is tapping such processes or, at the least, the relation of such processes to the cognitive responses we call "answers to scale items."

It took psychology a long time to recognize that conventional intelligence tests reflected a number of different mental processes or factors rather than a single "thing" or process. Paradoxically, it took psychology a long time *because* intelligence tests were found to have practical value, i.e., their usefulness tended to inhibit criticism of the basic assumptions underlying the tests and to play down data and observations which were contrary to existing conceptions of intelligence. "Intelligence is what intelligence tests measure"—this kind of attitude was conducive to changing neither ideas nor practices. It was a splendid "defense" against the need for intellectual struggle. May we not be at a similar point in anxiety research? We have a number of scales appropriately labeled (anxiety, lie, defensiveness) to communicate what we hope we are measuring. The scales have been rather fruitful in demonstrating certain relationships with other variables (also having clear labels), and it even seems that they can be developed to the point where they may have practical value in that they will contribute to decisions affecting the lives of people. This is no small accomplishment, and neither was the development and use of conventional intelligence tests. After a certain point conventional intelligence tests contributed little to our understanding of intellectual development and processes. Similarly, anxiety and defensiveness scales in their present formats and formulations may contribute less and less to our understanding of anxiety and defense.

Some Suggestions Concerning the Interpretation
of Anxiety Scales

My first suggestion is that we take seriously the implications of the possibility that high anxiety scores, except perhaps in a small number of instances, do not reflect what may be termed unambiguous anxiety or even some attenuated manifestation of it. Our own studies (Sarason *et al.,* 1960) indicate that from the overt behavior of high anxious children (in a situation in which they see themselves as "anxious") one may infer dependent, direction-seeking, conforming tendencies and, occasionally, a marked reduction in responsiveness. Rather than considering such behavior as "anxious," the behavior may be viewed as a successful mode of avoiding the experience of anxiety. That is to say, dependent behavior, for example, may be a learned, ego-syntonic way of avoiding experiences of anxiety. From this point of view a high anxious score may be tapping not anxiety but coping tendencies. The consequences for performance or problem solving may be the same as when anxiety is present.

One can assume, however, that there are variations among children in the degree to which past experience has facilitated and reinforced dependency as an ego-syntonic way of thinking about self and relating to others. In the successful case, the dependency "works" in that it is manifested and responded to by others in ways which in one way or another are satisfying—it may well be that these are the children who in the teacher-rating study discussed earlier were viewed in the most favorable terms. In the unsuccessful case, the dependent tendencies are there but the consequences of their expression do not lead to a satisfying state of affairs, thus requiring other maneuvers to avoid the experience of anxiety. It is easy to overlook the fact that a defense against anxiety may have consequences which then require further defensive maneuvers.

In this connection attention should be directed to a type of child, not large in number, that has been somewhat of a puzzle. I refer to the child who gets a high anxiety score but who overtly behaves in a hostile and aggressive manner, which in our way of thinking is atypical for those with high anxiety scores. On the basis of informal and scattered observations it is my impression that in these cases hostile and aggressive behavior are consequences of the lack of success of dependent tendencies. This is not to say that they are not dependent but that the lack of satisfaction gives rise to other ways of responding which also vary in the degree to which they allow the avoidance of the experience of anxiety. I should add that the problem-solving behavior of these children tends to be poor and markedly erratic.

Although the above clinical speculations may be in error, I will be surprised if the assumption that high anxiety scores primarily tap defensive tendencies, rather than anxiety, turns out to be largely wrong. In any event, at the present time we have no good basis for assuming that high anxiety scores primarily reflect in any clear way the tendency to experience and manifest anxiety frequently.

TABLE III

RELATION OF TASC AND LSC IN THE FIFTH GRADE TO TEST SCORES FROM THE
FOURTH AND FIFTH GRADE FOR LOWER-GRADE BOYS[a]

Group (anxiety–lie-tendency levels)	Grade 4 IQ verbal (standard)	Grade 5				
		IQ verbal (Otis) (standard)	EQ total (months)	Reading general (months)	Arithmetic concepts (months)	Arithmetic problem solving (months)
LA–LL	129.2	121.8	81.8	85.4	76.2	72.3
LA–HL	116.8	116.3	72.6	76.4	68.3	66.3
HA–LL	118.8	115.2	73.8	71.6	73.4	68.2
HA–HL	110.6	108.0	65.4	63.2	66.2	65.3
Combined	118.9	115.4	73.4	74.1	71.1	68.0

[a] $N = 20$ in all cells (Hill & Sarason, 1966).

TABLE IV

RELATION OF TASC AND LSC IN THE THIRD GRADE TO IQ AND EQ SCORES FROM
THIRD, FOURTH, AND FIFTH GRADE FOR LOWER-GRADE BOYS[a]

Group (anxiety–lie-tendency levels)	IQ verbal (standard)			EQ total	
	Grade 3	Grade 4	Grade 5 (Otis)	Grade 4 (standard)	Grade 5 (months)
LA–LL	122.9	128.0	119.6	118.7	80.0
LA–HL	113.3	117.4	113.6	111.0	73.4
HA–LL	115.3	115.8	114.2	112.6	73.8
HA–HL	109.6	113.6	108.6	107.9	68.6
Combined	115.3	118.7	114.0	112.6	73.9

[a] $N = 20$ in all cells (Hill & Sarason, 1966).

The tendency to view HA and LA children as different types of individuals, and to consider each group as relatively homogeneous, has been reinforced by the fact that in many studies their performances differ in expected ways. The most recent data from our longitudinal study (Hill & Sarason, 1966) suggest that such views are very likely oversimplifications. Tables III and IV contain data from our lower-grade boys' sample in which subjects are grouped on the basis of both extreme anxiety and extreme lie scores. The trends contained in these tables are also found in analyses with other grade and sex groupings, although not always with such clarity. The data suggest that within each anxiety group (HA and LA) those with low lie (LL) scores outperform those with high lie (HL) scores. Put in another way, within each anxiety grouping those who tend not to admit to universal worries (e.g., nobody has ever been able to scare me) outperform those who tend to admit such worries.

Since there is a very significant tendency in all our studies for anxiety and lie scores to be negatively correlated, it is the statistically deviant groups (LA-LL, HA-LL) within the HA and LA groups who excel in performance. At the very least, these data suggest that those who obtain extreme anxiety scores are probably not homogeneous on important personality variables. This is not a surprising conclusion and could be derived from either observation or systematic personality theory. The data in Tables III and IV raise a number of questions. Is the child who tends not to admit to what are considered universal anxiety experiences consciously keeping them private and, if so, is this related to a more general tendency to keep disturbing experiences from manifesting themselves? Is this tendency to keep private what other children can acknowledge publicly related to the use and content of fantasy, style of relating to other people, and affect expression? To characterize these children as "high liars" or "malingerers," or with other labels, should be the start rather than the end of investigation concerned with personality development and organization.

It can (or should) be assumed that not all individuals with HL scores are consciously aware of what they are doing when they persist in answering "no" to the scale items. Is it not likely that there are children who tend not to admit to what are considered universal anxiety experiences because of "faulty" recall of past experiences? Are we dealing with distortions of recall and not, for example, with something like "amnesias?" Are we dealing less with memory distortions of one kind or another and more with inadequate testing of reality in the here and now? In connection with the last question, it should be noted that one of the more consistent findings in the anxiety literature is that HA and LA groups tend to differ in the appropriateness or realism of their responses to inkblots. Here, too, we are dealing with between-group differences which tend to divert one's attention from the role of within-group variables which would lead one to a better understanding of the complex of variables which are always interacting with each other. How to conceptualize the interactions among variables is a problem to any systematic theory of personality. The practice of designing studies productive of between-group differences is not to be derogated, but it is a practice which theoretically is justified only if it leads to conceptions broad enough to encompass, better understand, and lead to studies of the sources of within-group differences.

I have already indicated that I seriously doubt that scores on anxiety scales reflect the tendency to experience anxiety frequently, except in a minority of individuals. I have no doubt that in the early years of life unambiguous anxiety is a frequent and highly upsetting experience. As the child grows older, however, such experiences become increasingly infrequent as a result of the different ways a child has of coping with anxiety. It is not only that a child defends against anxiety (in the psychoanalytic sense of that word) but also that the consequences of such defense lead to cognitive processes and cognitive interrelationships which vary widely in *their* consequences. To clarify this point I present the following observations of a child by Freud (1959, p. 12).

. . . I have been able, through a chance opportunity which presented itself, to throw some light upon the first game played by a little boy of one and a half and invented by himself. It was more than a mere fleeting observation, for I lived under the same roof as the child and his parents for some weeks, and it was some time before I discovered the meaning of the puzzling activity which he constantly repeated.

The child was not at all precocious in his intellectual development. At the age of one and a half he could say only a few comprehensible words; he could also make use of a number of sounds which expressed a meaning intelligible to those around him. He was, however, on good terms with his parents and their one servant-girl, and tributes were paid to his being a "good boy". He did not disturb his parents at night, he conscientiously obeyed orders not to touch certain things or go into certain rooms, and above all he never cried when his mother left him for a few hours. At the same time, he was greatly attached to his mother, who had not only fed him herself but had also looked after him without any outside help. This good little boy, however, had an occasional disturbing habit of taking any small objects he could get hold of and throwing them away from him into a corner, under the bed, and so on, so that hunting for his toys and picking them up was often quite a business. As he did this he gave vent to a loud, long-drawn-out "o-o-o-o", accompanied by an expression of interest and satisfaction. His mother and the writer of the present account were agreed in thinking that this was not a mere interjection but represented the German word "*fort*" ["gone"]. I eventually realized that it was a game and that the only use he made of any of his toys was to play "gone" with them. One day I made an observation which confirmed my view. The child had a wooden reel with a piece of string tied round it. It never occurred to him to pull it along the floor behind him, for instance, and play at its being a carriage. What he did was to hold the reel by the string and very skilfully throw it over the edge of his curtained cot, so that it disappeared into it, at the same time uttering his expressive "o-o-o-o". He then pulled the reel out of the cot again by the string and hailed its reappearance with a joyful "*da*" ["there"]. This, then, was the complete game—disappearance and return. As a rule one only witnessed its first act, which was repeated untiringly as a game in itself, though there is no doubt that the greater pleasure was attached to the second act.

A further observation subsequently confirmed this interpretation fully. One day the child's mother had been away for several hours and on her return was met with the words "Baby o-o-o!" which was at first incomprehensible. It soon turned out, however, that during this long period of solitude the child had found a method of making *himself* disappear. He had discovered his reflection in a full-length mirror which did not quite reach to the ground, so that crouching down he could make his mirror-image "gone".

For the purposes of the present discussion I shall make the assumption that this child's play, particularly in its initial stages, was a response to some kind of separation anxiety. One of the significances of the observations of this little boy is the light it sheds on the strength of his coping behavior with a particular problem. It is not only the repetitiveness which suggests a strong effort to cope, but also the variety of situations in which the problem is experienced and the degree of interest which these have for him. Equally important is the variety of cognitive functions which become involved in the experience and resolution of the problem, i.e., language, eye-hand coordination, curiosity, and perception of self, body, and others.[1] I am not maintaining, of course, that these cognitive features are intrinsically a part of the experience and the coping with this particular problem-solving task. For example, in the case of Freud's grandson the availability of the mirror and certain toys may have brought into the experience certain cognitive variables (e.g., perception of self and body, eye-hand coordination) which ordinarily are either missing or play a very minor role. In any event, the point I wish to stress is that there are probably wide variations in the cognitive consequences of an anxiety experience and that these consequences can play as fateful a role in development as anxiety itself. I would go so far as to say that the cognitive consequences of anxiety in children affect personality development to a greater degree than does the anxiety to which they were a response. It is these cognitive consequences— involving attitude formation, social perceptions, fantasy, judgmental processes, and the like—which take on a kind of pattern or organization that will itself affect the nature of subsequent experience at the same time that it will be changed by it. From this standpoint, verbal responses to items of an anxiety scale take on significances not contained in conceptions which view such responses as measures or indicators of the expression of a particular affect. This statement is no more than a glimpse of the obvious: a *self*-report about an affect involves processes not contained in a definition

---

[1] Following the completion of this paper I read a monograph by White (1963) in which he described and discussed inadequacies in psychoanalytic theorizing stemming from conceptualizations about instinctual energies. In addition to describing these inadequacies, White developed his own concepts of effectance and sense of competence as means for handling these inadequacies. The significance of his concepts seems to be clearly illustrated in Freud's description of the play of his grandson. White's monograph put in broader perspective some of the points I try to make in this paper about anxiety and anxiety scales, particularly the point that the avoidance of anxiety takes on a strength, or plays a role, as important as the experience of anxiety itself.

of the affect. What I have been suggesting is that the verbal response to our scales may be telling us more about the self than about the affect.

REFERENCES

Barnard, J. W., Zimbardo, P. G., & Sarason, S. B. Bias in teacher's ratings of student personality traits due to IQ and social desirability. Unpublished study, 1965.

Freud, S. *Beyond the pleasure principle.* New York: Bantam Books, 1959.

Hill, K., & Sarason, S. B. A further longitudinal study of the relation of test anxiety and defensiveness to test and school performance over the elementary school years. *Child Develpm. Monogr.,* 1966, in press.

Sarason, S. B., Davidson, K. S., Lighthall, F. F., Waite, R. R., & Ruebush, B. K. *Anxiety in elementary school children.* New York: Wiley, 1960.

Sarason, S. B., Hill, K., & Zimbardo, P. G. A longitudinal study of the relation of test anxiety to performance on intelligence and achievement tests. *Child Develpm. Monogr.,* 1964, No. 98.

White, R. W. Ego and reality in psychoanalytic theory: A proposal regarding independent ego energies. *Psychol. Issues,* 1963, **3**, No. 3.

CHAPTER 4

Affect and Behavior: Anxiety as a Negative Affect

Carroll E. Izard[1,2] *and Silvan S. Tomkins*

DEPARTMENT OF PSYCHOLOGY AND COUNSELING CENTER,
VANDERBILT UNIVERSITY,
NASHVILLE, TENNESSEE

AND

DEPARTMENT OF PSYCHOLOGY,
CITY UNIVERSITY OF NEW YORK,
NEW YORK, NEW YORK

For a number of years the authors have argued for the significance of affect in human motivation and for its status as a major personality subsystem, autonomous, yet interdependent with other subsystems of personality. Tomkins (1962; 1963) has presented a general model for human personality in which the affect system is the primary motivational component. As will be apparent, his *Affect, Imagery, Consciousness,* Vols. I and II, furnished much of the substance of this chapter. Izard (1959; 1960; Izard, Wehmer, Livsey, & Jennings, 1965b) has developed the thesis that the positive affects constitute the motivating experiences or conditions that instigate and sustain the behavioral functions requisite to effective functioning and creative activity. He has presented empirical evidence demonstrating the significance of positive affect for learning, perception, and

[1] I want to express deep appreciation to my father, W. Lee Izard, who is confronting death from leukemia as he has lived his 77 years—with great interest and affection for people, and without fear.

[2] The senior author's work on this paper was supported by Vanderbilt-ONR Contract Nonr 2149(03), Carroll E. Izard, Principal Investigator. The opinions and conclusions do not necessarily reflect those of the United States Department of the Navy.

constructive personality change (1965; Izard, Randall, Nagler, & Fox, 1965a; Izard et al. 1965b). He has also shown the disrupting and suppressive effects of negative affect (1964; Izard et al., 1965a; Izard et al., 1965b).

The central purpose of this paper is to present our conceptual analysis of the relationship between affect and behavior. The explication of this fundamental relationship requires that we begin with an overview of our general theory of personality. Then we shall present a detailed discussion of the affect system as the primary motivational system. Finally, we shall state our theory of anxiety—defining it as a negative affect, describing its development and socialization, and showing its relationship to other major affects and to behavior. As with any "new" theoretical position, this one includes many things from the past, but these are incorporated in a framework that calls for a different way of thinking about cause and effect relationships in psychology.

Affect and Personality

Personality is a complex organization of five subsystems: homeostatic, drive, affect, cognitive, and motor. Each system has a degree of autonomy or independence, but all are complexly interrelated. The homeostatic and drive systems are of primary importance in biological maintenance, reproduction, and the regulation of body functions; however, they interact with and influence the other subsystems of the personality. For example, the drive system may frequently be dependent upon the cognitive and motor systems in order to effect consummatory behavior and drive reduction. As long as body functions are normal and biological needs are met, these two subsystems are of little significance in the functioning of the human personality. Indeed, homeostatic processes generally occur without the individual's awareness or voluntary action. And so it is with drive processes (e.g., hunger), until physiological deficit creates tissue changes that demand awareness, cognition, coping, and consummatory activity. Even then, the cognitive processes and gross muscular actions required for drive satisfaction (body maintenance and safety) are so simple (certainly in a modern, affluent society) that they can become almost automatic. Most nonautomatic or complex behavior seen at cocktail parties is more a function of the affect system than of the thirst drive.

The three subsystems most important in social behavior and higher-order human functions are the affect, cognitive, and motor systems. These three systems are the underpinning for behavior which may be viewed as uniquely human. The affect system is the primary motivational system, the cognitive system is the primary communication system, and the motor system is the primary action system.

Any one of the five personality subsystems may dominate the personality and become the primary determinant of behavior. In a crisis situation, the homeostatic system may place the organism in a state of alarm and bring about a high degree of organismic arousal. Until homeostatic balance is regained, the individual may be dominated by the dysfunction. In cases of severe deprivation resulting in physiological deficit, the drive system may become dominant and remain in focus as the primary determinant of behavior until tissue needs are satisfied. Such situations are relatively infrequent in affluent societies, but more frequent in cultures where people are chronically deprived.

Under extreme conditions the affect system or a given affect may be amplified to such a degree that it becomes a unilateral determinant of behavior. In such cases there is no effective interaction between affect, cognition, and other personality subsystems, and hence the behavior is likely to be maladaptive, and certainly noncreative. Integrated behavior results when there is appropriate interaction among the subsystems of the personality. Most personality theories emphasize one subsystem of the personality to the neglect of the others. All must be taken into account in any comprehensive theory of behavior.

It is important to note that, in our conceptual framework, personality is defined in terms of process. Personality or any personality variable can be adequately understood only as process within the larger socio-cultural environmental process. This does not vitiate the concepts of separateness and uniqueness, which we feel are central in significance for personality. Indeed, uniqueness and separateness are concepts that depend upon social and environmental context for definition and differentiation. The important point here is that a great deal of affect (motivation) is fully understood only by viewing personality as process, where a central part of the process is two-way communication with the social and physical environment. This suggests the need for an increasing emphasis on the study of affect in interpersonal situations.

Considering the vast gulf that separates the few effective, creative personalities from the many inadequate and/or malfunctioning personalities, we must conclude that a great deal of human behavior is inefficient, unproductive, and maladaptive. We assume that the problem centers around the way our society has conceptualized affects, the methods we have adopted for the socialization of affects in our children, and the ill-conceived and gross procedures we have utilized in dealing with affects gone awry.

The basic assumption that the affect system is the primary motivation system cannot be overemphasized. Much of what we present in the way of a new conceptual framework derives directly from this central proposition. This assumption departs from contemporary psychological theory in two ways. It focuses on affect as the primary motivational system of the personality and thereby relegates the homeostatic and drive systems to secondary status (at least for higher-order human behavior); and it underscores the necessity of conceptually differentiating the various personality subsystems. At the theoretical level it is important to make a clear distinction between motivation (affect) and subsequent behavior (cognition, communication, action).

The fundamental assumption that the affects constitute the primary motivation system has wide-ranging implications for psychological theory. It calls for a new way of thinking about emotion and hence a new way of thinking about motivation. It calls for a reconsideration of many of the axioms that permeated psychology during the heyday of drive theory. For example, the prevailing conception of drive as the most widely accepted motivational construct leads psychologists to believe that organisms behave as they do in order to reduce drive. Our conceptualization of affect as the basis of motivation finds the notion of drive reduction not only inadequate but frequently 180 degrees off course. Individuals often behave as they do in order to amplify affect (motivation). We have had support from many sources (e.g., White, 1961) in questioning the power of the drive-reduction concept. Yet the notion that drive reduction is a comprehensive explanatory construct in motivation and behavior theory still persists and is represented subtly and otherwise in much psychological thought.

Our basic assumption has equally important implications for the application of psychology—in assessment, behavior modification, teaching, and in programs designed to foster the growth of creative personalities and effective social systems. We believe that any effort to understand, assess, and change behavior will be facilitated if we work on the assumption that the affect system is the primary motivational system, that any affect—anxiety, hostility, guilt, interest—is *motivational in nature*. This means that, at the beginning of any effort to understand and change the behavior of individuals, groups, or societies, there must be an "affect analysis." Affect analysis requires careful study of the structure and dynamics of the affect system. A complete affect analysis would begin with an assessment of each of the eight primary affects in much the same way that we might assess eight basic personality characteristics or traits. It would also be necessary to measure affective states under varying conditions. We would then determine the relationship between affects, between affects and drives, and between affects, cognition, and action.

THE THREE MOTIVATIONAL SUBSYSTEMS OF PERSONALITY

There are three subsystems of the organism that have inherent motivational properties: the homeostatic system, the drive system, and the affect system. Under unusual or emergency conditions any one of the three systems *may* become critically important in initiating behavior.

The Homeostatic System

The homeostatic system is part of the survival equipment of the individual. As a rule the mechanisms that constitute this system are silent, unconscious, physiological processes. They are automatic in that they function without awareness or voluntary action. Their principal function is to maintain equilibrium of biochemical conditions (concentrations of sugar, salt, oxygen and carbon dioxide in the blood, body temperature, etc.) necessary to sustain life. The homeostatic system is critical for the maintenance of a healthy body, and thus in a very general way it may contribute to personality characteristics that are strongly related to energy level. A highly efficient, sensitive homeostatic system may play an important role in determining an individual's pace or activity level, factors which in turn may be significantly related to more specific personality characteristics such as n achievement. (McClelland, 1965).

Regardless of the sensitivity and efficiency of the homeostatic system, even the vital biochemical equilibria (the "steady states" of body functioning) obviously cannot be maintained for long by internal processes alone. Disequilibria or deficits resulting from shortage of oxygen, food, or water require effective exchange between the organism and the environment. We view the self-sustaining individual's part in this exchange as purposive behavior, which in addition to the homeostatic system requires the drive system, affect system, cognitive system, and motor system.

The Drive System

The basic physiological and safety needs of the organism—hunger, thirst, sex, warmth, etc.—constitute the drive system. The primary function of the drive system is to provide *motivating information*. The drive system tells the organism where to behave, when to behave, what to do, and what to be responsive to. It is important to note that while drives have motivational properties, the drive system is primarily *informational* and not motivational in nature. (A detailed elaboration of this view of the drive system has been presented in Tomkins, 1962, p. 29 ff.) Whereas the homeostatic system is silent and unconscious in its operation, the drive system is basically a signal-sending system.

Drive mechanisms may send signals which pain or please, and Tomkins (1962) has distinguished three types of drive mechanisms classified in terms of their relationship to pain and pleasure. Some drives emit pain signals only, e.g., nausea, anoxia, and pain. Some drive activities initiate pleasure signals and are terminated by pain signals, e.g., eating. Finally, there are drives which are initiated by both pain and pleasure and terminated by concurrent reduction of both, e.g., thirst.

While a drive has motivational characteristics, it can act as a motivator only while it is operating. Memory of yesterday's hunger pangs do not instigate eating today. Since the memory of pain does not "hurt," it cannot produce learning or avoidance behavior. The memory of pain requires an accompanying negative affect (fear, distress) in order to motivate learning, or anticipatory avoidance behavior in the absence of actual drive stimulation (pain). For a burned child to learn to shun the flame, the following sequence of events is required: flame → pain (drive) → fear (affect) → association of flame with the combination of pain and fear (i.e., flame → pain-fear) via cognition → fear (continuing after cessation of pain) via postication or memory → association of flame or memory of flame with fear via cognition, i.e., the relationship between flame, pain, and fear is contracted so that flame (or memory of flame) leads to fear (of flame and/or flame-induced pain).

Thus, for a burned child to learn to shun the flame, he must first learn to connect the flame with the combined responses of pain and fear. Then, after the flame is no longer burning him, he must connect the flame or his memory with the fear response so that perception of flame induces fear. This entire sequence, as diagramed above, takes place in a matter of seconds. After these events, the following sequence is possible: perception or memory of flame → fear → awareness of relationship between flame, pain, and fear → anticipatory avoidance behavior.

Now, on perceiving the flame, fear is instigated and awareness of the relationship between flame, fear, and pain produces the desired anticipatory avoidance behavior. Such avoidance is not simply a consequence of a contiguity of flame and fear. There is drive (pain) amplified by affect and followed by motor behavior (avoidance). The interaction of the drive, affect, and motor systems is mediated in the main by cognitive processes.

The Affect System

The detailed definition and delineation of affect and the affect system, and the differentiation of affect from other personality functions will be presented in the next section. Here we shall frame the definitional problem with a series of general statements that constitute a summary definition of affect and the affect system.

Affect is a complex concept that has neurophysical, behavioral, and phenomenological aspects. At the neurophysical level, affect is defined in terms of density of neural firing or stimulation and changes in stimulation. At the level of behavioral or motor expression, affect is primarily facial response and secondarily visceral and bodily response. At the phenomenological level, affect is essentially motivating experience. To activate an affect is to motivate. When neural firing via innate programs produces affective (facial, bodily, visceral) responses, and the feedback from these responses is transformed into conscious form, affect is both a motivating and a cue-producing experience. Phenomenologically, positive affect has inherent characteristics that tend to enhance one's sense of well-being and to instigate and sustain approach toward and constructive relations with the object, while negative affect tends to be sensed as noxious and difficult to tolerate and to instigate avoidance of and/or nonconstructive relations with the object.

The affect system consists of the eight major affects and their inter-relationships. We refer to the affective component of personality as a system since, on the basis of both innate and learned characteristics, the affects are organized in certain hierarchical relationships. Due to the nature of the innate mechanisms, a given condition will activate startle, fear, or interest depending on the gradient of stimulation or density of neural firing. In turn, from idiosyncratic experience and learning, fear may activate distress, shame, or terror, i.e., extreme fear. Further, the affects have certain characteristics or qualities in common (e.g., generality, flexibility) and they tend to relate to other personality subsystems in a similar, regulatory fashion. One of the important and frequent functions of affect is that of an amplifier in the motivational system complex. Drives that are not reduced within the tolerance limits of the organism tend to instigate and recruit affects, which in turn amplify the drive.

The interest-excitement affect may bring the sex drive to high pitch; the affects of disgust, fear, or distress may modulate, mask, reduce, or completely inhibit the sex drive. Even behaviors motivated by homeostatic mechanisms are continually modulated by such affects as fear, joy, depression, grief, startle, distress, and anger.

The Affect System as the Primary Motivational System

A comprehensive theory of personality focusing on affect, imagery, and consciousness has been presented by Tomkins (1962; 1963) and the role of affect in learning, perception, interpersonal relating, and personality change by Izard (1959; 1960; 1964; 1965; Izard *et al.*, 1965a; Izard *et al.*, 1965b). Our aim in this section is to present a systematic summary of our conceptual framework as it relates to affect and the affect system, together with refinements and extensions of some of the earlier theoretical formulations.

GENERAL CHARACTERISTICS OF THE AFFECT SYSTEM

1. The affect system is the primary motivational system; affect is inherently motivating.

2. At the neurological level, affect is correlated with density of neural firing. At the behavioral level, affect is primarily facial response and secondarily bodily and visceral response. At the phenomenological level, affect may be considered a motive. Motive is defined as a "feedback report of a response which governs processes other than itself to maintain itself, to produce a duplicate of itself, or to reduce itself" (Tomkins, 1962, p. 42).

3. The affect system is the principal provider of blueprints for cognition, decision, and action. Thus, affect enters integrally into the development of the *Image* (Tomkins, 1962) that governs man's purposive, goal-seeking behavior.

4. Affects do not necessarily occur in their pure form. In fact, admixtures of affective responses are probably the rule, even in the experimental laboratory.

5. The affect system has a significant degree of independence from the other systems.

THE NEUROLOGICAL BASIS OF AFFECT: NEURAL FIRING, AFFECT, AND AMPLIFICATION

The relationship between neural firing or stimulation and the activation of affect is complex, though differences in affect activation are accounted for by variants of a single principle: the density of neural firing or stimulation. Density is the number of neural firings per unit time. There are three general classes of activators of affect: stimulation increase, stimulation level, and stimulation decrease. Thus, three distinct classes of affects are guaranteed: affects instigated by stimulation which is on the increase (surprise, fear, interest), by stimulation which maintains a steady level of density (distress, anger), and by stimulation which is on the decrease (enjoyment). With respect to density of neural firing or stimulation, then, the human being is equipped for affective arousal for every major contingency. If internal or external sources of neural firing suddenly increase he will startle, or become afraid, or become interested, depending on the suddenness of increase of stimulation. If internal or external sources of neural firing reach and maintain a high, constant level of stimulation he will respond with distress or anger, depending on the level of stimulation. If internal or external sources of neural firing decrease he will probably laugh or smile with enjoyment, depending on the suddenness of decrease of stimulation.

The general advantage of affective arousal to such a broad spectrum of levels and changes of level of neural firing is to make the individual care about quite different states of affairs in different ways. Stimulation increase may be disturbing and difficult to tolerate or may enhance inner harmony and sense of well-being, depending on whether it is a more or less steep gradient and therefore activates fear or interest. A constantly maintained high level of neural stimulation is invariably punishing inasmuch as it activates the cry of distress or anger, depending on how high the particular density of neural firing is above optimal levels of stimulation. A suddenly reduced density of stimulation is likely to enhance the experience of the moment, whether the stimulation which is reduced is itself positive or negative in quality. Stated another way, such a set of mechanisms guarantees sensitivity to whatever is new, to whatever continues for any extended period of time, and to whatever is ceasing to happen, in that order.

We have indicated that stimulation increase may result in positive or negative affect and that continuing unrelieved high level of stimulation results only in negative affect. In the case of stimulation decrease, we have said that the result is *typically* positive affect; however, we recognize the possibility that stimulation decrease may result in negative affect when a moderate stimulation level sustaining positive affect is decreased and the resulting reduction of stimulation or interruption of positive affect is experienced as mild negative affect. Such an occasion might be the loss from the perceptual field of an esthetically pleasing scene, sound, or tactual impression. It is plausible that this loss of enjoyment could take place with a concurrent loss (reduction) of stimulation, and it is not reasonable that loss of joy would activate joy.

Further, the interruption or incomplete reduction of excitment may produce shame. The interruption of excitement may also produce distress or anger as a secondary response to a greatly increased contraction of the skeletal muscles, as in the case of interruption of children's games by adults. Yet, it is possible that in the event of sudden and substantial decrease in stimulation this change might result in enhancement of the experience of the moment, followed by a condition that instigates negative affect. It is also possible that any interruption or reduction of positive

affect may in fact result in stimulation increase even though phenomenologically a decrease of joy or excitement may seem to be followed by a
condition that by comparison is both unpleasant and less "stimulating"
(dull, boring, etc.).

Whether the interruption or reduction of positive affect per se can
instigate negative affect (without mediation by stimulation increase) is a
problem which will require empirical investigation.

Affect and Amplification

Affect serves as a general amplifier to all motivational systems. Affect
intensifies any neural message which it accompanies.

The affect system can influence activation via the reticular formation.
In turn, the reticular formation and the hippocampus have amplifier-attenu-
ator functions in relation to the affects and the drives. There is a difference
between affect on the one hand and nonspecific amplification on the other.
There can be amplification without affect. The reticular formation amplifies
sensory and motor responses as well as affective responses. Amplification
and affect both have distinct and overlapping subcortical representation,
with a closer interdependency between negative affect and amplification
than between positive affect and amplification.

The difference between nonspecific amplification and affect is an important one. The reticular formation is a general amplifier which boosts
the gain of *any* message, be it a sensory, motor, memory, or affect message,
transmitted by the nervous system. In general, it is conceived to sustain
the state of alertness by generally amplifying all messages and to stand
in the same relationship to affect as affects do to drives.

Affective responsiveness, like amplification level, depends upon the
basic energies of the organism. Individuals vary considerably with regard
to level of energy mobilization.

THE BEHAVIORAL BASIS OF AFFECT: AFFECT AS FACIAL RESPONSE

Behaviorly, affects are primarily facial responses such as the smile
and the cry. The feedback from such facial expression, when transformed
into conscious form, has self-enhancing (positive affect) or disturbing
(negative affect) characteristics. These organized sets of facial responses
are triggered at subcortical centers where specific "programs" for each
distinct affect are stored. These programs are innately endowed and have
been genetically inherited. They are capable, when activated, of simultaneously capturing such widely distributed organs as the face, the heart, and
the endocrines, and imposing on them a specific pattern of correlated re-

sponses. One does not learn to be afraid, or to cry, or to startle, any more than one learns to feel pain or to gasp for air. Of course, one does learn to fear specific things, to be angry or ashamed or excited under certain conditions.

Most contemporary investigators have pursued the inner bodily responses, after the James-Lange theory focused attention on their significance. Important as these undoubtedly are, they are of secondary importance to the expression of emotion through the face. The relationship between the face and the viscera is analogous to that between the fingers and forearm, upper arm, shoulders, and body. The fingers do not "express" what is in the forearm, or shoulder, or trunk. They lead rather than follow the movements in these organs to which they are an extension. Just as the fingers respond both more rapidly and with more precision and complexity than the grosser and slower-moving arms to which they are attached, so the face expresses affect, both to others and to the self via feedback, more rapidly and more complexly than is possible for the slower-moving visceral organs. It is the very gross and slower-moving characteristic of the inner organ system which provides the counterpoint for the melody expressed by the facial solo. In short, behaviorally, affect is primarily facial. Secondarily, it is bodily behavior, outer skeletal and inner visceral behavior. When we become aware of these facial and/or visceral responses we are aware of our affects. We may respond with these affects, however, without becoming aware of the feedback from them. Finally, we learn to generate, from memory, images of these same responses of which we can become aware with or without repetition of facial, skeletal, or visceral responses.

The Major Affects

If the affects primarily are expressed behaviorally as facial responses, what are the major affects? Eight innate affects have been defined. They are listed here, along with a description of their facial expression. For each affect we list two descriptive terms denoting the end points on a continuum. There are three positive affects: First, interest-excitement, with eyebrows down and stare fixed or tracking an object. Second, enjoyment-joy, the smiling response. Third, surprise-startle, with raised eyebrows and eyeblink. There are five negative affects: First, distress-anguish, the crying response. Second, fear-terror, with eyes frozen open in fixed stare or moving away from the dreaded object to the side, with skin pale and cold, and with sweating, trembling, and hair erect. Third, shame-humiliation, with eyes and head lowered. Fourth, contempt-disgust, with the upper lip raised in a sneer. Fifth, anger-rage, with a frown, clenched jaw, and red face.

AFFECT AND FEEDBACK

Feedback and affect are two different mechanisms which may operate independent of each other. The infant passively enjoys or suffers the experience of his own affective responses long before he is capable of employing a feedback mechanism in instrumental behavior. He does not know "why" he is crying, that it might be stopped, or how to stop it. Even many years later he will sometimes experience passively, without knowledge of why or thought of remedial action, deep and intense objectless despair. Without initial awareness that there might be a specific cause that turns affect on and a specific condition which might turn it off, there is only a remote probability of using his primitive capacities to search for and find these causal conditions. The affect system will remain independent of the feedback system until the infant discovers that something can be done about such vital matters. Even after he has made this discovery it will be some time before he has achieved any degree of control over the appearance and disappearance of his affective responses. Indeed, most human beings never attain precise control of their affects. The individual may or may not learn to reduce his fear, or maintain or recapture his joy. Although the affects constitute the basic wants and don't-wants of the human being, it is only gradually that they become the targets for the feedback control system. It is a long step from the consummatory pleasure of eating and the affect of joy at the sight of the mother's face to the "wish" for these, and a still longer step to the instrumental behaviors necessary to satisfy any wish. Nonetheless, there is a high probability that the human being will ultimately utilize his feedback mechanisms to maximize his positive affects, such as excitement and joy, and to minimize his negative affects, such as distress, fear, and shame, and to maximize his drive pleasure and to minimize his drive pain.

AFFECTS, IMAGES, INTENTIONS, AND MOTIVES

There is a sharp distinction between affects as the primary motives and the aims or intentions of the feedback system. The purpose of an individual is a centrally emitted blueprint called the *Image*. This Image of an end state to be achieved may be compounded of diverse sensory, affective, and memory imagery, or any combination or transformation of them.

In many Images what is intended is conceived not as the maintenance or reduction of any affect, but rather as doing something (such as taking a walk) or achieving something (such as writing a book). Despite the fact that there may be intense affect preceding and following the achievement of any Image, there may yet be a high degree of phenomenological independence between what is intended and the preceding, accompanying, and consequent affect. Indeed, an individual may intend something nonaffective and experience quite unintended and unexpected affect upon the achievement of his purpose or Image. In the case of predominantly habitual action it is the rule rather than the exception that affect plays a minimal role. Driving an automobile, while engaged in conversation, represents the operation of an Image which is minimally represented in awareness. In the Image the individual is conceived to project a possibility which he hopes to realize and that must precede and govern his behavior if he is to achieve it.

Affect is conceived as a motive or motivating experience (phenomenological level) mediated by receptors (neurological level) activated by the individual's own responses (behavioral level). Motives or motivating experiences may or may not become organized with cognitions to form purposes. Ordinarily they do, and they generally tend to support strategies of maximizing reward and minimizing punishment. Human beings are so designed that they prefer to repeat positive affects and to reduce negative affects, but they may or may not act on these preferences.

AFFECT, AWARENESS, AND COGNITION

There is a kind of variable interdependency between affect and awareness of affect. It is not unusual for a person to respond in terms of an affect without being aware of it.

It is possible that attention to internal processes such as autonomic activity may interfere with complex intellectual processes such as those involved in learning and problem solving. It is incorrect, however, to equate autonomic feedback with negative affect, and the latter with only interfering properties. Certainly positive affects, such as excitement and its accompanying autonomic activity, may sustain rather than interfere with performance.

The ". . . relationship between the affects, their activators, and consciousness must specify both the density of the affect activator and the density of the activated affect" (Tomkins, 1962, p. 274). Specific hypotheses concerning the relationship between affects, awareness, and cognition have been detailed by Tomkins (1962, pp. 282–304). Here we shall give the more general principles.

1. In the case of competing affects, the one that becomes conscious is the one that has the greatest density of neural firing or stimulation.

2. The gradient of stimulation density is highly correlated with density of affect; hence the affect experience is similar in profile to its activator, e.g., the experience of startle is as peaked and sudden and brief as its characteristic activator.

3. Affects instigated by peak stimulation will achieve consciousness in competition with affects activated by absolute density levels at the moment of the peak stimulation. The affect associated with absolute density level will override the affect associated with peak stimulation over any period of time when there is a lapse of peak stimulation.

4. Continuing novelty will support continuing emission and selection of gradient affects in consciousness over absolute density-level affects and density-reduction affects. This is the principle that enables the human being to experience substantial periods of excitement in relation to anything having sufficient complexity, novelty, or uncertainty.

5. The affect system is the primary provider of blueprints for cognition, decision, and action. The human being's ability to duplicate and reproduce himself is guaranteed not only by a responsiveness to drive signals but also by a responsiveness to whatever circumstances activate positive and negative affect. Some of the triggers of interest, joy, distress, startle, disgust, anger, fear, and shame are unlearned. At the same time the affect system is also capable of being instigated by learned stimuli. In this way, the human being is born biased toward and away from a limited set of circumstances, and he is also capable of learning to acquire new objects of interest and disinterest. By means of a variety of unlearned activators of these wanted or unwanted responses and their feedback reports, the human being is urged to explore and to attempt to control the circumstances which seem to evoke his positive and negative affective responses.

The ultimate combinations (in the human being) of affect with the receptor, analyzer, storage, and effector systems produces a much more complex set of combinations than could have been built into the affect system alone, or into any predetermined affect "program." The gain in information from the interaction of relatively independent parts or subsystems within the organism is likened to the gain in information from a set of elements when these are combined according to the rules of a language.

No sooner do memory and analysis come into play than they too become activators of affect as potent as any of the inherited mechanisms. Indeed, it is the inheritance of a flexible, varying central assembly structure capable of activating and combining affect with varying components of this assembly that guarantees the basic freedom of the human being.

AFFECTS AND DRIVES: CONTRASTS AND RELATIONSHIPS

1. In contrast to the specificity of the drive system, the affect system has those more general properties which permit it to assume a central position in the motivation of human beings. The drive system is necessarily

a secondary motivational system because the drive alone is weak in motivational power and requires amplification from the affects; but the affects are sufficient motivators in the absence of drives. Much of the apparent urgency of a drive is an artifact of the *combined* strength of both affect and drive. Thus, if one is excited and sexually aroused, the excitement (which is in the chest and face, and not in the genitals) sustains potency; but if one is guilty or afraid about sexuality, the individual may lose his potency. One needs to be excited to enjoy the sexual drive, but one need not be sexually aroused to be excited—one can be excited about anything under the sun.

2. Affects may amplify, attenuate, mask, interfere with, or reduce drives. For example, positive affect is capable of blocking or masking pain impulses. Pain not amplified by affect and unattended is not experienced as painful.

3. Drive (e.g., pain) alone will not motivate learning (avoidance). Drive plus affect (e.g., fear or distress) will motivate anticipatory behavior or learning.

4. Drive pleasure and the positive affect of enjoyment are different responses even though highly correlated. Drive pleasure may under certain conditions arouse distress or fear, as in *anorexia nervosa*.

INHERENT RESTRICTIONS ON THE AFFECT SYSTEM

1. The affect system in comparison with the motor system is quite difficult to control. Control is most difficult and arousal inertia is lowest for stimuli over which the individual has little control.

2. Affects instigated by and linked to drive conditions are restricted in freedom.

3. There is a restriction on the affect system because of the syndrome character of its neurological and biochemical organization. Once an affect is instigated, all parts of the affect system tend to be innervated at once in very rapid succession.

4. There is a restriction on the freedom of affect due to the inherent limitation in the cognitive system. There are only so many channels available for the reception and transmission of information.

5. Memory of past experience of affect places another limit on affect freedom. The human being has the mixed blessing of being constrained and pushed by the vividness of past affective experience that can be present in memory and thought.

6. A final restriction on freedom of affect can be imposed by the nature of the object of affect investment, as in the case of the unrequited lover.

GENERALITY, FLEXIBILITY, AND REDUCED VISIBILITY OF THE
AFFECT SYSTEM

1. The inherent generality and flexibility of the affect system reduces its visibility and distinctness. The generality of site, response, and object of affect and the variation due to learning reduce the visibility of affect.

2. The visibility of affects is reduced by the fact that as a result of learning an individual may experience and express two affects simultaneously. These affects may continue as moods relatively independent of the environment.

3. The visibility of affect is reduced by the taboo on looking at the face.

4. Another problem contributing to the reduced visibility of affects is the complex relationship between language and affects as compared to the relatively simple relationship between language and the drive system. We have not been taught to accurately verbalize our affective experience.

FREEDOMS OF THE AFFECT SYSTEM AND THE FREEDOM OF MAN

Affects are motives that are more free than drives. The pseudoproblem of the freedom of the will and the general controversy concerning man's freedom has stemmed in part from this failure to distinguish between motives that are more or less free. Tomkins has described the role of affect in this sphere as follows: "Out of the marriage of reason with affect there issues clarity with passion. Reason without affect would be impotent, affect without reason would be blind. The combination of affect and reason guarantees man's high degree of freedom" (Tomkins, 1962, p. 112). Although most human beings never become able to control their affects with a high degree of precision, it is the complexity of the affect system that gives rise to man's freedom and competence. The affect system has some ten types of freedom not characteristic of the drive system.

1. The first of these is freedom of time; there is no essential rhythm or cycle as with the drives.

2. Affect has freedom of intensity. Whereas drives characteristically increase in intensity until they are satisfied, the intensity curve or profile of an affect may vary markedly in time.

3. Affect has considerable freedom in the density with which it is invested. Density of affect is the product of intensity and duration. On the density dimension, affects may either be much more casual than any drive or much more monopolistic.

4. The freedom of the affect system is such that affect can be invested in "possibility." Thus, affect underwrites anticipation, the central process in learning. It is the affect of fear that enables the burnt child to avoid

the fire; he will avoid it only if he is afraid of it. Affect can also be invested in positive possibility.

5. The affect system has freedom of object. Although affects which are activated by drives and by special releasers have a limited range of objects, the linkage of affects to objects through cognition enormously extends the range of the objects of positive and negative affect.

6. Affect may be invested in a monopolistic way in a particular mode of experience, such as in one of Jung's types. Affect may be monopolistically invested in action, achievement, decision making, etc.

7. Affects are free to combine with, modulate, and suppress other affects.

8. There is considerable freedom in the way affects may be instigated and reduced. As a general rule the organism strives to maximize positive affects and minimize negative affects, but even different aspects of the same activity may instigate or reduce negative and positive affects.

9. Affect enjoys considerable freedom in the substitutability of consummatory objects. It is the transformability of the affects, not of the drives, that accounts for the Freudian concept of sublimation.

10. Affects have great freedom in terms of "consummatory" response or response sequence alternatives, whereas drives as motives are quite specific in this regard. "There is no strict analog in the affect system for the rewarding effect of drive consummation. It is rather the case that affect arousal and 'reward' are identical in the case of positive affects; what activates positive affects 'satisfies,' and these satisfiers are spatially widely distributed" (Tomkins, 1962, p. 139).

AFFECT AS MOTIVATING EXPERIENCE

It should be noted that the term *reward* in relation to affect cannot mean the same as reward in relation to drive. In the case of drive reward there is typically a cyclical, fixed pattern: increasing drive → increasing goal-directed activity → consummatory response → drive reduction → period of cessation or decrease of drive-related activity → increasing drive → repetition of cycle. The case of affect "reward" is different. Affect activation is *not* followed by a fixed and irreversible pattern of events; there is no consummatory response followed by affect reduction and decrease in affect-related activity. For the affects the sequence is this: affect-activation → motivating/cue-producing experience → affect instigated/sustained/ cue-producing activity → 1 . . . n possible events.

In the case of positive affect, the motivating experience can be best described, not as rewarding, but as experience that tends to be enhancing and self-perpetuating. Such experiences instigate and sustain adient behavior—behavior that involves approach toward, attention to, and communion with the object of the affect when there is an object. In the case of negative affect, the motivating experience can be best described, not as punishing, but as experience that tends to be psychologically noxious and difficult to tolerate. Such experience instigates abient behavior—behavior that tends to produce avoidance and to reduce attention to and/or communion with the object of the affect when there is an object. While the terms rewarding and punishing may sometimes partially describe affect, they are always incomplete and often misleading. It is more nearly correct and more heuristic to define affect as motivating, cue-producing experience.

Psychological theory and research need to become more concerned with *how* affects and affect combinations *motivate,* and what behaviors they can instigate and sustain most efficiently and effectively. Attention to rewards or to rewarding and punishing reinforcing agents is more appropriate in the study of animals, young children, and the maladjusted, but even in these areas there is need for perspective.

Among the 1 . . . n possible events in the affect → behavior sequence, there could be: (1) events that amplify, attenuate, or sustain the original affect; (2) events that instigate a complementary affect (e.g., interest may heighten enjoyment or make anxiety more tolerable); (3) events that instigate a conflicting or competing affect (shame might interrupt enjoyment); (4) events that are mainly cognitive; (5) events that are mainly motor; or (6) any combination of these events. For example, consider a cognitive event. It would most likely obtain in situations where the affect instigator is cognitive in nature, a symbol or symbolic process such as a name or label, a word, phrase, sentence, or idea. If we instigate positive affect with a word there would be a motivating, cue-producing experience. The motivating aspect of the experience would instigate and sustain cognitive processes—the production of other words, phrases, thoughts. The cue-producing function of the affect selects or limits the range of words produced.

Through socialization and life experiences we develop ways of symbolizing ways-of-affect-experiencing or ways of thinking about ways-of-feeling. A given way of symbolizing or way of thinking might be termed an associative network, after McClelland (1965). A stimulus word that instigates positive affect will tend, via the cue-producing function of affective experience, to produce a positive-word associative network. Similarly, a stimulus word that instigates negative affect tends to produce a negative-word associative network. We would predict that a positive word would tend to produce a looser and more variable associative network than negative words, if relevant cognitive factors such as word frequency are held constant. Our reasoning is this: joy and excitement are generally accompanied by feelings of expansiveness and freedom, while negative affects are accompanied by constriction. This is the basis for the well-known observation that anxiety produces tunnel vision. Fear reduces subsequent cognitive and behavioral alternatives; enjoyment and excitement increase them.

Fear-Terror: Anxiety as an Affect

It is not new new to consider anxiety an affect. Most psychologists would probably concede that anxiety has an affective component. The novelty of our conceptualization of *anxiety as an affect* becomes meaningful only when we put it in context:

1. Anxiety is a negative affect, but anxiety and negative affect are *not* interchangeable terms. We posit five negative affects: (1) fear-terror, (2) distress-anguish, (3) shame-humiliation, (4) anger-rage, and (5) contempt-disgust.

2. Anxiety is subsumed under the affect fear-terror; it may be generated by innate activators, drives, other affects, cognition, and external conditions.

3. Fear-terror (anxiety), like each of the eight primary affects, is subserved by its own innate mechanisms.

4. Fear-terror (anxiety), as one of the eight primary affects, is part of the affect system. To determine the significance of anxiety, it must be considered *one* of the major affects.

Fear and anxiety are terms we shall use interchangeably on the conviction that there are no theoretically useful distinctions between them. The need for such distinctions is, instead, between anxiety and other affects or between anxiety affect and anxiety-generated cognitive and/or motor processes.

THE DETERMINANTS OF FEAR

The determinants of fear must be delineated into two realms, the physiological and the psychological. In the physiological realm, we are concerned with the mechanism of fear affect and with fear activation (the neurophysical triggering of the mechanism). In the psychological realm, we are concerned with the internal and external stimuli or conditions that evoke fear. In the psychological realm, there is a need to distinguish between the objective and the phenomenological levels. Fear may be activated physiologically, be observable objectively, but may not exist in awareness for the individual.

In considering the physiology of fear activation, we would like to add one note of caution. When we speak of fear activation we do not mean arousal as it is generally understood. Arousal is an ambiguous term, used variously to refer to affect activation, drive activation, orientation-reflex activation, and general organismic arousal. In our usage there are distinct mechanisms for each of the first three of these. We consider the function of the reticular formation to be primarily that of a nonspecific amplifier of drive, affect, or any neural message; thus its function is best described as amplification, not activation or arousal.

Fear Activation

At the neurophysiological level, we consider fear to be a stimulation or neural density-increase affect. Fear is activated by an increase in the density of neural firing. As previously indicated, there are three density-increase affects, surprise-startle, fear-terror, and interest-excitement. The innate and learned differentiation of these three affects equips the human being for every major contingency of stimulation increase. The most sudden and sharpest increases in density of neural firing activate startle. The next sharpest increases activate fear. Less sudden, less sharp increases in stimulation activate interest. Tomkins (1962) has presented the case for the differentiation of these three distinct affects based on differences in the gradient of stimulation.

Startle appears to be activated by a critical rate of increase in the density of neural firing. The differences between startle (or surprise, in its weaker form) and interest is a difference in the steepness of the gradient of stimulation. The same stimulus therefore may evoke surprise or interest, depending on the steepness of the rise of stimulation (which in turn depends on numerous factors, prominent among which is the degree of unexpectedness), or it may evoke first surprise, then interest, or it may evoke interest and then surprise, or surprise and then some affect other than interest. Let us consider each of these possibilities.

Whether a stimulus activates surprise or interest will depend on just how rapidly density of stimulation increases. Thus a gunshot will evoke startle rather than interest. An unexpected tap on the back of the shoulder by someone who is not seen will also evoke startle rather than interest. In the case of the gunshot the suddenness of increase of stimulation was primarily in the auditory stimulus itself. In the tap on the shoulder the suddenness of this stimulus might have been sufficient but the overall density of stimulation was so low as to have been insufficient to activate the startle in the competition between messages for transformation into reports. We assume that such a weak stimulus must recruit from memory information in the form of neural messages that have a steep rate of increase of neural firing to activate a sequence of further rapid retrievals which summate to activate startle. If the same person is somewhat less unexpected and seen gradually approaching, such stimulation may be just steep enough in increased density of stimulation which it recruits to activate interest or even excitement (the more intense form of interest) without preliminary startle or surprise.

If the stimulation rises in density so steeply that startle is evoked, the further exploration of this object may recruit, from the combined sensory and memory sources, perceptual messages of sufficient acceleration of stimulation density to evoke interest in the continued exploration of the object. The affect of interest may itself also activate startle rather than the converse. As we have noted before, the "double take" is such a case. Here the individual first responds with interest in looking at an object, which is weak and very brief, but sufficient to activate further retrieval from memory which produces a sudden-enough change in stimulation to evoke interest, which, combined with the on-going retrieval of further information, now provides a sufficiently steeper increase of stimulation to startle the individual and then to support further interest and a second look at the object. Startle need not of course be followed necessarily by interest.

There are at least two other possibilities. One is that as soon as the startling object is identified and it proves to be a very familiar object interest can be sustained only momentarily. The other possibility is that the object evokes some affect other than interest or excitement. Thus the identified person may turn out to be a familiar person who evokes the smiling response, since one of the activators of the smile is the relatively sudden reduction of startle or interest. The individual who appears unexpectedly may also activate fear rather than interest immediately after the startle. Our theory of the mechanism of fear activation is that it lies midway between startle and interest among the density of stimulation gradients. If a stimulus or set of stimuli, internal, external, or both, increases with a maximum acceleration, startle is activated. If the density of stimulation increase is less steep, fear is activated, and if it is still less steep, interest or excitement is activated. The intensity of each of these affects, whether it is surprise or startle, whether it is fear or terror, whether it is interest or excitement, depends, we think, on the absolute level of density of stimulation rather than the gradient of the rate of change. Thus a change from one loudness to another might startle, frighten, or interest, depending on the gradient of change of stimulation, but whether it evoked surprise or startle, or interest or excitement, or fear or terror would depend on the absolute density of stimulation involved. A gunshot would startle, whereas a toy cap pistol would surprise, though both involve the same gradient of sudden stimulation.

If startle, fear, and interest differ with respect to activation essentially only in the rate at which stimulation or neural firing increases, then we can account for the unstable equilibrium which there seems to be between them. First, it would illuminate the familiar sequence of startle, fear, interest. The same object which first startles quickly passes over into fear and this somewhat less quickly is transformed into interest or excitement. Lorenz (1956) has reported the characteristic lability of fear and excitement in the raven who, on first encountering anything new, flies away, up to an elevated perch and stares at the object for hours, after which he gradually approaches the object, still showing considerable fear. As he comes closer, he hops sideways with wings poised for immediate flight. Finally he strikes one blow at the object and flies right back to his perch. This sequence is repeated until eventually he loses interest in it. Harlow and Zimmermann (1959) have also noted the alternation between escape from and exploration of the feared object when the model mother is present. The infant monkey alternates between clinging to the mother and, when the fear has somewhat abated, going forth to explore the object and then returning to the mother.

This lability, which is based on a similarity of activators, would also account for the paradoxical conversion of electric shock into an activator of interest rather than fear. Pavlov reported that by appropriate gradualness of training procedure he could produce in dogs conditioned salivation to an electric shock which preceded the presentation of food. It could further account for the self-conscious titillation of excitement in human beings through the confrontation of danger which is sufficiently threatening to arouse a delicately balanced ultra-labile compound of excitement and fear. Sexual excitement may also be intensified through the pursuit of the tabooed, feared object if the fear can be kept within bounds (Tomkins, 1962, p. 252 ff.).

There are undoubtedly overlapping components in the affects of startle, fear, and excitement. This, plus the fact that there exists an unstable equilibrium between them, has important implications for anxiety theory and research. We shall reutrn to this in a later section.

Fear Activators

By fear activators we mean the internal and external stimuli, conditions, or situations that instigate the fear affect. We shall consider mainly the sources of fear in general psychological terms, thus from an objective or external frame of reference. However, in studying fear in a given individual we must remain cognizant of the need to take into account the internal frame of reference of the person considered.

Before considering the various classes of fear activators, we would like to emphasize the differences between an activator or cause of fear on the one hand and an object of fear on the other. Tomkins has discussed the distinctions between affect cause and affect object, with particular reference to shame-humiliation (1963, pp. 426–428); here we shall present these differences as they relate to fear-terror.

There is always an activator or cause of fear, but fear may or may not have an object. First, there may be fear activation with cause but no object. This is experienced phenomenologically as objectless anxiety. A person may wake up feeling afraid and describe his mood as one of apprehension. He may be able to verbalize the fact that he is tense and jittery, and this mood may have one of a great variety of causes. It may result from a distress-fear linkage formed in childhood. During socialization a punitive parental attitude toward distress may have made him literally afraid to cry as a child and afraid to feel like crying or to express distress as an adult. Thus, if the person awoke feeling sad and lonely, this distress may have activated the fear. It is obvious that this distress-activated fear would have no object. Because of the ubiquity and frequency of distress, an early and strong linkage of distress and fear may produce an anxiety neurosis.

Second, an object of fear may or may not be perceived as the cause of the fear. Take the person who awoke in the distress of sadness and loneliness and whose distress activated anxiety. He may begin to contemplate a tough examination on which he wants badly to make a good showing. His anxiety may now be perceived as being sharply increased by the exam. However, he may sense that his anxiety preceded his awareness of the exam. Then, he may be able to verbalize the fact that his anxiety must have some cause independent of the present object (exam), though the cause may be unknown to him if the distress-fear bind was unconscious or at a low level of awareness.

Third, the identification of objects as causes may or may not be correct. On occasion the tough exam may be both cause and object of fear. However, in our example where the fear activator was distress, the individual may have mistaken the exam or proximal cause of his *heightening anxiety* as the sole and original cause of his fear.

As we shall indicate in our discussion of the differences between distress-anguish and fear-terror, fear has a highly intolerable effect. Consequently, optimal functioning requires that fear activation be reserved for life-and-death emergencies—situations having high threat value because of their implication for the safety of the body or the integrity of the psychological self.

The specific fear activators may be divided into four classes: innate releasers, drives, affects, and cognitive processes (thinking, remembering, imagining).

Special Innate Releasers. From research such as that of Tinbergen (1951) we are just beginning to learn how special "releasers" evoke affect in animals. He reported that a gosling will emit fear to a model of a flying bird if the model has a short neck like a hawk but not if the model has a long neck like a goose. Whether there are any innate "releasers" of human affects is questionable. It is more probable, according to Tomkins, that the innate activators of human affects depend more on the general properties of neural stimulation than on the stimulus configurations of specific releasers.

Drives. In comparison with affect and cognition, drive is the least significant class of activators. Drive alone is often insufficient motivation for adaptive action, though any drive that increases to a point where it is signaling a critical deficit will activate affect.

Since the drive system is primarily a signal-sending system with relatively low motivational power, emergency action typically requires the activation of affect. The affect will in turn amplify the drive and increase the probability of drive-reducing or adaptive responses. For example, consider the need for air. "Ordinarily this is attended to without drive signals and without awareness. When the need for air becomes critical enough to require drive activation it also activates affect, ordinarily a massive fear reaction, which quickly reaches panic proportions if the obstruction to drive satisfaction is not immediately removed. The need is so vital that the massive affect in addition to the awareness of suffocation represents an important safety factor in guaranteeing immediate attention to drive satisfaction" (Tomkins, 1962, p. 46).

Pain, whether deficit-determined or exogenous, may instigate fear. To the degree that an individual's affects are monopolistically linked to drives, his freedom is restricted. Drive activity must necessarily be channelled toward drive-reducing objects, thus drastically limiting behavioral alternatives.

Other Affects. The activation of one affect by another may be mediated either by innate mechanisms or learned behavior. Almost nothing is known about the innate relationships among affects in humans. Based mainly on his theory of innate activators, Tomkins (1962, pp. 283–304) has constructed 19 hypotheses relating to affect-affect dynamics. Two of these, concerning fear, will be given here. (1) "All affects, with the exception of startle, are specific activators of themselves—the principle of *contagion*. This is true whether the affect is initially a response of the self, or a response of another. By this we mean that the experience of fear is frightening, the experience of distress is distressing, the experience of anger is angering, the experience of shame is shaming, the experience of disgust is disgusting, the experience of joy is joying, the experience of excitement is exciting. These are innate relationships. One may experience fear when one feels angry, but this is ordinarily a learned response" (p. 296).

The next hypothesis is related to fear reduction. (2) "The sudden reduction of intense, enduring fear, if complete, releases joy, but if incomplete releases excitement" (Tomkins, 1962, p. 290). Indirect support for the close relationship of fear and excitement can be found in Bull's (1951) study of hypnotically induced fear. She reported that her frightened subjects were caught in a conflict between the wish to investigate and the wish to escape. She considered this as evidence of the dual nature of fear. We would interpret the conflicting behavior as a result of the oscillation between fear-terror (motivating the wish to escape) and interest-excitement (motivating the wish or need to investigate).

Cognitive Processes. Fear (or any affect) may be activated by a cognitively constructed cause. Indeed, cognitive processes constitute the most general and pervasive fear-instigators. First we shall present a general picture of the way cognitive processes—purposes, aims—function as affect activators.

The human being has purposes, intends to achieve these purposes, and does achieve them through the feedback principle. Man's purpose is primarily a conscious purpose, a centrally emitted blue print which has been designated as the *Image* (Tomkins, 1962, p. 17). The Image is a projected possibility or end state which the person wishes to realize or duplicate. The Image, constituted of memory, percepts, or any combination of these, must precede and govern behavior if it is to be achieved. A feedback system is one in which a predetermined state, or Image, is achieved by utilizing information about the difference between the achieved or present state and the Image. Feedback from the cognitive constructions that constitute the Image activates affect. The affect which is activated instigates and sustains behavior that narrows the gap between achieved state and end state or Image.

Fear of a specific object may be activated by a cognitive construction, e.g., memory or anticipation. Unfortunately, such a cognition may not be accurate or precise, thus, one may learn to fear the wrong situation or too many situations or all situations and life in general. The memory or anticipation of fear itself is sufficient to activate fear. If an individual mistakenly identifies a person as a source of fear, he may nonetheless experience fear in thinking about this person, then in anticipating meeting him, and for the third time in actually seeing him again. In this way a person, object, or situation may become a source of fear first through hypothesis formation, then through anticipation, and finally through confrontation of the constructed dread object (Tomkins, 1963, p. 66).

A cognitive construction having great power to evoke anxiety (and shame) can develop in early childhood, if the individual, say a firstborn, construes the mother's response to a child born later as betrayal and desertion. Tomkins has presented a cogent example of this situation in his analysis of castration anxiety. The stage is set by inner conflict—the conflict between affect expression and the internalized demand for affect inhibition. Freud mistook this anxiety-producing conflict as one between the drives and the threat of castration.

Psychoanalytic theory, in its central concepts of the Oedipus complex, castration anxiety and penis envy, is an expression of Freud's paranoid posture. In Freud's world there is humiliation and terror, and the threat of castration is an extraordinarily appropriate symbol not simply of anxiety as Freud represented it but of the conjoint threats of terror and humiliation.

Consider that castration is not simply a punishment which terrorizes, but a symbol of an emasculated, inferior male who has been forced into a permanent, irreversible submissiveness to male and female alike. It is certainly not the most extreme punishment which we find in Freud's mythology. In the Oedipus myth it is the son who exacts the most extreme punishment against the father. He kills the father. If the father threatens the son, it is not to kill him but rather to humiliate him as much as to frighten him. Castration, actual or psychological, cannot, in fact, kill the son. To have called it castration anxiety concealed from Freud and others the dual nature of the dual threat. If Freud was more aware of the role of anxiety than humiliation in his and others' relations to their mother and father, he was also more aware of the threat from the father than from the mother.

If the mother will not continue to give her son her undivided love because she gives birth to another child and thus turns away from her favorite, the favored son is castrated by his mother. If she was unfaithful even in bringing him into the world, she was a whore even while she appeared to love only her son. The discovery of the primal scene was doubly painful for Freud, for he had half-convinced himself that it had been his half-brother Philip rather than his father who had impregnated his mother. He had deliberately urinated in his parents' bedroom at the age of seven or eight, and his recollection of his father's displeasure as we have noted was his father's statement, "That boy will never amount to anything." It will be remembered that Freud's dreams concerning this incident revolved about disproving his father's prophecy: "You see, I have amounted to something after all."

It would seem that the shock of the primal scene for Freud was the witnessing of a double betrayal which deepened the already severe feelings of humiliation. This was further reinforced by the nature of the reproof from his father. Freud's reaction, as ever, was counteractive—he *would* amount to something. Freud's recollection of the primal scene is, however, noteworthy in its absence of feelings of betrayal, when one considers his general intolerance of any kind of rival and his interpretation of its significance for others.

The meaning of the concepts of castration anxiety and penis envy must be understood in the context in which they originated for Freud. They did not originate at the age of five, when the young hero contested the king for the love of the queen. They originated when the mother turned to the infant intruder, weaning and "poisoning" her first-born. This is how he was "dethroned" and emasculated. He now develops castration anxiety for the first time—not because his mother has no penis, but because she has no breast—she has withdrawn the milk of human kindness and poisoned him.

Now he knows both terror and humiliation. She has betrayed him because she is not a good mother who always offers the good milk of human kindness but a narcissist, a whore who takes from the father, as from her son, as from the infant, what she must have, because she is empty of love and therefore envious of her son and her husband who have offered her their love for what they thought was her love.

You, my mother who have taken from me, must have some terrible lack in you which consumes you with envy of me. The mechanism is common among children. If one child calls another a "thingumabob" with intent to derogate, it is only a moment before the other child, stung to the quick, replies in kind, "*You're* a thingumabob." I am not bad because you rejected me—you are the bad one. I am not envious of the newborn infant. It is you, and all women who betray the love of their sons, who are envious of their sons, and wish to rob them of everything which is precious to them. Thereafter it will be a war between the sexes, in which I must suffer castration anxiety lest your penis envy devour and poison me. You will not again seduce me to betray me, to castrate me and humiliate me.

We do not believe with the English school of psychoanalysis that because the pre-Oedipal early years are critical in development that they are therefore necessarily "oral" in nature. The prominence of oral imagery in Freud and others we take to be symbolic of the positive affects of excitement and enjoyment and of negative affects of distress, shame, anger and fear occasioned not only by hunger but by the varieties of discomforts which infants and children suffer, not the least of which is the absence of the familiar and exciting face of the mother.

Castration anxiety and penis envy are not, to our way of thinking, genital masks for oral dangers; both are symbols of the threat to positive affect from negative affect—in short, the danger to love from hate (Tomkins, 1963, pp. 526–529).

FEAR PHENOMENOLOGY

Fear is an affect of great potency in determining what the individual will perceive, think, and do. Fear is the most constricting of all the affects. It can result in perceiving that is characterized as "tunnel vision," where the victim becomes functionally blind to a large proportion of the potential perceptual field. It can produce thinking that is slow, narrow in scope, and rigid in form. It brings about a tensing and tightening of muscles and other motor apparatuses and in terror a "frozen," immobile body. Fear greatly reduces behavioral alternatives.

Fear is experienced as apprehension, uneasiness, uncertainty, insecurity. The person has the feeling that he lacks safety, a feeling of danger and impending disaster. He feels a threat to the existence of the person-he-is; this may be sensed as a threat to the body, the psychological self, or both.

In his review of major philosophical and psychological formulations in the area of emotion, Hillman (1961, p. 154 ff.) points to a number of theorists who have considered anxiety as the most important, most basic emotion. He concluded from his analysis that ". . . in one respect emotions can ultimately be traced to a root concept of non-being," a concept usually associated with anxiety (Hillman, 1961, p. 163).

Despite the vast importance attributed to anxiety, very little is available on the phenomenology of this affect. Major works on emotion (Arnold, 1960; Knapp, 1963; May, 1950; Reymert, 1950) contain scarcely anything in the way of subjects' own descriptions of anxiety experiencing. A notable exception is the work of Bull (1951), who studied individuals in whom she had induced a "pure" experience of fear via hypnotic trance. After the emotion subsided but while still in the hypnotic state, subjects described the experience. Bull maintained that her seven subjects reported a consistent pattern of events. Perhaps the most prominent feature of the experience was a tensing-up or freezing of the body. Equally salient was a strong feeling of wanting or needing to escape, to run, to hide, to get away. Here are some examples from the subjects' reports. Subject B: "I wanted to turn away . . . I couldn't . . . I was too afraid to move . . . I couldn't move my hands . . . ." Subject D: "I wanted to turn away . . . I became very tense . . . ." Subject F: "My whole body stiffened . . . wanted to run away . . . I was petrified and couldn't move . . . ." Subject E (II): "First my jaws tightened, and then my legs and feet . . . my toes bunched up until it hurt . . . I wanted to shrink away, make myself as inconspicuous as possible" (Bull, 1951, pp. 58, 59). Bull interpreted her data as indicative of a conflict, experienced as a freezing-up in fear on the one hand and wanting to escape on the other.

As we have already indicated, Bull believes there is another duality in the nature of fear. "Thus the feeling of fear in its simplest form is definitely dual in character, and owes its existence to an uncomfortable struggle between the reflex of investigation (the 'what is it?' reflex of Pavlov) and the reflex of escape. These competing tendencies give fear a unique position in a sequence between the primary start or shock of surprise and eventual specific adaptive behavior, for which it is a kind of fumbling in the dark before a wholly satisfactory appraisal of the danger has been made. It means that fear is primarily bound up with the feeling of *uncertainty* as to (a) the exact nature of the danger stimulus and, therefore, (b) how to act with reference to it" (Bull, 1951, p. 100). We agree that adaptive, effective behavior in the face of a fear-evoking object or situation requires cognitive processes to appraise and differentiate the object or situation. Cognition is also required to generate or select a plan of escape or appropriate action. Motor responses are required to execute the plan. The sequence of fear–cognition–action is basically the same even in those situations where we are able to talk our way out of danger. We do not believe that the "reflex of investigation" is adequate to support these cognitive and motor activities in a complex and prolonged fear experience. Under such conditions extended, adaptive effort in perceiving, attending, planning, and acting would require the motivational experience of the interest-excitement affect.

DEVELOPMENT AND SOCIALIZATION OF FEAR

Since fear is one affect among several, its role in the personality depends upon the frequency and duration of fear experiences relative to the frequency and duration of experiences of shame, distress, anger, contempt, excitement, and enjoyment. For those whose developmental years have made the world terrifying, fear is of far greater significance than it is for those for whom the world is a vale of tears or an exciting, enjoyable adventure land. Looking at affect developmentally should help us determine the degree of constriction and rigidity or openness and responsiveness that describes the various affects.

Tomkins has detailed these general patterns that describe the development of the affect system or of a given affect. To summarize briefly, any ". . . affect may be so reinforced and generalized during development that we may speak of a snowball effect. Or it may be submerged, and outgrown but with vulnerability to intrusions so that we may speak of an iceberg effect. It may continue to co-exist with other conflicting affects to be finally integrated so that we may speak of the late bloomer" (1963, p. 156).

During development each affect that is experienced becomes associated with various cognitive symbols, i.e., images, words, thoughts. Such affect-cognition interactions result in a complex set of ideo-affective organizations or affect "theories." The influence of any experience on the total personality depends primarily on how it is processed in the cognitive-affective interactions that it instigates. That is, the significance of the given experience for personality development depends upon the transformations the existing ideo-affective organizations make upon the experience and vice versa.

We are continually behaving on the basis of ideo-affective organizations or affect theories. "A commonplace example is the pause of the individual at a curb before he crosses the street. It is certain that most of us at the curb learn to anticipate not only danger but fear. Few individuals experience fear at the sight of automobiles on the street. One of the reasons for this is an ideo-affective organization which informs the individual of the relevance of a broad band of contingencies for danger and for fear, and a set of strategies for coping with each of these contingencies. Thus on the curb of a city street, if automobiles do not exceed 35 or 40 miles an hour and do not deviate from relatively straight paths by more than a few degrees and if the individual allows a few hundred feet between himself and the oncoming automobiles, he characteristically crosses the street without the experience of either danger or fear.

The affect theory (a fear theory) here operates so silently and effectively that it would surprise everyman if the question of fear about crossing the street were even to be raised. He would say, quite self-persuasively, that he uses his common sense so that he doesn't need to be afraid. This is one of the major functions of any negative affect theory—to guide action so that negative affect is not experienced. It is affect acting at a distance. Just as human beings can learn to avoid danger, to shun the flame before one is burnt, so also can they learn to avoid shame or fear before they are seared by the experience of such negative affect.

This is one of the primary functions of affect theory. Without such ideo-affective organization the individual could at best escape after the dreaded experience like the child who can only pull his finger from the flame. The individual's affect theory enables him to act as if he were afraid or ashamed, so that he need not in fact become afraid or ashamed (Tomkins, 1963, pp. 320, 321).

Contrary to the Freudian position, a strong childhood affect theory may become a weak though adaptive and effective affect theory in adulthood. This can be illustrated with the crossing-the-street example.

It is clear enough that such a theory will not gain in strength as the individual grows older, if he is never endangered, because he observes the appropriate avoidance strategies. However, we can envision a strong theory growing weaker and thereby fitting the iceberg model.

Let us suppose that the individual had in fact been hit by automobiles not once but several times in his childhood, while crossing the street. Such a child might develop a strong fear theory, in which he became afraid not only of passing automobiles but of moving through space and of other human beings in general. Let us further suppose that gradually such a child is persuaded that human beings can be trusted, that mobility can be exciting, that even the dread automobile is not as dangerous as it appeared and that his experience had been truly atypical. As his positive experience grew in scope and he developed stronger and stronger excitement and enjoyment theories, the relative strength of his fear theories grew weaker and weaker. If now, as he stepped off the curb to cross a street, a prankster were to blow his horn unexpectedly, we might expect an intrusion from the past and a momentary panic lest he be hit again.

It would be intrusive in the present, despite the massive reactivation of former affect, so long as the further consequences of such reactivation were limited and constituted a minor episode in the life of the adult. It is, of course, always possible that such a reactivation would produce a major regression to the earlier monopolistic status of the strong fear theory, or an ultralabile oscillation between this state and the adult personality. In the latter case there would be a transformation from the iceberg to the coexistence model in which two relatively strong medium affect theories are in enduring competition between the present and the past (Tomkins, 1963, pp. 324, 325).

One of the most common of parental techniques for the socialization of affect involves the use of one affect to influence another. Many affects are socialized by shaming techniques. Fear may be attenuated by the evocation of shame: "You ought to be ashamed for acting like a scaredy-cat." If fear is habitually controlled by shame, the individual becomes vulnerable to shame whenever he senses danger or any threat which frightens.

Tomkins (1964, 1965) has discussed the role of socialization in the acquisition of knowledge and the development of ideologies. He posits a basic ideological polarity in Western thought. The issues in the polarity are these: "Is man the measure, an end in himself, an active, creative, thinking, desiring, loving force in nature? Or must man realize himself, attain his full stature only through struggle toward, participation in, conformity to, a norm, a measure, an ideal essence basically prior to and independent of man?" (Tomkins, 1965, p. 79). He maintains that the patterns of affect socialization play a vital role in determining whether an individual will develop ideo-affective organizations that resonate to the left-wing humanistic ideology or the right-wing normative ideology. Here we shall present a brief definition of terms and a description of right-wing and left-wing socialization of fear.

Ideology is used in a special sense to designate any set of ideas about which a person is at once most articulate and most passionate, and for which there is no evidence and about which he is least certain. Ideo-affective posture (e.g., a permissive attitude) is any *loosely organized* set of feelings and *ideas about feelings*. An ideological posture (e.g., a liberal democratic political position) is any *highly organized* set of ideas about anything. An ideo-affective resonance is the engagement of an ideo-affective posture by an ideology, when there is sufficient similarity between the two so that they reinforce and strengthen each other (see Tomkins, 1965, p. 72 ff.). During developmental years all individuals acquire ideo-affective postures, but not all attain an organized ideological posture. Whether an individual makes a given ideological commitment depends upon his acquaintance with the particular realm and his affective experiences therein, particularly those occurring during socialization.

Left-Wing Socialization of Fear

Socialization of fear which will produce ideo-affective postures resonant with left-wing ideology will include one or more of the following components.

1. The experience of fear is minimized. The child is exposed to a parent who refrains from terrorizing the child. Even when the parent himself may be frightened for the safety of the child he tries to protect the child without communicating his own fear. The parent believes and communicates to the child that fear is noxious and not to be invoked except under emergency conditions.

2. There is a verbalized ideology exaggerating the noxiousness of fear. The child's exposure to fear is not only minimized but he is also exposed to a verbalized ideology which exaggerates the noxiousness of fear and which is in some measure self-defeating, since the child is made more timid about fear than he need be. However, the general benevolence of the intention somewhat limits this secondary effect.

3. The parent makes restitution for fear. If the parent has willingly or unknowingly frightened the child, he atones for this by apology or explains that this was not his intention. He also reassures and reestablishes intimacy with the child.

4. Tolerance for fear per se is taught. If the child becomes afraid, the parent attempts to teach the child not to be overwhelmed by the experi-

ence, to accept it as part of human nature, and to master it. This presupposes a parent who is somewhat at home with his own fear, who can tolerate it in himself and others sufficiently to teach tolerance of it to his child. In particular, the masculinity of the father must not hinge excessively on shame about being afraid.

5. Counteraction against the source of fear is taught. Not only is the child taught to tolerate the experience of fear, but he is also taught to counteract the source of fear while he is experiencing fear. Such a technique was used in World War II to prepare combat troops to face fire; they were required to crawl forward while being shot at just above their heads. The child is similarly taught to confront various sources of fear, first with the aid of the parent as an ally, and then gradually more and more on his own. Visits to the doctor and dentist, confrontation of bullies among his peers, and confrontation of parental authority are all occasions for learning to counteract fear by going forward rather than retreating; and in the type of socialization we are describing these steps are graded to the child's ability to master them.

6. There is concern that the child not become chronically anxious. The parent, upon detecting any signs of anxiety in the child, attempts some type of therapy or refers the child to a therapist. Anxiety is regarded as an alien symptom and is treated as any other problem might be treated, with speed and concern. He is generally concerned lest the child's spirit be broken.

Right-Wing Socalization of Fear

Socialization of fear which will produce ideo-affective postures resonant with right-wing ideology will include one or more of the following components.

1. The experience of fear is not minimized. The child is exposed to a parent who relies upon terror as a technique of socialization. When the parent himself is frightened he communicates this to the child. The parent may be chronically anxious so that the child becomes anxious through identification. When the socialization is normative, terror may be used to guarantee norm compliance. The child may be terrorized into goodness or manners.

2. There is a verbalized ideology minimizing noxiousness of fear. The child is exposed to a parent whose verbalized ideology minimizes the noxiousness of fear, which has a double consequence. On the one hand the child is made less afraid of fear through identification with such a parent, but he is also made more anxious because this parent has no hesitancy in using fear frequently as a way of socializing him.

3. There is no restitution for the use of fear. If the parent has willingly or unknowingly frightened the child, he makes no restitution. There is no apology or explanation that this was not his intention. Nor does he attempt to reassure or reestablish intimacy with the child. If the fear has taught the child norm compliance the parent regards it as entirely justified.

4. Tolerance for fear is not taught. If the child becomes afraid, tolerance for fear is not taught. Either the child is permitted to "sweat it out" alone or the burden is increased by shaming the child for his fear. Some normative socializations, especially those aiming at toughness or independence, do attempt to teach the child to overcome his fear, but this is frequently done by invoking shame and other negative sanctions for cowardice. Other types of normative socialization emphasize the value of fear as a deterrent, so there is no motive to attenuate the experience of terror.

5. Counteraction against the source of fear is not taught. When the child shows fear, counteraction against the source of fear is not taught. It is either disregarded or derogated. If it is derogated, the parent may also force the child to counteract his fear by such humiliation that the child would rather be still more frightened than suffer further humiliation. The child so socialized may seem on the surface similar to the one who has been taught to counteract fear by graded doses and with the parent as an ally, but the difference is quite deep and will become evident under those circumstances in which counteraction proves impossible. Under these conditions the individual socialized through contempt will suffer deep humiliation, whereas one socialized by an ally will not.

6. There is no concern about anxiety in the child. The parent characteristically is insensitive to signs of anxiety in the child and disregards or minimizes them. He deprecates as an alarmist anyone who suggests the child might need help. So long as the child is meeting the norm the parent is not concerned with the hidden costs (Tomkins, 1964).

In the foregoing schema, we have depicted the socialization process at the right and left extremes, neither of which is intended to represent the ideal or correct form. Actual parental techniques of socialization vary widely and often include right- and left-wing elements. Determining optimal socialization attitudes and procedures remains one of the greatest challenges to psychological science.

FOUR OF THE MAJOR AFFECTS THAT INTERACT WITH FEAR

The list of primary affects and a description of their facial expressions were given earlier. In order to complete an adequate context for our theory of anxiety, we shall present a fuller discussion of four of these: enjoyment-joy, interest-excitement, distress-anguish, and shame-humiliation. All of these affects play an important role in the affect-affect dynamics involving anxiety.

Enjoyment-Joy

The smile of joy is innately activated by any relatively steep reduction of the density of stimulation or neural firing. Thus, sudden relief from negative stimulation such as pain, fear, distress, or aggression will produce the smile of joy. In the case of pain, fear, or distress reduction, the smile of joy is a smile of relief. In the case of sudden anger reduction, it is the smile of triumph. The same principle operates with the sudden reduction of pleasure, as after the orgasm or the completion of a good meal. Further, the sudden reduction of positive affect, such as excitement, also activates the smile of joy, in this case usually the smile of recognition or familiarity. In all these cases it is the steepness of the gradient of stimulation reduction which is critical. Also, a steep gradient reduction in density of stimulation necessarily requires a prior level of sufficient density of stimulation, so that the requisite change is possible.

There is a reciprocal relationship between excitement and enjoyment such that enjoyment can be activated by the postication or anticipation of what has previously given excitement. This can happen when the recognition of familiarity of the exciting experience in imagination suddenly reduces the excitement. Excitement can be activated by the anticipation or postication of sudden enjoyment, since the sharp gradient of a sudden smile of enjoyment may be sufficiently peaked to activate the affect of excitement. As a rule rather than an exception, one can enjoy excitement and be excited by enjoyment.

The smiling response and the enjoyment of its feedback serves several functions in the psychological economy of the individual and his society. First, the potency of the human face as a stimulus for the smiling response and the affect of enjoyment-joy makes it highly probable that man will be a social animal. Second, by accompanying a wide variety of stimuli and responses, the smiling response broadens, through learning, the spectrum of objects and activities which human beings can enjoy. In this way non-social objects and activities also become the objects of enjoyment, somewhat attenuating man's purely social responsiveness. Third, it places limits on the investment of the competing positive affect of excitement in the inanimate environment and in achievement as an impersonal motive which might otherwise assume monopolistic significance. Fourth, it reduces and offers competition to negative stimulation from drives and from negative affects. Fifth, it is instrumental in the creation of familiar objects in the perceptual domain and in concept formation. Sixth, it provides an enhancing experience subsequent to the sudden reduction of noxious stimulation from drives or negative affects and is thereby instrumental in producing positive commitments to objects which have conjointly produced and reduced negative affect. Seventh, by virtue of the cognitive elaboration of repeated joy in the presence of the object and negative affect in the absence of the same object, psychological addictions are created. We are arguing that the smile in response to the human face makes possible many varieties of human communion which are independent of eating and of touching the other.

The general role of enjoyment is critical in promoting courage to cope with fear and pain, in promoting frustration tolerance and persistence in coping with distress from excessive difficulty in goal attainment or from drive discomfort, and in promoting confidence in dealing with shame and other threats to a sense of competence.

Interest-Excitement

Interest-excitement is activated through a range of optimal rates of neural increase of neural stimulation density. A range of optimal rates is specified rather than a specific rate of increase, since it seems probable that interest is aroused by *varying* magnitudes of increase of stimulation.

The subjective experience accompanying the affect of interest can be described as a desire to extend the self. This is felt as a curiosity and sense of inquisitiveness accompanying amplification.

The primary purpose of the interest affect in terms of biological utility is as a necessary condition for the physiological support of long-term effort. There can be no long-term effort without the presence of the interest affect, for otherwise there will be no amplifier of the physiological basis for prolonged and fatiguing functioning.

The interest affect will often, but not always, combine with the orienting reflexes, enabling the individual to sustain interest and attention to complex objects. This is different from the startle affect, which serves to clear the central assembly for new information. Interest affect serves not to clear but rather to provide the motivation to continue gathering information about the same or similar source of interest.

The function of this very general positive affect is to "interest" the human being in what is necessary and in what is possible. Without interest the development of thinking and the conceptual apparatus would be seriously impaired. The interrelationships between the affect of interest and the functions of thought and memory are so extensive that absence of the affective support of interest would jeopardize intellectual development no less than would destruction of brain tissue. To think, as to engage in any other human activity, one must care, one must be excited, one must be continually motivated. *There is no human competence that can be achieved in the absence of a sustaining interest.* Not only are the drives and perceptual and conceptual apparatuses critically dependent on the continuing support of interest, but so too is the motor system.

Interest is a function of novelty such that as novelty drops, the affect of excitement abates. Interest is not the only response to novelty (e.g., startle, fear), but it is the only positive affective response and therefore is most suited to power creativity. Surprise is a response to novelty, but surprise interrupts ongoing activity; fear is too intolerable to enable the individual to explore the novel object and prompts escape from it.

Distress-Anguish

The crying response is the first response the human being makes upon being born. The birth cry is a cry of distress. It is not the prototype of anxiety. It is a response of distress at the excessive level of stimulation to which the neonate is suddenly exposed upon being born.

Distress is as general a negative affect as excitement is a positive one. Between them they account for a major part of the posture of human beings toward themselves, toward each other, and toward the world they live in.

Since we emphasize the distinction between distress-anguish and fear-terror, and since this distinction is not commonly made, we should at this time examine the distinction between these two responses. One of the critical distinctions between distress crying and fear is the difference between the wide-open eyes of fear versus the characteristic contraction of the muscles around the eye which produces the arched eyebrow and which protects the eyeball from excessive pressure and engorgement with blood. The second difference is the frozen immobility and lack of tonus of facial and leg muscles alternating with extreme tonus of facial and leg muscles, which produces the characteristic trembling features of the face as well as the hands and legs, in fear. In distress crying there is neither extreme tonus or loss of tonus, nor alternation.

Fear and terror evoke massive defensive strategies which are as urgent as they are gross and unskilled. Further, they motivate the individual to be as concerned about the re-experience of fear or terror as he is about the activator of fear or terror. In contrast, the lower toxicity[3] of distress permits the individual to mobilize all his

---

[3] Toxicity is used here in a special sense that goes beyond its simple pharmacological meaning; thus, a toxic condition is a highly intolerable, debilitating experience which, if prolonged, can be severely damaging and eventually fatal to the existential or physical self or to both.

resources including those which take time (e.g., thinking through a problem) to solve the problems which activate distress.

Thus if I am distressed at my poor performance as a public speaker, I can usually tolerate this sufficiently to work upon improving my skill. But if I become stage-frightened, I may freeze so that I cannot speak; or so that I then avoid the entire public-speaking situation lest I re-experience panic. Again, if failure in work is very distressing, I can try again and succeed. But if failure activates intense fear, of whatever content (e.g., that I never will succeed, or that I will be punished severely), then if I try again, it is with competence impoverished by the excessive drain on the channel capacity of the central assembly which the injuriousness and intolerableness of fear entails.

If I am completely intimidated by fear, then I will not try again, and there is no possibility of solving this particular problem. What is more serious, my development as a general problem-solver is thereby jeopardized. Again, if in general social relationships an individual is rebuffed or is left alone and responds with distress, he can re-examine this particular instance, and decide to seek friendship elsewhere, or tolerate the distress of loneliness or change his own behavior to please the other. If, however, the rebuff or the indifference produces intense fear, the individual may more readily generalize his experience so that there is a withdrawal from interpersonal relationships of any kind; or, in attempting to master such anxiety he may provoke more rejection and then more anxiety because of the grossness, incompetence, and craven submissiveness obvious to those towards whom such overtures are made.

In short, fear is an affect designed to rapidly minimize acquaintance with its source, whereas distress is designed to reduce such acquaintance but with less urgency and therefore with more mobilization of the best resources of the individual and so with more competence. Under emergency conditions, distress would be a luxury which most organisms could not afford.

If one wishes to guarantee commitment to any object, be it a person, an institution, a profession, or a way of life, one must not only provide intense motivation but also sufficient distress, in the form of challenges, separations, and deprivations so that excitement is continually sustained by these sources of uncertainty, and by the continual redefinition of the object, and enjoyment heightened by the overcoming of these impediments, by reunion with the love object, and by the attainment of the redefined "new" object now seen in another perspective following distress.

Because of the freedom of objects of distress, and because distress is a necessary condition for the formation of stable commitment to objects, distress can continually enlarge the spectrum of objects which can concern the human being. The objects of distress are in no way limited to what we have learned to be disturbed by in childhood. Development necessarily entails new objects of distress as much as it entails new objects of excitement and enjoyment. If I do not learn to become distressed by what can happen to my friends, to my wife, to my children, to my profession, to my community, to my nation, and to my world, then I have certainly failed to become completely human (Tomkins, 1963, p. 5 ff.).

Shame-Humiliation

The shame response is an act which reduces facial communication. It stands in the same relation to looking and smiling as silence stands to speech and as disgust, nausea, and vomiting stand to hunger and eating. By dropping his eyes, eyelids, head, and sometimes the whole upper part of his body, the individual calls a halt to looking at another person, particularly the other person's face, and to the other person's looking at him, particularly at his face. In self-confrontation the head may also be hung in shame symbolically, lest one part of the self be seen by another part and become alienated from it. Blushing is a frequent response auxiliary to the shame complex. The shame response is literally an ambivalent turning of the eyes away from the object and toward the face, toward the self. The adult modifies the response because it is not acceptable for him to express shame too openly, intensely, or often.

The innate activator of shame is the incomplete reduction of interest or joy. Hence, any barrier to further exploration which partially reduces interest or the smile of enjoyment will activate the lowering of the head and eyes in shame and reduce further exploration or self-exposure powered by excitement or joy. The experience of shame is inevitable for any human being insofar as desire outruns fulfillment sufficiently to attenuate interest without destroying it.

The pluralism of desire may be matched by a pluralism of shame. We have noted the extraordinary range of objects of excitement and enjoyment. Insofar as there may be impediments, innate or learned, to any of the extraordinary range of objects that activate excitement or enjoyment, there is a perpetual vulnerability to idiosyncratic sources of shame.

If distress is the affect of suffering, shame is the affect of indignity, defeat, transgression, and alienation. Though terror speaks to life and death and distress makes of the world a vale of tears, shame strikes deepest into the heart of man. While terror and distress hurt, they are wounds inflicted from outside which penetrate the smooth surface of the ego; but shame is felt as an inner torment, an indignity to selfhood. It does not matter whether the humiliated one has been shamed by derisive laughter or whether he mocks himself. In either event he feels himself naked, defeated, alienated, and lacking integrity or worth.

Shyness, shame, and guilt are one and the same affect. It is the differences in the other components which accompany shame in the central assembly which make the three experiences different at the conscious level. Shame is the most reflexive of affects in that the phenomenological distinction between the subject and object of shame is lost.

The nature of the experience of shame guarantees a perpetual sensitivity to any violation of the dignity of man. Men have exposed themselves repeatedly to death and terror, and have even surrendered their lives in the defense of their dignity, lest they be forced to bow their heads and bend their knees in shame. The heavy hand of terror itself has been flouted and rejected in the name of pride. Many have had to confront death and terror all their lives lest their essential dignity and manhood be called into question. Better to risk the uncertainties of death and terror than to suffer the deep and certain humiliation of cowardice (Tomkins, 1963, p. 118 ff.).

FEAR DYNAMICS: THE INTERRELATIONSHIPS OF FEAR, OTHER AFFECTS, AND BEHAVIOR

The experiencing of "pure" fear in the absence of any other affect is probably of secondary importance in day-to-day behavior. When it does so occur it is likely to be an isolated event of limited duration. In personality dynamics, fear or anxiety is often linked with other affects. A person who is frequently afraid is also frequently distressed, ashamed, digusted, or angry. In this section we shall describe the relationships between fear and other affects and the effects of these affect dynamics; first, the negative affects, then the positive.

The Distress-Fear Bind

Distress is a negative affect of less disturbing, less debilitating effect than fear. Problems that distress us can be confronted and solved much more easily than those which frighten us. Distress is ubiquitous, fear more an emergency reaction. Thus, the linkage of distress and fear is of signal importance for adjustment. We showed how such a linkage could occur in our discussion of affect activators. For example, if a child who is afraid to go to sleep in the dark is spanked and made to cry, fear may become a learned activator of distress. If this fear-distress bind generalizes so that whenever this person faces a difficult, distressful problem or situation he becomes afraid, he is indeed maladjusted. Such a person is likely to stop trying to solve difficult problems, to live in dread of the new situations and uncertainties each day may bring, and to become very cautious about trusting and liking himself and other people. "Avoidance of the distress experience itself and of the circumstances which provoked it would become a much more likely strategy than attempting to control the sources of distress. A generalized pessimism which contaminates achievement motivation and communion enjoyment, and which produces a pervasive hypochondriasis, is not infrequently the consequence of the linkage of distress to fear" (Tomkins, 1963, p. 91). When an early and strong linkage of distress and fear snowballs, the result is likely to be severe maladjustment.

The distress-fear bind may produce a lack of physical courage. Pain, unadulterated by negative affect, is difficult enough for the human being to tolerate. Pain experience is an amalgam of pain, distress, and/or fear.

If there is a strong distress-fear linkage, then the sequence is likely to be pain → distress → fear, with subsequent panic reaction rather than courageous action.

The linkage of fear to distress also radically increases the difficulty of solving the essential problems of individuation and the sense of identity and the toleration of loss of love. It is difficult, because distressing, to tolerate the threat of loss of love and communion, which is part of the price of achieving a firm sense of one's own identity, that is to say, a part of the problem of becoming individuated from one's parents, from one's wife and friends, and from humanity in general. The addition of fear to distress favors more radical strategies of submission and conformity or rebellion and deviance, lest one experience the terror of loneliness and difference. Loneliness and alienation are no doubt distressing to most human beings, but they need not be terrifying if fear has not been closely tied to distress. The child who has been made to experience fear whenever he feels like crying is peculiarly vulnerable to the threat of separation from the parent who produced the distress-fear bind.

Nor is the impact of fear on distress limited to an increased sensitivity to the threat of separation from others. In addition, any sign of distress in others may also arouse anxiety in the self. Thus such an individual may become anxious if another person gives expression to his tiredness or illness, if another person expresses his discouragement and apparent failure, or if another person expresses his feeling of loneliness. All such attempts at communion through the expression of distress may evoke from the distress-frightened listener not sympathy but fear.

Further, since the experience of fear is so toxic, repeated distress-fear sequences can eventually power massive defensive strategies lest such experiences be repeated. Thus a person who is distress-frightened may deny that he or others are ever tired or sick, are ever defeated or seriously challenged in competitive striving and problem-solving, or ever lonely. Such a linkage may also power compulsive athleticism or withdrawal from the risks of life, compulsive achievement or passivity, and compulsive communication or isolation.

The punitive socialization of the distress cry then not only produces the serious problem of learning how to cry without being seen and heard, but may add to this problem the even more difficult one of coping with affects such as fear, which are more threatening than distress (Tomkins, 1963, pp. 94, 95).

Self-Contempt: Self-Disgust and Self-Fear

If a parent frequently responds to his child with disgust or contempt, the child will learn to expect such disgust or contempt. If the expected parental contempt is internalized, the self may be bifurcated, with one part of the self as judge and the other part as offender. The judging self finds the offending self disgusting. In this case the accused self may become afraid of the judging self, fearing that the accuser is right. He now fears himself as he once feared the tongue-lashing from his parent.

Fear of Fear and the Neurotic Paradox

As we have shown, cognitively constructed causes of fear may be both inaccurate and imprecise. This tends to make the individual develop a more comprehensive system of defenses than is demanded by reality. He has to defend himself against dangers that exist only in his perceived world. Effective defense or avoidance of these dread objects is rewarding in that it results in anxiety reduction. The continuing reward for avoidance makes it difficult for him to reevaluate the source of his anxiety and thereby discover its impotency and learn not to be afraid. He *fears the fear* that confrontation of the object would evoke. These imprecise, inaccurate cognitively constructed sources of fear and the avoidance behavior that precludes confrontation and mastery of them create the neurotic paradox, the resistance to extinction of such unrealistically exaggerated fears.

But even when the neurotic "knows" that as an adult he need no longer fear what might have constituted a real threat for him when he was a child, this knowledge rarely helps. We would suggest that a major part of this invulnerability to relearning is due to the fact that negative affect is usually learned not only to the innate or even learned activators of negative affect, but also to the experience of negative affect itself. It is as frightening to be afraid as to be threatened. It is as distressing to experience distress as to be in pain.

Since the neurotic is one who has had the continuing experience of severe negative affect about experiencing negative affect, it is insufficient to demonstrate that he need no longer fear or be distressed by the *object* which presumably originally frightened or distressed him. He is in fact now quite as afraid or distressed of reexperiencing the fear or distress which has happened to him hundreds of times in the absence of the supposed cause of fear or distress. We are suggesting that the fear or distress has long ago ceased to be activated by the original activator, therefore the knowledge that this activator no longer has the power it was once endowed with is not therapeutic. The neurotic must now be taught to tolerate his own negative affect, since it is the anticipation of his own fear or distress which has become the major activator of further fear or distress (Tomkins, 1963, p. 67).

The Fear-Shame Bind

If the socialization of fear has been accomplished by means of shaming techniques, the individual may be vulnerable to shame whenever he senses any threat which frightens. A strong fear-shame bind can result in a high degree of psychological entropy. If the fear expands to terror and the shame to humiliation, the combined effects of the two debilitating affects can produce paranoid schizophrenia.

The paranoid's shame may center around either the problem of immorality or the problem of inferiority. It is our opinion that in the last hundred years perceived inferiority has become a relatively more important source of shame-humiliation than immorality. The paranoid's fear is that he will be caught and found guilty of sexual or hostile intent or deed or that he will be made to feel more and more inferior until his perceived impotence brings on humiliation.

The Relationships between Fear and the Positive Affects

We believe that fear and excitement have overlapping components at both the neurophysiological and phenomenological levels. As we hypothesized earlier, the sudden but incomplete reduction of intense, enduring fear releases excitement. The lure of death-defying sports, such as automobile racing and bull fighting, represents excitement released by partially reduced fear.

On the other hand, when intense, enduring fear is completely reduced suddenly we commonly observe the smile of joy on the face of both children and adults . . . . There is also possible a combination of fear, excitement, and joy, in which fear is incompletely reduced, leading to excitement which is then suddenly reduced and produces joy. When, after much experimentation with a source of fear which has resulted in only incomplete reduction and therefore produced continuing excitement this latter is suddenly reduced, joy will be experienced . . . . When human beings are suddenly confronted with an enemy who collapses in the midst of battle or who flees, there is joy characteristically evoked. Any sudden mastery of a source of hitherto incompletely mastered fear will also produce joy. (Tomkins, 1962, p. 292).

Fear-Terror → Avoidance; Interest-Excitement → Creativity

We believe that Kierkegaard's (1844) provocative and insightful analysis of anxiety is a precursor of our concept of the relationship between anxiety and the positive affect of interest-excitement. Kierkegaard maintained that anxiety was the possibility of freedom, the result of man confronting choice or possibilities. Such possibilities involve unknowns, uncertainties, and hence anxiety. For Kierkagaard, the more "possibility" a man has, the more creativity he is capable of, and the more likely he will experience anxiety. In linking anxiety with freedom and creativity, Kierkegaard was laying the groundwork for differentiating anxiety and the positive affect of interest-excitement. He came very close to making the differentiation when he distinguished between fear as the affect that supports avoidance or retreat from the object and anxiety as the basis of an ambivalent relation to the object. This ambivalence is what we have described as an oscillation between anxiety (or fear) and excitement. The anxiety may result from the unknown, uncertain qualities or possibilities in the object, or choice; the excitement from the novelty and possibility itself, from investigation that reduces the uncertainty, and hence the fear. The anxiety places some limits on man's thrust into the unknown; interest-excitement sustains the exploration.

Thus, we draw sharp distinctions beween fear-terror or anxiety and the other negative affects and between anxiety and the positive affect of excitement. The distinction between anxiety and other negative affects is necessary if anxiety is to be delineated as a precise and scientifically useful construct in psychological theory and research. The distinction between fear and excitement should help clarify the ambiguity resulting from the seemingly paradoxical effects of anxiety as sometimes facilitating and sometimes inhibiting or incapacitating. Fear facilitates *only* defense or escape behavior not perception, learning, or performance (except as these effect avoidance of the object of fear), and not creativity or positive inter-personal relating, all realms where fear would be inhibiting or incapaci-tating. Whenever "anxiety" has been shown to facilitate behavior other than avoidance, there has been a failure to differentiate between fear-terror and the positive affects, particularly interest-excitement, the principal source of power for sustaining constructive, effective functioning and creative living.

Summary

We have presented a brief synopsis of a model of the human being, stressing the importance of relatively independent but interacting person-ality subsystems. The homeostatic system, the drive system, and the affect system are the three motivational systems. The homeostatic system under normal circumstances is the silent, "automatic" regulator of vital functions. The drive system is concerned with physiological and safety needs. The affect system is the primary motivational system, the principal provider of blueprints for cognition and action. Drives, though necessary for bio-logical survival, are relegated to a place of little importance in the behavior we consider uniquely human: constructive interpersonal relating, complex cognitive processes, creative activity. These kinds of human behavior can be understood and predicted only when we conceive affect as the dynamic, motivating, cue-producing experience. Similarly, maladjustments that are peculiarly human, the personality disturbances of neurosis and functional psychosis, are adequately explained in terms of affects gone awry, typically as a result of maladaptive affect socialization.

We presented the principal characteristics of the affect system, dis-cussing its relations with drives, its role as an amplifier of any neural message, and its relation to auxiliary amplifying systems such as the reticu-lar formation; we discussed the activation of the affect system, its generality, flexibility, and inherent restrictions and freedoms. It is the flexibility and complexity of the affect system that give rise to man's freedom and competence.

Anxiety, or the affect of fear-terror, was discussed as one of the eight major affects, five of which are negative. The activation of fear was dis-tinguished from that of startle and the positive affect of excitement. We consider the problem of innate activators and learned activators of fear. We emphasized the importance of cognitively constructed causes of fear and the distinction between causes of fear and objects of fear. We considered the area of fear phenomenology, though systematic evidence here is sparse.

We gave special attention to the socialization of fear. We described socialization techniques that cause the individual to resonate with right-wing normative ideology and techniques that lead to resonance with left-wing humanistic ideology.

We discussed affect-affect dynamics, the relationships of fear to other affects in both adaptive and maladaptive functioning. We showed the effects of fear and of fear in combination with other negative affects on personality malfunctioning, particularly as these are expressed in the neurotic paradox and paranoid schizophrenia.

We drew sharp distinctions between fear-terror (anxiety) and other negative affects and between fear-terror and the positive affect of interest-excitement. We maintained that anxiety facilitates *only* defense or escape and that interest-excitement is the chief facilitator of constructive behavior and creative living.

REFERENCES

Arnold, M. B. *Emotion and personality.* New York: Columbia Univer. Press, 1960.

Bull, Nina. The attitude theory of emotion. *Nerv. ment. Dis. Monogr.,* 1951, No. 81.

Harlow, H. F., & Zimmermann, R. R. Affectional responses in the infant monkey. *Science,* 1959, **130**, 421-432.

Hillman, J. *Emotion.* Illinois: Northwestern Univer. Press, 1961.

Izard, C. E. Positive affect and behavioral effectiveness. Duplicated manuscript, Vanderbilt Univer., 1959.

Izard, C. E. Personality similarity and friendship. *J. abnorm. soc. Psychol.,* 1960, **61**, 47-51.

Izard, C. E. The effects of role-played emotion on affective reactions, intellectual functioning and evaluative ratings of the actress. *J. clin. Psychol.,* 1964, **20**, 444-446.

Izard, C. E. Personal growth through group experience. In S. S. Tomkins & C. E. Izard (Eds.), *Affect, cognition, and personality.* New York: Springer, 1965. Pp. 200-241.

Izard, C. E., Randall, D., Nagler, S., & Fox, J. The effects of affective picture stimuli on learning, perception and the affective values of previously neutral symbols. In S. S. Tomkins & C. E. Izard (Eds.), *Affect, cognition, and personality.* New York: Springer, 1965. Pp. 42-70. (a)

Izard, C. E., Wehmer, G. M., Livsey, W., & Jennings, J. R. Affect, awareness, and performance. In S. S. Tomkins & C. E. Izard (Eds.), *Affect, cognition and personality.* New York: Springer, 1965. Pp. 2-41. (b)

Kierkegaard, S. *The concept of dread.* Transl. by W. Lowrie, Princeton, N.J.: Princeton Univer. Press, 1944. (Originally published in Danish, 1844).

Knapp, P. (Ed.). *Expression of the emotions in man.* New York: International Univer. Press, 1963.

Lorenz, K. F. Plans and vacuum activities. In *L'Instinct dans le comportement de l'animal et de l'homme.* Paris: Masson, 1956.

McClelland, D. Toward a theory of motive acquisition. *Amer. Psychologist,* 1965, **20** (5), 321-333.

May, R. *The meaning of anxiety.* New York: Ronald Press, 1950.

Reymert, M. L. (Ed.). *Feelings and emotions.* New York: McGraw-Hill, 1950.

Tinbergen, N. *The study of instinct.* London & New York: Oxford Univer. Press (Clarendon), 1951.

Tomkins, S. S. *Affect, imagery, consciousness.* Vol. I. *The positive affects.* New York: Springer, 1962.

Tomkins, S. S. *Affect, imagery, consciousness.* Vol. II. *The negative affects.* New York: Springer, 1963.

Tomkins, S. S. Psychology of knowledge. Invited address, Amer. Psychol. Ass., 1964. (Duplicated manuscript)

Tomkins, S. S. Affect and the psychology of knowledge. In S. S. Tomkins & C. E. Izard (Eds.), *Affect, cognition, and personality.* New York: Springer, 1965. Pp. 72-97.

White, R. W. Motivation reconsidered: The concept of competence. In D. Fiske & S. Maddi (Eds.), *Functions of varied experience.* Illinois: Dorsey, 1961. Pp. 278-325.

Part III
ANXIETY AND PSYCHOPATHOLOGY

CHAPTER 5

The Psychosomatic Aspects of Anxiety[1]

Roy R. Grinker, Sr.

INSTITUTE FOR PSYCHOSOMATIC AND PSYCHIATRIC RESEARCH AND TRAINING,
MICHAEL REESE HOSPITAL AND MEDICAL CENTER,
CHICAGO, ILLINOIS

In this chapter, I shall present my own research on the psychosomatic aspects of anxiety and that of the various co-workers who have collaborated with me in these investigations during their stay in my institute. The studies which will be cited will describe only a portion of the findings of a long-lasting research program on anxiety and other emotions.

Observations of Anxiety in Men under Stress

My experiences with anxiety began during the second world war which, as a natural experiment, stimulated interest in the human being under stressful conditions (Grinker & Spiegel, 1945). We observed that persons who experienced the holocaust of war were often stirred to increased and more efficient activity if anxiety were moderate. In this sense anxiety is facilitative; it stimulates better performance. Those of you who know public performers, or who have performed in public yourselves, recognize that if you do not experience a certain amount of anxiety you are likely to be ineffective. But excessive amounts of anxiety produce disturbances in performance, inefficiency, and often serious consequences. During the second world war there was much of the latter, and many individuals regressed both psychologically and physiologically in response to extreme

---

[1] This chapter has been edited from the transcribed tape recording of an extemporaneous presentation.

stress. When anxiety reached a certain level the whole world seemed to be a dreaded, dangerous place. There was a marked decrease in perceptual efficiency and a tendency to react with startle as if the slightest noise were an indication of some overwhelming threat.

The only retreat available under such stress was psychological flight (regression) which was often accompanied by a state of dependency characterized by a great need to rely on other people. Often there was an accompanying physical regression evidenced by a fetal-like position with the trunk flexed forward, the arms hanging down at the sides. Many of these severely anxiety-ridden soldiers looked as if they had adopted simian postures. Often there was generalized stiffness and sometimes a tremor resembling the Parkinsonian syndrome.

After the cessation of the stress stimuli, there was often an increase in felt-anxiety and an increase in its physiological and psychological concomitants. This occurred after the danger was over. We have seen this a number of times, not only during the war but also during our studies of soldiers training to become paratroopers. We viewed this as an "end phenomenon" which indicated that when the stress stimulus was at an end, defenses against reactions to the stress were weakened or abrogated and the phenomena of anxiety were intensified.

Thus, we can say in general as a result of our war experiences that anxiety is a curvilinear phenomenon in that it is associated with both differentiation and dedifferentiation. Some people who are stimulated by anxiety become more proficient and efficient; those who are overwhelmed with anxiety regress and react as if they were no longer adults in that they are unable to maintain the levels of emotional stability which they had previously achieved.

Early Investigations of Anxiety

When we returned to this country, we saw the same phenomena that we had observed overseas in soldiers who had returned after completing their tours of duty. Soldiers who had had some degree of anxiety became worse. We observed that many had severe physiological disturbances such as loss of hair, great loss of weight, and difficulty in maintaining body weight even though fed large quantities of food and stimulated with insulin (Grinker, Willerman, Bradley, & Fastovsky, 1946). We attempted to make a physiological survey of these returned soldiers and called for help.

The first Macy Conference was held at our request to give some leads as to how to deal with the serious psychophysiological problems of psychiatric casualties. To our disappointment the talent assembled had no hunches and suggested only that we survey bodily functions from A to Z. This would have been a costly procedure, but we did a few minor surveys suggested by the subjects' symptoms. One of these surveys was to determine whether or not the liver was damaged in cases of prolonged anxiety; the positive findings gave us our first significant lead to further research. We also noted that the breath-holding time of subjects with anxiety was reduced (Mirsky, Lipman, & Grinker, 1946).

We then developed a test which enabled us to evaluate the state of ego functions in the process of recovery from anxiety and called it the "stress tolerance" test (Harrower & Grinker, 1946). A Group Rorschach Test was administered and war pictures demonstrating the kinds of stress situations that these people had experienced were then flashed on the screen. Finally, a second group Rorschach was obtained. Those patients with considerably weakened ego or boundary functions had a great number of personalized failures and inferior responses. Those who were very much disturbed could not stand the sight of the war pictures and fled from the room. Thus, the stress tolerance test provided an indication, an index, of the ego's capacity to tolerate stress stimuli and, thereby, a measure of the degree of recovery. In subsequent studies of paratroopers in training we utilized specific pictures for that situation in order to measure ego strength. This technique has broad applicability.

When we returned from the military services, we started a research program which will be discussed here in some detail. It has general application to psychophysiological research as well as utility for the study of anxiety. This research program was undertaken originally because we felt there was a need for a methodological model generally applicable to the problems of psychosomatic research. We felt that if this model was fruitful in the study of a single emotion such as anxiety, it might be utilized in studies of other emotions and perhaps eventually lead to the formulation of more general laws (Grinker, 1956b).

Anxiety and Stress

We chose to investigate anxiety because of its great importance in the economy of human existence. Anxiety has a special role in the adjustive processes of the human organism, as both an indicator of response to stress and a precursor of further stress responses. This is so because anxiety has a tendency to feed upon itself, to become more intensive (Grinker, 1956a). As the ineffectiveness of the psychological and physiological organism becomes clearer, anxiety mounts. We become more anxious as we see our own ineptitude. We believe that anxiety is a signal to the self and others which indicates that organismic adjustments to present or expected situations are being made in dynamically related somatic, psychological,

and behavioral processes. A distinction between psychological and behavioral processes is made only in the sense that behavior is the action of
the total organism whereas psychological processes involve those aspects
which have to do with the organism's cognitive and emotional functions.
At higher levels of anxiety, as in war or unexpected catastrophe, equilibrium becomes so disorganized that adequate behavior, psychological efficiency, and somatic functions are profoundly disturbed. However, milder
anxiety is of great significance as a signal of threat for it precedes or
accompanies active preparation for adjustment.

Psychologically, defensive responses against chronic anxiety may be
manifested in such maneuvers as counterphobic activity, magical ritualistic
behavior or thought, withdrawal, or character alteration. Thus, anxiety at
some time may be responsible for the development of psychiatric syndromes and personality deformation. In the therapeutic process, and for
any form of insight therapy, we attempt to penetrate beneath the characterological defenses. Whenever we do, we come upon the phenomena of
anxiety. Without anxiety there is no fundamental shift in psychological
forces, actual insight, or emotional learning; therefore, the defenses which
hide anxiety must be penetrated. One of the best examples of the relation
between anxiety and defensive maneuvers is seen in our work on depression
(Grinker, Miller, Sabshin, Nunn, & Nunnally, 1961). We observed that
anxiety as a feeling experienced by the subject indicated that the individual
was moving into or out of a depression and that the other factors which
developed were defenses against the presence of anxiety.

Subsequent work has shown that when anxiety appears, the person who
is diagnosed as depressed is not as he looks—withdrawn and hibernating
physiologically. Instead, the patient is biologically active as evidenced by
the fact that adrenal cortical hormones are maintained at a very high level.
The degree of activity in depression may be ascertained by measuring these
hormones and observing the level of anxiety (Board, Persky, & Hamburg,
1956; Board, Wadeson, & Persky, 1957). Recent work has indicated that
when the patient begins to move out of the depression, as evidenced by his
anxiety and the elevated level of his hormones, he then presents the greatest suicidal risk of any time during his depression (Bunney, Mason, &
Hamburg, 1963). I think there is no question that anxiety is the central
focus of psychiatric investigation because of its dynamic importance.

Threatening recrudescence of anxiety in the present may intensify
previous defenses or evoke new types of defenses, because free anxiety is
one of the most unendurable afflictions of man. Man attempts to deal with
the anxiety, at least at first, by attributing it to some external source. He
likes to call it fear and signifies some object that he is afraid of, hanging

the reason for his anxiety on an external hook. There is constant confusion between the terms fear and anxiety, because man attempts to attribute his anxiety to external sources of which he says he is afraid, and when he is afraid it is because the external objects have some particular personal meaning to him, with some exceptions. In extremely stressful situations, all of us become frightened and anxious.

The Nature of Anxiety

As a signal of danger, anxiety is accompanied by a host of interrelated somatic processes which are in the nature of activity preparatory to emergency action. Often these are patterned in individual ways which are derived from the subject's early learning. Whatever the later stimulus, the personal pattern is evoked and recognizable. With decrease in psychological defenses and loss of control, anxiety mounts and the somatic processes tend to become less discrete in pattern and more diffuse, global, and undifferentiated. Similarly, the same dedifferentiation of function can be seen in the cognitive, conative, and behavioral processes as the defensive responses to the anxiety signal break down.

Anxiety can be identified as an affect in interpersonal behavior that is objectively experienced by the subject and communicated by him to an observer (Grinker, 1959). Such anxiety is experienced as an inexplicable foreboding of danger or disintegration. In our research we have never been concerned with unconscious anxiety. Although you will read about such phenomena, unconscious anxiety has no external reference—we cannot measure it—it cannot be reported because it is unconscious. It really means that, with the loosening of a certain defense, anxiety *will* appear. It is unconscious because at the time it isn't present. All of us are anxiety-prone; the problem is to find out what makes our proneness actual.

Unfortunately, much of psychosomatic research has been based upon these assumed affects which are but vaguely implicit in consciousness and expressed only indirectly in symbolic form. Anxiety in some subjects in stressful conditions can be nascent, that is, overt anxiety can appear in time after certain other indicators have made their presence known. For example, the excretion of hippuric acid, which I will speak about later as a delicate index of anxiety, may appear first in increased amounts and later result in conscious, reportable anxiety. We would say, then, that anxiety was nascent or latent because its appearance was not yet evident.

In research on anxiety, and in all psychosomatic research, we require a clear and consistent definition of the affect we are talking about rather than considering it as an inferred psychological state. We believe it important to define different qualities of anxiety related to the time of onset, the life history of the individual, and the conditions under which it appears. However, for the subject himself, anxiety is unitary in the sense that no matter what its source or how it came into being the experience is dreadful and foreboding. For our purposes, we try to differentiate its qualities and quantities. For the former, we still have only vague notions of the qualities of anxiety related to shame, possible harm to self, and the anticipation of personal disintegration.

Producing and Measuring Anxiety

When we returned from military service, we found that it was very difficult to obtain subjects who had free anxiety. I should like in passing to say that this is characteristic of the whole field of psychiatry. The kinds of patients that we see have changed remarkably and no longer fit into the accepted nosological categories. The classic hysterias, the anxiety neuroses, the people with free anxiety are rarely met. Instead, we see chronically restricted, inhibited characters which we have now lumped together in a wastebasket category called "borderline." These people reveal little in the way of free anxiety.

Very shortly after the war, we sent a crew of investigators to Fort Benning, Georgia, to see if we could work with subjects who were made anxious by having to jump from heights and ultimately from airplanes (Basowitz, Persky, Korchin, & Grinker, 1955). There was very little free anxiety in these paratrooper trainees. Therefore, we had to turn to manufacturing anxiety, that is, to take anxiety-prone individuals, find out what they were susceptible to, and make them anxious.

First, let me indicate that we tried to categorize anxiety in degrees short of what we later developed as our quantitative range. The phases of anxiety that I speak of are alertion, apprehension, free anxiety, and panic. We must be alert, otherwise we would be killed any day crossing the street. We are all from time to time apprehensive, and this facilitates our responses under certain conditions of strain. Free anxiety, which is a chronic, destructive kind of anxiety, is always neurotic (Korchin & Levine, 1957). Panic is an anxiety state in which the organism runs wildly in total behavior away from a supposedly dangerous situation.

Our first experiments involved studying the liver functions. We found that the liver's detoxifying function was highly correlated with the degree of free anxiety (Persky, 1952; Persky, 1953; Persky, Gamm, & Grinker, 1952; Persky, Grinker, & Mirsky, 1950). By measuring the amount of hippuric acid excreted after the injection of a substance which has to be broken down, we found that the rapidity and the degree with which this substance was broken down was an index of the height of anxiety. Anxious patients were treated and, as their anxiety decreased, hippuric acid excretion went down. In psychotic patients who were catatonic and withdrawn the hippuric acid was low; as they were coming back to life as it were the hippuric acid was high. At the time we did not know what it meant. But we do, I think, know more about it now. It would seem that the anxiety response in human beings is different than those responses that have been called "The Wisdom of the Body."

The anxiety response is an indicator of the stupidity of the body (Hamburg, 1961). To what avail does the human organism develop such a massive endocrine reaction (Korchin & Herz, 1960; Persky, 1962; Persky, Hamburg, Basowitz, Grinker, Sabshin, Korchin, Herz, Board, & Heath, 1958) and such violent increases in cardiac rate and blood pressure (Glickstein, Chevalier, Korchin, Basowitz, Sabshin, Hamburg, & Grinker, 1957) in order to mobilize for action in response to the slight stimuli that are imposed upon us? It is the detoxifying effect of the liver that confirms our speculation that all these stuffs are secreted only to have to be detoxified by the liver because they are not utilized. True, the adrenocortical steroids do potentiate the action of the sympathetic nervous system. But this is not necessary to the degree evoked by the slight stress stimuli about which we are talking.

We then tried to analyze the components of what we called "system anxiety" (Grinker, 1953a). We can view anything we want to as a system provided we recognize that its total structure has parts, that it has an enduring pattern over time, that it has capacity for maintaining its parts in some gradient within the whole system, that it has defenses against disintegration, and that it has a function in relation to other systems (Spiegel, 1953). So we attempted to determine the component parts of anxiety. That meant measuring a number of variables, not only the biological, psychological, and behavioral, but also the degree of anxiety itself (Grinker, 1961; Grinker, 1964). Here is where our methodological advances became most clear. In most psychophysiological or psychosomatic research, investigators carefully measure various physiological and biochemical variables and correlate these measurements with statements that the patient either is or is not anxious. We felt it was necessary to develop a system for measuring or estimating the degree of anxiety (Hamburg, Sabshin, Board, Grinker, Korchin, Basowitz, Heath, & Persky, 1958).

At first I worked on this alone with a 4-point scale, testing myself over and over again. After a period of time my estimates of the degree of anxiety correlated with the amount of hippuric acid excreted by the subject. Then, as we progressed to other research which I will describe later, additional people were added to the team to observe quantities of anxiety.

We were able to achieve a high reliability, not only within members of the team, but over time. If we took unknown protocols and estimated the degree of anxiety on a given day and then the same unknown protocols 6 months later, our reliability was high. In the correlations of the anxiety ratings with the best physiological indicators of anxiety available, namely, increase in heart rate, increase in blood pressure, and increase in adreno-cortical secretion, we then had both reliability and validity.

We estimated anxiety by: (1) observing the patient and developing sentences which described the behavior associated with varying degrees of anxiety; (2) interviewing the subject and obtaining from him statements regarding the level of his anxiety; and (3) having the subject himself rate his own anxiety. Subjects who are prone to anxiety and who have experienced anxiety are exquisite raters of their own level of anxiety. In the paratrooper studies, the self-ratings of anxiety by the young soldiers just about to enter the airplane were as good as those of trained observers whose reliability was previously proven (Basowitz et al., 1955).

We did not evoke anxiety by some common stimulus which was generally regarded as being capable of evoking a stress response. We are all prone to respond to stress with anxiety, providing the proper stimulus occurs. Therefore, the task of the investigator is to determine the appropriate stimulus for evoking a stress response. We did not start with the preconceived notions that shooting a gun or producing white noise would produce anxiety. Rather, one of the investigators in a transactional relationship with the subject probed to find out what disturbed him. Through the processes of communication (Grinker, Sabshin, Hamburg, Board, Basowitz, Korchin, Persky, & Chevalier, 1957), cues or clues of disturbances appeared, pressure was maintained, and the subjects became anxious. We found that the best way to produce anxiety was to impede communication, to block communication in a dyadic relationship. We pretended not to understand who the subject was; we made all kinds of stupid mistakes. Blocking of communication was the best means of evoking anxiety (Korchin, Basowitz, Grinker, Hamburg, Persky, Sabshin, Heath, & Board, 1958).

Methods of producing anxiety, such as threatened harm, or shaming, were relatively ineffective. Furthermore, producing anxiety seems to depend upon the personality traits of the individual. Some subjects become anxious when left alone in a room while hooked to machinery and have little anxiety when with people. Others have more anxiety when they are with people than when left alone. This in itself is a problem in group dynamics. We are sure that supposedly graded stimuli do not evoke corresponding grades of response.

We were interested in insuring proper controls. One way in which anxiety can be produced is through novelty or strangeness in a situation. We soon found that the preliminary day of an experiment could not be used as the control day; there was too much anxiety (Sabshin, Hamburg, Grinker, Persky, Basowitz, Korchin, & Chevalier, 1957). Indeed, it became feasible to use the first day during which the subject was in the laboratory to help us produce anxiety. The strangeness of the situation was one added variable which helped produce anxiety. The control day or quiescent day was always the last day of experimentation because, by this time, the subject had become familiar with the technical aspects of the experiment.

One of our greatest problems in psychosomatic research is the timing of the measurement of variables. It takes some time to produce anxiety experimentally. The adrenal medullary responses such as epinephrine or norepinephrine appear very quickly and have a very short half-life. Adrenal cortical steroids are elevated very slowly (Persky, 1957). Heart rate, blood pressure, and respiration have different time factors (Oken, Grinker, Heath, Herz, Korchin, Sabshin, & Schwartz, 1962). It has not been resolved in psychosomatic research whether these variables are simultaneously activated or whether one is a donor to another, or whether there is a series of chain reactions or compensatory cyclic systems which vary in speed and direction. The numbers which we use for each variable probably do not mean the same thing, and the number of variables involved creates many problems in data analysis, not the least of which is the "law of initial values" (Heath & Korchin, 1963; Heath & Oken, 1962; Heath, Oken, Korchin, & Towne, 1960).

Finally, because a single subject cannot be involved in an experimental session for more than 2 or 3 hours, we cannot extrapolate the findings from experiments involving the induction of acute anxiety in the laboratory to chronic conditions in man or say that one sort of anxiety response is related to the development of hypertensive syndromes, cardiac neuroses, etc. Another difficulty in stress work is that one does not evoke a single, isolated emotional response. As a matter of fact, in research in which psychologists, psychiatrists, and biologists attempt to evoke and relate variables in the anxiety system, a mixture of anger, depression, and anxiety is generally produced. Anger (Oken, 1960) and anxiety are emotions which are relatively easy to rate, but depression is not. It is very difficult to rate depression, and even the subject himself has difficulty in rating degrees of sadness. Some investigators have attempted to resolve this problem by considering all of these emotions as one variable, emotional turbulence, without dissecting it into its component parts.

Anxiety and Defense

We have observed that anxiety protects against both sleep and cerebral excitability. This was implied in the earlier discussion of facilitory and destructive anxiety. Although anxiety is a protector against sleep, patients who can't sleep because they are anxious are obviously not going to use that expression. However, protection against sleep which brings up horrifying dreams is important. Evidence that anxiety protects against cerebral excitability may be found by measuring the latency period before convulsions induced by electric shock. The higher the degree of anxiety, the longer is the latency. Patients with elevated anxiety require larger doses or repeated stimuli (Jeans & Toman, 1956).

I would like to point out that both in psychological stimulation and in the use of intravenous adrenalin to produce anxiety, we find a number of individuals who do not become anxious (Basowitz, Korchin, Oken, Goldstein, & Gussack, 1956). Here, we felt that we were dealing with a phenomenon that had something to do with defenses against anxiety. This, of course, brought us up against a whole series of problems with which we attempted to deal by defining degrees and types of defenses and rating them as we had rated emotional states (Oken, 1962; Oken, Grinker, Heath, Sabshin, & Schwartz, 1960). We have developed a series of rating scales for various types of defenses: situational cathexis, defense intensity, defense primitivity, defenses against awareness, and general coping defenses. These rating scales are not very well worked out, but I think they are important for future studies of stress responses. It should be emphasized, however, that anxiety response was not considered simply as the inverse of defense. There are some defenses which cannot prevent anxiety and, in fact, facilitate its development.

The problem of personality traits and states in relation to the evocation of anxiety has become very important. Classifications such as the hysterical personality, the compulsive personality, and so on are not fruitful. What we have found to be useful and effective are personality categories which we have called EMB. "E" represents the Thurstone emotional stability scale; "M" is the Rorschach inner fantasy movement; and "B" is the barrier score—the clear sense of body limits. Character strength, inner ideation, and a clear sense of boundaries are associated with high muscle tension because subjects with active fantasy have inner restraint against action; hence, muscle tension is increased (Goldstein, 1964a; Goldstein, 1964b; Goldstein, 1965; Shipman, Oken, Goldstein, Grinker, & Heath, 1964).

This brings us to the subject of muscle tension which we felt we had to study. Some of you may have come across the term "psychomotor rigidity." It is an old term without clear operational meaning, but it obviously had something to do with muscle tension. We set out to measure muscle tension on the simple hypothesis that degree of muscle tension may have something to do either with the expression of emotion or with the defense against emotion. We found a high degree of personality-patterned responses. Given a certain number of muscles with heightened tension in response to a particular stimulus, or as a part of a response pattern associated with anxiety or anger, they become tense no matter what the stimulus nor what the emotion may be. This also holds true in general for cardiac, respiratory, and skin responses. There is an individually patterned (ideographic) response no matter what the stimulus, or what the fear (Engel, 1960). These observations lead me back to a basic problem in the psychosomatic field.

The Etiology of Psychosomatic Disorders

In the 1930's, Franz Alexander (1950) developed hypotheses which promised a breakthrough in the psychosomatic field. Many people were excited about Alexander's theory that there were specific emotional factors involved in degenerative diseases not associated with bacterial infection, such as rheumatoid arthritis, migraine, hypertension, peptic ulcer, and ulcerative colitis (Grinker & Robbins, 1954). According to this view, if people suffered from certain emotional factors over a long period of time, they would develop symptoms of a particular psychosomatic disorder. To give a few examples, repressed rage was believed to lead to hypertension, repressed dependency to peptic ulcers, and repressed chronic anger of a low degree of intensity to migraine. The only relationship that we have been able to find consistently is: if a person, in the presence of an adequate stimulus, represses or suppresses his anger, his diastolic blood pressure will rise. Diastolic blood pressure is the important concomitant of essential hypertension. However, since our experiments involved acute emotional states, we cannot extrapolate readily to the chronic state.

It has been observed over a period of time that the various so-called psychosomatic diseases do *not* have a specific emotional etiology, but are characterized by response specificity. This pushed us into the general research in psychophysiology that I have described in this chapter. It also brought us back to the conception which I first published in 1953 in a book called *Psychosomatic Research* (Grinker, 1953a). At that time, I suggested that it was the individual patterning or conditioning of responses in an organism at an early period of life that was the critical factor in psychosomatic disorders rather than the specific emotional constellation. The only time we can speak legitimately of psychosomatic unity is in the undifferentiated phase of infancy, before the organism has been differentiated into psyche and soma. Never again is there such unity. In the undifferentiated state, aspects of the environment which impinge upon the organism's constitutional tendencies influence the whole undifferentiated structure and function, producing effects which are carried into the differentiated phase of both soma and psyche. Both become marked, both have become conditioned together, and both carry the imprint of these early experiences (Grinker, 1953b).

The feeling states can be stimulated and the appropriate biological response will occur. The appropriate biological state can be stimulated and the psychological response will occur. They have become welded together even though they belong to two different systems. Our task then, as pointed out in *Psychosomatic Research,* is to study the development of the idiosyncratic responses. This is being pursued in the new field of psychophysiological research in child development. Measurements are being made of heart rate and amplitude in infants during and after specific handling by the mother. The mother influences the specific cardiac rate pattern. In our laboratory, specific kinds of ego functions are observed as responses to different types of bodily manipulation in young children. It is through such observations and their appropriate interpretation that we will eventually gain a better understanding of the nature of anxiety and the relationships of mind to body, in health and illness.

REFERENCES

Alexander, F. *Psychosomatic medicine.* New York: Norton, 1950.

Basowitz, H., Korchin, S. J., Oken, D., Goldstein, M. S., & Gussack, H. Anxiety and performance changes with a minimal dose of epinephrine. *Arch. Neurol. Psychiat.,* 1956, **76**, 98-105.

Basowitz, H., Persky, H., Korchin, S. J., & Grinker, R. R., Sr. *Anxiety and stress.* New York: McGraw-Hill, 1955.

Board, F. A., Persky, H., & Hamburg, D. A. Psychological stress and endocrine functions. Blood levels of adrenocortical and thyroid hormones in acutely disturbed patients. *Psychosom. Med.,* 1956, **18**, 324-333.

Board, F. A., Wadeson, R., & Persky, H. Depressive affect and endocrine functions. *Arch. Neurol. Psychiat.,* 1957, **78**, 612-620.

Bunney, W. E., Jr., Mason, J. W., & Hamburg, D. A. Correlations between behavioral variables and urinary 17-hydroxycorticosteroids in depressed patients. *Psychosom. Med.,* 1963, **25**, 488.

Engel, B. T. Stimulus-response and individual-response specificity. *Arch. gen. Psychiat.,* 1960, **2**, 305-313.

Glickstein, M., Chevalier, J. A., Korchin, S. J., Basowitz, H., Sabshin, M. A., Hamburg, D. A., & Grinker, R. R., Jr. Temporal heart-rate patterns in anxious patients. *Arch. Neurol. Psychiat.,* 1957, **78**, 101-106.

Goldstein, I. B. Physiological responses in anxious women patients. *Arch. gen. Psychiat.,* 1964, **10**, 382-388. (a)

Goldstein, I. B. Role of muscle tension in personality theory. *Psychol. Bull.,* 1964, **61**, 413-425. (b)

Goldstein, I. B. The relationship of muscle tension and automatic activity to psychiatric disorders. *Psychosom. Med.,* 1965, **27**, 39-44.

Grinker, R. R., Sr. *Psychosomatic research.* New York: Norton, 1953. (a) [New York: Grove Press, 1961 (paperback)]

Grinker, R. R., Sr. Some current trends and hypotheses of psychosomatic research. In F. Deutsch (Ed.), *The psychosomatic concept in psychoanalysis.* New York: International Univer. Press, 1953. Pp. 37-81. (b)

Grinker, R. R., Sr. Psychosomatic approach to anxiety. *Amer. J. Psychol.,* 1956, **113**, 443-447. (a)

Grinker, R. R., Sr. *Toward a unified theory of human behavior.* New York: Basic Books, 1956. (b)

Grinker, R. R., Sr. Anxiety as a significant variable for a unified theory of human behavior. *Arch. gen. Psychiat.,* 1959, **1**, 537-545.

Grinker, R. R., Sr. The physiology of emotions. In A. Simon, C. C. Herbert, & R. Strauss (Eds.), *The physiology of emotions.* Springfield, Ill.: Thomas, 1961. P. 248.

Grinker, R. R., Sr. Psychoanalytic theory and psychosomatic research. In J. Harmorston & E. Stainbrook (Eds.), *Psychoanalysis and the human situation.* New York: Vantage Press, 1964.

Grinker, R. R., Sr., Miller, J., Sabshin, M. A., Nunn, R., & Nunnally, J. C. *The phenomena of depressions.* New York: Harper (Hoeber), 1961.

Grinker, R. R., Sr., & Robbins, F. B. *Psychosomatic case book.* New York: McGraw-Hill (Blakiston), 1954.

Grinker, R. R., Sr., Sabshin, M. A., Hamburg, D. A., Board, F. A., Basowitz, H., Korchin, S. J., Persky, H., & Chevalier, J. A. The use of an anxiety-producing interview and its meaning to the subject. *Arch. Neurol. Psychiat.,* 1957, **77**, 406-419.

Grinker, R. R., Sr., & Spiegel, J. P. *Men under stress.* Philadelphia: Blakiston, 1945. [New York: McGraw-Hill, 1963 (paperback)]

Grinker, R. R., Sr., Willerman, B., Bradley, A. D., & Fastovsky, A. A study of psychological predisposition to the development of operational fatigue. *Amer. J. Orthopsychiat.,* 1946, **16**, 191-214.

Hamburg, D. A. The relevance of recent evolutionary changes to human stress biology. In S. Washburn (Ed.), *Social life of early man.* Chicago: Aldine Press, 1961. P. 654.

Hamburg, D. A., Sabshin, M. A., Board, F. A., Grinker, R. R., Sr., Korchin, S. J., Basowitz, H., Heath, H. A., & Persky, H. Classification and rating of emotional experiences. *Arch. Neurol. Psychiat.,* 1958, **79**, 415-426.

Harrower, M., & Grinker, R. R., Sr. The stress tolerance test: Preliminary experiments with a new projective technique utilizing both meaningful and meaningless stimuli. *Psychosom. Med.,* 1946, **8**, 3-15.

Heath, H. A., & Korchin, S. J. Clinical judgements and self-ratings of traits and states. *Arch. gen. Psychiat.,* 1963, **9**, 390-399.

Heath, H. A., & Oken, D. Change scores as related to initial and final levels. *Ann. N.Y. Acad. Sci.,* 1962, **98**, 1242-1256.

Heath, H. A., Oken, D., Korchin, S. J., & Towne, J. C. A factor analytic study of multivariate psychosomatic changes over time. *Arch. gen. Psychiat.,* 1960, **3**, 467-477.

Jeans, R. F., & Toman, J. E. P. Anxiety and cerebral excitability. *Arch. Neurol. Psychiat.*, 1956, **75**, 534-547.

Korchin, S. J., Basowitz, H., Grinker, R. R., Sr., Hamburg, D. A., Persky, H., Sabshin, M. A., Heath, H. A., & Board, F. A. Experience of perceptual distortion as a source of anxiety. *Arch. Neurol. Psychiat.*, 1958, **80**, 98-113.

Korchin, S. J., & Herz, M. Differential effects of "shame" and "disintegrative" threats on emotional and adrenocortical functioning. *Arch. gen. Psychiat.*, 1960, **2**, 640-651.

Korchin, S. J., & Levine, S. Anxiety and verbal learning. *J. abnorm. soc. Psychol.*, 1957, **54**, 234-240.

Mirsky, I. A., Lipman, E., & Grinker, R. R., Sr. Breath-holding time in anxiety states. *Fed. Proc.*, 1946, **5**, 1-3.

Oken, D. An experimental study of suppressed anger and blood pressure. *Arch. gen. Psychiat.*, 1960, **2**, 441-456.

Oken, D. The role of defense in psychological stress. In R. Roessler & N. S. Greenfield (Eds.), *Physiological correlates of psychological disorder*. Madison: Univer. of Wisconsin Press, 1962. Pp. 193-210.

Oken, D., Grinker, R. R., Sr., Heath, H. A., Herz, M., Korchin, S. J., Sabshin, M. A., & Schwartz, N. B. Relation of physiological response to affect expression. *Arch. gen. Psychiat.*, 1962, **6**, 336-351.

Oken, D., Grinker, R. R., Sr., Heath, H. A., Sabshin, M. A., & Schwartz, N. Stress response in a group of chronic psychiatric patients. *Arch. gen. Psychiat.*, 1960, **3**, 451-466.

Persky, H. Hippuric acid synthesis, plasma glycine level and tissue gutathione concentration of healthy persons under psychological stress. *Fed. Proc.*, 1952, **11**, 268-270.

Persky, H. Response to a life stress: An evaluation of some biochemical indices. *J. appl. Physiol.*, 1953, **6**, 369-372.

Persky, H. Adrenal cortical function in anxious human subjects. *Arch. Neurol. Psychiat.*, 1957, **78**, 95-100.

Persky, H. Adrenocortical function during anxiety. In R. Roessler & N. S. Greenfield (Eds.), *Physiological correlates of psychological disorder*. Madison: Univer. of Wisconsin Press, 1962. Pp. 171-191.

Persky, H., Gamm, S. R., & Grinker, R. R., Sr. Correlation between fluctuation of free anxiety and quantity of hippuric acid excretion. *Psychosom. Med.*, 1952, **14**, 34-40.

Persky, H., Grinker, R. R., Sr., & Mirsky, I. A. Excretion of hippuric acid in subjects with free anxiety. *J. clin. Invest.*, 1950, **29**, 110-114.

Persky, H., Hamburg, D. A., Basowitz, H., Grinker, R. R., Sr., Sabshin, M. A., Korchin, S. J., Herz, M., Board, F. A., & Heath, H. A. Relation of emotional responses and changes in plasma hydrocortisone level after stressful interview. *Arch. Neurol. Psychiat.*, 1958, **79**, 434-447.

Sabshin, M. A., Hamburg, D. A., Grinker, R. R., Sr., Persky, H., Basowitz, H., Korchin, S. J., & Chevalier, J. A. Significance of preexperimental studies in the psychosomatic laboratory. *Arch. Neurol. Psychiat.*, 1957, **78**, 207-219.

Shipman, W. G., Oken, D., Goldstein, I. B., Grinker, R. R., Sr., & Heath, H. A. Study in psychophysiology of muscle tension. *Arch. gen. Psychiat.*, 1964, **11**, 330-345.

Spiegel, J. P. Psychological transactions. In *Situations of acute stress*. Army Med. Service, Washington, D.C., 1953. P. 622.

CHAPTER 6

The Basis of Psychopathology:
Malconditioning or Misbehavior?[1]

O. Hobart Mowrer
DEPARTMENT OF PSYCHOLOGY,
UNIVERSITY OF ILLINOIS,
URBANA, ILLINOIS

The view most often espoused by those who have approached the domain of psychopathology from the standpoint of learning theory has been to this effect: that here the basic trouble lies in some anomaly in the *emotional* (or "attitudinal") life of the afflicted individual and that any irregularities in overt behavior are merely "symptomatic" of the underlying affective problem. More specifically, the assumption has been that psychoneurotic individuals have suffered from "traumatic" emotional malconditioning of some sort, as a result of physical accidents or overly harsh, perverse "training" at the hands of others. Irrational or irresponsible behavior on the part of the victims of such unfortunate treatment is thus merely an expression of the irrationality and abnormality of their emotions. This, then, is supposed to be the essence of "neurosis" and "mental illness" in the most pervasive sense of these terms.

Despite the great insight and practical control which this (essentially Freudian) way of conceptualizing the problem is supposed to have provided, sober appraisal of our situation suggests that, in point of fact, it has contributed very little to the more effective management and prevention

---

[1] This paper is a slightly modified version of Section I of a chapter entitled "Learning Theory and Behavior" which appears in Wolman, B. B. (Ed.) *Handbook of Clinical Psychology*. New York: McGraw-Hill, 1965.

of psychopathology. A plausible case can, indeed, be made for the surmise that this theoretical position merely reinforces a perception which the neurotic is himself almost certain to have. He will be quick to tell you how bad he *feels,* and he will not be averse to the suggestion that *others* are somehow responsible for his present unfortunate state and thus ought to "treat" him in such a way as to make him "feel better." Also, he will readily fall in with the idea, which flows naturally from the foregoing assumptions, that he himself is *not responsible* for what *he* now does. This type of theory—to the effect that so-called neurotic individuals *act* strangely ("compulsively," "irrationally") because their emotions have been perverted and warped—is thus part and parcel of the "disease" itself, and by no means its cure. Increasingly we are today getting reports of "iatrogenic" (treatment-exacerbated) personality disorder. And it also appears that great social institutions (for example, the home, church, school, and courts) which have assimilated this philosophy are afflicted by a mysterious, creeping paralysis and loss of confidence—to such a degree that our whole society is commonly said to be *sick* (LaPiere, 1959; Schoeck & Wiggins, 1962).

A New Conception of Emotional Disturbance

Where, then, can we find a sounder and more effective way of thinking about this type of problem? On the basis of various clinical reports and experimental studies (see, for example, Mowrer, 1964), the induction is emerging that so-called emotional disturbance, discomfort, or "dis-ease," is the lawful, well earned, and eminently *normal* result of abnormal (in the sense of socially and morally deviant) behavior—and not the other way round, as has been so often assumed. Once an individual becomes fearful and guilt-ridden because of his misconduct, it is true that he may then develop "symptoms" which reflect his inner malaise and apprehension. But this is not to say that his emotional responses are the original source of his difficulty. It will instead be our thesis that in psychopathology the primary, basic cause is deliberate, choice-mediated behavior of a socially disapproved, reprehensible nature which *results* in emotional disturbance and "insecurity" (because the individual is now objectively "guilty," socially vulnerable, and, if "caught," subject to criticism or punishment). The "symptoms" which then ensue represent ways in which the individual is trying to "defend" himself against *and hide* his "disturbing" and suspicion-arousing emotions (of moral fear and guilt). Thus, a deliberate misdeed is the original, or primary, cause, and emotional disturbance follows, which may then produce symptoms of a more or less "behavioral" type. That is, we assume that "emotional" disturbance is the *second* in a three-link chain of consequences, rather than the original or *first* link in a two-link chain.

Or, to be more precise, we should perhaps put the matter a little differently and say that *both* approaches imply three links in the "chain of circumstances" which eventuates in the more manifest aspects of what we call psychopathology. If one wishes, one can easily think of "emotional disturbance" (or "disturbing emotions") as the *second* link in both frames of reference; but in the one case the first link would be the foolish, unthinking, harmful behavior *of others,* whereas in the other case the first link is the foolish, unthinking, harmful behavior of the individual *himself.* This is the distinction which is behind the suggestion of certain contemporary writers to the effect that in "neurosis" and "functional psychosis" the element of *personal responsibility* is probably far greater than has been commonly supposed; and if this be true, there is also a corresponding opportunity—indeed obligation—for the individual to "help himself" if he has fallen into a pathological state.

Or, to epitomize the matter still further, one might say that it is not the emotions that are being experienced by patients in mental hospitals which constitute their "craziness." Given their personal history and "life style," the presumption is that (in the absence of gross neurological lesions, toxic states, and hormonal disorders) their emotions (however turbulent and painful) are, in an ultimate sense, reasonable and proper. What *is* crazy is *the behavior* which these persons have previously engaged in—*and* the ways in which they (*and,* very likely, their therapists) are now trying to deal with the resulting anxiety or emotional "dis-ease."

This perception of the situation is in direct contrast to the still widespread view that the essence of "mental illness" lies in the "inappropriate," "disproportional," and "irrational" nature of the individual's emotional reactions. Our assumption is rather that it is the individual's *behavior,* both originally and now "symptomatically," that has been "off" and that his emotions have been, and are, in no way unsuited to the circumstances, when the latter are fully known and understood. By this route we arrive at the view that the therapy of choice is necessarily *behavior therapy,* in the sense of (1) changing the behavior which originally got the individual into "trouble" and (2) changing what the individual has since been trying to do about his "trouble" or "dis-ease," i.e., his symptoms. This approach is manifestly different from the view that a neurotic's "trouble" is the fact that he is *having* trouble, emotional trouble (troubling emotions), a view which still dominates large segments of both psychiatric and psychological precept and practice. Our assumption is that the capacity to *be* "troubled"

in this way is the hallmark of the individual's basic humanity and potentially his salvation and deliverance (see Fig. 1).

Our view, in short, is that the "sick" individual's problem lies not in
how he is *feeling,* but in what he has been, and perhaps still is, *doing.* And
we further assume that no therapy can be ultimately successful which involves a *direct* attack (by chemical or whatever other means) upon the
patient's emotions, as such. They can be effectively modified, it seems, only
through systematic changes *in behavior.* As Glasser (1963) succinctly
says: "No one can help another person feel better." Neurotic persons do
not act irresponsibly because they are sick; instead they are sick (sick of

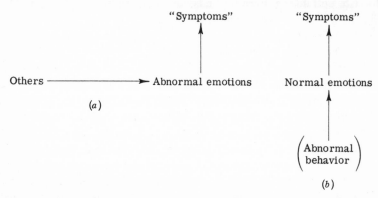

Fig. 1. Schematic representation of two conceptions of psychopathology. According to the more conventional of these [(a), diagramed at the left], the essence
of "neurosis" or "mental illness" is an *emotional* disturbance or disorder which has
been produced by inappropriate, irrational behavior on the part of others (parents,
teachers, husbands, wives, employers, etc.). The alternative position [(b), depicted
on the right] holds that the crux of the problem is not emotional but *behavioral.*
Given the deviant, duplicitous life style of the individual himself, his emotional suffering (insecurity, anxiety, inferiority feelings, guilt) is seen as thoroughly natural,
appropriate, and normal. The abnormality in the situation consists of the individual's
secret deviations from the norms, standards, rules, and "values" of this reference
group. In the first conceptual scheme, one's own behavior is never seen as "causal,"
only the behavior of others (which, if one is consistent, must in turn have been
caused by others, and so on to an infinite regress). And whatever the individual does, if
it is in any way objectionable or "bad," is interpreted as "merely symptomatic of deep,
underlying emotional problems." Thus, attention is focused almost exclusively upon
emotions, with little or no responsibility accruing to the individual. In the other
frame of reference, so-called symptoms (see Fig. 2) arise from emotional discomfort
which is appropriate and well "earned," considering what the individual has done in
the past, is still doing, and is *hiding* (a fact denoted by the parentheses). Attention
is thus shifted from emotions to conduct and from what others have done to one's
own actions. Reprinted from B. B. Wolman (1965) with permission from McGraw-
Hill (see footnote 1).

themselves and *feel* bad) because they act badly, irresponsibly. So the strategy of choice for the therapist is to help the other person become *more responsible* (even though it temporarily "hurts"). This, of course, is in direct contradiction to the more traditional (but manifestly unsatisfactory) view that human beings become "emotionally ill" because they have been morally overtrained and are, in consequence, trying to be "too good."[2]

Choice, Responsibility, and Identity Crisis

If *others* are truly responsible for our emotional difficulties, then it would perhaps follow that we could recover only through "treatment" (that is, a so-called "corrective emotional experience") which would likewise have to come from "without." This, of course, is tantamount to saying that psychopathology is due to *false,* unrealistic guilt, a mere "guilt complex." But a kind of revolution is now in progress which puts the responsibility—both for one's having gotten into a "neurotic" impasse in the first place *and* for one's getting *out* of it—much more squarely upon the individual himself. That is, we are here assuming that psychopathology *in*-volves *real* guilt: i.e., fear of being "found out" which is generated by actions which the individual's reference group condemns and negatively sanctions.[3]

In other words, this newly emerging point of view attributes to human beings the capacity for *choice:* capacity, in the first place, to choose either

---

[2] Twenty-five years ago, in the heyday of Freudianism, most psychologists, if they were interested in the phenomenon of conscience at all, were concerned only to the extent of discovering how to get rid of it (on the assumption that it was likely to be the repository of all manner of unrealistic, "archaic" fears and scruples). As further indication of the collapse of this tendency to derogate conscience, and of the collapse of the whole Freudian philosophy, attention should be called to a small but rapidly growing literature on the question of how conscience and character and moral competence are *acquired*. This literature (mainly in the area of "child development" and "child training") is manifestly pertinent to our general thesis, but only tangentially, so will not be specifically considered here.

[3] Our view does not for a moment overlook or deny the fact that others may be the source of great anguish and heartache for a given individual, but *this* is not "neurosis" and is not what "destroys" us. The assumption is rather that we are destroyed (in the sense of losing self-esteem and self-acceptance) only as a result of those things for which we, personally, are responsible. Society holds no one accountable, and is in no sense inclined to punish one, for what others have done *to* him. It is our *own conduct* which, if deviant, can be our downfall. If others are unreasonable, harsh, or unfair, the whole, healthy person may suffer acutely; but he will have durability and resiliancy. Objective stress is usually episodic; and when it is over, the person whose self-regard is intact soon "bounces back." (The question of "autism" and childhood schizophrenia has been considered elsewhere: Mowrer, 1964, Chapter 13.)

to "behave" or not to behave; and, having chosen misbehavior, the further capacity to choose either to conceal or reveal this fact. Manifestly, we do not, cannot choose or control *our emotions,* directly or voluntarily. Given the "appropriate" ("conditioned") stimulus, *they* occur automatically, reflexly. So the question of control and choice exists only at the level of overt, voluntary behavior. And this is why "behavior therapy" opens up vistas and potentialities which are forever closed if one thinks of the problem of psychopathology as essentially "emotional." But there has been, in recent decades, some question as to whether the concept of choice or volition is justified even in respect to overt, "instrumental" behavior. We shall have to pause momentarily to consider this matter, for the validity of our whole analysis importantly hinges on it.

Much of the skepticism concerning the possibility of human "freedom of choice" comes from stimulus-response psychology, or Primitive Behaviorism, which held that, given a specific stimulus, S, the organism (be he man or mouse), must respond with whatever R (response) happens to be most directly "connected," or "conditioned," to S. On the basis of evidence which has been reviewed in detail elsewhere (Mowrer, 1960a; Mowrer, 1960b; Mowrer, 1961a), it can now, with good reason, be maintained that stimuli never "produce" or "cause" *behavioral* (as opposed to emotional) responses in the manner implied by S-R connectionism or reflexology. A stimulus (S) may *suggest* (i.e., provide an image or memory of) a particular response (R). But the fact that the S is present does not at all mean that the subject is obliged or "forced" (cf. Loeb, 1918) to make a particular R—or, indeed, any R at all. A given S may, as noted, suggest a particular R, that is, it may "remind" the subject of a certain *possibility;* but whether or not the individual responds to the suggestion ("yields to the temptation") is dependent on prudential factors (hopes and fears) which are complexly determined, by the individual's total life experience, knowlege (including that which is gained vicariously), and objectives—in a word, by "character." Whatever else Gestalt psychologists may have meant when they spoke of an organism's responding "as a whole," *totally,* rather than segmentally, this is surely an important part of what they *should* have meant.

Here, in the foregoing analysis, we are not repudiating "determinism" in the sense of denying that the universe (including the principles governing the human mind) is orderly and lawful; but we *are* saying that as far as the overt responses which human beings make are concerned, they are very *intricately,* very *compexly* "determined." Their occurrence is dependent, not merely upon the presence or absence of any given S, or even upon a particular pattern or concatenation of stimuli comprising a "situation," but also upon everything which, as Krechevsky (1932) has phrased it, the organism "brings to" the situation—*and,* we may add, upon the information (sensory feedback) which is provided while a response is *in progress.* In other words, the reflexological, connectionistic *model* of behavior which was postulated by Pavlov, Watson, Thorndike, and others is grossly inadequate, that is, not isomorphic, or "iconic," with the reality it is supposed to represent; instead we must have a model which, at the very least, recognizes the reality of mediating processes and higher-order "habits" (even the Russian "reflexologists" are now speaking of "the *second* signal system") which make possible the "deliberate" weighing and balancing of alternative possibilities (Dulany, 1964; Miller, Galanter, & Pribram, 1960; Mowrer, 1960b, especially Chapter 6; Osgood, 1953). This way of thinking about the problem very largely resolves the conflict between "determinism" and "teleology" or "purpose." We may say, in effect, that we have now discovered (in contemporary learning theory) the "mechanics of teleology." As long as we are able to respond to the circumstances of our existence with flexibility and intelligence, rather than in a fixed and essentially "stupid" manner, do we not have all the "freedom" we need—or should, for that matter, desire?

Now we are in a position to ask what it is that human beings *do,* i.e., what choice, or choices, they make, which precipitate the state known, ambiguously, as "neurosis." Manifestly, this term is just a medical euphemism and does not at all mean what it would literally seem to mean, namely, an "osis" or disorder of the nerves or the nervous system. The term "psychosis" comes closer to carrying the implication which is obviously in point here. And it would not, perhaps, be too bad if it gradually replaced the term "neurosis." However, Eriksen (1958) has suggested an expression which is more appropriate still, namely, *identity crisis.* For it fits in nicely with the answer to the question: What is it that human beings *do* which leads to the personal condition with which we are here concerned? The answer to this question seems to be: (1) they choose to do socially forbidden things and then (2) they hide and deny what they have done. In other words, they refuse to say who they "really are," i.e., they deny their true identity *to others.* Francis Thompson ends the first stanza of his "Hound of Heaven" with this memorable line: "All things betray Thee who betrayest Me." That is, if we for long deny who we are to others (that is, "betray" *them*), the time comes when we no longer know ourselves (cf. Jourard, 1964); and this is the state of psychic nonbeing or "anxiety" (cf. Frankl's concept of "existential vacuum" or "meaninglessness") which we commonly call neurosis or psychosis, and which could, it seems, so much more pertinently and precisely be called "identity crisis."

This way of thinking about the problem obviously represents a radical departure from the prevailing "medical" emphasis. In mental hospitals, both public and private, the "doctor" typically tries to reassure the patient (i.e., make him or her *feel* better) by saying something like this: "Now you should realize, first of all, that you do *have a disease*. And this is just like any other disease or sickness, of an organic nature, which you might have. It is not associated with anything you have done or not done. That is, you are in no way responsible for it—and you can't do anything about it, yourself. In other words, you should not worry or blame yourself for anything—instead, just relax and leave everything to us. We understand these things, and will completely take over the 'treatment.' Simply do as you are told." If it is true that the individual does have a responsibility, and perhaps a very sizeable one, for both the cause and the cure of the condition under discussion here, how tragically nonfunctional all this is! Such an approach has served to create what someone has aptly called "the healing industry," but it has not, it seems, accomplished much else.

Understandably, there is thus growing skepticism concerning the appropriateness of the "medical model" (of illness, sickness, and "treatment") in the whole psychiatric area (cf. Glasser, 1965; Szasz, 1961). And psychologists, while probably willing enough to accept *this* development, are, however, faced by the necessity of deciding whether they will go on trying to keep the "patient" (see how inveterate the medical language is!) in *another* deterministic frame of reference—not that of "disease" but of S-R "bondage"—or liberate him, in the sense of granting to him a significant role in both the production and the elimination of his difficulties. As already noted, the simple, unelaborated S-R learning model can only make a robot of man; but, for reasons cited, this model is inherently unsatisfactory and is today being replaced by a model in which "freedom of choice" is a definite (though qualified) possibility. The real element of determinism, compulsion, constraint, and necessity comes, it seems, not so much from the biological, neurological, or even psychological nature of the individual himself as from the fact that man is a *social* being, operating within a social *system,* and that this system puts very definite and inevitable constraints and restraints upon him.

In such a system, the individual still has a number of choices open to him. He can, for example, choose (at least within limits) the particular social system in which he is going to function (cf. the concept of "social mobility"). And he can also choose whether he is going to function, within a given system, honestly or dishonestly. But if he chooses the latter course, there is, it seems, an *inevitable* consequence: he becomes prey to that special variety of fear and personal misery which we call *guilt,* and if he does not deal with this in a realistic and constructive way—that is, by confession and restitution—he will soon be trying to deal with it in ways which we call "symptomatic." This is not the place to elaborate on the meaning of the latter term (cf. Mowrer, 1964, Chapter 11), but it can be said that so-called symptoms represent (1) an effort on the part of the guilty (uneasy, dis-easy, apprehensive, "anxious") individual to deny and

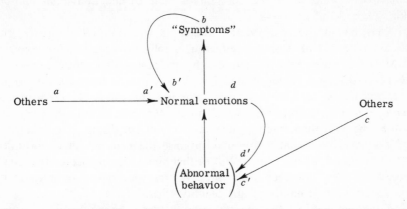

FIG. 2. Combination and elaboration of the two diagrams shown in Fig. 1. If, in the conventional frame of reference, the basic problem is an abnormality of emotions which has been produced by others, then "therapy" ($a \longrightarrow a'$) would require some sort of treatment by others which would offset the mistreatment to which the individual has been previously exposed. Oddly, this is precisely what the individual's own symptomatic efforts ($b \longrightarrow b'$) are designed to do, i.e., make him *feel* better, without necessarily *being* better. Thus, "symptoms" may be defined as an individual's own attempt at self-cure, which, like most professional treatment, assumes that the basic problem is wrong emotions, bad "nerves." If, however, the other hypothesis is correct and if the neurotic individual's emotional reactions (considering his ongoing life style) are essentially normal, we see how sadly misdirected such treatment is. Surely it is suggestive in this connection that, on the average, the apparent effectiveness of professional treatment does not exceed the incidence of "spontaneous remissions" in untreated persons. But if it is really the individual's behavior rather than his emotions which is abnormal, then "therapy," i.e., the efforts of others to help him, ought to be directed toward behavior change ($c \longrightarrow c'$) rather than emotional reeducation. And to the extent that this point of view begins to make sense to the suffering person himself, he will then start letting his emotional discomfort motivate him ($d \longrightarrow d'$) to eliminate the questionable behavior and life strategies which have been producing the emotional upset, rather than seeking to eliminate the emotional discomfort directly ($b \longrightarrow b'$). When an emotionally disturbed person is able to see his predicament in this light, he will actively, independently, effectively set about "curing" himself (through confession and restitution) and will not need protracted treatment from others. Instead of continuing to be weak and needing to "receive," he will become strong and able to *give*. Reprinted from B. B. Wolman (1965) with permission from McGraw-Hill (see footnote 1).

hide such feelings, lest they arouse suspicion—"*Why* are you so fearful?"— and (2) an effort to lessen the subjective intensity of such feelings, because they are inherently unpleasant and painful. Hence, the appropriateness of referring to symptoms as "defenses," not against a fear of a return of repressed impulses of sex and hostility (as Freud supposed), but against the danger of having one's guilty secrets known to others *and* against the subjective experience of the emotion of guilt by the individual himself (Fig. 2).

Thus, one arrives at the view that there is no possibility of a successful *private* treatment of neurosis (either in a religious or a secular context; cf. Mowrer, 1963a; Mowrer, 1963b), for the reason that privacy, concealment, secrecy, and "defensiveness" is the essence of the difficulty. Here both psychiatrists and psychologists have, it seems, made the error of engaging in treatment procedures which are more congruent with the premises of the "disease" than those of health. It is not surprising that such procedures have been salable, for they promise the neurotic an opportunity to "get well" *on his own terms*. But neither should it surprise us that such procedures have not been truly effective, for they have not adequately recognized the true nature of an "identity crisis."

A rational and effective therapy must, it seems, be a behavior therapy, which involves (1) admission rather than denial, to the significant others in one's life, of who one genuinely is and (2) rectification of and restitution for past deviations and errors. Thus, one must again traverse the same path which led him "into neurosis" in the first place, but now in the *reverse* direction. If it is by sinning and then trying to conceal the sinning that one progressively destroys his social relatedness (i.e., his "identity"), the only possibility of recovering it is to move back in the opposite direction toward openness, cooperation, community, and "fellowship."

Psychological Science, Ancient Wisdom—and Folly

But is *this* the shape of science in the domain of psychopathology or an awful retrogression? In the story of the temptation and fall of Man, as set forth in the Third Chapter of Genesis, the essential facts of the case are, familiarly, that Man (Adam, Everyman) sins and then hides his sin. If, after violating the one rule (remember, this was Paradise) that had been put upon him, Man had gone to the Lord (his "significant others") and admitted his mistake, the outcome would presumably have been very different. But instead, after having chosen to eat of the forbidden fruit, Man, and Woman, further decided to deny and conceal what they had done. Banishment from Eden is the penalty that is inflicted upon them, just as loss of "peace of mind" and a pervasive "insecurity" is the price that is still exacted of all of us if we violate our social obligations and then pretend that we have not done so. We, too, are "banished," no longer *belong,* because we have thus disqualified ourselves for the privilege of membership and group participation. But we alone *know* this. And our "neurosis" consists of this knowledge, and the fear of being "found out" which it engenders, and the constant vigilance which is needed lest this should happen.

But why should man, if he is truly free, ever choose to violate rules? Rules always involve a restriction or sacrifice which has the effect of insuring a long-term advantage of some sort; and whenever an individual is not experienced or intelligent enough to see the "logic" of a rule, he is, understandably, tempted to violate it. In a land of wonderful abundance it was certainly no great physical imposition upon Adam and Eve not to eat of the forbidden fruit, but it was perhaps something of an affront to their vanity and pride to be told there was something they should *not* do.[4] So, they ate. And then, instead of admitting what they had chosen to do, each, in his own way, denied it: "And the man said, The Woman whom thou gavest to be with me, she gave me of the tree, and I did eat. . . . And the woman said, The serpent beguiled me, and I did eat" (Genesis, 3:13). Because they both refused to confess their mistake and to accept the responsibility for it, they found no restoration, no redemption, no recovery, no reconciliation, no return to Innocence: "Therefore the Lord God sent [Man] forth from the Garden of Eden, to till the ground from whence he was taken . . . and he placed at the east of the Garden of Eden Cherubims, and a flaming sword which turned every way, to keep the way to the tree of life" (Genesis, 3:23-24).

The story of the Fall of Man is one of the great allegories of all time. It is like a finely cut diamond: no matter how one turns and looks at it, it reflects a bright and illuminating light. So, taking the particular facet of the story which we have chosen, does it not suggest that so many of our current efforts to help "fallen" ("neurotic") individuals to *rise* ("recover") are to no avail because we do not sufficiently recognize Man's true nature and destiny?

On the assumption that Man is today no less (potentially, at least) than the author of Genesis understood him to be, we shall use this classic conception as the standard of comparison for latter-day theories and practices in this domain.[5]

---

[4] Not long ago, a "sick" college girl said to me: "But if I confess this thing to my parents, I will lose my independence," meaning the complete autonomy and authority she had arrogated unto herself. Is *this* the age-old "sin of pride?"

[5] It is interesting to observe how many psychologists (*and* psychiatrists) are today asking the "existential" question: "What, then, is man?" See, for example, the book by Meehl *et al.* (1958).

The reader should perhaps be reassured that the conception of neurosis and recovery (or "sin and salvation") which is here delineated is not conventionally "religious." In one sense, of course, this approach is deeply and inveterately religious. One of the roots of the word "religion" is the Latin term *ligare,* from which our words *ligament* and *ligature* come. Religion thus, literally, implies a binding-to, a connectedness, a relationship, a belonging; and in this sense, we shall assume that the normal, "healthy" man is necessarily "religious" and that an abnormal, "sick" one is suffering from a tragic form of brokenness and alienation.

But religion, in the more institutional sense—particularly Protestant religion (which I am best qualified to appraise)—suffers, it seems, from some of the same presuppositions that have so seriously handicapped secular therapeutic approaches. Perhaps the most fatal of these is the assumption that in an identity crisis the individual's *emotions* are in some way out of kilter, inappropriate, disordered. As we have seen, an excellent case can be made for the alternative view that the "neurotic" is suffering, not from an emotional disorder, but from a disorderly, irresponsible way of life. And, as we have also seen, it is in itself "neurotic" to view the emotions as the source of "the trouble." Thus, we are led to the inference that much contemporary religion is itself sick, just as psychiatry and clinical psychology, and the neurotic himself, are (Mowrer, 1961b).

But is it true, is it *fair* to say that contemporary Protestantism stresses wrong emotions as the source of suffering man's condition? Protestantism has long taken a dim view of "works" (your own efforts and actions) as a means of salvation ("lest any man should boast," as Paul put it); and now we find that many ministers have become so advanced in their thinking that they don't even mention sin and guilt. All is forgiveness and love, first love of God, then one's fellowmen, and then oneself. And what is "love?" As ordinarily understood it is *an emotion.* And if you don't *have* it, can't *experience* it, you are quite as helpless as you are if you have some negative "emotion" and want to get rid of it. Operationally, such a "theology" hamstrings the lost, alienated, suffering individual about as effectively as do the doctrines of disease (in psychiatry) or reflexology (in psychology). The main difference is that now, in the religious context, one is supposed to "see" a theologian for "help," instead of a secular healer of some sort.

The present approach exemplifies the much discussed but seldom actualized Protestant doctrine of "the priesthood of all believers," i.e., the ability and the obligation, on the part of everyone, to be a priest ("therapist") to himself and to others.

Actually, there is excellent Biblical support for this point of view. In classic Judaism, and in Orthodox Judaism of today, one appears before

God (on the Day of Atonement) only after having spent a week making right one's transgressions against one's fellowmen during the preceding year. And in the New Testament we read: "Therefore if thou bring thy gift to the altar, and there rememberest that thy brother hath aught against thee, leave there thy gift [to God] before the altar, and go thy way; *first be reconciled to thy brother, and then come and offer thy gift*" (Matthew, 5:23-24, italics added).

There is a familiar couplet which goes:

> I sought my soul, I sought my God; but neither could I see;
> But then I sought my brother, and then I found all three.

This may not be very exalted poetry; but it is, it seems, excellent psychology and also "theology." It puts *behavior,* interpersonal, social, *moral* behavior first, and says that everything else will follow from this. ["Seek first his Kingdom, and all these things shall be yours as well" (Matthew 6:33).] Why have we professionals, in both psychology and religion, been so reluctant to acknowledge and emphasize this time-honored approach? Can it be that we have disliked it precisely because it gives the laymen—Adam, Everyman—more freedom and responsibility and "power" than we wish him to have? Does it, in other words, make him too independent *of us?* If there is even a trace of professional chauvinism in this transcendentally important human area, we should surely divest ourselves of it as promptly and completely as possible. "Behavior Therapy," as it has been outlined in this chapter, can, hopefully, be a useful instrument to this end.

REFERENCES

Dulany, D. E., Jr. The separable effects of the information and affect conveyed by a reinforcer. Paper read at Psychonom. Soc. meeting, Niagara Falls, Canada, 1964.

Eriksen, E. H. *Young man Luther.* New York: Norton, 1958.

Glasser, W. Reality therapy—a new approach. Paper read at Thirty-second Annu. Governors Conf. on Youth, Chicago, 1963.

Glasser, W. *Reality therapy: A new approach to psychiatry.* New York: Harper, 1965.

Jourard, S. M. *The transparent self.* Princeton, N. J.: Van Nostrand, 1964.

Krechevsky, I. "Hypotheses" in rats. *Psychol. Rev.,* 1932, **39**, 516-532.

LaPiere, R. *The Freudian ethic.* New York: Duell, Sloan, & Pearce, 1959.

Loeb, J. *Forced movements, tropisms, and animal conduct.* Philadelphia: Lippincott, 1918.

Meehl, P. E. *et al. What, then, is man?* St. Louis: Concordia, 1958.

Miller, G. A., Galanter, E., & Pribram, K. H. *Plans and the structure of behavior.* New York: Holt, 1960.

Mowrer, O. H. *Learning theory and behavior.* New York: Wiley, 1960. (a)

Mowrer, O. H. *Learning theory and the symbolic processes.* New York: Wiley, 1960. (b)

Mowrer, O. H. The rediscovery of moral responsibility. *Atlantic mon.,* 1961, **208,** 88-91. (a)

Mowrer, O. H. *The crisis in psychiatry and religion.* Princeton, N. J.: Van Nostrand, 1961. (b)

Mowrer, O. H. Transference and scrupulosity. *J. Relig. Hlth.,* 1963, **2,** 313-343. (a)

Mowrer, O. H. Payment or repayment? The problem of private practice. *Amer. Psychologist,* 1963, **18,** 577-580. (b)

Mowrer, O. H. *The new group therapy.* Princeton, N. J.: Van Nostrand, 1964.

Osgood, C. E. *Method and theory in experimental psychology.* London & New York: Oxford Univer. Press, 1953.

Schoeck, H., & Wiggins, J. W. *Psychiatry and responsibility.* Princeton, N. J.: Van Nostrand, 1962.

Szasz, T. S. *The myth of mental illness.* New York: Harper (Hoeber), 1961.

CHAPTER 7

Studies of Anxiety: Some Clinical Origins
of the Activation Concept

Robert B. Malmo

ALLAN MEMORIAL INSTITUTE,
MCGILL UNIVERSITY,
MONTREAL, CANADA

Anxiety is a term which has been used rather loosely and for which there is no widely accepted general definition (Malmo, 1957; Malmo, 1962). In this chapter, anxiety will refer to *pathological* anxiety, i.e., the emotional responses of pathologically increased intensity and duration which may be observed in certain psychoneurotic patients (Malmo, Shagass, & Davis, 1950). As I view anxiety, it can probably best be understood in the context of what has come to be called "activation theory." Indeed, at least for some of my colleagues and myself, important roots of activation theory are to be found in clinical observations of psychoneurotic patients suffering from severe anxiety.

There is terminological confusion between "activation" and "arousal" that cannot easily be avoided at the present time. Most authors have treated these terms as synonyms. However, Feldman and Waller (1962) suggested that "activation" should be confined to the EEG change and that the term "behavioral arousal" should be used in connection with changes along the sleep-walking continuum as reflected in observations of the subject's behavior. The fact that Feldman and Waller (1962) have demonstrated these two kinds of phenomena to be dissociable makes their terminological distinction a very reasonable one. There are, however, other changes in the subject such as autonomic nervous system (ANS) reactions that are very difficult to classify in terms of the Feldman and Waller distinction. For any general treatment of the topic, it seems that, for the present at least, terminology cannot be very strict. In this chapter the term *activation* (following Duffy, 1962; Lindsley, 1951) will be used in references to the general theory and, on the empirical side, to levels of reaction (*activation levels*) as gauged by physiological indicators. *Arousal* will be used chiefly in reference to the work of others who used this term, e.g., *arousal function* and *arousal system* (Hebb, 1955), and in reference to the important dissociation discovered by Feldman and Waller (1962).

In order to clarify the relations between anxiety and activation, a brief outline of current activation theory will first be presented. I will then proceed to describe a number of empirical studies, carried out in our laboratory, in which psychiatric patients showing high anxiety were compared with various patient and normal control groups. The findings in these studies will be considered as they relate to the concept of activation and to the neural mechanisms which are believed to provide the basis for anxiety and for behavioral arousal.

Activation

Behavior may be analyzed into two broad categories: the first is characterized chiefly by organization, in which ordering and timing of events is important; the second is characterized primarily by diffuseness rather than organization. Hebb (1955) termed the former "cue function" and the latter "arousal function," and this distinction seems basically the same as that implied by the classic terms "phasic" and "tonic" (Herrick, 1928).

Cue function in mammals is, in all probability, largely dependent upon the cerebral cortex along with related subcortical neural mechanisms which are organized for the mediation of sequential, timed responses. Speech apparently depends upon such mechanisms. In a study by Penfield and Rasmussen (1950) it was demonstrated that speech may be completely arrested by stimulating the motor speech areas in patients undergoing craniotomies carried out under local anesthesia. Under such conditions, Hebb (1950) has theorized that the stimulating electrode fires *all at once* neurons that must fire in sequence in order to mediate the sequential activity of speech.

Arousal function, on the other hand, is presumably influenced chiefly through diffuse discharges of the ascending reticular activating system (ARAS). This system came into prominence following the dramatic demonstration by Moruzzi and Magoun (1949) that stimulation of the reticular region of the midbrain had the effect of changing cortical EEG activity from a synchronous, relatively high amplitude pattern to one characterized by low amplitudes and fast frequencies. The great importance of this observation lay in the fact that the change in the EEG pattern following reticular stimulation was essentially the same kind of EEG change which was known to occur when a resting subject was unexpectedly exposed to an "arousing" stimulus (see Lindsley, 1951, p. 497). Furthermore, a persisting, low-level, fast-frequency EEG pattern is also considered characteristic of patients with pathological anxiety (see Lindsley, 1951, p. 499). It is not surprising, therefore, that the Moruzzi and Magoun discovery focused considerable attention on the ARAS, and especially on its facilitatory functions.

On the basis of recent evidence, especially from experiments in which microelectrodes have been used to study single cells, Jasper (1963) has pointed out the dangers inherent in regarding reticular mechanisms as entirely "unspecific," and in neglecting the inhibitory side of these mechanisms. Furthermore, the functions of the descending parts of the brain-stem reticular formation (both facilitatory and inhibitory) have been relatively ignored in theoretical discussions of activation, and these may turn out to be as important as the ARAS for our understanding of behavioral phenomena such as pathological anxiety. (Henceforth in the present context, "pathological anxiety" will be shortened to "anxiety" and this term will be restricted in meaning to the denotation of pathological anxiety in psychoneurotic states.)

The descending brain-stem reticular system is divided into a midbrain part and a bulbar part (see Magoun, 1958, p. 23 ff.). Facilitatory effects have been experimentally demonstrated for the former and inhibitory effects for the latter. For example, the amplitude of reflexes, such as the knee jerk or eyeblink, is increased by stimulating the facilitatory area of the brain-stem reticular formation and decreased by stimulating the inhibitory area (Magoun, 1958). As we shall see presently, there is also evidence from experiments with psychoneurotic patients which suggests that, in states of anxiety, there may be defective regulatory control of skeletal-motor reaction. These observations suggest that in anxiety states, following strong or stressful stimulation, there may be failure in some homeostatic mechanism that normally acts to bring excessive skeletal-motor tension back toward the homeostatic baseline. It seems reasonable to speculate that the inhibitory part of the descending brain-stem reticular system may be a major component of such a homeostatic mechanism.

Just as the descending part of the reticular system has been neglected in theoretical discussions of the relations between the reticular system and behavior, the importance of the hypothalamus in the arousal system has not been sufficiently appreciated until very recently. In an important paper by Feldman and Waller (1962, p. 1321), the following statement pointed up the complexity of the relations between the hypothalamus, the reticular system, and behavioral arousal: "(a) . . . behavioural arousal is lost following posterior hypothalamic lesions despite the functional integrity of an ascending pathway from the midbrain reticular formation which can provide ECG [electrocorticographic] desynchronization; (b) . . . slow ECG activity is the dominant pattern following lesions of the midbrain reticular formation, despite the integrity of a conducting pathway [through the hypothalamus] which can mediate [behavioural] arousal and alert behaviour. This leads to the conclusion that although behavioural arousal requires the integrity of the posterior hypothalamic region, induced ECG activation is not critically dependent on pathways funnelling through this region."

RELATIONS BETWEEN ACTIVATION AND PERFORMANCE

A major tenet of activation theory states that: (a) there is an optimal condition or point of activation for best performance; (b) on either side of this point, performance is relatively impaired; and (c) impairment of performance increases with the distance from the optimal point of activation. In short, the hypothetical function relating performance to activation is that of an inverted U. Direct and indirect evidence for this relation has been thoroughly reviewed by Duffy (1962); further discussions related to this question have been published elsewhere (Malmo, 1957; Malmo, 1958; Malmo, 1962; Malmo, 1963).

As a neuropsychological concept, activation must be approached experimentally on both the neural and behavioral levels of description. First, with regard to the neural side of the question, recent advances in neurophysiology point up deficiencies in the methods used in earlier attempts to derive the inverted U relation from neurophysiological phenomena. These methodological deficiencies stemmed from limitations in the theoretical conceptions which guided research, because the earlier models were based only on the postulation of excitatory mechanisms. It is now clear, as Jasper (1963) has pointed out, that the inhibitory mechanisms also play an important part. Furthermore, although the basic distinction between phasic and tonic processes seems still to hold, evidence from neurophysiological experiments (Jasper, 1963) clearly indicates that the neural mechanisms underlying such processes are much more complicated than those posited in the earlier formulations. In particular, as previously mentioned, the importance of inhibitory influences has now been established. In short, according to this revised view, the sequential neural activity essential for a given sequence of organized (phasic) behavior is supported by tonic neural activation in at least two ways: (a) through optimal *excitatory* facilitation of the focal neural activity required for efficient performance, and (b) through concomitant *inhibition* of neural activity elsewhere that would otherwise interfere with the smooth running off of the focal (phasic) neural sequences. These revisions in the conception of the neurophysiological model are based mainly on the results of unit recording experiments (Jasper, 1963).

In order to deal with the other side of the neuropsychological concept of activation, the neurophysiological data must be placed in the context of behavioral and psychophysiological findings. Experimental manipulation of certain variables, e.g., varying number of hours of water deprivation in animals *under controlled conditions of environmental stimulation,* has been shown to produce monotonic changes in level of drive or motivation as gauged by means of physiological measures such as heart rate (HR) and muscle potentials (for reviews of these areas, see Malmo, 1962; Malmo, 1963). The italicized phrase above requires some explanation. The point requiring emphasis is that physiological changes associated with deprivation of a need (e.g., need for water, food, or sleep) are a product of at least two factors: (a) the state of bodily need produced by depriving the animal; and (b) the relevant environmental stimulating situation (e.g., bar pressing for water or food) which is absolutely essential for the interaction which yields measurable physiological change. In the absence of (b), the (a) factor produces no such change. This is what is meant by the multifactor theory of activation. Strong emphasis is laid on this point, because, when it is lost sight of, serious misunderstandings arise.

The same manipulations of experimental conditions that have produced monotonic effects on physiological functions (e.g., HR) have been shown to produce nonmonotonic effects on performance measures, as would be predicted by activation theory. For example, Bélanger and Feldman (1962) showed that, with increasing hours of water deprivation, HR rose monotonically but bar-pressing rate (recorded simultaneously) showed the predicted inverted-U curve. Conclusions from the Bélanger and Feldman (1962) experiment have been confirmed and extended in later investigations carried out in Bélanger's laboratory. For a recent summary of some of this work see Malmo and Bélanger (1966). The behavioral and physiological evidence from these and other experiments seem to indicate that, with rising drive or motivational level, the net tonic effect is one of increased excitation (reflected in increased HR and muscle tension, for example). Precisely how inhibitory and excitatory components combine in the total tonic process is, of course, a problem for further research.

Experiments with Psychiatric Patients Showing High Anxiety

A selected review based on experiments carried out in our laboratory on patients with pathological anxiety follows. Related investigations of anxiety have been reviewed elsewhere (Duffy, 1962; Martin, 1961). In our investigations, anxiety was defined as "a tensional state of such severity that work efficiency was interfered with and medical advice was sought, and which was characterized by one or more of the following complaints: persistent feelings of tension and strain, irritability, unremitting worry, restlessness, inability to concentrate, feelings of panic in everyday life situations" (Malmo & Shagass, 1949a, p. 9). In keeping with this clinical criterion of anxiety, it was possible to group patients according to the predominance of anxiety in the symptom picture as described in the patient's case history.

It is important to point out that the experiments to be reviewed here were carried out over a decade ago and prior to the general availability of tranquilizing drugs. We were able, therefore, to make observations on the relatively unaltered condition of pathological anxiety. Such observations would be difficult to obtain at the present time, given the widespread routine prescription of tranquilizers by psychiatrists and other physicians.

ANXIETY-PRODUCED INTERFERENCE IN SERIAL ROTE LEARNING

In the first study to be reported here, the performance of anxiety patients on a serial rote learning task was compared with that of a normal control group (Malmo & Amsel, 1948). The patient group consisted of nonpsychotic subjects in whom severe anxiety was noted as one of the most prominent symptoms. The control group was drawn largely from the hospital staff and matched with the patient group for age, sex, last grade completed in school, occupation, and vocabulary level. Both groups were required to learn a list of eight nonsense syllables by the serial anticipation method to a final criterion of one errorless repetition.

The number of trials required by the patient and control groups to reach successive levels of performance is indicated in Fig. 1. It should be noted that although the control group is slightly superior to the patient group in requiring fewer trials to go from each successive criterion to the next, the curves for the two groups were parallel up to the seven-syllable-correct criterion. Furthermore, the differences between groups for successive criteria up to the final one were not statistically significant. However, there was a large difference between the patient and control groups in the number of trials required to go from the seven-syllable to the eight-syllable (final) criterion and this difference was statistically significant. The absence of any tendency toward progressive divergence of the curves should be especially noted.

One possibility of accounting for the end decrement in the performance of the patient group is that it resulted from anxiety-produced overactivation. Assuming that the anxiety patient, unless completely at rest, is generally operating at an activation level that is higher than normal (see Malmo, 1957, p. 283), it follows that any condition which moves the patient still

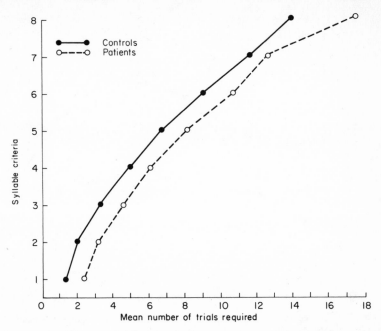

Fig. 1. Learning curves showing mean number of trials to reach successive criteria of performance by patients and controls. Each point is based upon the mean of 32 learning scores. From Malmo and Amsel (1948, Fig. 4, p. 448).

further out on the activation continuum will also probably have the effect of lowering his proficiency. Introspections reported by subjects in rote learning experiments suggest a plausible basis for inferring heightened activation in the patient group. When subjects in serial learning experiments have nearly satisfied the learning criterion (in this experiment one errorless repetition of the eight-syllable list), they frequently feel "uneasy" lest they miss a syllable on what could be the last (criterion) trial. When this "uneasiness" augments the anxiety patients' higher-than-normal mean level of activation, this augmentation is apparently sufficient to produce a critical difference in level of activation between patients and controls, resulting in lower proficiency in the performance of the patients relative to that of the controls.

Another factor responsible for the lower learning proficiency in the anxiety-patient group is indicated in Fig. 2 which presents the mean number of failures (errors) for the patient and control groups at each of the eight positions in the serial list. Statistical analyses of these data showed

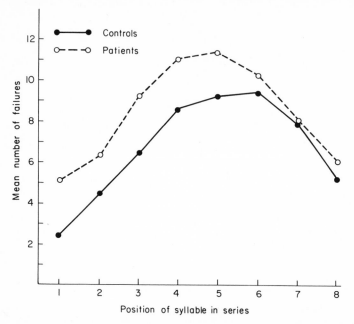

Fig. 2. Curves showing mean number of failures at each syllable position during learning by patients and controls. Each point is based upon the mean of 32 learning scores. From Malmo and Amsel (1948, Fig. 1, p. 443).

that the differences between patients and controls were statistically significant only for the syllables which appeared in the first two serial positions, suggesting that there is an "impact effect" associated with the onset of each new trial. Although the patient group continued to make consistently more errors in positions 3, 4, and 5 than did the controls, as may be noted in Fig. 2, the differences between groups for these positions were not significant. On the last three units of the list, performance was about the same for both groups.

That anxiety-produced "interference" may be distinguished from *intraserial* interference is indicated in Fig. 3 which presents data from an article by Hovland (1940). It may be noted that the locus of the increased intraserial interference, produced in Hovland's study by the massing of trials, occurred after the middle of the list, and that maximum differences between Hovland's massed and distributed practice groups occurred for syllables in the fifth and sixth serial positions. Comparison of Fig. 3 with Fig. 2 clearly reveals that the intraserial interference produced by massed practice was quite different from the anxiety-produced interference observed in the present study.

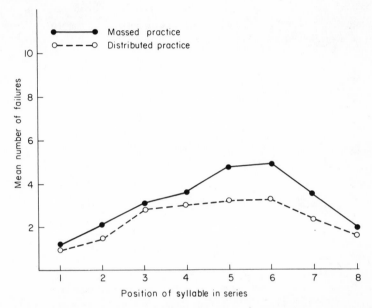

FIG. 3.   Curves showing mean number of failures at each syllable position during learning by massed and distributed practice. Each point is based upon the mean of 64 learning scores. Data from Hovland (1940), reported in Malmo and Amsel (1948, Fig. 2, p. 444).

This first experiment in the series of investigations from our laboratory was a behavioral study in which no physiological measures were employed. The significant differences between groups and the discovery of distinct anxiety-produced effects on serial learning raised questions concerning differences which these groups might show on physiological measures. The next step in our research program, therefore, was an investigation of physiological differences between anxiety patients and controls.

EVIDENCE FOR DEFECTIVE REGULATION OF SOMATIC LEVELS IN ANXIETY PATIENTS FOLLOWING "NORMAL" STARTLE REFLEX

In our early investigations of anxiety patients, it was clear that physiological recordings made under resting conditions were much less successful in differentiating patients from normal controls than were measures taken under conditions of (controlled) stimulation. One very effective form of stimulation for differentiating between anxiety patients and normal persons was that of startle induced by a strong auditory stimulus (Malmo *et al.*, 1950). The subject, reclining in bed, was stimulated at intervals through binaural earphones by a very loud 1000-cycle tone. The tone was 80 decibels above threshold and lasted for 3 seconds. Throughout the experiment electromyograms (EMGs) were continuously recorded from the extensor muscles of the right forearm.

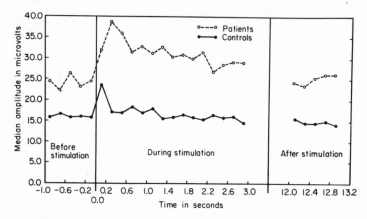

FIG. 4. Comparison of patients and controls with respect to median EMG amplitudes before, during, and after stimulation. Interval of measurement = .2 second. From Malmo *et al.* (1950, Fig. 1, p. 327).

Figure 4 presents results of the EMG recording. Although patients showed somewhat greater muscle tension levels at the beginning of the experiment, the difference betwen patients and controls before stimulation was not statistically significant. Furthermore, the mean rise in tension was nearly identical for the two groups during the reflex period (0–.2 seconds) of the startle reaction. However, the difference in the EMGs of patients and controls immediately following the startle reaction (.2–.4 seconds) was statistically significant. It will be noted in Fig. 4: (a) that the controls' curve started downward at the .2–second point and returned to prestimulation tension levels, whereas the patients' curve continued to rise, and (b) that the tension levels for the two groups remained widely separated for some time afterwards. Figure 5 presents the data of this experiment plotted in terms of median percent change in EMG. From this figure it is readily apparent that the groups were practically identical in their immediate reaction to the loud sound, but that they differed markedly with respect to EMG level in the after-response period. On the basis of these findings, Malmo *et al.* (1950) concluded as follows.

"These results are what might have been expected from the hypothesis that, in anxiety, inhibition of cortical afterdischarge, through some regulatory mechanism, such as the reticular system (thalamic and/or brainstem) is defective. The term afterdischarge is used on the assumption that *normally* the initial impact of . . . [the stimulus] . . . has higher stimulating value (startle) than the continuation of the tone for the remainder of the

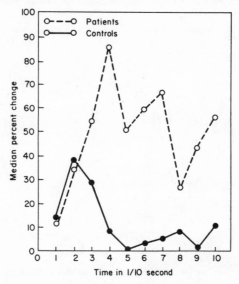

FIG. 5. Percent change in EMG response during first second of stimulation. Interval of measurement = .1 second. From Malmo *et al.* (1950, Fig. 2, p. 327).

3-second stimulation interval. This assumption is based on our present finding with normal control subjects" (p. 328).

Essential confirmation of the Malmo *et al.* (1950) experiment was provided by the results of an experiment by Davis, Malmo, and Shagass (1954) who again found that ". . . there is less deviation (from normal) in psychoneurotics' primary startle reflex reaction than in secondary [after-response] aspects of the total reaction mechanism" (p. 186). A likely explanation of the abnormally high after-reaction observed in anxiety patients in these experiments is that the sustained tension is due to the failure of a homeostatic mechanism located in the reticular systems. Moreover, it seems reasonable to speculate that this faulty mechanism is located in the descending branch of the reticular system, probably the bulbar inhibitory system.

IRREGULARITIES IN MOTOR ACTION: FURTHER EVIDENCE OF A FAULTY
REGULATORY MECHANISM IN ANXIETY PATIENTS

Malmo and Shagass (1949a) investigated the effects of stress on several
indexes of motor control in anxiety patients. A Hardy-Wolff thermal-pain
stimulation apparatus, shown in Fig. 6, was employed to induce stress. A
series of 12 thermal stimuli were presented at 1½ minute intervals. These
consisted of light from a 500-watt lamp (upper left) that was focused by
means of a condensing lens on the subject's forehead which was blackened

FIG. 6. Subject with head in frame ready for stimulation. Note left hand strapped
down for GSR recording and right forefinger resting on button. In the actual experiments electrodes were attached to the neck, right arm, and left leg, and a pneumo-
graph was employed. From Malmo and Shagass (1949a, Fig. 1, p. 10).

beforehand to increase heat absorption. Finger-movement (or "tremor")
and respiratory irregularity were recorded along with other physiological
measures (which will not be reported here). Polygraph tracings of each
of these measures are compared in Fig. 7 for an anxiety patient and a
normal control. The finger-movement tracings (see subject's finger resting
on tremor recorder in Fig. 6) clearly differentiated between anxiety patients
and normal controls. In Fig. 7, the disturbed appearance of the patient's
finger-movement tracing may be noted in contrast to the control's undisturbed tracing.

Finger-movement data for controls and for three groups of patients are presented in Figs. 8 and 9. Note the marked difference between anxiety patients and controls. Note also the resemblance here between anxiety patients and early schizophrenics. (Discussion of the data for schizophrenics is beyond the scope of this paper; for an account of these data see Malmo

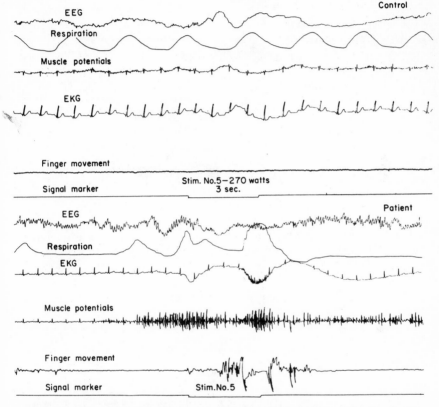

FIG. 7. Comparison of patient and control. Control: 33-year-old male physician; patient: 33-year-old male chemist with chronic anxiety neurosis. Note disturbances in the respiratory, muscle-potential, and finger-movement tracings of the patient. Note also anticipatory muscle responses of the patient. These are typical findings. In this case the patient showed relative tachycardia (rate = 100 per minute). From Malmo and Shagass (1949a, Fig. 2, p. 12).

and Shagass (1949a); for data on *chronic* schizophrenics see Malmo, Shagass, and Smith (1951c). The finding of significantly increased finger-movement irregularity for anxiety patients as compared with controls was confirmed in a later study in which a nonpainful "stress" situation was used with different subjects (Malmo, Shagass, Bélanger, & Smith, 1951a).

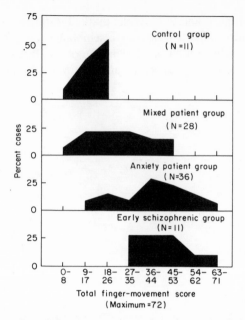

Fig. 8.   Range of total finger movement scores for each of three patient groups and the control group. Note complete absence of overlap between controls and early schizophrenics. From Malmo and Shagass (1949a, Fig. 5, p. 14).

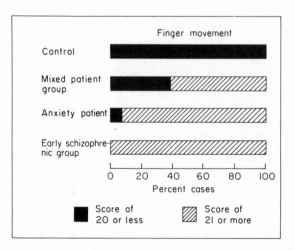

Fig. 9.   Amount of disturbance in finger-movement records. The greater the disturbance, the higher the score. From Malmo and Shagass (1949a, Fig. 6, p. 14).

Irregularity in respiration also clearly differentiated anxiety patients from controls and other patient groups. In Fig. 10 it may be noted that respiratory irregularity was produced in nearly 60% of the anxiety patients by the thermal stimuli on eight or more occasions, whereas this degree of irregularity was not found in a single control subject. As may be noted in Fig. 10, the other patient groups fell between the anxiety patients and the controls.

The increased frequency of disturbances in anxiety patients in comparison with other groups, which was reflected in finger-tremor and re-

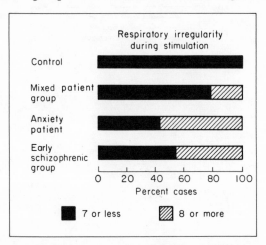

FIG. 10. Respiratory irregularity during stimulation. Score is expressed in terms of number of stimulations during which irregularities occurred. Maximum score was 12 (irregularity produced by every stimulus). From Malmo and Shagass (1949a, Fig. 12, p. 19).

spiratory irregularity, is regarded as further evidence of tonic background activity resulting from defective regulatory control in anxiety patients. As in the case of the findings in the startle experiments, the excessive (and prolonged) motor reactions of anxiety patients to stress stimuli seem to reflect the breakdown in a homeostatic mechanism whose general function is to inhibit such reactions. Again the inhibitory components of the reticular systems seem implicated by these findings.

The physiological findings described thus far have dealt mainly with observations of skeletal-motor changes. In the studies presented next, evidence of anxiety-produced overreaction in effectors primarily under the control of the autonomic nervous system (ANS) will be examined.

EVIDENCE OF DEFECTIVE AUTONOMIC NERVOUS SYSTEM (ANS)
CONTROL IN ANXIETY

Blood-pressure and heart-rate data were obtained for psychoneurotic
and psychotic patients and normal controls while these subjects were performing on a mirror drawing test and a rapid discrimination test (Malmo
& Shagass, 1952; Malmo et al., 1951c). The blood-pressure reactions during the mirror drawing test of psychoneurotic patients, in whom anxiety
was a prominent symptom, are compared in Fig. 11 with those of chronic

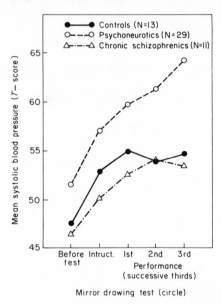

FIG. 11. Mean blood pressure during mirror drawing test (circle). Note continuous rise in curve for psychoneurotics. From Malmo and Shagass (1952, Fig. 5,
p. 90).

schizophrenics and normal controls. It may be noted that the systolic blood
pressure of the psychoneurotic group was higher before the mirror drawing test began and continued to rise throughout the test in contrast to the
blood pressure of the other groups which tended to level off. The mean
blood-pressure scores obtained for the psychoneurotic group during the
rapid discrimination test were quite comparable with those obtained by this
group on the mirror drawing test (see Malmo & Shagass, 1952, Fig. 4,
p. 89). A similar failure of psychoneurotics to show what might be considered "normal" habituation of blood-pressure reaction in response to
repeated stresses was found by Malmo, Shagass, and Heslam (1951b).

Heart-rate data on the same mirror drawing test for essentially the same groups of subjects as those whose blood-pressure data were presented in Fig. 11 are presented in Fig. 12. Here again the psychoneurotics have higher HRs than the comparison groups, and much higher HRs than the normal controls. Similar HR findings were obtained for these patient groups during a rapid discrimination test, as may be noted in HR data presented in Fig. 13.

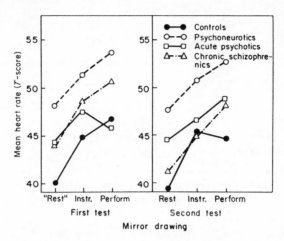

FIG. 12.   Mean heart rate during mirror drawing tests. From Malmo *et al.* (1951c, Fig. 5, p. 369).

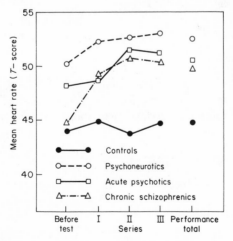

FIG. 13.   Mean heart rate during rapid discrimination test. From Malmo *et al.* (1951c, Fig. 4, p. 368).

The evidence for anxiety-produced overreaction in the cardiovascular system indicated by the blood-pressure and HR findings described above seems quite clear. Since central nervous system control of cardiovascular activity is organized at different levels of the neuraxis, there are a number of alternative possibilities which must be considered in attempting to account for the observed deficiencies in the regulation of the cardiovascular system in anxiety patients. Although detailed consideration of these possibilities is beyond the scope of this paper, it may be noted that, in the regulation of cardiovascular activity, increasing emphasis is being placed on the role played by the limbic system (Covian, Antunes-Rodrigues, & O'Flaherty, 1964).

FACTORS OF AGE AND SEX

It is important to stress the dangers inherent in research with clinical patients where precise matching of groups for age and sex is sometimes almost impossible to achieve. In the studies reviewed in this chapter the groups were either carefully matched or the influences of age and sex variables were evaluated in order to avoid erroneous conclusions. In the course of determining the influences of age and sex factors, some interesting relationships were obtained between these variables and various psychophysiological indexes.

(1) Heart-rate variability under stress decreased linearly with age, a finding which may be interpreted as indicating diminished autonomic nervous system influences, both vagal and sympathetic, with increasing age (Malmo & Shagass, 1949b).

(2) In comparing male and female subjects with respect to the adaptation of systolic blood pressure, male controls consistently showed more rapid adaptation than female controls (Malmo et al., 1951b). This was found for four successive periods of performance on a psychomotor task, and for three successive periods of immersion in the cold pressor tests.

(3) There was a tendency for the finger movements of younger patients to show more disturbance than those of older ones (Malmo & Shagass, 1949a, p. 22).

GSR AS A "MEASURE" OF ANXIETY

There is a rather prevalent misconception that the galvanic skin response (GSR) and palmar conductance (PC) level are superior to all other physiological measures in differentiating between anxiety patients and controls. To the best of my knowledge there is no evidence to support such a conclusion. In the comprehensive review of Duffy (1962) there is no indication that skin conductance is superior to other physiological measures in differentiating between anxiety patients and controls. In the study by Malmo, Shagass, Davis, Cleghorn, Graham, and Goodman (1948), cited by Duffy, analysis of skin conductance records showed a higher frequency of GSR oscillations in anxiety patients than in controls during an anticipatory period preceding pain stimulation. However, a measure of finger movement also employed in this experiment appeared even more effective in differentiating between anxiety patients and controls. This indication was borne out in a follow-up study (Malmo & Shagass, 1949a). In this later study carried out with a larger number of patients, the results with the finger-movement measure were amply confirmed, but (possibly because of a change in the electrical circuit that likely produced more oscillations in both groups) no significant differences were found between patients and controls in frequency of GSR oscillations. With regard to level of palmar conductance, contrary to what might have been expected, anxiety patients' mean conductance level was lower than that of controls, before the start of the test. Increase in skin conductance from pretest to posttest was greater for anxiety patients than for controls, but this finding could easily have been due to the lower initial level in the anxiety-patient group. Taking the results of the two studies together it was clear that compared with GSR the finger-movement measure was significantly more differentiative between anxiety patients and controls. Furthermore, in comparison with various other physiological measures employed in the second study, GSR seemed a relatively poor differentiator, particularly when compared with measures of skeletal-motor functions. It is true that we later revised our method for recording skin conductance (Malmo & Davis, 1961), but the method used with anxiety patients had previously been successfully employed by Andrews (1943) in a study of reaction to pain.

To repeat, as far as reaction to pain is concerned, measures of skeletal-motor activity appear superior to GSR in differentiating between anxiety patients and controls. Because anxiety patients have been shown to condition more rapidly than normals in GSR conditioning experiments, it has sometimes been assumed that the GSR is particularly sensitive with respect to detecting anxiety. But review of the conditioning literature shows that a skeletal-motor reaction (eyeblink) appears at least as effective as GSR in differentiating anxiety patients from controls. Franks (1956, 1961) has reviewed GSR and eyeblink conditioning studies in relation to anxiety. In these reviews there is certainly no indication of superior differentiation by GSR. In Franks' own experiments he actually found less marked differences between groups for GSR than for eyeblink conditioning; but he believed the relatively poor differentiation by GSR conditioning may have been due to the low intensity of the unconditioned stimulus which he used (Franks, 1956, p. 147).

Summary

In this chapter I have attempted to provide a brief sketch of my conception of certain selected aspects of activation theory as it has developed thus far, and to show some of the clinical origins of the activation concept in early investigations of pathological anxiety observed in psychoneurotic patients. A review of the findings in these studies, which were carried out prior to the introduction of tranquilizing drugs, pointed up the probable deficiency of homeostatic mechanisms in pathological anxiety. It was argued that such homeostatic mechanisms normally prevent physiological overactivation and related losses in behavioral efficiency. Inhibitory components of the reticular and limbic systems, which have been relatively neglected in theories relating the reticular system and behavior, were considered as probably playing a major role in the homeostatic control of physiological overreaction in response to stress.

REFERENCES

Andrews, H. L. Skin resistance changes and measurements of pain threshold. *J. Clin. Invest.*, 1943, **22**, 517-520.

Bélanger, D., & Feldman, S. M. Effects of water deprivation upon heart rate and instrumental activity in the rat. *J. comp. physiol. Psychol.*, 1962, **55**, 220-225.

Covian, M. R., Antunes-Rodrigues, J., & O'Flaherty, J. J. Effects of stimulation of the septal area upon blood pressure and respiration in the cat. *J. Neurophysiol.*, 1964, **27**, 394-407.

Davis, J. F., Malmo, R. B., & Shagass, C. Electromyographic reaction to strong auditory stimulation in psychiatric patients. *Canad. J. Psychol.*, 1954, **8**, 177-186.

Duffy, Elizabeth. *Activation and behavior.* New York: Wiley, 1962.

Feldman, S. M., & Waller, H. J. Dissociation of electrocortical activation and behavioral arousal. *Nature*, 1962, **196**, 1320-1322.

Franks, C. M. Conditioning and personality: A study of normal and neurotic subjects. *J. abnorm. soc. Psychol.*, 1956, **52**, 143-150.

Franks, C. M. Conditioning and abnormal behavior. In H. J. Eysenck (Ed.), *Handbook of abnormal psychology.* New York: Basic Books, 1961. Pp. 457-487.

Hebb, D. O. Animal and physiological psychology. *Annu. Rev. Psychol.*, 1950, **1**, 173-188.

Hebb, D. O. Drives and the C.N.S. (conceptual nervous system). *Psychol. Rev.*, 1955, **62**, 243-254.

Herrick, C. J. *An introduction to neurology.* (4th ed.) Philadelphia: Saunders, 1928.

Hovland, C. I. Experimental studies in rote-learning theory. VII. Distribution of practice with varying lengths of list. *J. exp. Psychol.*, 1940, **27**, 271-284.

Jasper, H. H. Studies of non-specific effects upon electrical responses in sensory systems. In G. Moruzzi, A. Fessard, & H. H. Jasper (Eds.), *Brain mechanisms. Progress in brain research,* Vol. 1. Amsterdam: Elsevier, 1963. Pp. 272-293.

Lindsley, D. B. Emotion. In S. S. Stevens (Ed.), *Handbook of experimental psychology*. New York: Wiley, 1951. Pp. 473-516.

Magoun, H. W. *The waking brain*. Springfield, Ill.: Thomas, 1958.

Malmo, R. B. Anxiety and behavioral arousal. *Psychol. Rev.*, 1957, **64**, 276-287.

Malmo, R. B. Measurement of drive: an unsolved problem in psychology. In M. R. Jones (Ed.), *Nebraska symposium on motivation*. Lincoln: Univer. of Nebraska Press, 1958. Pp. 229-265.

Malmo, R. B. Activation. In A. J. Bachrach (Ed.), *Experimental foundations of clinical psychology*. New York: Basic Books, 1962. Pp. 386-422.

Malmo, R. B. On central and autonomic nervous system mechanisms in conditioning, learning, and performance. *Canad. J. Psychol.*, 1963, **17**, 1-36.

Malmo, R. B., & Amsel, A. Anxiety-produced interference in serial rote learning with observations on rote learning after partial frontal lobectomy. *J. exp. Psychol.*, 1948, **38**, 440-454.

Malmo, R. B., & Bélanger, D. Related physiological and behavioral changes: What are their determinants? *Res. Publ. Ass. nerv. ment. Dis.*, 1966, in press.

Malmo, R. B., & Davis, J. F. A monopolar method of measuring palmar conductance. *Amer. J. Psychol.*, 1961, **74**, 106-113.

Malmo, R. B., & Shagass, C. Physiologic studies of reaction to stress in anxiety and early schizophrenia. *Psychosom. Med.*, 1949, **11**, 9-24. (a)

Malmo, R. B., & Shagass, C. Variability of heart rate in relation to age, sex and stress. *J. appl. Physiol.*, 1949, **2**, 181-184. (b)

Malmo, R. B., & Shagass, C. Studies of blood pressure in psychiatric patients under stress. *Psychosom. Med.*, 1952, **14**, 82-93.

Malmo, R. B., Shagass, C., Bélanger, D. J., & Smith, A. A. Motor control in psychiatric patients under experimental stress. *J. abnorm. soc. Psychol.*, 1951, **46**, 539-547. (a)

Malmo, R. B., Shagass, C., Davis, J. F. A method for the investigation of somatic response mechanisms in psychoneurosis. *Science*, 1950, **112**, 325-328.

Malmo, R. B., Shagass, C., Davis, J. F., Cleghorn, R. A., Graham, B. F., & Goodman, A. Joan. Standardized pain stimulation as controlled stress in physiological studies of psychoneurosis. *Science*, 1948, **108**, 509-511.

Malmo, R. B., Shagass, C., & Heslam, R. M. Blood pressure response to repeated brief stress in psychoneurosis: A study of adaptation. *Canad. J. Psychol.*, 1951, **5**, 167-179. (b)

Malmo, R. B., Shagass, C., & Smith, A. A. Responsiveness in chronic schizophrenia. *J. Pers.*, 1951, **19**, 359-375. (c)

Martin, Irene. Somatic reactivity. In H. J. Eysenck (Ed.), *Handbook of abnormal psychology*. New York: Basic Books, 1961. Pp. 417-456.

Moruzzi, G., & Magoun, H. W. Brain stem reticular formation and activation of the EEG. *Electroencephalography clin. Neurophysiol.*, 1949, **1**, 455-473.

Penfield, W., & Rasmussen, T. *The cerebral cortex of man*. New York: Macmillan, 1950.

CHAPTER 8

The Conditioning and Deconditioning of Neurotic Anxiety

Joseph Wolpe
DEPARTMENT OF BEHAVIORAL SCIENCE,
TEMPLE UNIVERSITY SCHOOL OF MEDICINE,
PHILADELPHIA, PENNSYLVANIA

Today it is generally accepted that neuroses result from certain kinds of experience and are thus in some sense learned. But experts disagree about the manner and the details of this learning process. Most American psychiatrists and clinical psychologists accept the psychoanalytic view that what is learned is essentially a habit of "repressing" painful complexes into an "unconscious" region of the mind and that the manifestations of a neurosis are due to discharges from the "repressed complex" and from the "repressive forces."

In this chapter an opposing view will be put forward—that neurotic responses are established by simple conditioning. Since anxiety is central to most neuroses, our exposition will be concerned mainly with the conditioning of neurotic anxiety. We shall first survey the circumstances in which the conditioning and deconditioning of neurotic anxiety occurs, then consider the mechanisms of learning that are conceived to operate, and finally give a conspectus of the results so far attained by the use of therapeutic methods based on the conditioning model (behavior therapy).

Experimental Neuroses

The idea that neurotic anxiety is nothing but a conditioned emotional habit had its origin in observations made in the laboratory in connection with experimental neuroses. Experimental neuroses were first produced in

Pavlov's laboratories about 60 years ago and subsequently by various workers in the United States, the most notable being Gantt (1944), Liddell (1944), and Masserman (1943). There are two basic methods for producing an experimental neurosis. The oldest consists of subjecting a spatially confined animal to ambivalent stimulation in the context of a powerful drive such as hunger. In Pavlov's famous circle-and-ellipse experiment (1927), a circle was conditioned as a positive stimulus to feeding and an ellipse as a food-negative stimulus; then the ellipse was changed in shape in stages until it was almost indistinguishable from the circle. The animal's response then became ambivalent, opposing action-tendencies were simultaneously evoked, and rising anxiety was generated. This anxiety was conditioned to the experimental chamber and was henceforth evoked whenever the animal was brought back there.

The other basic method for producing an experimental neurosis involves the use of noxious stimuli. To the spatially confined animal one applies either a large number of weak noxious stimuli (usually in the form of electric shocks) or a small number of stronger noxious stimuli. About a quarter of a century ago, extensive series of experiments employing noxious stimulation were carried out by Liddell and Masserman. Misled by various features of their experimental arrangements, these workers believed that the neuroses thus produced were also due to conflict. Masserman (1943), for example, ascribed the neuroses of his cats to a conflict between food-approach motivation and avoidance-of-shock motivation; he applied a high-voltage low-amperage shock to the animal when it was approaching food in response to a conditioned stimulus. However, in 1947, in a similar experimental setting, I demonstrated that neursoses could be produced by shocks administered to cats that had never been fed in the experimental cage. Recently, Dr. Reginald G. Smart (1965) has reported a study of variations on this experimental model. He has shown that there is very little difference on 16 measures of neurotic behavior between cats who receive only shock and those who are shocked either while approaching food or while eating in the experimental cage.

The fact that at least some experimental neuroses can be induced without conflict negates the supposition that neuroses must result from conflict-induced neural damage or "strain" and leads one to examine the presumption that learning is their basis. If neuroses are learned they will have the features common to all learned behavior:

(1) Neurotic behavior will be closely similar to the behavior evoked in the precipitating situation.

(2) Neurotic responses will be under the control of stimuli that were

present in the precipitating situation; that is, the responses will occur upon the impingement on the organism of the same or similar stimuli.

(3) Neurotic responses will be at greatest intensity when the organism is exposed to stimuli most like those to which the behavior was originally conditioned and will diminish in intensity as a function of diminishing resemblance in accordance with the principle of primary stimulus generalization.

All three of these features were found in my neurotic cats. Neurosis-inducing shocks evoked a variety of motor responses as well as autonomic responses (pupillary dilation, erection of hairs, and rapid respiration, inter alia). After a number of shocks, the animal would be continuously disturbed in the experimental cage, and then no more shocks would be given. The disturbance in each case consisted of just such responses as had been evoked by the shocks. Reactions of the sympathetic division of the autonomic nervous system were found in all animals, and vocalizing and clawing at the netting in most. But some displayed special reactions which, invariably, had been observed previously as reactions to electric shocks. For example, one cat who had urinated while being shocked always urinated subsequently within a few seconds of being put into the experimental cage.

The control of the neurotic reactions by stimuli involved in the causal situation was evident in several ways. First, the reactions were always at their strongest in the experimental cage, and the animals strongly resisted being put into it. Then, the sounding of a buzzer that had preceded the shocks invariably intensified whatever neurotic reactions were going on. Finally, if the experimenter had been visible to the animal at the time of shocking, his entry into the animal's living cage could at once evoke the neurotic reactions.

Primary stimulus generalization was manifested along several dimensions. Each animal displayed neurotic reactions in the experimental room outside the experimental cage because, it may be presumed, stimuli from the room had been acting upon him at the time of shocking. When placed in various other rooms he would manifest neurotic reactions at an intensity corresponding to the physical similarity between the experimental room and the other room. Another instance of primary stimulus generalization was on an auditory intensity continuum. Presentation of the buzzer at close quarters would always disturb an animal greatly, and the farther away the buzzer was when it sounded, the weaker were the animal's reactions.

Thus, experimental neuroses in animals exhibited all three of the characteristics of learned behavior for which they were examined. Human neuroses also possess these characteristics, as will be seen.

Human Neuroses as Learned Behavior

The commonest human neurotic-response constellation is anxiety, which is, broadly speaking, a sympathetic-dominated pattern of autonomic response. In most human neuroses anxiety is in the forefront, but it is also at the root of syndromes in which its role is not always obvious, such as impotence, asthma, and the so-called character neuroses. In neurotic patients, in a large majority of whom a history of the onset of unadaptive anxiety reactions can be obtained, one finds the origin of the neurosis almost always related to single experience or recurrent occasions of high anxiety, or to a chronic anxiety-evoking state of affairs. Symonds (1943) found a history of high anxiety arousal at the onset of 99% of anxiety states in 2000 flying crew members of the British Royal Air Force. The nature and degree of stress needed to evoke significantly high degrees of anxiety varied according to preexistent factors in the individual; this is also true of experimental animals.

Stimuli making impact on the individual at the time of causation of the neurosis are always the ones to become conditioned to human neurotic anxiety responses. For example, a lawyer's fear of public speaking had its origin in an incident in law school when he was humiliated by the lecturer when speaking before a class; a woman's fear of expressing anger originated in the heavy punishment which expression of anger had elicited from her foster parents. Of course, it is not true that *only* stimuli present at the original precipitating events can be cues to neurotic reactions. It is very common for second-order conditioning to take place. For example, a young woman with a neurotic fear of crowds was sitting in a half-empty movie house when it rapidly filled with a crowd of students. After this she feared all public interiors, even if empty.

The strength of human neurotic reactions is very often a function of primary generalization, but sometimes also of secondary generalization. In almost all phobias of the classic kind there is primary stimulus generalization. For example, a fear of crowds usually increases according to the number of people in the crowd, and claustrophobia increases in inverse relation to available space and in direct relation to duration of confinement. In secondary generalization, the stimuli are not similar, but evoke a common mediating response (Osgood, 1962). Thus, in one patient, lack of communion with her husband and going away from home by car each produced a desolate feeling that mediated anxiety.

The Deconditioning of Neurotic Anxiety

Animal and human neuroses have another similarity. Both differ from almost all other examples of learned behavior in their extraordinary persistence. The neurotic anxiety response is unadaptive in that it does not promote the satisfaction of the needs of the organism—and in fact often obstructs such satisfaction—being, to the human at least, unpleasant in itself. And yet, unlike other unadaptive habits, neurotic anxiety is not extinguished by its repeated evocation. The neurotic cat continues to be anxious in the cage in which he was shocked, no matter how often and for how long he is kept there; and similarly, the phobic human patient is usually not benefitted by being driven or coaxed into the situations that terrify him. On the contrary, this may make him worse. The mere evocation of anxiety is often found clinically to augment the anxiety habit. Campbell, Sanderson, and Laverty (1964) have demonstrated this experimentally. The evocation of anxiety also leads, under some circumstances, to the conditioning of anxiety to new stimuli (second-order conditioning). The "spread" of human neuroses is due to this process which has also been directly demonstrated in animals (Wolpe, 1958, p. 60).

Both animal and human neurotic anxiety-response habits can, however, be eliminated relatively easily by counterconditioning. This involves presenting anxiety-evoking stimuli to the organism when a response that can inhibit the anxiety is also present. In experimental neuroses the anxiety-inhibiting response has most often been eating (Masserman, 1943; Wolpe, 1952a; Wolpe, 1958) but sexual responses have also been used (Napalkov & Karas, 1957). Since anxiety of high intensity will inhibit eating, no matter how hungry the animal may be, one utilizes a generalization gradient to procure a low level of anxiety that will permit eating to occur in its presence. In the case of the anxiety conditioned to a buzzer, one animal would at first not eat closer than 40 feet from the source of the sound. But eating several pellets of meat at a point 40 feet from the buzzer brought about the gradual disappearance of his anxiety at that distance. It was then possible to feed him at 30 feet from the buzzer, and so on. Thus, when the food-approach impulse was the stronger, it inhibited the anxiety, and each time it did so, weakened to some extent the anxiety-response habit. This is what is meant by therapy of neurosis on the reciprocal inhibition principle.

In human neuroses feeding has so far been employed as the anxiety-inhibitor only in children by a technique very similar to that applied to the animals (Jones, 1924; Lazarus, 1959) but at least a dozen other anxiety inhibitors have proved effective (Wolpe & Lazarus, 1966). I shall briefly describe the use of three that are particularly frequently applied to adult neuroses: assertive responses, sexual responses, and deep muscle relaxation. It is actually quite common for several anxiety-inhibitors to be used on the same patient. The choice of an anxiety-inhibitor and the manner of its use is determined mainly on the basis of a thorough unraveling of the stimulus-response relations of the neurotic habit. I shall outline when and how the three most used anxiety-inhibitors are usually employed.

The Use of Assertive Responses

The term "assertive" is applied to any behavior which gives overt expression to spontaneous and appropriate feelings other than anxiety. The therapist instigates the expression of such feelings in a patient who is made so anxious by his interchanges with other people that he is unable to perform appropriately, for example, he is unable to ask for the repayment of an overdue loan. The therapist encourages him to express his desire for repayment. Each time the patient succeeds in expressing himself he inhibits his anxiety to some extent and thus somewhat weakens the anxiety-response habit. The feelings most commonly involved in such activities are anger and resentment, but anything from affection to revulsion may be relevant.

Mrs. T., age 42, was a typical case. She was exceedingly diffident in all her dealings with other people and suffered from frequent tension headaches. Assertive responses had to be instigated in a wide range of situations, some of which involved her elder brothers and sisters who frequently criticized her. She would resent this, seething inwardly but saying nothing for she had been the youngest in a Victorian-type household where respect for one's elders was rated the highest virtue. I impressed on her that her siblings had no business to try to run her life and that she should exteriorize the resentment that she so appropriately felt. The day after I spoke to her in this way, a brother thrust some advice upon her about the handling of her child to which she responded by telling him to "keep his nose out" of her affairs. Similar acts of appropriate assertion toward her siblings put an end to their interfering and, what was more important, at the same time conquered her anxieties with people. Her tension headaches also ceased, their emotional basis having been removed. Three years later she was still well and at the helm of her own life.

The Use of Sexual Responses

Sexual responses, not unexpectedly, are chiefly of use for treating neurotic reactions conditioned to sexual situations. Impotence and premature ejaculation, the commonest of all sexual problems, are in the great majority of cases due to anxiety having been conditioned to aspects of the sexual situation. Erection of the penis is subserved by the parasympathetic division of the autonomic nervous system and tends to be impaired by anxiety. In most cases of impotence or premature ejaculation sexual feelings are preserved, and the behavior therapist uses them to inhibit anxiety by arranging the regulation of sexual approaches. In run-of-the-mill cases of this kind, recovery in a matter of weeks can be almost guaranteed if there is enough opportunity for carrying out the maneuvers prescribed. The patient is enjoined to restrict his sexual advances to the stage of minimal anxiety. With repetition the anxiety diminishes to zero, and the patient then goes on to the next stage at which anxiety begins to be felt, advancing no farther until anxiety disappears. After several stages coitus becomes possible and its details are similarly controlled until performance becomes entirely satisfactory. A fully cooperative partner is of course indispensable to this procedure.

THE USE OF DEEP RELAXATION

Deep muscle relaxation (Jacobson, 1938) is a widely applicable means of inhibiting anxiety. It has autonomic accompaniments that are exactly opposite to those of anxiety (Jacobson, 1939; Jacobson, 1940). Its main use in behavior therapy is in relation to phobialike sources of anxiety. For example, if a man is anxious in crowds, or at heights, or at signs of stormy weather, relaxation may be used as the anxiety-inhibitor to overcome his phobia. About 14 years ago, a technique was introduced (Wolpe, 1954; Wolpe, 1958; Wolpe, 1961) that came to be called *systematic desensitization*. This requires a total of about 1½-hours' training in relaxation consisting of half a dozen sessions each taking about 15 minutes. During these sessions, various situations belonging to an area of disturbance are listed and then placed in rank order, the most disturbing being listed first. The ranked list is called a *hierarchy*. (An individual, may, of course, have several hierarchies.)

When relaxation has become adequate and the hierarchies determined, desensitizing can begin. The weakest scene from a hierarchy is presented to the imagination of the deeply relaxed patient for a few seconds, and the procedure is repeated until the imagined item no longer evokes anxiety at all. For example, a patient with a fear of crowds may first be asked to imagine entering a room in which two other people are seated. When repetition has reduced the anxiety this evokes to zero, the therapist proceeds to the next scene, perhaps a room containing three people, and so on, until as high a number as necessary is reached. There is almost always complete transfer of the deconditioning of anxiety from the imaginary situation to the corresponding situation in reality.

While in some cases, such as most classic phobias, desensitization is quite a straightforward matter, in others it is exceedingly complicated. For example, Mrs. A., age 30, had been afraid of going into crowds or public places like shops for over 11 years. She was also anxious when speaking to anybody other than her husband, because involvement in conversation gave her a feeling of being tied down and unable to get away. Her neurosis had started 11 years earlier when, after drinking at a party, she had become nauseous and had been seized with a great fear that she might be seen vomiting. Her treatment involved desensitization of several hierarchies (including social scrutiny, vomiting, driving cars, and being enclosed in space) that had to be treated both singly and in combination.

Controlling Factors in the Conditioning and Deconditioning of Neurotic Anxiety Reactions

The major factors that determine both the conditioning and the deconditioning of neurotic anxiety reactions are conveniently portrayed in a simple diagram (Fig. 1) that covers all the known kinds of learning and unlearning.

The manner in which an organism responds to a stimulus depends on the identity of the synaptic connections between the sensory pathways activated by that stimulus and the pathways serving response systems. (A synapse is a *functionally transmissive* point of contact between neurons.) Learning is manifested by change in the character of the response to a stimulus (given the same surrounding conditions) and implies change in the synaptic connections of the pathways that the stimulus activates. Learning always involves the attenuation (often to the point of elimination) of a preexisting habit of response to the particular stimulus. In other words, all positive learning involves counterconditioning.

There is a second way in which a habit can be eliminated: repeated evocation of the response without reinforcement (reward). This kind of elimination (or weakening) of a habit is, of course, known as experimental extinction and has been far more extensively studied than counterconditioning up to the present time. Our diagram (Fig. 1) illustrates the Hullian view (Hull, 1943) that extinction is due to reflex effects associated with muscle fatigue (reactive inhibition) on neural pathways that have been in action (Mowrer-Miller hypothesis; see Wolpe, 1952b). Reactive inhibition and its effects in the direction of extinction follow *every* motor response, but reinforcement can negate these effects.

The details of stimulus and response given in Fig. 1 relate to the conditioning and subsequent deconditioning of a neurotic anxiety response habit in the cat experiments referred to earlier. The stimulus that is the main focus of interest throughout is S_1, the sound of a buzzer. Before the conditioning experiment is begun the animal responds to S_1 by turning his head in the direction of the sound (R_1). This action leads to reactive inhibition in the muscles concerned; stimuli (S_4) set up by products of muscle activity excite sensory neurons, and this excitation has inhibitory consequences upon the S_1-R_1 chain. (In Fig. 1 the inhibitory pathway is represented by a single neuron, n_{17}, though in fact there must be a se-

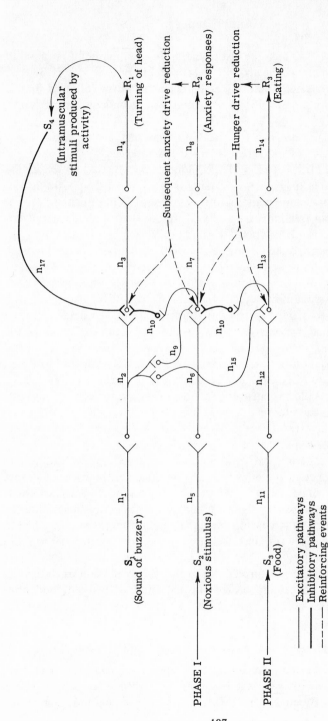

FIG. 1. Depiction of the major factors that determine the conditioning and deconditioning of neurotic anxiety reactions. In Phase I, when the animal (a cat) is shocked in temporal contiguity with stimulus S_1 (a buzzer) so that S_1 becomes conditioned to the responses (R_2) evoked by the shock, there is a correlated development of conditioned inhibition of the original head-turning response (R_1) to S_1. In Phase II the conditioning of an alimentary response (R_3) to S_1 is accompanied by conditioned inhibition of the "anxiety" responses (R_2). (See text for complete explanation.) The neuronal representations are not strictly necessary to this exposition but reflect the author's predilection to "think neuronally" because neurons and synapses are the real channels of behavior.

187

quence of neurons, and only the last of these, the one that delivers impulses at the $n_2 \cdot n_3$ synapse, would actually be an inhibitory neuron.) If S_1 were to be presented repeatedly and the S_1-R_1 sequence never followed by any reinforcing state of affairs, the S_1-R_1 habit would undergo experimental extinction.

S_2 represents the noxious electrical stimulus that evokes anxiety and avoidance responses (R_2). When S_1 has been followed by S_2 on several occasions (Phase I), it is found that S_1 alone evokes R_2 *and no longer R_1.* This means that neuron n_9, whose ending is in anatomical apposition with synapse $n_6 \cdot n_7$, has acquired the ability to transmit impulses to n_7. At the same time, n_{10} (an inhibitory neuron) is presumed to have delivered impulses that have brought about a conditioned inhibition at the $n_2 \cdot n_3$ synapse. The diagram assumes that anxiety-drive reduction following each cessation of S_2 has reinforcing effects on both the development of the new habit (S_1-R_2) and the elimination of the old one (S_1-R_1), but it is needless to insist on this assumption.

When the S_1-R_2 habit has been established, it would ordinarily be expected that repeated presentations of S_1 would lead to an extinction of the habit if there is no further reinforcement. However, experience has shown that repeated evocation of a strong anxiety response does not lead to weakening of the anxiety response habit (Campbell *et al.*, 1964; Wolpe, 1958). There are two possible explanations for this. First, on the face of it, autonomic responses generate very little reactive inhibition; and second, each cessation of S_1 involves anxiety-drive reduction (Farber, 1948; Miller, 1948) which could reinforce the S_1-R_2 sequence.

In Phase II, experimental conditions are arranged so that eating can occur in the presence of the buzzer, which is sounded at a distance so that some anxiety is evoked but not enough to inhibit eating. It becomes possible to bring the sound progressively nearer with repeated feedings. Thus, S_1 becomes conditioned in increasing "doses" to an alimentary response and to inhibition of the anxiety response. The essential events are parallel to those of Phase I.

Some animals were put through a third phase: extinction of the eating response to S_1 by repeatedly presenting that stimulus without food reinforcement (Wolpe, 1952b; Wolpe, 1958). There was no recurrence of anxiety.

Results of Therapy of Neurosis on a Conditioning Theory

Virtually any conventional form of therapy of the neuroses, from psychoanalysis to simple suggestion, is substantially successful in about 40% of all cases (e.g., Eysenck, 1952; Eysenck, 1965). Apparently this is due to nonspecific anxiety-inhibiting emotions evoked in patients by the therapeutic situation. If conditioning therapy (behavior therapy) is to merit any special consideration, its success must be significantly superior to the common average. There are strong indications of this.

In the first place there are the bare facts of clinical outcome studies. Dr. A. A. Lazarus (1963; 1965) and I (1958) have between us found in over 600 unselected neurotic patients (in most of whom anxiety was prominent) that almost 90% of those to whom the techniques were actually applied either recovered or improved markedly. The mean number of interviews was about 30. The experience of all who become skilled in the techniques has so far been similar. These results must be contrasted with the 60% recovery rate for completely analyzed patients after 3 or 4 years of treatment which consisted of three or four sessions per week—according to the report of the Fact Finding Committee of the American Psychoanalytic Association (Brody, 1962).

Impressive as this casual comparison seems, it would obviously be more satisfactory to have properly controlled comparative studies. One highly significant report has recently come from the University of Illinois (Paul, 1965). Finding that many students in a class on public speaking were very fearful before audiences, Paul got five *psychoanalytically oriented* psychotherapists to participate in an experiment in which they each treated nine of the students—three by systematic desensitization, three by their own kind of insight therapy, and three by a kind of direct suggestion. After five sessions, 86% of the desensitization group were *much improved,* 20% of the insight group, and none of the suggestion group.

Psychoanalytic theory tells us that recovery obtained by such methods as outlined here cannot endure, that there will be relapse or symptom-substitution because of alleged "deep unconscious conflicts" which are not resolved. The available facts contradict this supposition. Of 45 patients who had been treated solely by behavior therapy and who were followed up for periods ranging from 2 to 7 years, only one had relapse (Wolpe, 1958). I have been in personal contact with several people who have remained completely well 12–17 years after behavior therapy.

REFERENCES

Brody, M. W. Prognosis and results of psychoanalysis. In J. H. Nodine & J. H. Moyer (Eds), *Psychosomatic medicine.* Philadelphia: Lea & Febiger, 1962. Pp. 729-733.

Campbell, D., Sanderson, R. E., Laverty, S. C. Characteristics of a conditioned response in human subjects during extinction trials following a single traumatic conditioning trial. *J. abnorm. soc. Psychol.,* 1964, **68,** 627-639.

Eysenck, H. J. The effects of psychotherapy: An evaluation. *J. consult. Psychol.,* 1952, **16,** 319-324.

Eysenck, H. J. The effects of psychotherapy. *Int. J. Psychiat.*, 1965, **1**, 99-142.

Farber, I. E. Response fixation under anxiety and non-anxiety conditions. *J. exp. Psychol.*, 1948, **38**, 111-131.

Gantt, W. H. Experimental basis for neurotic behavior. *Psychosom. Med. Mongr.*, 1944, **3**, Nos. 3 & 4.

Hull, C. L. *Principles of behavior.* New York: Appleton, 1943.

Jacobson, E. *Progressive relaxation.* Chicago: Univer. of Chicago Press, 1938.

Jacobson, E. Variation of pulse rate with skeletal muscle tension and relaxation. *Ann. intern. Med.*, 1939, **12**, 1194.

Jacobson, E. Variation of blood pressure with skeletal muscle tension and relaxation. *Ann. intern. Med.*, 1940, **13**, 1619.

Jones, M. C. Elimination of children's fears. *J. exp. Psychol.*, 1924, **7**, 382.

Lazarus, A. A. The elimination of children's phobias by deconditioning. *Med. Proc.*, 1959, **5**, 261-265. (Reprinted in Eysenck, 1965.)

Lazarus, A. A. The results of behavior therapy in 126 cases of severe neuroses. *Behav. Res. Ther.*, 1963, **1**, 69-79.

Lazarus, A. A. Personal communication, 1965.

Liddell, H. D. Conditioned reflex method and experimental neurosis. In J. McV. Hunt (Ed.), *Personality and the behavior disorders.* New York: Ronald Press, 1944. Pp. 389-412.

Masserman, J. H. *Behavior and neurosis.* Chicago: Univer. of Chicago Press, 1943.

Miller, N. E. Studies of fear as an acquirable drive: I. Fear as motivation and fear reduction as reinforcement in the learning of new responses. *J. exp. Psychol.*, 1948, **38**, 89-101.

Napalkov, A. V., & Karas, A. Y. Elimination of pathological conditioned reflex connections in the experimental hypertensive state. *Zh. vyssh. nerv. Deyatel. I. P. Pavlov,* 1957, **7**, 402-409.

Osgood, G. E. Studies on the generality of affective meaning systems. *Amer. Psychologist.*, 1962, **17**, 10-18.

Paul, G. L. *Insight versus desensitization.* Stanford, Calif.: Stanford Univer. Press, 1965.

Pavlov, I. P. *Conditioned reflexes.* Transl. & edited by G. V. Anrep. London & New York: Oxford Univer. Press, 1927.

Smart, R. G. Conflict and conditioned aversive stimuli in the development of experimental neuroses. *Canad. J. Psychol.*, 1965, **19**, 208-223.

Symonds, C. P. The human response to flying stress. *Brit. med. J.*, 1943, **2**, 703-706.

Wolpe, J. Experimental neurosis as learned behavior. *Brit. J. Psychol.*, 1952, **43**, 243-268. (a)

Wolpe, J. The formation of negative habits: a neurophysiological view. *Psychol. Rev.*, 1952, **59**, 290-299. (b)

Wolpe, J. Reciprocal inhibition as the main basis of psychotherapeutic effects. *Arch. Neurol. Psychiat.*, 1954, **72**, 205-226.

Wolpe, J. *Psychotherapy by reciprocal inhibition.* Stanford, Calif.: Stanford Univer. Press, 1958.

Wolpe, J. The systematic desensitization treatment of neuroses. *J. nerv. ment. Dis.*, 1961, **112**, 189-203.

Wolpe, J., & Lazarus, A. A. *Behavior therapy techniques.* London: Pergamon Press, 1966.

Part IV

THE DETERMINANTS OF ANXIETY

CHAPTER 9

The Interaction of Cognitive and Physiological Determinants of Emotional State[*,1]

Stanley Schachter
Department of Social Psychology,
Columbia University,
New York, New York

Introduction

Many years ago, piqued by the disorderly cataloguing of symptoms which, in his time, characterized the classic works on emotion, William James offered what was probably the first simple, integrating, theoretical statement on the nature of emotion. This well-known formulation stated that "the bodily changes follow directly the perception of the exciting fact, and that our feeling of the same changes as they occur *is* the emotion" (James, 1890). Since James' proposition directly equates bodily changes

* *Editor's note:* This chapter is reprinted from L. Berkowitz (Ed.), *Advances in Experimental Social Psychology,* Vol. 1, 1964, with the permission of Professor Berkowitz and Academic Press, New York. Other important work on anxiety is reported by Professor Schachter in *The Psychology of Affiliation,* Stanford University Press, Stanford, California, 1959.

[1] Much of the research described in this paper was supported by Grant MH 05203 from the National Institute of Mental Health, United States Public Health Service, and by Grant G 23758 from the National Science Foundation.

and visceral feelings with emotion, it must follow, first, that the different emotions are accompanied by recognizably different bodily states and second, that the direct manipulation of bodily state, by drugs or surgery, also manipulates emotional state. These implications have, directly or indirectly, guided much of the research on emotion since James' day. The results of such research, on the whole, provided little support for a purely visceral formulation of emotion and led Cannon (1927, 1929) to his brilliant and devastating critique of the James-Lange theory—a critique based on the following:

1. Total separation of the viscera from the central nervous system does not alter emotional behavior.

2. The same visceral changes occur in very different emotional states and in nonemotional states.

3. The viscera are relatively insensitive structures.

4. Visceral changes are too slow to be a source of emotional feeling.

5. Artificial induction of the visceral changes typical of strong emotions does not produce them.

Though new data have weakened the cogency of some of these points, on the whole Cannon's logic and findings make it inescapably clear that a completely peripheral or visceral formulation of emotion, such as the James-Lange theory, is inadequate to cope with the facts. In an effort to deal with the obvious inadequacies of a purely visceral or peripheral formulation of emotion, Ruckmick (1936), Hunt et al. (1958), Schachter (1959), and others have suggested that cognitive factors may be major determinants of emotional states. It is the purpose of this paper to spell out the implications of a cognitive-physiological formulation of emotion and to describe a series of experiments designed to test these implications.

THE INTERACTION OF COGNITIVE AND PHYSIOLOGICAL PROCESSES

To begin, let us grant on the basis of much evidence (see Woodworth and Schlosberg, 1958, for example) that a general pattern of sympathetic discharge is characteristic of emotional states. Given such a state of arousal, it is suggested that one labels, interprets, and identifies this stirred-up state in terms of the characteristics of the precipitating situation and one's apperceptive mass. This suggests, then, that an emotional state may be considered a function of a state of physiological arousal[2] and of a cognition appropriate to this state of arousal. The cognition, in a sense, exerts a steering function. Cognitions arising from the immediate situation as interpreted by past experience provide the framework within which one understands and labels his feelings. It is the cognition which determines whether the state of physiological arousal will be labeled "anger," "joy," or whatever.

In order to examine the implications of this formulation, consider the fashion in which these two elements, a state of physiological arousal and cognitive factors, would interact in a variety of situations. In most emotion inducing situations, of course, the two factors are completely inter-related. Imagine a man walking alone down a dark alley when a figure with a gun suddenly appears. The perception-cognition "figure with a gun" in some fashion initiates a state of physiological arousal; this state of arousal is interpreted in terms of knowledge about dark alleys and guns, and the state of arousal is labeled "fear." Similarly, a student who unexpectedly learns that he has made Phi Beta Kappa may experience a state of arousal which he will label "joy."

Physiological Arousal Not Sufficient

Let us now consider circumstances in which these two elements, the physiological and the cognitive, are, to some extent, independent. First, is the state of physiological arousal alone sufficient to induce an emotion? The best evidence indicates that it is not. Marañon (1924), in a fascinating study (replicated by Cantril and Hunt (1932) and Landis and Hunt (1932)), injected 210 of his patients with the sympathomimetic agent adrenaline and then asked them to introspect. Seventy-one % of his subjects reported physical symptoms with no emotional overtone; 29% responded in an apparently emotional fashion. Of these, the great majority described their feelings in a fashion that Marañon labeled "cold" or "as if" emotions; that is, they made statements such as "I feel *as if* I were afraid" or "*as if* I were awaiting a great happiness." This is a sort of emotional *déjà vu* experience; these subjects are neither happy nor afraid, they feel "as if" they were. Finally, a very few cases apparently reported a genuine emotional experience. However, in order to produce this reaction

---

[2] Though the experiments to be described are concerned largely with the physiological changes produced by the injection of adrenaline—which appear to be primarily the result of sympathetic excitation—the term physiological arousal is used in preference to the more specific "excitement of the sympathetic nervous system" because there are indications, discussed later, that this formulation is applicable to a variety of bodily states.

in most of these few cases, Marañon pointed out

one must suggest a memory with strong affective force but not so strong as to produce an emotion in the normal state. For example, in several cases we spoke to our patients before the injection of their sick children or dead parents and they responded calmly to this topic. The same topic presented later, during the adrenal commotion, was sufficient to trigger emotion. This adrenal commotion places the subject in a situation of "affective imminence."

Apparently, then, to produce a genuinely emotional reaction to adrenaline, Marañon was forced to provide such subjects with an appropriate cognition.

Though Marañon was not explicit on his procedure, it is clear that his subjects knew that they were receiving an injection, in all likelihood knew that they were receiving adrenaline, and probably had some order of familiarity with its effects. In short, although they underwent the pattern of sympathetic discharge common to strong emotional states, at the same time they had a completely appropriate cognition or explanation as to why they felt this way. This, it is suggested, is the reason so few of Marañon's subjects reported any emotional experience.

The Need To Evaluate One's Feelings

Consider next a person in a state of physiological arousal for which no immediately explanatory or appropriate cognitions are available. Such a state could result were one covertly to inject a subject with adrenaline or, unknown to him, feed the subject a sympathomimetic drug such as ephedrine. Under such conditions a subject would be aware of palpitations, tremor, face flushing, and most of the battery of symptoms associated with a discharge of the sympathetic nervous system. In contrast to Marañon's subjects, he would, at the same time, be utterly unaware of why he felt this way. What would be the consequence of such a state?

Schachter (1959) suggested that just such a state would lead to the arousal of "evaluative needs" (Festinger, 1954). That is, pressures would act on an individual in such a state to understand and label his bodily feelings. His bodily state grossly resembles the condition in which it has been at times of emotional excitement. How would he label his present feelings? It is suggested, of course, that he will label his feelings in terms of his knowledge of the immediate situation.[3] Should he at the time be with a beautiful woman, he might decide that he was wildly in love or sexually excited. Should he be at a gay party, he might, by comparing himself to others, decide that he was extremely happy and euphoric. Should he be

---

[3] This suggestion is not new, for several psychologists have suggested that situational factors should be considered the chief differentiators of the emotions. Hunt et al. (1958) probably made this point most explicitly in their study distinguishing among fear, anger, and sorrow in terms of situational characteristics.

arguing with his wife, he might explode in fury and hatred. Or, should the situation be completely inappropriate, he could decide that he was excited about something that had recently happened to him or, simply, that he was sick. In any case, it is my basic assumption that emotional states are a function of the interaction of such cognitive factors with a state of physiological arousal.

THEORETICAL PROPOSITIONS

This line of thought leads to three propositions. One, given a state of physiological arousal for wh'ch an individual has no immediate explanation, he will "label" this state and describe his feelings in terms of the cognitions available to him. To the extent that cognitive factors are potent determiners of emotional states, it could be anticipated that precisely the same state of physiological arousal could be labeled "joy" or "fury" or any of a great diversity of emotional labels, depending on the cognitive aspects of the situation.

Two, given a state of physiological arousal for which an individual has a completely appropriate explanation (e.g., "I feel this way because I have just received an injection of adrenaline"), no evaluative needs will arise, and the individual is unlikely to label his feelings in terms of the alternative cognitions available.

Finally, consider a condition in which emotion inducing cognitions are present but there is no state of physiological arousal; an individual might, for example, be aware that he is in great danger, but for some reason (drug or surgical) remain in a state of physiological quiescence. Does he then experience the emotion "fear"? This formulation of emotion as a joint function of a state of physiological arousal and an appropriate cognition, would, of course, suggest that he does not, which leads to our final proposition. Three, given the same cognitive circumstances, the individual will react emotionally or describe his feelings as emotions only to the extent that he experiences a state of physiological arousal.[4]

Cognitive, Social and Physiological Determinants

The experimental test of these propositions requires (1) the experimental manipulation of a state of physiological arousal or sympathetic activation; (2) the manipulation of the extent to which the subject has an appropriate or proper explanation of his bodily state; and (3) the creation of situations from which explanatory cognitions may be derived.

In order to satisfy these experimental requirements, Schachter and

---

[4] In his critique of the James-Lange theory of emotion, Cannon (1929) made the point that sympathectomized animals and patients do seem to manifest emotional behavior. This criticism is, of course, as applicable to the above proposition as it was to the James-Lange formulation. The issues involved will be discussed later in this chapter.

Singer (1962) designed an experiment cast in the framework of a study of the effects of vitamin supplements on vision. As soon as a subject arrived, he was taken to a private room and told by the experimenter:

> In this experiment we would like to make various tests of your vision. We are particularly interested in how certain vitamin compounds and vitamin supplements affect the visual skills. In particular, we want to find out how the vitamin compound called "Suproxin" affects your vision.
>
> What we would like to do, then, if we can get your permission, is to give you a small injection of Suproxin. The injection itself is mild and harmless; however, since some people do object to being injected we don't want to talk you into anything. Would you mind receiving a Suproxin injection?

If the subject agreed to the injection (and all but one of 185 subjects did), the experimenter continued with instructions described below, then left the room. In a few minutes a doctor entered the room, briefly repeated the experimenter's instructions, took the subject's pulse, and then injected him with Suproxin.

Depending upon condition, the subject received one of two forms of Suproxin—epinephrine or a placebo.

Epinephrine or adrenaline is a sympathomimetic drug whose effects, with minor exceptions, are almost a perfect mimicry of a discharge of the sympathetic nervous system. Shortly after injection systolic blood pressure increases markedly. Heart rate increases somewhat, cutaneous blood flow decreases, muscle and cerebral blood flow increase, blood sugar and lactic acid concentration increase, and respiration rate increases slightly. For the subject, the major subjective symptoms are palpitation, tremor, and sometimes a feeling of flushing and accelerated breathing. With a subcutaneous injection, (in the dosage administered) such effects usually begin within three to five minutes of injection and last anywhere from ten minutes to an hour. For most subjects these effects are dissipated within 15–20 minutes after injection.

Subjects receiving epinephrine received a subcutaneous injection of ½ cc of a 1:1000 solution of Winthrop Laboratory's Suprarenin, a saline solution of epinephrine bitartrate.

Subjects in the placebo condition received a subcutaneous injection of ½ cc of saline solution.

Manipulating an Appropriate Explanation

"Appropriate" refers to the extent to which the subject has an authoritative, unequivocal explanation of his bodily condition. Thus, a subject who had been informed by the physician that as a direct consequence of the injection he would feel palpitations, tremor, etc. would be considered to have a completely appropriate explanation. A subject who had been informed only that the injection would have no side effects, would have no appropriate explanation of his state. This dimension of appropriateness was manipulated in three experimental conditions which shall be called: (1) Epinephrine Informed (Epi Inf), (2) Epinephrine Ignorant (Epi Ign), and (3) Epinephrine Misinformed (Epi Mis).

Immediately after the subject had agreed to the injection and before the physician entered the room, the experimenter's presentation in each of these conditions went as follows:

Epinephrine Informed

"I should also tell you that some of our subjects have experienced side effects from the Suproxin. These side effects are transitory, that is, they will only last for about 15 or 20 minutes. What will probably happen is that your hand will start to shake, your heart will start to pound, and your face may get warm and flushed. Again these are side effects, lasting about 15 or 20 minutes."

While the physician was giving the injection, she told the subject that the injection was mild and harmless and repeated this description of the symptoms that the subject could expect as a consequence of the shot. In this condition, then, subjects had a completely appropriate explanation of their bodily state. They knew precisely what they would feel and why.

Epinephrine Ignorant

In this condition, when the subject agreed to the injection, the experimenter said nothing more about side effects and left the room. While the physician was giving the injection, she told the subject that the injection was mild and harmless and would have no side effects. In this condition, then, the subject had no experimentally provided explanation for his bodily state.

Epinephrine Misinformed

"I should also tell you that some of our subjects have experienced side effects from the Suproxin. These side effects are transitory, that is, they will only last for about 15 or 20 minutes. What will probably happen is that your feet will feel numb, you will have an itching sensation over parts of your body, and you may get a slight headache. Again these are side effects lasting 15 or 20 minutes." And again, the physician repeated these symptoms while injecting the subject.

None of these symptoms, of course, are consequences of an injection of epinephrine and, in effect, these instructions provided the subject with a completely inappropriate explanation of his bodily feelings. This condition was introduced as a control condition of sorts. It seemed possible that the description of side effects in the Epi Inf condition might turn the subject introspective, self-examining, possibly slightly troubled. Differences on the dependent variable between the Epi Inf and Epi Ign conditions might, then, be due to such factors rather than to differences in appropriateness. The false symptoms in the Epi Mis condition should similarly turn the subject introspective, etc., but the instructions in this condition do not provide an appropriate explanation of the subject's state.

Subjects in all of the above conditions were injected with epinephrine. Finally, there was a placebo condition in which subjects who were injected with saline solution were given precisely the same treatment as subjects in the Epi Ign condition.

PRODUCING AN EMOTION-INDUCING COGNITION

We initially hypothesized that given a state of physiological arousal for which the individual has no adequate explanation, cognitive factors can lead the individual to describe his feelings with any of a variety of emotional labels. In order to test this hypothesis, it was decided to manipulate emotional states which can be considered quite different—euphoria and anger.

There are, of course, many ways to induce such states. In this program of research, we have concentrated on social determinants of emotional states. Other studies have demonstrated that people evaluate their own feelings by comparing themselves with others around them (Wrightsman, 1960; Schachter, 1959). In the experiment described here, an attempt was again made to manipulate emotional state by social means. In one set of conditions, the subject was placed together with a stooge who had been trained to act euphorically. In a second set of conditions, the subject was with a stooge trained to act angrily.

Euphoria

Immediately[5] after the subject had been injected, the physician left the room and the experimenter returned with a stooge whom he introduced as another subject. The experimenter then said, "Both of you have had the Suproxin shot and you'll both be taking the same tests of vision. What I ask you to do now is just wait for 20 minutes. The reason for this is simply that we have to allow 20 minutes for the Suproxin to get from the

---

[5] It was, of course, imperative that the sequence with the stooge begin before the subject felt his first symptoms. Otherwise the subject would be virtually forced to interpret his feelings in terms of events preceding the stooge's entrance. Pretests had indicated that, for most subjects, epinephrine caused symptoms began within three to five minutes after injection. A deliberate attempt was made then to bring in the stooge within one minute after the subject's injection.

injection site into the bloodstream. At the end of 20 minutes when we are certain that most of the Suproxin has been absorbed into the bloodstream, we'll begin the tests of vision."

The room in which this was said had been deliberately put into a state of mild disarray. As he was leaving, the experimenter added apologetically, "The only other thing I should do is to apologize for the condition of the room. I just didn't have time to clean it up. So, if you need any scratch paper, or rubber bands, or pencils, help yourself. I'll be back in 20 minutes to begin the vision tests."

As soon as the experimenter left, the stooge introduced himself again, made a series of standard icebreaker comments and then went into his routine. He reached first for a piece of paper, doodled briefly, crumpled the paper, aimed for a wastebasket, threw, and missed. This led him into a game of "basketball" in which he moved about the room crumpling paper, and trying out fancy basketball shots. Finished with basketball, he said, "This is one of my good days. I feel like a kid again. I think I'll make a plane." He made a paper plane, spent a few minutes flying it around the room, and then said, "Even when I was a kid, I was never much good at this." He then tore off the tail of his plane, wadded it up, and making a slingshot of a rubber band, began to shoot the paper. While shooting, he noticed a sloppy pile of manila folders. He built a tower of these folders, then went to the opposite end of the room to shoot at the tower. He knocked down the tower, and while picking up the folders he noticed a pair of hula hoops behind a portable blackboard. He took one of these for himself, put the other within reaching distance of the subject, and began hula hooping. After a few minutes, he replaced the hula hoop and returned to his seat, at which point the experimenter returned to the room.

All through this madness an observer, through a one-way mirror, systematically recorded the subject's behavior and noted the extent to which the subject joined in with the stooge's whirl of activity.

Subjects in each of the three "appropriateness" conditions and in the placebo condition were submitted to this setup. The stooge, of course, never knew in which condition any particular subject fell.

Anger

Immediately after the injection, the experimenter brought a stooge into the subject's room, introduced the two, and after explaining the necessity for a 20-minute delay for "the Suproxin to get from the injection site into the bloodstream" he continued, "We would like you to use these 20 minutes to answer these questionnaires." Then handing out the questionnaires, he concluded: "I'll be back in 20 minutes to pick up the questionnaires and begin the tests of vision."

The questionnaires, five pages long, started off innocently, requesting face sheet information and then grew increasingly personal and insulting, asking questions such as:

"With how many men (other than your father) has your mother had extra-marital relationships?"

4 and under_____ : 5–9_____ : 10 and over_____.

The stooge, sitting directly opposite the subject, paced his own answers so that at all times subject and stooge were working on the same question. At regular points in the questionnaire, the stooge made a series of standardized comments about the questions. His comments started off innocently enough, grew increasingly querulous, and finally he ended up in a rage, ripping up his questionnaire, slamming it to the floor, saying "I'm not wasting any more time. I'm getting my books and leaving," and stomping out of the room.

Again an observer recorded the subject's behavior.

In summary, this was a seven-condition experiment which, for two different emotional states, allowed us (1) to evaluate the effects of "appropriateness" on emotional inducibility, and (2) to begin to evaluate the effects of sympathetic activation on emotional inducibility. In schematic form, the conditions were:

Euphoria	Anger
Epi Inf	Epi Inf
Epi Ign	Epi Ign
Epi Mis	Placebo
Placebo	

The Epi Mis condition was not run in the Anger sequence. This was originally conceived as a control condition, and it was felt that its inclusion in the Euphoria conditions alone would suffice as a means of evaluating the possible artifactual effect of the Epi Inf instructions.

The subjects were all male college students, taking classes in introductory psychology at the University of Minnesota. The records of all potential subjects were reviewed by the Student Health Service in order to insure that no harmful effects would result from the injections.

MEASUREMENTS

Two types of measures of emotional state were obtained. Standardized observation through a one-way mirror was used to assess the subject's behavior. To what extent did he join in with the stooge's pattern of behavior and act euphoric or angry? The second type of measure was a self-report questionnaire in which, on a variety of scales, the subject indicated his mood of the moment.

These measures were obtained immediately after the stooge had finished his routine, at which point the experimenter returned saying, "Before we proceed with the vision tests, there is one other kind of information we must have. We have found that there are many things beside Suproxin that affect how well you see in our tests. How hungry you are, how tired you are and even the mood you're in at the moment—whether you feel happy or irritated at the time of testing will affect how well you see. To understand the data we collect on you, then, we must be able to figure out which effects are due to causes such as these and which are caused by Suproxin." He then handed out questionnaires containing a number of questions about bodily and emotional state. To measure mood the following two were the crucial questions:

1. How irritated, angry, or annoyed would you say you feel at present?

I don't feel at all irritated or angry	I feel a little irritated and angry	I feel quite irritated and angry	I feel very irritated and angry	I feel extremely irritated and angry
(0)	(1)	(2)	(3)	(4)

2. How good or happy would you say you feel at present?

I don't feel at all happy or good	I feel a little happy and good	I feel quite happy and good	I feel very happy and good	I feel extremely happy and good
(0)	(1)	(2)	(3)	(4)

THE EFFECTS OF THE MANIPULATIONS ON EMOTIONAL STATE

Euphoria

The effects of the several manipulations on emotional state in the euphoria conditions are presented in Table I. The scores recorded in this table were derived, for each subject, by subtracting the value of the point he checked on the "irritation" scale from the value of the point he checked on the "happiness" scale. Thus, if a subject were to check the point "I feel a little irritated and angry" on the "irritation" scale and the point "I feel very happy and good" on the "happiness" scale, his score would be $+2$. The higher the positive value, the happier and better the subject reports himself as feeling. Though an index is employed for expositional simplicity, it should be noted that the two components of the index each yield results completely consistent with those obtained by use of this index.

Let us examine first the effects of the "appropriateness" instructions. Comparison of the scores of the Epi Mis and Epi Inf conditions makes it immediately clear that the experimental differences are not due to artifacts resulting from the "informed" instructions. In both conditions the subject was warned to expect a variety of symptoms as a consequence of the injection. In the Epi Mis condition, where the symptoms were inappropriate to the subject's bodily state, the self-report score is almost twice that in the Epi Inf condition, where the symptoms were completely appropriate to the subject's bodily state. It is reasonable, then, to attribute differences between informed subjects and those in other conditions to differences in manipulated appropriateness, rather than to artifacts such as introspectiveness or self-examination.

TABLE I

SELF-REPORT OF EMOTIONAL STATE IN THE EUPHORIA CONDITIONS

Condition	N	Self-report scales
Epi Inf	25	.98
Epi Ign	25	1.78
Epi Mis	25	1.90
Placebo	26	1.61
Comparison		p values[a]
Epi Inf vs. Epi Mis		$< .01$
Epi Inf vs. Epi Ign		.02
Plac vs. Epi Mis, Ign or Inf		n.s.

[a] All p values reported throughout this paper are two-tailed.

It is clear that, consistent with expectations, subjects were more susceptible to the stooge's mood and consequently more euphoric when they had no explanation of their own bodily states than when they did. The means of both the Epi Ign and Epi Mis conditions were considerably greater than the mean of the Epi Inf condition.

Comparing the placebo to the epinephrine conditions, we note a pattern which repeated itself throughout the data. Placebo subjects were less euphoric than either Epi Mis or Epi Ign subjects, but somewhat more euphoric than Epi Inf subjects. These differences were not, however, statistically significant. The epinephrine-placebo comparisons are considered in detail in a later section of this paper, following the presentation of additional relevant data. For the moment, it is clear that, by self-report, manipulating "appropriateness" had a very strong effect on euphoria.

The analysis of the observational data was reported in detail elsewhere (Schachter and Singer, 1962). Here it is sufficient to note that on all behavioral indices devised—e.g. the amount of time the subject spent on stooge-initiated activity; "creative euphoria" (the extent to which the subject initiated euphoric activities of his own devising)— the same pattern of between-condition relationships held. Subjects in the Epi Mis and Epi Ign conditions behaved more euphorically than subjects in the Epi Inf condition. Placebo subjects again fell between Epi Ign and Epi Inf subjects.

Anger

In the anger conditions, we should again expect the subject to catch the stooge's mood only in those conditions where he was injected with epinephrine and had no appropriate explanation for the bodily state thus created. Subjects in the Epi Ign condition should, then, be considerably angrier than those in the Epi Inf or Placebo conditions. Data on behavioral indications of anger are presented in Table II. These figures were derived

TABLE II
BEHAVIORAL INDICATIONS OF EMOTIONAL STATE IN THE ANGER CONDITIONS

Condition	N	Anger index
Epi Inf	22	− .18
Epi Ign	23	+2.28
Placebo	22	+.79
Comparison		p value
Epi Inf vs. Epi Ign		< .01
Epi Ign vs. Placebo		< .05
Placebo vs. Epi Inf		n.s.

from coding the subject's comments and behavior during the experimental session with the angry stooge. The nature of the index devised is described in detail elsewhere (Schachter and Singer, 1962). For present purposes, we can note that a positive value to this index indicates that the subject agreed with the stooge's comments and was angry. The larger the positive value, the angrier the subject. A negative value indicates that the subject either disagreed with the stooge or ignored him.

It is evident in Table II that expectations were confirmed. The value for the Epi Ign condition is positive and large, indicating that the subjects became angry; while in the Epi Inf condition, the score is slightly negative, indicating that these subjects failed to catch the stooge's mood at all. Placebo subjects fall between Epi Ign and Epi Inf subjects. On the self-report scales of mood, this pattern repeated itself, though on this measure

Placebo subjects do not differ significantly from either Epi Ign or Epi Inf subjects.

DISCUSSION OF RESULTS

Having presented the basic data of this study, let us examine closely the extent to which they conform to theoretical expectations. If the hypotheses are correct, and if this experimental design provided a perfect test for these hypotheses, it should be anticipated that in the euphoria conditions, the degree of experimentally produced euphoria should vary in the following fashion:

$$\text{Epi Mis} \geq \text{Epi Ign} > \text{Epi Inf} = \text{Placebo}$$

In the anger conditions, anger should conform to the following pattern:

$$\text{Epi Ign} > \text{Epi Inf} = \text{Placebo}$$

In both sets of conditions, emotional level in the Epi Inf condition was considerably less than that achieved in any of the other Epi conditions. The results for the placebo condition, however, were ambiguous, for consistently the placebo subjects fell between the Epi Ign and the Epi Inf subjects. This is a particularly troubling pattern, making it impossible to evaluate unequivocally the effects of the state of physiological arousal and indeed raising serious questions about the entire theoretical structure. Though the emotional level was consistently greater in the Epi Mis and Epi Ign conditions than in the Placebo condition, this difference was significant at acceptable probability levels only on the behavioral indices in the anger conditions.

In order to explore the problem further, let us examine experimental factors which might have acted to restrain the emotional level in the Epi Ign and Epi Mis conditions. Clearly the ideal test of the first two hypotheses requires an experimental setup in which the subject has no other means of evaluating his state of physiological arousal other than the experimentally provided cognitions. Had it been possible to produce physiologically a state of sympathetic activation by means other than injection, one could have approached this experimental ideal more closely than in the present setup. As it stands, however, there is always a reasonable alternative cognition available to the aroused subject—he feels the way he does because of the injection. To the extent that the subject seizes on such an explanation of his bodily state, we should expect that he will be uninfluenced by the stooge.

It is possible, fortunately, to examine the effect of this artifact. In answers to open-end questions in which subjects described their own mood and physical state, some of the Epi Ign and Epi Mis subjects clearly attributed their physical state to the injection, e.g. "the shot gave me the shivers." In effect, such subjects are self-informed. Comparing such subjects to the remaining subjects in a condition, one finds in the Anger-Epi Ign condition that self-informed subjects are considerably less angry than the remaining subjects. Similarly in the Euphoria-Epi Mis and Ign conditions, self-informed subjects are considerably less euphoric than are their non-self-informed counterparts. If one eliminates such self-informed subjects, the differences between the Placebo and Epi Ign or Epi Mis conditions become highly significant statistically in both the Anger and the Euphoria set of conditions. Clearly, indications are good that this self-informing artifact has attenuated the effects of epinephrine.

Consider next the fact that the emotional level in Placebo conditions was greater than that in the Epi Inf conditions. Theoretically, of course, it should be expected that the two conditions will be equally low, for by assuming that emotional state is a joint function of a state of physiological arousal and of the appropriateness of a cognition we are, in effect, assuming a multiplicative function: if either component is at zero, emotional level is at zero. This expectation should hold, however, only if one can be sure that there is no sympathetic activation in the placebo conditions. This assumption, of course, is completely unrealistic, for the injection of placebo does not prevent sympathetic activation. The experimental situations were fairly dramatic and certainly some of the Placebo subjects must have experienced physiological arousal. If this general line of reasoning is correct, it should be anticipated that the emotional level of subjects who give indications of sympathetic activity will be greater than that of subjects who do not.

Since, in all conditions, a subject's pulse was taken before the injection and again after the session with the stooge, there is one index of sympathetic activation available—change in pulse rate. The predominant pattern in the Placebo conditions was, of course, a decrease in pulse rate. It is assumed, therefore, that in the Placebo conditions, those subjects whose pulses increase or remain the same give indications of sympathetic arousal, while those subjects whose pulses decrease do not. Comparing, within Placebo conditions, such self-aroused subjects with those who give no indication of sympathetic activation, we find in the Anger condition that those subjects whose pulses increase or remain the same are considerably and significantly angrier than those subjects whose pulses decrease. Similarly, in the Euphoria Placebo condition, the self-aroused subjects are considerably and significantly more euphoric than the subjects who give no indication of sympathetic activation. Conforming to expectations, sympathetic activation accompanies an increase in emotional level.

It should be noted, too, on the several indices, that the emotional level of subjects showing no signs of sympathetic activity is quite close to the emotional level of subjects in the parallel Epi Inf conditions. The similarity of these sets of scores and their uniformly low level of indicated emotionality would certainly make it appear that both factors are essential to an emotional state. When either the level of sympathetic arousal is low or a completely appropriate cognition is available, the level of emotionality is low.

Let us summarize the major findings of this experiment and examine the extent to which they support the propositions offered in the introduction of this paper. It has been suggested, first, that given a state of physiological arousal for which an individual has no explanation, he will label this state in terms of the cognitions available to him. This implies, of course, that by manipulating the cognitions of an individual in such a state, his feelings can be manipulated in diverse directions. Experimental results support this proposition, for following the injection of epinephrine, those subjects who had no explanation for the bodily state thus produced, proved readily manipulable into the disparate feeling states of euphoria and anger.

From this first proposition, it must follow that given a state of physiological arousal for which the individual has a completely satisfactory explanation, he will not label this state in terms of the alternative cognitions available. Experimental evidence strongly supports this expectation. In those conditions in which subjects were injected with epinephrine and told precisely what they would feel and why, they proved relatively immune to any effects of the manipulated cognitions. In the anger condition, such subjects did not become at all angry; in the euphoria condition, such subjects reported themselves as far less happy than subjects with an identical bodily state but no adequate knowledge of why they felt the way they did.

Finally, it has been suggested that given constant cognitive circumstances, an individual will react emotionally only to the extent that he experiences a state of physiological arousal. Without taking account of experimental artifacts, the evidence in support of this proposition is consistent but tentative. When the effects of "self-informing" tendencies in epinephrine subjects and of "self-arousing" tendencies in placebo subjects are partialed out, the evidence strongly supports the proposition.

Physiological Arousal and Emotionality

The pattern of data, then, falls neatly in line with theoretical expectations. However, the fact that it was necessary to some extent to rely on internal analyses in order to partial out the effects of experimental artifacts inevitably makes these conclusions somewhat tentative. In order further to test these propositions on the interaction of cognitive and physiological determinants of emotional state, a series of additional experiments was designed to rule out or overcome the operation of these artifacts.

The first of these experiments was designed by Schachter and Wheeler (1962) to test the proposition that emotionality is positively related to physiological arousal by extending the range of manipulated sympathetic activation. It seemed clear from the results of the study just described that the self-arousing tendency of placebo subjects tended to obscure the differences between placebo and epinephrine conditions. A test of the proposition at stake, then, would require comparing subjects who have received injections of epinephrine with subjects who, to some extent, were incapable of self-activation of the sympathetic nervous system. A class of drugs known generally as autonomic blocking agents makes such blocking possible to some degree. If it is correct that a state of sympathetic discharge is a necessary component of an emotional experience, it should be anticipated that whatever emotional state is experimentally manipulated should be experienced most strongly by subjects who have received epinephrine, next by placebo subjects, and least of all by subjects who have received injections of an autonomic blocking agent.

PROCEDURE

In order to conceal the purposes of the study and the nature of the injection, the experiment was again cast in the framework of a study of the effects of vitamins on vision. As soon as a subject—a male college student —arrived, he was taken to a private room and told by the experimenter:

"I've asked you to come today to take part in an experiment concerning the effects of vitamins on the visual processes. Our experiment is concerned with the effects of Suproxin on vision. Suproxin is a high concentrate vitamin C derivative. If you agree to take part in the experiment, we will give you an injection of Suproxin and then subject your retina to about 15 minutes of continuous black and white stimulation. This is simpler than it sounds: we'll just have you watch a black and white movie. After the movie, we'll give you a series of visual tests.

"The injection itself is harmless and will be administered by our staff doctor. It may sting a little at first, as most injections do, but after this you will feel nothing and will have no side effects. We know that some people dislike getting injections, and if you take part in the experiment, we want it to be your own decision. Would you like to?" (All subjects agreed to take part.)

Drugs Used

There were three forms of Suproxin administered—epinephrine, placebo, and chlorpromazine.

1. Epinephrine. Subjects in this condition received a subcutaneous injection of $\frac{1}{2}$ cc of a 1:1000 solution of Winthrop Laboratory's Suprarenin.

2. Placebo. Subjects in this condition received a subcutaneous injection of $\frac{1}{2}$ cc of saline solution.

3. Chlorpromazine. Subjects in this condition received an intramuscular injection of a solution consisting of 1 cc (25 mg) of Smith, Klein and French Thorazine and 1 cc of saline solution.

The choice of chlorpromazine as a blocking agent was dictated by considerations of safety, ease of administration, and known duration of effect. Ideally, one would have wished for a blocking agent whose mechanism and effect were precisely and solely the reverse of those of epinephrine —aperipherally acting agent which would prevent the excitation of sympathetically innervated structures. Though it is certainly possible to approach this ideal more closely with agents other than chlorpromazine, such drugs tend to be dangerous, difficult to administer, or of short duration.

Chlorpromazine is known to act as a sympathetic depressant. It has a moderate hypotensive effect, with a slight compensatory increase in heart rate. It has mild adrenergic blocking activity, for it reverses the pressor effects of small doses of epinephrine and depresses responses of the nictitating membrane to preganglionic stimulation. Killam (1959) summarizes what is known and supposed about the mechanism of action of chlorpromazine as follows: "Autonomic effects in general may be attributed to a mild peripheral adrenergic blocking activity and probably to central depression of sympathetic centers, possibly in the hypothalamus." Popularly, of course, the compound is known as a "tranquilizer."

It is recognized that chlorpromazine has effects other than the sympatholytic effect of interest to us. For purposes of experimental purity this is unfortunate but inevitable in this sort of research. It is clear, however, that the three conditions do differ in the degree of manipulated sympathetic activation.

Emotion Induction

Rather than the more complicated devices employed in the previous experiment, an emotion-inducing film was used as a means of manipulating the cognitive component of emotional states. In deciding on the type of film, two extremes seemed possible—a horror, fright or anxiety-provoking film or a comic, amusement-provoking film. Since it is a common stereotype that adrenaline makes one nervous and that the tranquilizer, chlorpromazine, makes one tranquil and mildly euphoric, the predicted pattern of results with a horror film would be subject to alternative interpretation. It was deliberately decided, then, to use a comedy. If the hypothesis is correct, epinephrine subjects should find the film somewhat funnier than placebo subjects who, in turn, would be more amused than chlorpromazine subjects.

The film chosen was a 14-minute excerpt from a Jack Carson movie called "The Good Humor Man." This excerpt is a self-contained, comprehensible episode involving a slapstick chase scene.

Three subjects (one from each of the drug conditions) always watched the film simultaneously. The projection room was deliberately arranged so that the subjects could neither see nor hear one another. Facing the screen were three theatre seats, separated from one another by large, heavy partitions. In a further attempt to maintain the independence of the subjects, the sound volume of the projector was turned up so as to mask any sounds made by the subjects.

Measures

The subjects' reactions while watching the film were used as the chief index of amusement. During the showing of the movie an observer, who had been introduced as an assistant who would help administer the visual tests, systematically scanned the subjects and recorded their reactions to the film. He observed each subject once every ten seconds, so that over the course of the film 88 units of each subject's behavior were categorized. The observer simply recorded each subject's reaction to the film according to the following scheme: (a) neutral—straight-faced watching of film with no indication of amusement; (b) smile; (c) grin—a smile with teeth showing; (d) laugh—a smile or grin on face accompanied by bodily movements usually associated with laughter, e.g., shaking shoulders, moving head; (e) big laugh—belly laugh; a laugh accompanied by violent body movement such as doubling up, throwing up hands.

In a minute by minute comparison, two independent observers agreed in their categorization of 90% of the 528 units recorded in six different reliability trials.

The observer, of course, never knew which subject had received which injection.

RESULTS

The observation record provides a continuous record of each subject's reaction to the film. As an overall index of amusement, the number of units in which a subject's behavior was recorded in the categories "smile," "grin," "laugh," and "big laugh" are summed together. The means of this amusement index are presented in Table III. The larger the figure, the more amusement was manifest. Differences were in the anticipated direction. Epinephrine subjects gave indications of greater amusement than did

TABLE III

THE EFFECTS OF EPINEPHRINE, PLACEBO, AND CHLORPROMAZINE ON AMUSEMENT

Condition	N	Mean amusement index
Epinephrine	38	17.79
Placebo	42	14.31
Chlorpromazine	46	10.41
Comparison		p value
Epi vs. Plac		n.s.
Epi vs. Chlor		< .01
Plac vs. Chlor		< .05

placebo subjects who, in turn, were more amused than chlorpromazine subjects.

Though the trend is clearly in the predicted direction, epinephrine and placebo subjects do not differ significantly in this overall index. The difference between these two groups, however, becomes apparent when we examine strong ("laugh" and "big laugh") reactions to the film; we find an average of 4.84 such units among the epinephrine subjects and of only 1.83 such units among placebo subjects. This difference is significant at better than the .05 level of significance. Epinephrine subjects tend to be openly amused at the film, placebo subjects to be quietly amused. Some 16% of epinephrine subjects reacted at some point with belly laughs, while not a single placebo subject did so. It should be noted that this is much the state of affairs one would expect from the disguised injection of epinephrine—a manipulation which, as has been suggested, creates a bodily state "in search of" an appropriate cognition. Certainly laughter can be considered a more appropriate accompaniment to the state of sympathetic arousal than quiet smiling.

It would appear, then, that degree of overt amusement is directly related to the degree of manipulated sympathetic activation.

Sympathetic Activity and Emotionality in Rats

A further test of the relationship of emotionality to sympathetic activity was made by Singer (1963) who, in a deliberate attempt to rule out the operation of the self-informing artifact, conducted his study on rats—a species unlikely to attribute an aroused physiological state to an injection. Among other things, Singer examined the effects of injections of epinephrine (an intraperitonial injection of epinephrine suspended in peanut oil in a concentration of .10 mg. per kg of body weight) and placebo on the reactions of rats to standard frightening situations. His technique was simple. In fright conditions, he placed his animals in a box containing a doorbell, a door buzzer, and a flashing 150 watt bulb. After a brief interval, a switch was tripped setting off all three devices simultaneously for a one-and-a-half minute interval. In nonfright conditions, of course, the switch was never tripped.

Singer's results are presented in Table IV. The figures presented in

TABLE IV
THE RELATIONSHIP OF EPINEPHRINE TO FRIGHT

Condition[a]	Epinephrine	Placebo	p value of difference
Fright	13.15	11.49	.025
Nonfright	7.47	7.17	n.s.

[a] $N = 12$ in each of the four conditions.

this table represent an index whose components are generally accepted indicators of fright such as defecation, urination and the like. The larger the figure, the more frightened the animal. Clearly there is a substantial drug-related difference in the fright condition and no difference at all in the nonfright condition. The drug × stress interaction is significant at better than the .01 level of significance. It would certainly appear that under these experimental circumstances the state of fear is related to sympathetic activity. Further evidence for this relationship is found in a study conducted by Latané and Schachter (1962) which demonstrated that rats injected with epinephrine were notably more capable of avoidance learning than were rats injected with a placebo. Using a modified Miller-Mowrer shuttlebox, these investigators found that during an experimental period involving two hundred massed trials, 15 rats injected with epinephrine avoided shock an average of 101.2 trials, while 15 placebo-injected rats averaged only 37.3 avoidances.

Discussion and Implications

Taken together, this body of studies does give strong support to the propositions which generated these experimental tests. Given a state of sympathetic activation, for which no immediately appropriate explanation is available, human subjects can be readily manipulated into states of euphoria, of anger, and of amusement at a movie. Varying the intensity of sympathetic activation serves to vary the intensity of a variety of emotional states in both rat and human subjects. Clearly the line of thought guiding these experiments is modified Jamesianism, for emotion is viewed as visceral activity in interaction with cognitive or situational factors. Let us examine the extent to which the addition of cognitive elements allows us to cope with the shortcomings of a purely visceral formulation. Since Cannon's critique (1927, 1929) has been the most lucid and influential attack on a visceral view of emotion, I shall focus discussion around Cannon's five criticisms of the James-Lange theory.

A RE-EXAMINATION OF CANNON'S CRITIQUE OF A VISCERAL FORMULATION OF EMOTION

Criticisms Overcome by Cognitive Considerations

a. Cannon's criticism that "artificial induction of the visceral changes typical of strong emotions does not produce them" is based on the results of Marañon's (1924) study and its several replications. The fact that the injection of adrenaline produces apparently genuine emotional states in only a tiny minority of subjects is, of course, completely damning for a theory which equates visceral activity with affect. This is, on the other hand, precisely the fact which inspired the series of studies described earlier. Rather than a criticism, the fact that injection of adrenaline, in and of itself, does not lead to an emotional state is one of the strong points of the present formulation; for, with the addition of cognitive propositions, we are able to specify and manipulate the conditions under which such an injection will or will not lead to an emotional state.

b. Cannon's point that "the same visceral changes occur in very different emotional states" is again damning for a purely visceral viewpoint. Since we are aware of a great variety of feeling and emotion states, it must follow from a purely visceral formulation that the variety of emotions will be accompanied by an equal variety of differentiable bodily states. Though the evidence as of today is by no means as one-sided as it appeared in Cannon's day, it does seem that the gist of Cannon's criticism is still correct. Following James' pronouncement, a formidable number of studies were undertaken in search of the physiological differentiators of the emotions. The results, in those early days, were almost uniformly negative. All of the emotional states experimentally manipulated were characterized by a general pattern of activation of the sympathetic nervous system but there appeared to be no clearcut physiological discriminators of the various emotions.

More recent work, however, has given some indication that there may be differentiators. Ax (1953) and Schachter (1957) studied fear and anger. On a large number of indices both of these states were characterized by a similar high level of sympathetic activation, but on several indices they did differ in the degree of activation. Wolf and Wolff (1947) studied a subject with a gastric fistula and were able to distinguish two patterns in the physiological responses of the stomach wall. It should be noted, though, that for many months they studied their subject during and following a great variety of moods and emotions, but were able to distinguish only two patterns.

Whether there are physiological distinctions among the various emotional states must still be considered an open question. Recent work might be taken to indicate that such differences are at best rather subtle, and that the variety of emotion, mood, and feeling states are by no means matched by an equal variety of visceral patterns—a state of affairs hardly compatible with the Jamesian formulation. On the other hand, the question of the physiological differentiability of the various emotions is essentially irrelevant to the present formulation, which maintains simply that cognitive and situational factors determine the labels applied to any of a variety of states of physiological arousal.

The experimental search for the physiological differentiators of emotional states has involved such substantial, long-time effort that the problem merits further comment. Viewed en masse, these experiments have yielded quite inconclusive results. Most, though not all of these studies have indicated no differences among the various emotional states. Since as human beings, rather than as scientists, we have no difficulty identifying, labeling, and distinguishing among our feelings, the results of these studies have long seemed rather puzzling and paradoxical. Perhaps because of this, there has been a persistent tendency to discount such results as due to ignorance or methodological inadequacy and to pay far more attention to the very few studies which demonstrate *some* sort of physiological differences among emotional states than to the very many studies which indicate no differences at all. It is conceivable, however, that these results should be taken at face value and that emotional states may, indeed, be generally characterized by a high level of sympathetic activation with few if any physiological distinguishers among the many emotional states. If this is correct, the cognitive-physiological formulation outlined here and the findings of the studies described may help to resolve the problem.

Obviously these studies do *not* rule out the possibility of differences among the emotional states. It is the case, however, that given precisely the same state of epinephrine-induced sympathetic activation, it has been possible, by means of cognitive manipulations, to produce in subjects the very disparate states of euphoria, anger, and amusement at a movie. It may, indeed, be the case that cognitive factors are major determiners of the emotional "labels" we apply to a common state of sympathetic arousal.

In *"Background to Danger,"* novelist Eric Ambler (1958) describes a fugitive who introspects this way:

Rather to his surprise, he found that being wanted for murder produced in him an effect almost identical to that of a dentist's waiting-room—a sense of discomfort in the intestinal region, a certain constriction in the chest. He supposed that the same glands discharged the same secretions into the blood stream in both cases. Nature could be absurdly parsimonious.

If these speculations are correct, nature may indeed be far more parsimonious than Ambler suggests.

c. Cannon's point that "the viscera are relatively insensitive structures" is again telling for a formulation which virtually requires a richness of visceral sensation in order to be able to match the presumed richness of emotional experience. For the present formulation, of course, the criticism is irrelevant. Just so long as there is *some* visceral or cardiovascular sensation, the cognitive-physiological hypotheses are applicable.

The introduction of cognitive factors does allow us, then, to cope with three of Cannon's criticisms of a purely visceral formulation. Let us turn next to Cannon's remaining two points which are quite as troublesome for the present view of emotion as for the Jamesian view.

Visceral Separation and Emotion

Effects of sympathectomies. Cannon's remaining criticisms are these: "Visceral changes are too slow to be a source of emotional feeling" (i.e., the latency period of arousal of many visceral structures is longer than the latency of onset of emotional feelings reported in introspective studies); and "total separation of the viscera from the central nervous system does not alter emotional behavior." Both criticisms make essentially the same point, for they identify conditions in which there are apparently emotions unaccompanied by visceral activity. The data with which Cannon buttresses his latter criticism are based on his own studies (Cannon et al., 1927) of sympathectomized cats, and Sherrington's (1900) study of sympathectomized dogs. For both sets of experimental animals "the absence of reverberation from the viscera did not alter in any respect the appropriate emotional display; its only abbreviation was surgical." In the presence of a barking dog, for example, the sympathectomized cats manifested almost all of the signs of feline rage. Finally, Cannon notes the report of Dana (1921) that a patient with a spinal cord lesion and almost totally without visceral sensation still manifested normal emotionality.[6]

---

[6] More recent work supporting Cannon's position is that of Moyer and Bunnell (Moyer, 1958a,b; Moyer and Bunnell, 1959, 1960a,b) who, in an extensive series of studies of bilaterally adrenalectomized rats, have consistently failed to find any indication of differences between experimental and control animals on a variety

Prior learning. For either the Jamesian or the present formulation, such data are crucial, for both views demand visceral arousal as a necessary condition for emotional arousal. When faced with this evidence, James' defenders (e.g., Wenger, 1950; Mandler, 1962) have consistently made the point that the apparently emotional behavior manifested by sympathectomized animals and men is well-learned behavior, acquired long before sympathectomy. There is a dual implication in this position: first, that sympathetic arousal facilitates the acquisition of emotional behavior and, second, that sympathectomized subjects act but do not feel emotional. There is a small but growing body of evidence supporting these contentions. Wynne and Solomon (1955) have demonstrated that sympathectomized dogs acquire an avoidance response considerably more slowly than do control dogs. Further, on extinction trials most of their 13 sympathectomized animals extinguished quickly, while not a single one of 30 control dogs gave any indications of extinction over two hundred trials. Of particular interest are two dogs who were sympathectomized after they had acquired the avoidance response. On extinction trials these two animals behaved precisely as did the control dogs—giving no indication of extinction. Thus, when deprived of visceral innervation, animals are quite slow in acquiring emotionally linked avoidance responses and, in general, rapid in extinguishing such responses. When deprived of visceral innervation only after acquisition, the animals behave exactly as do the normal dogs—they fail to extinguish. A true Jamesian would undoubtedly note that these latter animals have learned to act as if they were emotional, but he would ask: Do they feel emotional?

Autonomic dysfunctioning in humans. This apparently unanswerable question seems on its way to an answer in a thoroughly fascinating study of the emotional life of paraplegics and quadriplegics conducted by Hohmann (1962). Hohmann studied a sample of 25 patients of the Spinal Cord Injury Service of the Veterans Administration Hospital at Long Beach. The subjects were divided into five groups according to the height of the clinically complete lesions as follows:

Group I, with lesions between the second and eighth cervical segmental level, have only the cranial branch of the parasympathetic nervous system remaining intact.

Group II, with lesions between the first and fourth thoracic seg-

---

of emotionally linked behaviors such as avoidance learning. The effects of adrenalectomy are by no means clearcut, however, for other investigators (Levine and Soliday, 1962) have found distinct differences between operated and control animals.

mental level, have in addition to the above, at least partial innervation of the sympathetically innervated cardiac plexus remaining intact.

Group III, with lesions between the sixth and twelfth thoracic segmental level have, additionally, at least partial innervation of the splanchnic outflow of the sympathetics remaining intact.

Group IV, with lesions between the first and fifth lumbar segmental level, have in addition at least partial sympathetic innervation of the mesenteric ganglia.

Group V, with lesions between the first and fifth sacral segments have, in addition, at least partial innervation of the sacral branch of the parasympathetic nervous system.

These groups then fall along a dimension of visceral innervation and sensation. The higher the lesion, the less the visceral sensation. If the present conception of emotion is correct, one should expect to find decreasing manifestation of emotion as the height of the lesion increases.

With each of his subjects, Hohmann conducted an extensive, structured interview which was "directed to specific feelings in situations of sexual excitement, fear, anger, grief and sentimentality, and the subject's attention was directed toward their feelings rather than to the concomitant ideation." Hohmann asked his subjects to recall an emotion-arousing incident prior to their injury and a comparable incident following the injury. They were then asked to compare the intensity of their emotional experiences before and after injury. Changes in reported affect comprise the body of data. I have adapted Hohmann's data for presentation in Figure 1. Following Hohmann's coding schema a report of no change is scored as 0; a report of mild change (e.g., "I feel it less, I guess") is scored -1 for a decrease and $+1$ for an increase; a report of strong change (e.g., "I feel it a helluva lot less") is scored as -2 or $+2$.

Hohmann's data for the states of fear and anger is plotted in Figure 1. It can be immediately seen that the higher the lesion and the less the visceral sensation, the greater the decrease in emotionality. Precisely the same relationship holds for the states of sexual excitement and grief. The sole exception to this consistent trend is "sentimentality," which, I suspect, should be considered a cognitive rather than a "feeling" state. It is clear that for these cases deprivation of visceral sensation has resulted in a marked decrease in emotionality.

If, in an attempt to assess the absolute level of emotionality of these cases, one examines their verbalized introspections, we note again and again that subjects with cervical lesions described themselves as acting emotional but not feeling emotional. A few typical quotes follow:

". . . it's sort of cold anger. Sometimes I act angry when I see some injustice. I yell and cuss and raise hell, because if you don't do it sometimes, I've learned people will take advantage of you, but it just doesn't have the heat to it that it used to. It's a mental kind of anger."

"Seems like I get thinking mad, not shaking mad, and that's a lot different."

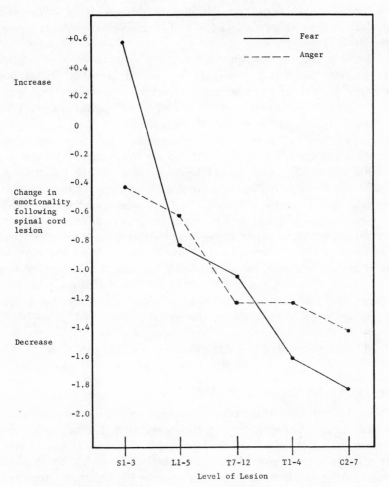

FIG. 1. Changes in emotionality as related to height of spinal cord lesion. (Adapted from Hohmann, 1962.)

"I say I am afraid, like when I'm going into a real stiff exam at school, but I don't really feel afraid, not all tense and shaky, with that hollow feeling in my stomach, like I used to."

In effect, these subjects seemed to be saying that when the situation demands it, they make the proper emotional-appearing responses, but they do not feel emotional. Parenthetically, it should be noted that these quotations bear an almost contrapuntal resemblance to the introspections of Marañon's subjects who, after receiving an injection of adrenaline, described their feelings in a way that led Marañon to label them "cold" or "as if" emotions. Many of these subjects described their physical symptoms and added statements such as, "I feel as if I were very frightened; however, I am calm."

The two sets of introspections are like opposite sides of the same coin. Marañon's subjects reported the visceral correlates of emotion, but in the absence of veridical cognitions did not describe themselves as feeling emotion. Hohmann's subjects described the appropriate reaction to an emotion-inducing situation but in the absence of visceral arousal did not seem to describe themselves as emotional. It is as if they were labeling a situation, not describing a feeling. Obviously, this contrasting set of introspections is precisely what should be anticipated from a formulation of emotion as a joint function of cognitive and physiological factors.

The line of thought stimulated by the Wynne and Solomon (1955) and Hohmann (1962) studies may indeed be the answer to Cannon's observation that there can be emotional behavior without visceral activity. From the evidence of these studies, it would appear, first, that autonomic arousal greatly facilitates the acquisition of emotional behavior but is not necessary for its maintenance if the behavior is acquired prior to sympathectomy; and, second, that in the absence of autonomic arousal, behavior that appears emotional will not be experienced as emotional.

Some Effects of Cognitive Factors on the Appraisal of Bodily States

Cognitions and Response to Marihuana

Let us turn now to the cognitive component of this view of emotion and examine further implications of the formulation. The key cognitive assumption underlying the human experiments described is that "given a state of physiological arousal for which an individual has no immediate explanation, he will label this state and describe his feelings in terms of the cognitions available to him." Obviously, this proposition implies that a drive exists to evaluate, understand, and label ambiguous body states. It is suggested that Festinger's (1954) theoretical invention—the "evaluative need," which he employs as the conceptual underpinning of his theory of social comparison processes—is as necessary and useful for an understanding of emotion and the perception of bodily states as it has proven for understanding of the opinions. Given a new, strange, or ambiguous bodily state, pressures will act on the individual to decide exactly what it is that he feels and to decide how he will label these feelings. In the Schachter and Singer (1962) study the differences between the Epi Ign and Epi Inf conditions would certainly indicate that it is useful to apply this notion of evaluative needs to bodily states.

These cognitive assumptions as worded clearly imply applicability to bodily states other than the epinephrine induced state of sympathetic activation. If these ideas are correct, it should be expected that any novel bodily state will give rise to pressures to decide what is felt, to decide how these feelings are to be labeled, and, perhaps, to decide whether these feelings are pleasant or unpleasant ones. Though I know of no experiments directly designed to test these ideas for states other than that induced by epinephrine, the extensive literature on the effects of drugs provides constant hints and bits of data which suggest that these ideas do have wide applicability.

As an example, consider the effects of smoking marihuana. Following the pharmacological texts, marihuana or cannabis produces the following physiological effects:

> Marihuana usually causes an increase in pulse rate, a slight rise in blood pressure, and conjunctival vascular congestion; the cardiovascular system is otherwise unaffected. The blood sugar and basal metabolic rate are elevated, but usually not beyond the upper limits of normal. Urinary frequency without diuresis occurs. A marked increase in appetite (especially for sweets) and hunger are characteristic, and hypergeusia may occasionally be prominent. Dryness of the mouth and throat is frequent. Nausea, vomiting, and occasionally diarrhea may be noted.
>
> Tremor, ataxia, vertigo, tinnitus, hyper-reflexia, increased sensitivity to touch, pressure, and pain stimuli, pupillary dilatation with sluggish light reflexes, and a sensation of floating are also observed. . . . Tremulousness of the eyelids, lips, and tongue and nystagamus on lateral gaze are common. (Goodman and Gilman, 1958, pp. 172–173.)

These are the measured physiological changes caused by smoking marihuana. In and of themselves, are such bodily feelings pleasant or unpleasant? Given such symptoms, should the smoker describe himself as "high" or as "sick"?

In an absorbing study of fifty marihuana users, the sociologist Becker (1953) reports an invariable sequence in learning to use marihuana for pleasure. Once he has learned the techniques of smoking, the smoker must learn to label his physiological symptoms as being "high." In Becker's words,

> . . . being high consists of two elements: the presence of symptoms caused by marihuana use and the recognition of these symptoms and their connection by the user with his use of the drug. It is not enough, that is, that the effects

be present; they alone do not automatically provide the experience of being high. The user must be able to point them out to himself and consciously connect them with his having smoked marihuana before he can have this experience. Otherwise, regardless of the actual effects produced, he considers that the drug has had no effect on him.

An example of learning that he is high is provided by this quotation from a novice who gets high for the first time only after he learned that intense hunger is one consequence of smoking marihuana:

> They were just laughing the hell out of me because like I was eating so much. I just scoffed (ate) so much food, and they were just laughing at me, you know. Sometimes I'd be looking at them, you know, wondering why they're laughing, you know, not knowing what I was doing. (Well, did they eventually tell you why they were laughing?) Yeah, yeah, I come back, "Hey, man, what's happening?" and all of a sudden I feel weird, you know. "Man, you're on you know. You're on pot (high on marihuana)." I said, "No, am I?" Like I don't know what's happening.

An instance of more indirect learning is the following: "I heard little remarks that were made by people. Somebody said, 'My legs are rubbery,' and I can't remember all the remarks that were made because I was very attentively listening for all these cues for what I was supposed to feel like."

Obviously, these are instances where the novice must literally learn to notice his feelings. Given that a user is made aware of his symptoms and has learned that what he is feeling is being "high," Becker notes that one further step is necessary for continued use of the drug:

> He must learn to enjoy the effects he has just learned to experience. Marihuana-produced sensations are not automatically or necessarily pleasurable. The taste for such experience is a socially acquired one, not different in kind from acquired tastes for oysters or dry martinis. The user feels dizzy, thirsty; his scalp tingles; he misjudges time and distances, and so on. Are these things pleasurable? He isn't sure. If he is to continue marihuana use, he must decide that they are. Otherwise, getting high, while a real enough experience, will be an unpleasant one he would rather avoid.

Becker supports this analysis with numerous instances of novice smokers being taught, in social interaction, that their feelings were pleasant.

This study, then, indicates that new marihuana users must be taught to notice and identify what they feel, must be taught to label the state as "high" and must be taught that the state is "pleasant." The marihuana induced state of feelings appears to be another instance of a bodily state which takes its meaning and labels in good part from cognitive and social factors.

I would guess that the labels and hedonic valuation attached to an amazing variety of bodily conditions are cognitively determined.

Obviously, there are limits. It is unlikely that anyone with undiagnosed peritonitis could ever be convinced that he was euphoric, high, or anything but deathly ill. I suspect, though, that the limits are astonishingly wide. Vomiting to us may seem unpleasant, but to a banqueting Roman gourmet, it may have been one of the exquisite pleasures.

LABELING OF BODILY STATES IN OBESITY

As a final point, if it is correct that the labels attached to feeling states are cognitively, situationally, or socially determined, it becomes a distinct possibility that an uncommon or inappropriate label can be attached to a feeling state. Where such is the case, we may anticipate bizarre and pathological behavior. As an example of this possibility, consider the state of hunger. We are so accustomed to think of hunger as a primary motive, innate and wired into the animal, unmistakable in its cues, that even the possibility that an organism would be incapable of correctly labeling the state seems too far fetched to credit. The physiological changes accompanying food deprivation seem distinct, identifiable, and invariant. Yet even a moment's consideration will make it clear that attaching the label "hunger" to this set of bodily feelings and behaving accordingly, is a learned, socially determined, cognitive act.

Consider the neonate. Wholly at the mercy of its feelings, when uncomfortable, in pain, frightened, hungry, or thirsty, it screams. Whether it is comforted, soothed, clucked at, fondled, or fed has little to do with the state of its own feelings, but depends entirely on the ability and willingness of its mother or nurse to recognize the proper cues. If she is experienced, she will comfort when the baby is frightened, soothe him when he is chafed, feed him when he is hungry, and so on. If inexperienced, her behavior may be completely inappropriate to the child's state. Most commonly, perhaps, the compassionate but bewildered mother will feed her child at any sign of distress.

It is precisely this state of affairs that the analyst Hilde Bruch (1961) suggests is at the heart of chronic obesity. She describes such cases as characterized by a confusion between intense emotional states and hunger. During childhood these patients have not been taught to discriminate between hunger and such states as fear, anger, and anxiety. If correct, these people are, in effect, labeling a state of sympathetic activation as hunger. Small wonder that they are both fat and jolly.

REFERENCES

Ambler, E. (1958). "Background to Danger." Dell, New York.
Ax, A. F. (1953). *Psychosomat. Med.* **15**, 433–442.
Becker, H. S. (1953). *Am. J. Sociol.* **59**, 235–242.

Bruch, H. (1961). *Psychiat. Quart.* **35,** 458–481.

Cannon, W. B. (1927). *Am. J. Psychol.* **39,** 106–124.

Cannon, W. B. (1929). "Bodily Changes in Pain, Hunger, Fear and Rage." 2nd ed. Appleton, New York.

Cannon, W. B., Lewis, J. T., and Britton, S. W. (1927). *Boston Med. and Surg. J.* **197,** 514.

Cantril, H., and Hunt, W. A. (1932). *Am. J. Psychol.* **44,** 300–307.

Dana, C. L. (1921). *Arch. Neurol. Psychiat.* **6,** 634–639.

Festinger, L. (1954). *Human Relat.,* **7,** 114–140.

Goodman, L. S., and Gilman, A. (1958). "The Pharmacological Basis of Therapeutics." Macmillan, New York.

Hohmann, G. W. (1962). The effect of dysfunctions of the autonomic nervous system on experienced feelings and emotions. Paper read at Conference on Emotions and Feelings at New School for Social Research, New York.

Hunt, J. McV., Cole, M. W., and Reis, E. C. (1958). *Am. J. Psychol.* **71,** 136–151.

James, W. (1890). "The Principles of Psychology." Holt, New York.

Killam, E. K. (1959). *Natl. Acad. Sci.—Natl. Res. Council Publ.* **583.**

Landis, C., and Hunt, W. A. (1932). *Psychol. Rev.* **39,** 467–485.

Latané, B., and Schachter, S. (1962). *J. Comp. Physiol. Psychol.* **55,** 369–372.

Levine, S., and Soliday, S. (1962). *J. Comp. Physiol. Psychol.* **55,** 214–216.

Mandler, G. (1962). *In* "New Directions in Psychology" (R. Brown *et al.,* eds.), pp. 267–343. Holt, Rinehart and Winston, New York.

Marañon, G. (1924). *Rev. Franc. Endocrinol.* **2,** 301–325.

Moyer, K. E. (1958a). *J. Genet. Psychol.* **92,** 17–21.

Moyer, K. E. (1958b). *J. Genet. Psychol.* **92,** 11–16.

Moyer, K. E., and Bunnell, B. N. (1959). *J. Comp. Physiol.* **52,** 215–216.

Moyer, K. E., and Bunnell, B. N. (1960a). *J. Genet. Psychol.* **96,** 375–382.

Moyer, K. E., and Bunnell, B. N. (1960b). *J. Genet. Psychol.* **97,** 341–344.

Ruckmick, C. A. (1936). "The Psychology of Feeling and Emotion." McGraw-Hill, New York.

Schachter, J. (1957). *Psychosom. Med.* **19,** 17–29.

Schachter, S. (1959). "The Psychology of Affiliation." Stanford Univ. Press, Stanford, California.

Schachter, S., and Wheeler, L. (1962). *J. Abnorm. Soc. Psychol.* **65,** 121–128.

Schachter, S., and Singer, J. (1962). *Psychol. Rev.* **69,** 379–399.

Sherrington, C. S. (1900). *Proc. Roy. Soc.* **66,** 390–403.

Singer, J. E. (1963). *J. Comp. Physiol. Psychol.* **56,** 612–615.

Wenger, M. A. (1950). *In* "Feelings and Emotions" (M. L. Reymert, ed.), pp. 3–10. McGraw-Hill, New York.

Wolf, S., and Wolff, H. G. (1947). "Human Gastric Function." Oxford Univ. Press, London and New York.

Woodworth, R. S., and Schlosberg, H. (1958). "Experimental Psychology." Holt, New York.

Wrightsman, L. S. (1960). *J. Abnorm. Soc. Psychol.* **61,** 216–222.

Wynne, L. C., and Solomon, R. L. (1955). *Genet. Psychol. Monogr.* **52,** 241–284.

CHAPTER 10

The Study of Psychological Stress: A Summary of Theoretical Formulations and Experimental Findings

Richard S. Lazarus and Edward M. Opton, Jr.

DEPARTMENT OF PSYCHOLOGY,
UNIVERSITY OF CALIFORNIA,
BERKELEY, CALIFORNIA

This chapter is basically a summary of research carried out in our laboratory during the past 5 years.[1] The studies we shall report deal with several of the substantive problems of psychological stress, but all have in common the use of a single method for producing stress and a single strategy for measuring the degree of stress produced. Motion picture films, and occasionally tape recordings, have been used to produce stress in all our experiments. The use of this method was dictated by the major difficulties inherent in the alternative approaches to laboratory stress induction. The usual laboratory approach involves deception of one kind or another to threaten the subject. But deception presents certain problems for laboratory research on stress. For one thing, the subject is likely to realize that

[1] This chapter is a revised version of a progress report submitted to the National Institute of Mental Health in January, 1965. The research reported here was supported by Research Grant NH-02136 from the National Institute of Mental Health, United States Public Health Service, and by other grants from this agency. Dr. Opton is presently co-Principal investigator on this project. Numerous graduate students and staff members (such as Dr. Joseph C. Speisman who was previously co-investigator), all listed in connection with individual studies, contributed indirectly to this summary of research which they performed under the project and to the ideas that are communicated.

the threat is based on deception, since he assumes the experimenter will not really allow any serious harm to come to him. If the deception succeeds fully, then serious ethical problems arise. Another limitation of deception tactics is that subjects cannot be fooled repeatedly; therefore, problems of adaptation to stress, consistency versus stimulus specificity in the response patterns among individuals, and other problems requiring repeated measurements are difficult to approach through deception techniques.

We have turned, therefore, to the use of motion pictures as sources of threat (see Lazarus, 1964). In vicarious situations such as movies, the content of the threats employed can be more serious in degree (e.g., death, mutilation, ostracism, etc.) and more salient to individuals' core motives than direct threats can afford to be, yet the experimenter avoids producing any real harm. Continuous measurement of reactions is possible, and experiments using repeated and/or multiple stressors are feasible. A wide variety of different stress situations are potentially available. And finally, the subject watching a movie is free from participation in any active task. This has two advantages: it keeps the subject free to give frequent verbal or other reports of his emotional response uncluttered by simultaneous task demands, and it avoids the confounding effects on the physiological stress reaction of the physical activity or mobilization which accompanies task performance and produces response effects not directly relevant to threat.

Of course, the use of films brings problems of its own, the most important of which is that we do not know the processes that are involved in the production of threat and stress by vicarious experience. Why should it be stressful to look at a picture of a surgical operation that took place long ago and far away or at a dramatized industrial shop accident which the viewer well knows never took place in reality at all? We have assumed from the beginning that *identification* with the film characters was the key process involved. But our data have not yet given firm support to this assumption. We apparently still have much to learn about the processes of identification and vicarious threat.

The ultimate justification for our laboratory approach to problems of psychological stress is the hope that the processes operative in the laboratory situation will prove generalizable to situations of real-life stress. We trust, in other words, that the stressful motion picture situation is, to a useful degree, analogous to real-life stress. The exact extent to which the analogy is valid must remain to be determined when a bridge of empirical work is built between laboratory and field research, but at least one limit on the analogy is suggested by a most evident fact about the vicarious stress situation: when watching the stress film, the subject is under strong social constraints to be a passive observer. The methods available to him for coping with the stress are perforce limited to internal cognitive and emotional processes. In real-life stress both physical escape ("leaving the field") and active manipulation of the situation are often feasible alternatives. Escape is socially difficult, although explicitly permitted, in the film experiment, and intervention in the events portrayed is impossible. We expect, therefore, that our experiments will yield results most relevant to knowledge of the *sources* of threat, the *internal* processes for coping with stress, and the psychological and physiological consequences of experiencing stress.

Some initial work on the motion picture analogue was first undertaken between 1957 and 1960, and limited progress was reported early (Lazarus, 1960; Lazarus & Speisman, 1960). The motion-picture-film approach to psychological stress was described and some of its potential advantages outlined. Limited early data as well as the findings of other investigators (Äas, 1958; Schwartz, 1956) encouraged us in the view that films could be used to study the processes and conditions of psychological stress. There remained, however, much to be learned about the systematic use of films and about the methodological issues to be faced in assessing film-induced stress reactions and relating them to antecedent conditions.

The original plan for the project involved three stages of experimentation. In the first stage several main types of interpersonal conflict were to be explored as sources of stress reaction. We were concerned with the capacity of these conflict-related stimulus areas to produce psychological stress in any given population of subjects, especially as a function of assessable personality characteristics which make the person especially sensitive to certain areas of human interaction.

The second phase involved the plan to manipulate "ego-defense" processes so as to reduce stress reactions while subjects watched a stressful film. The focus was to be on denial and intellectualization as modes of defensive thought. Not only did we intend to study coping processes as they occurred naturally in the subject, but we planned also to influence such strategies by the use of sound tracks created to channel defensive activity. These sound tracks were to be played along with the film in order to encourage particular ways of thinking about the events that were being portrayed.

The third phase of our research plan was to evaluate the extent to which the processes studied in the vicarious stress situation of watching films could be generalized to stress situations in which the subject was himself faced with a direct threat of harm. The question was to what extent the reaction pattern obtained for a subject under the film stressor conditions would be similar to that obtained if the subject were threatened directly.

Implicit in the plan that was outlined was the need for a systematic theoretical frame of reference within which to view psychological stress. Successful research is, to some degree, guided by concepts about process, and the conditions that one chooses to study reflect these concepts. Not only was a more systematic point of view required, but it was important to make it explicit.

Before we review the research progress over the past 5 years, we note the failure to make successful strides in one of the three planned phases of the project: that dealing with types of social stimuli as sources of stress reaction. It became apparent early that the task of locating or creating films dealing with a variety of social threats was more difficult than we had anticipated. At that time TV technology for producing relatively inexpensive kinescopes was not available to us. The alternative of using sound tape recordings had its own special problems. Although we did use two tapes made in our laboratory, they were not what was needed for a systematic attack on the problem of stimulus content. They did support the idea, however, that sound tapes, like films, are capable of producing substantial stress reaction, both physiological and behavioral.

Shortly after the project was undertaken, it seemed best to defer our plan to invest heavily in interpersonal threat themes. The decision was not entirely predicated on the difficulty of obtaining such materials, although this was an important factor. It became evident that larger resources than we had available would be necessary to launch a successful systematic attack on this problem.

There were other good arguments in favor of temporarily shifting our emphasis away from phase one of the planned program of research. Many important substantive and methodological problems of importance could be tackled with film materials that were already available. The resulting program over the past years reflects this temporary shift in emphasis. Phases two and three of the original proposal were advanced in priority, as well as some methodological issues not originally considered. What follows is organized into three categories: the theory of psychological stress, methodological advances, and empirical findings concerning the psychodynamics of stress. Since some of these findings have already appeared, there is a greater emphasis in this article on as yet unpublished work, although, of necessity, the published material is also noted.

The Theory of Psychological Stress

A theory of psychological stress has been described in full by the senior author in a forthcoming book, *Psychological Stress and the Coping Process* (Lazarus, 1966). The book also reviews a substatntial amount of clinical, field, and laboratory research, which is cited as it bears on the various theoretical and methodological issues. This theoretical viewpoint has, in part, guided the research to be summarized here (implicitly at least, since the above book has only recently been completed). With respect to this theoretical analysis, it is only possible here to do two things: first, to mention some of the main issues around which a theory of psychological stress must be built; and second, to give a very brief summary of the main analytic concepts.

The central issues in psychological stress are the conditions and processes that determine when stress reactions will be produced and when they will not. For example, how does the individual differentiate between benign conditions and damaging conditions? What processes are involved, and what factors influence them? A second class of issues concerns what happens when a stimulus is reacted to as stressful. How does the individual cope with stress and what factors influence the choice of these coping processes? A third has to do with the patterns of reaction that define the presence of the stress processes. Which ones are pertinent to psychological stress? What accounts for the variations in reaction? How are these variations related to intervening processes? Any theoretical system must not only distinguish between the various observable phenomena of psychological stress and provide terminology for them, but also postulate the processes intervening between the "stress" stimulus and "stress" response and identify the factors that influence these processes.

Psychological stress analysis is distinguished from other types of stress analysis by the intervening variable of *threat,* a state in which the individual anticipates harm. Stimuli resulting in threat or nonthreat reactions are cues that signify to the individual some future condition, either harmful, benign, or beneficial. These cues are evaluated by a cognitive process of *appraisal.* The process of appraisal depends on two classes of antecedents. One consists of factors in the stimulus configuration, such as the comparative power of the harm-producing condition and the individual's counterharm resources, the imminence of the harmful confrontation, and degree of ambiguity in the significance of the stimulus cue. The second class of factors that determine the appraisal are within the psychological structure of the individual, including motive strength and pattern, general beliefs about transactions with the environment, and intellectual resources, education, and knowledge. Threat is appraised on a continuum from complete absence to very intense levels.

Once a stimulus has been appraised as threatening, processes whose function it is to reduce or eliminate the anticipated harm are set in motion. They are called *coping* processes. They also depend on cognitive activity, but because they are influenced by special factors, we have termed the cognitive activity related to coping *secondary appraisal*.

The primary appraisal of threat and secondary appraisal of conditions relevant to coping with threat should not be regarded as necessarily sequential processes. They may overlap in time, since features of the stimulus configuration relevant to coping may be noted even before threat is appraised, as when long-standing awareness of road or street conditions determine what the individual does when suddenly confronted with the danger of floods. However, although information relevant to coping may be assimilated before or during the primary appraisal of threat as well as after, threat gives the secondary appraisal process its poignancy and urgency. We may always know roughly where the exits to a theater are, but a fire suddenly makes this knowledge urgent as a means of coping. Sometimes the secondary appraisal process informs us about factors in the situation not previously recognized which alter the significance of the situation so that there is no longer any reason to be threatened. In such an instance, the secondary appraisal process, in turn, influences threat appraisal itself, and we may speak of "reappraisal" on the basis of further evaluations by the individual, realistic or defensive. It should also be noted that appraisal is not a process of which an individual is necessarily fully aware or that is reportable by the individual.

Although primary and secondary appraisal of threat cannot always be distinguished phenomenologically or temporally, we think it important to make the distinction. In general, the cognitive style an individual uses to appraise the presence or absence of threat is one adapted not only to detecting and/or protecting against threat, but one that also must serve to discriminate between interesting and irrelevant stimuli; it must suit the individual's self-concept; and it must be open to satisfactions and pleasures. But when a threat is appraised as being present, the usual combination of purposes becomes much less salient, a different hierarchy of coping processes comes into use, and a different combination of cognitions becomes relevant. The more dangerous and immediate the threat, the more different from the ordinary will be the cognitive mechanisms used in secondary appraisal or reappraisal.

Three main classes of factors are involved in secondary appraisal. The first is degree of threat. The second consists of factors in the stimulus configuration such as the locatability and character of the agent of harm, the viability of alternative available routes or actions to prevent the harm, and situational constraints which limit or encourage the action that may be taken. A third class of factors influencing the secondary appraisal process lies within the psychological structure: for example, the pattern of motivation which determines the "price" of certain coping alternatives, ego resources, defensive dispositions, and certain beliefs about the environment and one's resources for dealing with it.

Secondary appraisal based on the above factors determines the form of coping process, i.e., the coping strategy adopted by the individual in attempting to master the danger. The end results observed in behavior (e.g., affective experiences, motor manifestations, alterations in adaptive functioning, and physiological reactions) may be understood in terms of these intervening coping processes. Each pattern of reaction—for example, actions aimed at strengthening the individual's resources against the anticipated harm, attack with or without anger, anger without attack, avoidance with fear, fear without avoidance, and the various defenses—is determined by a particular kind of appraisal.

Methodological Advances

Methodological advances with respect to our laboratory analogue of psychological stress processes have been made in a number of categories including continuous measurement of autonomic stress reaction, the relationship between different autonomic measures, near continuous measurement of level of affective disturbance, the mechanisms and conditions underlying discrepancies between self-report ratings of disturbance and autonomic measures, and the generality of the vicarious approach. We shall briefly summarize our work on each of these.

CONTINUOUS AUTONOMIC MEASUREMENT OF STRESS REACTION

When a person watches a stressful motion picture there is a continuous flux or ebb and flow of disturbance depending on the events momentarily being presented on the screen. The changing state of the subject is in this respect like real-life stress situations and must be captured in the response measures at each moment in time in order to properly understand it. It is important to observe not only the reactions to the specific, discrete threatening moments, but also the ups and downs of disturbance throughout the experience, in benign scenes as well as in highly threatening ones. To represent such a changing picture it is necessary to record continuously during the entire experience. Measures of autonomic activation offer a prime tool for this kind of analysis. No other stress-reaction indicator is as easily applied to a motion picture film situation.

An early problem was to determine the extent to which such autonomic measures as skin conductance and heart rate would, indeed, reflect the ups and downs of disturbance. A monograph by Lazarus, Speisman, Mordkoff, and Davison (1962) reported our first systematic study of this problem. A benign control film and a stressful film on Subincision (a ritual performed by the men of an Australian stone-age culture in which the penis and scrotum of male adolescents are cut deeply with a sharpened piece of stone) were employed to study the reactions of a large sample of college men and women. Continuous recordings of skin conductance and heart rate showed a low and declining level of arousal during the control film and markedly elevated levels of arousal during the Subincision film. Not only did the two films differ greatly in impact, but the level of autonomic disturbance in the Subincision film rose sharply during scenes that *a priori* had been defined as threatening and fell during benign scenes. Continuous recording of autonomic reactivity provided a reliable *group-average* profile of fluctuations in stress reaction (Fig. 1).

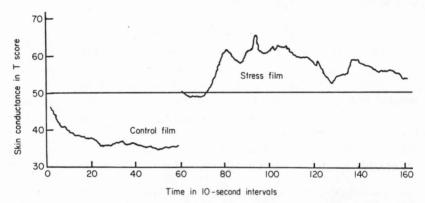

FIG. 1.   Skin conductance during neutral (control) and stress films. From Lazarus *et al.* (1962) and reproduced with the permission of the American Psychological Association.

Early difficulties in this type of procedure were posed by uncertainty about which of many types of autonomic variables should be used to reflect level of stress reaction. As part of the initial normative study, several large cluster analyses were performed on 63 skin-conductance variables and 53 heart-rate variables in order to select the most useful ones for later research. This analysis was reported separately (Speisman, Osborn, & Lazarus, 1961) and also summarized in the monograph cited above. It became clear in the course of this work that for both organ systems, heart rate and skin conductance, measures of level (rather than range, lability, etc.) were the most useful variables. Continuous autonomic measurement showed striking parallels between skin-conductance and heart-rate levels and *a priori* evaluations of the contents of the film stimulus. Since extraneous physical variables were controlled and the subject engaged in no systematic muscular exertion or task performance (he was seated in an easy chair, merely watching), the fluctuating stress reactions are attributable to psychological mediating processes linked to the particular events portrayed in the film.[2]

THE RELATIONSHIPS BETWEEN DIFFERENT AUTONOMIC MEASURES OF STRESS REACTION

The history of the psychophysiology of stress and emotion shows that disappointingly low agreement is typically found between the measured reactions of different end organs of the autonomic nervous system. While it can be observed, for example, that heart rate and skin conductance both usually rise under stressful situations, the correlations between these variables, both presumably measuring the same state, are reported to be very low (e.g., Lacey, 1959). This is an embarrassing problem to those interested in measuring stress reaction, since if the measures used do not agree, it is difficult to say that any single one is a valid basis of inference about stress or arousal. In consequence of the usual disagreement between indexes, the concepts of stimulus and response specificity have been introduced to refer to variance due to the stimulus and variance due to the constitutional makeup of the individual. To the degree that such sources of variation are important, the individual end-organ responses reflect less well a generalized condition of arousal or stress reaction.

In several papers we have argued that the usual methodology of assessing the degree of correspondence between autonomic measures is inadequate, since it is obtained interindividually, across individuals, rather than intraindividually, across conditions. Actually, in stress research the use of any single measure is predicated on the assumption that the various measures of reaction rise and fall together within the same individual physiological system. We must make the assumption that, to a significant degree, when heart rate in an individual rises, so will skin conductance, except perhaps under specifically defined situations (e.g., the conditions of specificity). The greater this degree of intraindividual correspondence, the more reliance we can place on any given measure of stress reaction. The smaller the correspondence, and in the absence of our ability to specify the conditions of high and low correlation between measures, the less valid is our reliance on any single measure.

The motion-picture-film methodology, with its continuous recording of autonomic levels of activity, lends itself ideally to *intraindividual* analysis

---

[2] In some studies we have also obtained continuous records of respiration and gross body movements, but in our experiments these have never seemed to add information to that obtained from heart-rate and skin-conductance records.

of the correspondence between measures. Data from the original monograph study were analyzed and reported by Lazarus, Speisman, and Mordkoff (1963) employing several kinds of intraindividual approach. An encouraging degree of correspondence was found between heart rate and skin conductance in certain intraindividual measures—high enough, in our view, to justify the assumption that a single autonomic measure could indeed be employed to infer general arousal. Such findings do not, of course, either invalidate the concepts of stimulus and response specificity or the notion that combinations of measures ought to be superior to single ones. The correlations are never high enough to rule out considerable degrees of specificity.

More recently, Malmstrom, Opton, and Lazarus (1966) introduced modifications in the scoring of heart rate which result in still better correspondence between its pattern and that of skin conductance. Data were taken from a study using a different threatening film, "It Didn't Have To Happen" (see p. 246). A "peak-rate" sampling of heart rate was employed, and the heart-rate curves were smoothed by the method of moving averages. As a consequence, heart rate appeared to correspond better not only with skin conductance, but also with the film contents. This latter point might well be underscored. Because we have much normative data on the various threatening films employed in our laboratory, and because the places in the film that result in subjective stress reaction in most subjects are also known, we are not merely relating two measures, heart rate and skin conductance, to each other, validating one unknown against another. Rather, we are linking both to a third variable, the stimulus events portrayed in the film. Thus, we feel justified in concluding that the agreement between heart rate and skin conductance reflects stress reaction.

On this methodological point of agreement between autonomic measures, a further study by Opton, Rankin, and Lazarus (1966) offered greater simplicity in scoring heart rate and encouraged the hope that additional efforts to improve and develop the scoring of autonomic variables will increase still further the intraindividual correspondence between them, up to some unknown maximum. It is also worth noting in passing that these findings not only have methodological value, but also provide some support for the theoretical concept of activation or arousal which would be difficult to maintain if no general state of arousal were empirically definable.

This is not to say that stress reaction can be adequately described in terms of a single dimension of arousal that includes what is common or general to all states of arousal. We view such a concept as oversimple, a generalization that is made at the expense of the obviously specific sources of variance in stress reactions. In our view, the most exciting new developments in the measurement of stress reactions concern the problem of *patterning or specificity,* and we make the assumption that intervening psychological processes of threat and coping are reflected in this patterning of response indicators (e.g., Lazarus, 1965a). The maximum correlations between various indicators of autonomic nervous system reaction are probably only modest even under the most favorable conditions. The discrepancies between stress-reaction indicators are even more marked and obvious when we compare different levels of analysis, for example, the physiological response and the behavioral response. We think that these discrepancies in large part can be analyzed and predicted.

For example, in the study by Lazarus and Alfert (1964), which is described more fully later in the section on appraisal, subjects were divided into two groups, high deniers and low deniers, on the basis of questionnaire scales derived from the MMPI. On a check list after watching the Subincision film, high deniers did exactly what that personality disposition implied: they reported significantly less anxiety than did low deniers. It is a sound inference that this report represents a form of denial, since the high deniers also showed significantly higher autonomic levels of reactivity, indicating greater stress than the low deniers. In effect, as judged by autonomic measures, they were under greater stress, but as judged by their reports, they were under less stress. Their ways of coping interpersonally and intrapersonally with the disturbance determined the pattern of stress-reaction indicators as measured at two levels of analysis, the physiological and the behavioral.

This sort of finding raises a question fundamental to theoretical conceptions of stress: Which indicator, if either, is correct? To put the question another way: How shall we conceptualize the state or process which underlies the several kinds of measures of stress? Our answer would not be that one measure, the physiological or the behavioral, is the true index of the underlying state and that the validity of the other measure depends on its correlation with the true index. Nor would we concede, as Krause (1961) and Martin (1961) tend to do, that since the different kinds of stress indicators disagree in the Lazarus and Alfert experiment neither is valid and that we have no adequate measure of stress response. Instead, we think it most useful to think of stress response as a multidimensional concept, with components of physiological arousal in the various organ systems, subjective phenomenology, and objective behavioral reactions. In defining stress response as a multidimensional concept, we might compare it to the concept of "growth," also a multidimensional concept. People grow physically in both height and girth, and the two measures are by no means perfectly correlated. People also grow intellectually and emotionally, and the indexes of these aspects of growth are completely different from (and minimally correlated with) tape measure or skeletal X-ray measures of physical growth. The concept of growth in all its multidimensionality is nonetheless a central concept in developmental psychology, and the patterns of correlations and disparities among the various indexes of growth make up much of the substantive content of developmental psychology. Likewise, we think stress response is best conceived as a set of different, but intimately related, processes. The discovery of the rules which determine the sometimes congruent, sometimes quite independent, pattern of these processes is the task of the investigator who does research on stress. Each pattern of response indicators permits different inferences about the underlying psychological processes (Lazarus, 1965b).

NEAR-CONTINUOUS MEASUREMENT OF LEVEL OF AFFECTIVE DISTURBANCE

We noted above the ease with which autonomic measurement could be made continuously while the subject watched a motion picture and how level of arousal rose and fell with shifts among benign and threatening scenes. There are important reasons for attempting also to measure the same ebb and flow in level of affective disturbance as reported by the subject. But the technical problems posed here are quite different from those of continuous autonomic measurement.

In our first studies affect was measured by an adjective check list of mood which provided an opportunity to evaluate the effects of threatening films on a number of categories of affect, such as anxiety, depression, aggression, pleasantness, etc. Check lists of mood have the great advantage of providing assessment of a rich pattern of affect. We know that different types of threatening films create different patterns of affective disturbance. The study of stress reaction is potentially greatly enriched by the ability to document these qualitative aspects of affect as well as to record the simple dimension of degree. In our theoretical view, affective variations also index some of the psychological processes that mediate between stimulus and stress reaction.

The trouble with the check-list approach, however, is that the measures are obtained at the beginning and at the end of the threatening film, or following discretely different types of stimuli, such as a control versus a stressful movie. The subject must recall how he felt during the movie to fill out the check list. It is impossible to determine the particular content of the film on which his rating is based. Affective reactions may sometimes be simple, but they are usually complex, as in real life, both in intensity and quality, varying with the content of each experience or each scene in the experimental film. The subject must somehow condense all this complex information into a single concept represented by his answer to each item of the scale. This is clearly unsatisfactory, and we should hardly expect any close correspondence between his self-reported affective disturbance and the autonomic measures of disturbance. The same arguments that favor continuous recording of heart rate and skin conductance also favor continuous recording of affect.

We have experimented with near-continuous recordings of affect by inserting a number of blank leads into the film. While they are on the screen for 5 seconds with no film content occurring during that period, the subject rates his tension, distress, pleasantness, or some other affective state on a seven-point scale. If sufficient numbers of occasions are provided for this task, a near-continuous curve of reported experience of that affect can be drawn, with its fluctuations resulting from changes in the threatening impact of particular film events, just as with autonomic measures. Such a procedure was first reported in a doctoral dissertation by Mordkoff (1964) using 44 blank leads during the Subincision film. When these blanks were on the screen, the subject rated his affective state on a scale anchored by one of three adjectives representing the three primary dimensions of Wundt's (1907) tridimensional theory of feeling. Mordkoff found that regardless of which dimension was rated, the self-report ratings corresponded quite closely in their ups and downs with the autonomic indicators of arousal and with *a priori* analysis of the film content.

The same type of procedure has now become standard in many experiments within the project, including research accomplished by the Principal Investigator in Japan.[3] The method is important because it permits intraindividual comparison of different indicators of stress reaction such as self-reports of affect and autonomic measures. At the same time as we record continuous physiological indications of arousal, we obtain subjectively based measures as well, measures that can be aligned in time to each stimulus event during the film. We are thus in a good position to study discrepancies as well as agreements between self-reports of distress and autonomic indications.

Discrepancies provide the main empirical grounds for speaking about defenses or about social maneuvers to protect self-esteem. Mordkoff's dissertation was designed to throw light on some of the conditions under which discrepancies between these levels of analysis would be large or small. Perhaps because of the implicit acceptance by the subject of the

---

[3] R. S. Lazarus, M. Tomita, E. M. Opton, and M. Kodama, unpublished manuscript, 1965.

implied "contract" with the experimenter in a scientific experiment, the variations in the social atmosphere created by Mordkoff did not influence the agreement between self-report and autonomic measurements. The issue is still unsettled and the method of near-continuous recording of affective disturbance provides a necessary method for attacking the problem, or for studying the affective impact of any film.

MECHANISMS AND CONDITIONS UNDERLYING DISCREPANCIES BETWEEN SELF-REPORT RATINGS OF DISTURBANCE AND AUTONOMIC MEASURES

In the monograph cited earlier (Lazarus et al., 1962) we reported on interviews following the viewing of the Subincision film. Questioning the subjects about their reactions to the film produced statements that were classifiable into expressions of denial of distress, intellectualization, and other reactions. We considered such statements as defensive efforts to master the film-induced threats, but we found no differences in the degree of arousal or disturbed affect as a function of the tendency to deny or intellectualize. Our impression is that sufficient time and opportunity to develop successful defenses had not been available to the subjects, and our attention was directed subsequently to the manipulation of defensive modes of thought by sound tracks and orientations prior to the film showing. We shall take up such manipulations a little later.

Poststress interviews as a source of data on defensive efforts are subject to a very serious limitation. The essence of successful defensive thought processes is that they are not readily open to inspection by the person using them. If defensive omissions, distortions, and reconstructions of perception have been successful, any attempt to study their operation by direct introspection is likely to be foiled by the operation of the very processes under study. The near-continuous technique of recording affective disturbance during the showing of the film, which was discussed above, may be a considerable step forward in the direction of obtaining accurate estimates of felt affective disturbance, but it is not suitable for inquiry about the psychological processes that produce or prevent the disturbance.

Recently, Dr. Opton has undertaken a study which should provide some access to observation of the coping processes as they are used while watching the film. Each subject is led to believe that he is watching the film along with a partner in another room. (The physical layout of our laboratories makes this procedure plausible.) The subject is asked to provide a "sound track" or commentary which will ease the distress of the other subject. This commentary is recorded, as is also an interview after the film in which the subject is asked to explain his strategy. In the control condition subjects are asked merely to talk during the film showing; no stress-reducing efforts are requested. Instead of asking the subject directly about how he coped with the stressful aspects of the film, we are eliciting verbalization of the coping processes in the form of "therapeutic" statements for the benefit of this fellow subject. Although we cannot expect the subjects' verbalizations under these conditions to assume exactly the pattern of coping the subjects do or would use for themselves, we do expect the commentaries to be indicative of the major modes of defensive coping employed by the subjects.

It is possible to ask a number of interesting questions by virtue of this method. For example, what types of strategies are associated with lowered or heightened disturbance in the subject? Do differential coping methods account for discrepancies between the affective tone of what is said and the physiological and behavioral evidences of stress reaction? Are subjects consistent in how they handle the problem during the film and how they conceive and describe their reactions in the interview following the film? In other words, to what extent does a retrospective account accurately reflect the states and processes that appear to be taking place during the stressful experience? Data for this study have been collected but not yet analyzed.

THE GENERALITY OF THE VICARIOUS APPROACH

The objective of phase three of the original research plan was to determine whether the processes studied in film-induced stress reactions were comparable to those found in everyday life. This is important since we are not interested merely in the limited, vicarious condition of drama, films, or television, but in principles that apply also when the individual is himself exposed to some direct threat.

The problem is a very difficult one to tackle, but there appear to be two ways in which it can be approached. One is to expose the subjects to both a vicarious threat and a laboratory direct threat of the same type of content and compare the extent to which the pattern of reaction is the same or different. Another is to test the principles that have been developed in the vicarious experimental laboratory situation in a life-stress context.

The former approach was employed in a doctoral dissertation by Alfert (1964). Her vicarious stressor was a woodshop safety film in which three accidents occur: fingers are lacerated and cut off and a man is killed. To produce stress by direct threat, she told subjects they would receive a painful electric shock after the last of seven clicks. The clicks were timed to provide an anticipation period equal in time to that of a crucial film accident scene. Thus, the two threats were similar in general type, both involving physical assault and pain. One group of subjects saw the film twice, one group faced the direct threat of shock twice, one saw the film followed by the threat of shock, and the last group was threatened first with shock, then watched the film segment.

Alfert found that there was a high degree of similarity between the affective reactions in the same subjects to both kinds of threat. She also obtained substantal interindividual correlations between psychological and physiological levels of reaction to both stressors. Subjects who showed a strong reaction to one situation were also likely to show it in the other. Thus, the evidence favors the assumption that the dynamics of the vicarious and direct threat situations are similar (though probably not identical). This single experiment by no means closes the question, and the specific processes that overlap or differ are not explored by this study. But the evidence points to a useful degree of generalizability between a vicarious laboratory threat and a direct, real threat.

Psychodynamics of Stress

At the outset we indicated that the real-life range of sources of psychological stress has not been our main concern. Suitable films using interpersonal sources of stress have not been available to us, so we have used instead two films, both of which capitalize on physical threats to life and limb. One might reasonably expect these films to be universally threatening and therefore minimally interesting for the psychologist concerned with individual differences in sensitivity to varied kinds of threat. However, even these two rather similar films do differ in some interesting ways. The Subincision film is highly complex and ambiguous. Speisman, Lazarus, Davison, and Mordkoff (1964a) found that some subjects are stressed mainly by the scenes of the crude, mutilative operations on the boys' genitals; other subjects also show stress response to the scenes of nudity without physical harm; some subjects appear to be in a state of stress throughout the film, even during "neutral" scenes such as landscapes; and some subjects show little or no evidence of stress response during any part of the movie. Speisman et al. found that responsiveness to the three kinds of film content (mutilation, nudity, neutral) was in part a function of personality variables and in part a function of order of presentation of the various scenes, but these interactions were complex and only marginally significant. We have as yet no convincing explanation of the wide individual differences in response to the Subincision film. (The clear patterns of physiological and psychological response to the Subincision film, Fig. 1 for instance, are averaged data from many subjects. Such average data do not convey the variability of response among individuals.)

In sharp contrast with the Subincision film, the shop safety film, "It Didn't Have to Happen," produces a comparatively uniform pattern of stress response. Almost all subjects show sharp rises in physiological activation and subjective stress ratings during the three accident scenes. One could tell, from inspection of almost any single subject's physiological record, where the accident scenes occur, whereas identification of the Subincision film scenes would be possible only from averaged records of a number of individuals. In effect, the concordance among subjects watching the shop safety film is high, while it is low for Subincision. Consequently, if one wishes to study individual differences in reaction, the Subincision film, by its very complex and somewhat ambiguous nature, has great advantages. But if the emphasis of a study is on normative data, the Subincision film, requiring large numbers of subjects for stability of data, is less appropriate, and a film like that of shop safety is ideal. The threats carried by the Subincision film are indeed complex and cannot entirely be explained on the basis of the theme of castration or mutilation. More clinically centered observation further suggests that unusual features of the past experience of some subjects account for strong reactions (e.g., Lazarus & Speisman, 1960); homosexual fantasies in some subjects may be stimulated by observing the physical intimacy of the natives during the ritual. The methodological problems inherent in separating the various types of threat content from a complex film of this sort make it unsuited to an effective attack on the issue of threat content.

A second study of stimulus content, but one with quite a different purpose, was carried out by McGurk.[4] This study attacked the question of whether there would be consistency of reaction within subjects across two different films; in other words, the study asked not whether a group of subjects would show similar responses to the two films, but whether individuals who reacted strongly to one film, relative to the group, would also react strongly to the other film. This is, of course, a crucial question for laboratory research on individual differences in stress response: the existence of stable individual differences implies some considerable degree of consistency of response across moderately similar kinds of stressor films.

The design of the study by McGurk[4] was simple: 10 subjects were shown the Subincision film followed by the shop safety film; 10 subjects saw the two films in the reverse order; 10 subjects saw Subincision twice; and 10 subjects saw the safety film twice. It was found that in spite of the previously described differences in the general effects of the two films, there was a high degree of consistency of response within subjects to the two films for the physiological measures, skin conductance and heart rate.

---

[4] E. McGurk, R. S. Lazarus, and E. M. Opton, unpublished data, 1964.

In other words, there was a strong tendency for the subjects who showed the greatest skin-conductance reaction to the Subincision film to also show the greatest conductance reaction to the safety film. The correlations of the various skin-conductance and heart-rate measures over the two different films were almost as high as the test-retest reliability correlations for the subjects who viewed the same film twice.

Unfortunately, high positive correlations were *not* found for the psychological measures of subjective stress response and mood changes. Hence, it remains a distinct possibility that the positive physiological correlations are mainly a product of stable individual differences in physiological lability which may be independent of stimulus conditions. On the other hand, our disappointing results from the psychological dependent variables may reflect the inadequacy of measures of affective reaction based solely on a poststimulus, subjective check list. Or it may be that the considerable differences between the two films are more important than the superficial similarity of physical-assault threat in each. We cannot go much further on this problem until a larger range of film-threat themes are available.

THE PROBLEM OF ADAPTATION

In the study of reactions to the Subincision film (Lazarus *et al.*, 1962), and in subsequent studies as well, we observed that autonomic measures of stress reaction (especially skin conductance) showed higher levels during the first three operations than in the last three. It was possible that some kind of adaptation was occurring during the second half of the film. An alternative possibility, however, was that these later operation scenes were inherently less threatening than the ones at the beginning of the film, or that, as has been suggested in the psychophysiological literature, skin conductance may be inhibited when strong arousal states persist for a considerable time. A study by Weinstein[5] was designed to evaluate these possibilities. The findings appear to support two of the hypotheses: that there is adaptation during the film, and that the second series of operations are also intrinsically somewhat less disturbing.

The matter of adaptation remains an open research issue at this point, and the mechanism of the adaptation remains unknown. What happens to the subject during the film or afterwards which reduces the film's impact on subsequent presentations? And what conditions influence the degree of adaptation?

Problems produced by adaptation influence almost all our research. For instance, in a doctoral dissertation Riess (1964) had planned to study the

---

[5] J. Weinstein, unpublished data, 1964.

role of different kinds of "therapeutic" interactions occurring between two administrations of the Subincision movie. In one type of interaction, the "therapist" is supportive and encourages expression of feelings; in another he denies the opportunity for such expression; and in a third, the subject can only speak into a tape recorder, thus obtaining little or no social interaction. Riess did find that the nature of the interaction between the subject and interviewer influenced degree of autonomic disturbance when the film was shown again following the interview (the positive, accepting relationship proving most stress reducing). However, the differences were not very striking, in large part because of the adaptation in autonomic reaction between the first and second showings of the film. Very little of the physiological disturbance was left in the second showing, regardless of the type of interaction between experimenter and subject.

Davison (1963), too, found dramatic adaptation effects on repeated showings of the Subincision film. In his dissertation, the film was presented once a week for 3 successive weeks. The stressful impact of the film virtually disappeared on the second showing. Some of Davison's findings concerning the relationship between defensive types and adaptation are similar to those reported by Goldstein, Jones, Clemens, Flagg, and Alexander (1965) in a similar type of study.

It appears likely that adaptation is not simply a function of repetition of the stimulus. In Alfert's dissertation (1964), for example, repetition of the film showing woodshop accidents twice in the *same* session resulted in no adaptation at all. And the study by McGurk referred to earlier showed that if one stressful movie is followed by a different stressful movie, the second film yields quite as much physiological stress reaction as the first. In current pilot data, the film impact is found to hold over three successive sessions if the films shown in each session are different. If the same movie is shown twice during the same session, there is little or no adaptation.

The import of all these observations is that time between administrations of the same stressful movie appears necessary in order for marked adaptation to occur. In Alfert's procedure with the shop safety film, both administrations occurred in the same session, as they did in the study by McGurk. When a different film is shown after the first stressful movie, the subject must cope with an altogether new and different set of threatening film events, and adaptation does not occur. In both Davison's (1963) and Riess' (1964) studies, in contrast with the others, the showings of the Subincision film were separated by about 1 week. It would seem that whatever happens to produce adaptation requires time; how much time we do not know. Perhaps showing the film in sessions 1 day apart would produce the same degree of adaptation, or perhaps longer periods are required.

The critical question, of course, is what psychological events happen between viewings that account for the adaptation or the lack of it?

APPRAISAL: ITS MANIPULATION AND STUDY

In our judgment, the most significant work done within the project concerns the cognitive activity underlying the production and reduction of stress reaction. A key theoretical concept of psychological stress is that of *appraisal,* the evaluation by the individual of the harmful significance of some event. Threat occurs when a cue signifies to the individual that a harmful confrontation or experience may be anticipated. As was noted in our first experimental report on this concept (Speisman, Lazarus, Mordkoff, & Davison, 1964b), "Thus, the same stimulus may be either a stressor or not, depending upon the nature of the cognitive appraisal the person makes regarding the significance for him" (p. 367).

There is a close link between the process of threat appraisal and the concept of defense mechanism. The former is an initial judgment concerning the harmful portent of a stimulus. The latter is a reappraisal of the significance of a stimulus that was once regarded as threatening, but whose threat now is denied, isolated, projected, etc. Viewed in this way, there is a close connection between appraisal and reappraisal, or defense. Depending on the interplay of these processes, the same objective stimulus may or may not be threatening. Even the gruesome Subincision film might be viewed in a relatively benign light if the defensive modes of thought were successfully employed.

The method of the first study on appraisal (Speisman *et al.,* 1964b) was to create experimental sound tracks for the silent Subincision film. One sound track denied the harmful features of the events portrayed in the film. Not only did the sound track assert in official-sounding, travelogue-like voice and words that the adolescent participants in the genital operation were not mutilated or harmed by it or in significant pain, but also it was emphasized that they viewed the ritual positively and happily (reaction formation), since it permitted them to become adult, respected members of the tribe. A second sound track encouraged intellectualizing modes of thought. An anthropological view of the affair was presented in intellectualized and emotionally detached words and style. Attention was not diverted from the operation scenes. Quite the contrary, the operation procedures were described, but much as one might in a technical manual, so as to encourage remoteness from the feelings of the boys who were exposed to the procedure. A third sound track, the trauma track, emphasized the horror of the situation, the dread of the boys, and the harmful consequences that would befall some of the victims. A fourth condition was the original silent version, undoctored in any way.

The key findings of the study were that both denial and intellectualization sound tracks significantly reduced the stress reaction as measured through autonomic levels of arousal. The trauma track elevated the level of disturbance even over the silent version. There was evidence that some subjects, inclined to denial as a characteristic mode of defense, were benefited most by the denial sound track, that is, showed the largest stress reduction, while subjects disposed to intellectualization were helped more by the intellectualization track. But the evidence for this interesting interaction was not fully convincing. In any case, the data offered strong support for the proposition that threat depends on the manner in which a stimulus is appraised or evaluated. "Objectively" distressing stimulus events can be viewed without great stress reaction if these events are interpreted in comparatively nonthreatening ways. It appeared that we had developed a feasible method for evaluating the role of concurrent cognitive factors in stress production and reduction.

The interpretation that the stress reduction observed resulted from an effect on the appraisal of the stimulus events was tentative. The study suffers from the feature that the stress-reducing conditions of denial and intellectualization involved a continuous distraction in the form of speech which occurs frequently and sporadically throughout the film. The fact that the trauma track had an opposite effect from the "defensive" sound tracks mitigates this difficulty somewhat. But the model of appraisal is not ideally represented by a narrative played simultaneously with the viewing of the film.

A study by Lazarus and Alfert (1964) dealt with this limitation by substituting orientation statements presented before the film instead of sound tracks during the film. In one of the experimental conditions, the denial sound track was presented before the film-showing with minor changes to make it suitable for this change in position. In a second condition, the original denial sound track procedure was employed, and a third condition consisted of showing the film with no interpretation of any kind provided. The denial orientation resulted in the greatest reduction of autonomic stress reaction. The denial sound track was less effective, but it still reduced the stress as compared to the nonorientation condition. We reasoned that the superiority of the orientation prior to the film over the sound track during the film arose from the greater opportunity in the former condition for the subject to assimilate the full denial argument.

This study provided still more support for the concept of appraisal as a process crucial to stress reaction. It was also found that subjects disposed to denial defenses (as inferred from any of four questionnaire assessment devices, i.e., Hy denial, K, R, and R-S scales derived from the MMPI) gained more from the denial passage than subjects low in "denial disposition," thus supporting the interaction suggested in the earlier study by Speisman et al. (1964b). In the discussion of these findings, Lazarus and Alfert (1964) introduced the term "short-circuiting" to refer to the lowering of the expected stress reaction resulting from the prior prophylactic indoctrination.

Up to this point we had shown how sound tracks representing denial and intellectualizing modes of thought reduce stress reactions to the Subincision film. We had also demonstrated that denial will work even better when it is presented as an orientation prior to the showing of the film. A third study was needed to demonstrate the same thing for an intellectualization orientation and to determine whether the principle of short-circuiting of stress can be generalized to other types of threatening movies. Larazus, Opton, Nomikos, and Rankin (1965) have made use of the film, "It Didn't Have to Happen," which shows a series of woodshop accidents. In this film, a man has the tips of his fingers lacerated through carelessness in the use of safety devices. A foreman then gives a lecture on safety, illustrating it with the sad experience of one of the men whose story is told in flashback. First he is seen, as of today, with a finger missing. Then we see him with his finger intact operating the machine without safety guards. The abrupt loss of his finger follows with its momentary horror and spurting blood. A third more serious accident is then anticipated because one of the men who had at first heeded the foreman's warnings now returns to his old careless ways. Through his carelessness, a board is caught by a circular saw and rammed with tremendous force through the midsection of a fellow worker who happens to be passing by. He dies writhing on the floor, his companions looking on stunned.

The film provides a more strenuous test of the appraisal hypothesis, for it is clear, unambiguous, and much more pertinent to the real life of our subjects than a film about an almost-vanished stone-age culture. It might be fairly easy to manipulate appraisal of the Subincision film, since the meaning of the ceremony and the feelings of the aborigines are not clear, and yet difficult or even impossible to influence the appraisal of something as clearly defined and unambiguous as North American workers having their fingers cut off.

It has been shown that the accident film produces strong stress reactions in the viewers as a result of the dissertation research of Birnbaum (1964) and Alfert (1964). Birnbaum had observed that the three accidents produced distinct increases in levels of autonomic reaction, beginning with the periods of anticipation of the accidents. The issue tackled by Lazarus, Opton, Nomikos, & Rankin was whether orientation passages could also be successfully employed to reduce these stress reactions.

Three passages were created. In denial, it briefly stated that the people were actors and that the accidents did not actually occur, but were only enactments, skillfully done and realistic looking. Such a statement made sense from a rational point of view since subjects never believe that cameramen lay in wait for real accidents to occur. In one sense, the statement that the accidents are not real is a denial of the visual evidence, but it could also be regarded as assisting the individual to test reality better.

Intellectualization was imposed by encouraging the subjects to analyze the psychodynamics of the shop situation, for example, how the foreman attempted to induce the shop workers to use the safety devices. The implicit assumption in the intellectualization passage is that the accidents really happened, but the viewpoint of the subject is specifically directed to a detached analysis of certain psychological features of the situation and of the movie as a propaganda vehicle. The expectation was that subjects would be able to watch the distressing accidents with less evidence of stress reaction because the threatening features of the situation are affectively isolated by means of the intellectual examination of the interpersonal events.

The third passage was a control in which a brief description of the film contents was given. The findings again showed that both the denial and intellectualization orientations were successful in reducing skin-conductance and heart-rate levels over those levels found in the control condition. These data are portrayed graphically in Figs. 2 and 3. The study supports the findings of Lazarus & Alfert regarding denial, showing that an intellectualization orientation also short-circuits stress reaction. Of even greater importance, however, it shows that the principle of short-circuiting can be extended to other film-induced threats and is not limited to the esoteric Subincision film.

Appraisal can be dealt with by means of experimental manipulation as above, or by attempting to infer it from behavior and relating it to stimulus conditions. The latter approach has been followed in an incomplete study by Gerver. Using the Semantic Differential and estimates reported by the subject of the affective distress assumed to be experienced by the adolescent boys exposed to genital operations in the Subincision film, the correspondence between the subject's cognitions of the situation and his autonomic disturbance level were examined. It was found, for example, that benign film scenes led to benign appraisals compared with scenes judged *a priori* to be threatening. Moreover, relatively benign ap-

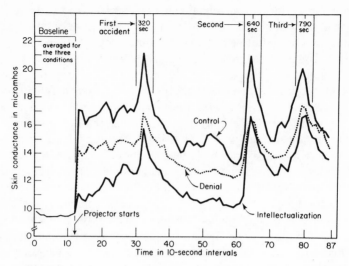

FIG. 2. Group-average skin conductance for three orientation treatments during the accident film. From Lazarus *et al.* (1965) and reproduced with the permission of Duke University Press.

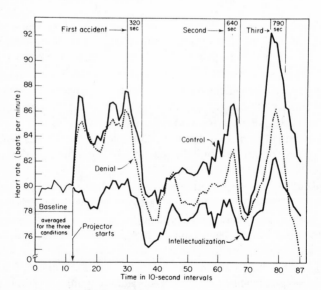

FIG. 3. Group-average heart rate for three orientation treatments during the accident film. From Lazarus *et al.* (1965).

praisals of the stressful operation scenes were associated with low levels of autonomic arousal, while threatening appraisals were associated with high levels of autonomic arousal. Here again, the intimate association between threat appraisal and stress reaction is observed.

Any condition that influences appraisal should also influence the degree of stress reaction. If an individual has had an immediately previous experience which weakens his estimate of his resources to master dangers, he should be more likely to appraise any new situation as threatening. In an incomplete study by Doyle, fraternity members were exposed to one of three kinds of social situations: rejection by their peers, acceptance by their peers, and a condition of no judgment by peers. Following this, they were shown the Subincision movie in the expectation that the supportive or damaging nature of this prior experience would influence the likelihood of subsequent threat appraisal of the film events. Individual differences in the importance of affiliation motives were also assessed to facilitate the prediction of degree of threat. Data collection has been completed and the autonomic data have been reduced, but the findings have not yet been fully analyzed.

Preliminary data from this study indicate that the prior treatments interacted with affiliation motivation to affect the level of autonomic arousal of subjects prior to and during the Subincision movie. Highest disturbance was found for the high affiliation group rejected by their peers, the next highest for the low affiliation rejected group, and the lowest levels of disturbance for high affiliation control subjects who were not exposed to peer judgments. The skin-conductance curves of each group are shown in Fig. 4. It appears that the effects occurred immediately following the prior treatment and influenced the "baseline" (*postrejection*) measurement of autonomic arousal. Since there is a very high correlation between baseline levels and Subincision-film levels, adjusting for these differences in baselines appears to remove the effects of the experimental treatments on level of arousal produced by the threatening movie itself. In other words, no effects could be observed on vulnerability to further threat as a result of the prior threatening experience. Instead, the entire level of disturbance was influenced, baseline period as well as Subincision-film period. Further analysis is needed to clarify these tentative observations.

Five other studies relevant to appraisal have been completed or are in progress. The first, a master thesis by Malmstrom (1963), provided weak evidence that expectation influences the degree of stress reaction. Subjects who had been led by prior experience in the experiment to expect a stressful film showed less stress reaction to the Subincision film than did subjects whose prior experience in the experiment had been with a benign film.

The second, a doctoral dissertation by Jones (1963), attempted two modifications in the defensive sound track approach to the Subincision film. One consisted of elaborating and employing only that portion of the intellectualization track which includes an abstract explanation of the meaning of the ritual. This sound track was compared with mere description of the film events. A second variable involved manipulation of degree

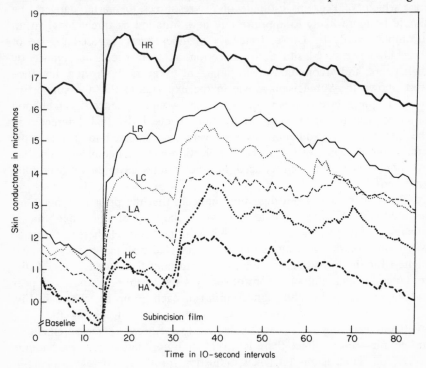

FIG. 4. Group-average skin conductance for combinations of affiliation need and peer judgment during baseline period and the Subincision film. H=high-need affiliation; L=low-need affiliation; R=rejection by peers; A=acceptance by peers; C=control (no peer judgment).

of positive identification with the boys on whom the subincision operation is performed. In one condition they were verbally portrayed as animal-like, deceitful, and treacherous. In another they were described positively in accordance with ego ideals. In a third condition, no characterization at all was offered. The two variables, type of explanation and type of identification, were factorially represented in the study. Our expectation had been that conditions which reduce degree of identification would also reduce degree of threat. However, interactions that were difficult to evaluate were observed between the two independent variables, leaving the main hypothesis about identification unsupported.

The two studies cited above leave the questions of the role of expectation and of identification in film-threat production and reduction still unresolved. In our view, these questions cannot be satisfactorily answered with films dealing only with physical danger or assault, but can be attacked through films dealing with a variety of interpersonal threats. Perhaps our negative findings with respect to identification occur because we identify readily even with the primitive man and share with him his human plight when he is attacked or suffers. Even a predatory beast would probably induce empathy if it were helpless and suffering. In other words, it is hard to make a suffering man or animal an unsuitable object of identification. Films dealing with interpersonal threats of different kinds should permit more effective variation in degree of identification on the part of different subjects, identification based on similarities and differences in the personal relevance of the experience and in the similarity of the identification object.

A third study (Weinstein, Lazarus, & Opton, 1965) was in part a pilot effort to work with interpersonal threat through specially created dramatic materials, and in part a replication of the dissertation by Jones (1963), using procedures which, it was hoped, would be more successful in manipulating degree of identification and its effect on stress response. In this experiment, women students listened to two tape recordings which purported to be psychotherapeutic counseling sessions with a female student. The first recording the subject heard was an initial session, in which the patient presented herself as a warm, sympathetic person (positive identification condition) or as a cold, hostile, sarcastic, disagreeable person (negative identification condition) or in which the therapist did most of the talking and one heard little from or about the patient (neutral identification condition). The second tape recording consisted of the cathartic recounting of a traumatic and humiliating escapade with a boy friend. The patient tells how she seduced the boy into a sexual attack on her, after which he left her in disgust. The "patient" breaks down in tears as she relives the experience.

One of the purposes of this experiment was to see whether it would be feasible to create and record original dramatic productions of selected stressful themes. The results, in terms of the effort required to produce the stimulus tapes, and in terms of the stressful effect of these tapes on our subjects, lead us to believe that the "made to order" stressful dramatization is practical.

On the main hypothesis of the experiment, that identification would determine the degree of stress induced by the tape recording, Weinstein *et al.* (1965) found no significant differences in stress response among identification conditions. However, since there were very large individual differences in actual degree of identification with the "victim" within each of the experimental manipulation conditions, the subjects were separated into new groups based on the actual degree of identification (independently measured), regardless of experimental condition. When the reported degree of identification by the individuals with the "victim" was thus used

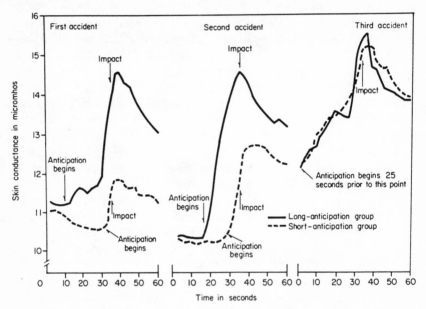

FIG. 5. Effects of long- and short-anticipation periods on skin conductance. The two groups differed in length of anticipation only for the first two filmed accident scenes; anticipation scenes for the third accident were the same for both groups.

as the criterion, some evidence was found that greater stress reaction occurred in individuals reporting more intense identification. This result cannot be taken as conclusive, because there were a small number of hypothesis-confirming results among a larger number of nonsignificant results. We must conclude, although we have found some tendency for degree of identification to influence appraisal of threat, that the tendency is either a very weak one or is obscured by inadequate measures of identification.

The fourth study[6] followed up on the finding by Speisman *et al.* (1964b) that two populations, airline executives and students, dif-

---

[6] C. A. Jones, Jr., E. M. Opton, and R. S. Lazarus, unpublished data, 1963.

fered in defensive disposition and in reaction to the denial and intellectualization sound tracks. We adopted the social psychological view that different
populations would have different preferred defensive modes. We tried to
test this by comparing a highly educated, presumably rather intellectualized
group of graduate students in the social sciences with an uneducated, labor-
ing group, presumably more likely to prefer denial as a defense. Subjects
in both groups were exposed to the Subincision film and treated in some

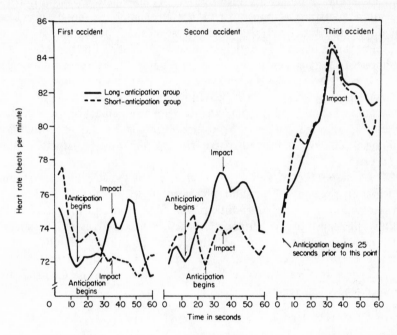

FIG. 6.   Heart-rate effects of long and short anticipation of filmed woodshop
accidents. Both experimental groups saw the same anticipatory scenes before the
third accident.

cases with the denial sound track and in other cases with the intellectualization sound track. The results failed to confirm the anticipated interaction
between socioeducational background and amount of stress reduction resulting from the different types of defensive sound tracks.

A fifth study on appraisal (Rankin, Nomikos, Opton, & Lazarus, 1965)
was concerned with the role of anticipation of harm in producing stress
reactions. For this study two versions of the industrial safety movie previously referred to were prepared. A "short-anticipation" version was
produced by deleting the footage in the film which leads the viewer to

anticipate the accidents. The deleted scenes, in which the workman's hands are seen approaching closer and closer to the blade, etc., amount to 15–30 seconds for each accident. A "long-anticipation" version of the film was created by splicing the footage removed from the short-anticipation version into the original film, after first reversing the spliced-in footage left to right so as to prevent detection of the duplication. The resulting film had prolonged anticipatory scenes lasting 30–60 seconds.

In the original film, with its normal-length anticipation scenes, much of the autonomic stress response occurs not at or after the bloody accidents, but during the anticipation of "danger" scenes. We thought that the appraisal of threat during the anticipation scenes might add to the total stressful impact of the accidents: the viewer not only watches the mutilation, he also must sit through the suspense of seeing the accident approaching and not knowing how serious it will be. On the other hand, we thought the appraisal of threat might also reduce the total stressful impact of the accidents, since it allows the viewer time to mobilize his psychological defenses (coping mechanisms) instead of confronting him with the stressful scene by surprise.

The results (Figs. 5 and 6) show clearly that the suspenseful, or long-anticipation version of the film produced more autonomic evidence of stress reaction than the short-anticipation film.[7] Even in the short-anticipation film, most of the autonomic reaction occurred in the very short anticipatory intervals, not in the impact and postimpact periods. This is consistent with the idea that it is the appraisal of threat—of potential or impending harm—rather than the confrontation with harm itself that produces the stress reaction.

Cross-Cultural Research

Dr. Lazarus spent the year 1963–1964 in Japan in order to begin an experimental examination of cultural influences in stress production and reduction. There is an absence of experimental work in which the same stimulus materials are presented to members of different societies and patterns of reaction directly compared.

Two interlocking experiments were performed.[8] In one experiment, the Subincision film was used, along with a Japanese control film portraying rice farming in Japan. The control film was presented first, followed by the

---

[7] The lengths of the anticipatory periods shown in Figs. 5 and 6 were different for the short-anticipation and long-anticipation groups for accidents one and two. For accident three, which was preceded by the same anticipatory period for all subjects, the two groups' autonomic curves were identical.

[8] Lazarus, Tomita, Opton, and Kodama, see footnote 3.

Subincision film, in a fashion similar to that followed in the study cited earlier (Lazarus *et al.*, 1962). However, four experimental conditions were imposed between the control and Subincision film. These were the denial orientation passage, the intellectualization passage, the trauma passage, and a no-orientation condition. The passages were translated into Japanese and recorded on tape. Near-continuous recording of degree of subjective distress was employed for both the control and Subincision films so that a curve of affective distress could be obtained, as well as a curve of skin conductance.

The experiments in Japan were designed to answer a number of questions relevant to cross-cultural comparison of the psychodynamics of stress. We wanted to know, for example, whether Japanese subjects would show as much stress reaction to the film as Americans; also, whether they would as frankly report their affective state, as judged by the degree of discrepancy between physiological and self-report measures; also we wanted to know whether their responses to the orientation passages of denial and intellectualization would be comparable to those found in the United States (perhaps, for example, their psychological makeup would favor reliance more on denial than on intellectualization). We also wanted to investigate whether the affective pattern in response to the Subincision film would be different in the two cultures.

Two experiments were performed, one with a college group comparable to Berkeley students, the other with an equally well educated, older group, 36–58 years of age, who had been reared within the older, prewar Japanese tradition. Because of limitations of time, the trauma orientation passage was omitted as a condition in the older sample.

The Japanese reported a pattern of subjective stress experience almost identical with American samples. At each operation scene reported distress was intense; in the benign scenes between operations, during a benign hair-tying sequence and during the control, rice-farming film, reported stress was very low. These ratings are shown for Japanese students, for the older Japanese sample, and for an American sample in Fig. 7.

Most of the questions we had originally posed could not be answered from the data collected in Japan because of a striking and unexpected difference between the Japanese and the Americans in their physiological reactions to the experiment as a whole. In the Japanese, unlike the Americans, skin-conductance changes paralleling subjective stress ratings did not appear. Instead, the Japanese group's skin conductance rose sharply at the outset of the control film and remained elevated until the baseline period between the films, when the subjects were told simply to relax, with the clear implication that the experiment was temporarily suspended. When the experiment was "resumed" with the start of the Subincision film, the conductance level rose again to a high level and remained high throughout the Subincision film. Figure 8 shows the skin-conductance data for the younger and the older Japanese, along with comparable American data.

The Japanese pattern of autonomic response appears similar to that found in a number of studies in psychiatric settings in which subjects with chronically high apprehension or anxiety and subjects low in anxiety were compared (Glickstein, Chevalier, Korchin, Basowitz, Sabshin, Hamburg,

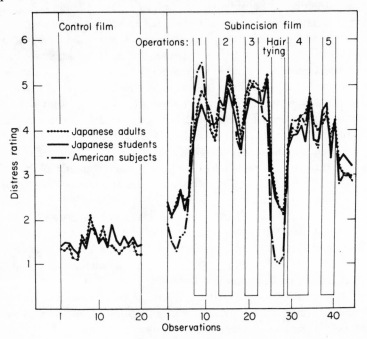

FIG. 7. Self-ratings of "distress" during neutral and stress films for Japanese college students, middle-aged Japanese, and an American student sample. The American data are reproduced from Mordkoff (1964) with the permission of the American Psychosomatic Society.

& Grinker, 1957; Persky, Korchin, Basowitz, Board, Sabshin, Hamburg, & Grinker, 1959). Highly anxious subjects in these studies appeared to react to the total experimental situation, showing no selective reaction to the specific threats imposed by the experimenters. Subjects low in anxiety, in contrast, showed a generally low level of physiological arousal, but reacted sharply to specific procedures designed to be threatening. The high-anxiety subjects were inclined to be generally apprehensive about new situations, but they did react to aspects of the experiment that threatened them.

Discussion with collaborating Japanese psychologists reinforced the impression that the Japanese subjects were indeed responding with apprehension to the total experimental situations. Impersonal observation by experimenters is a strange experience for the Japanese, rather alien to their social experience. There is also great sensitivity among the Japanese to

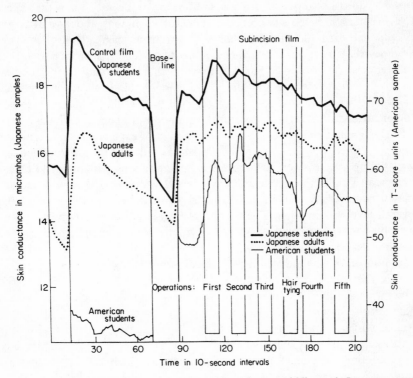

FIG. 8. Skin conductance for Japanese students, middle-aged Japanese, and American students during baseline periods, the neutral film, and the stress film. Note that the Japanese data are scaled in micromhos (left scale), while the American data are scaled in T scores (right scale); thus, only the patterns of the curves may be compared; the relative position of the American and Japanese data on the graph is arbitrary. The American data are from Lazarus *et al.* (1962) and are reproduced with the permission of the American Psychological Association.

being observed and evaluated by others. Placed in this experimental context, even though the experimenters were Japanese graduate students, it was the total experience of *being observed in the laboratory* that was threatening rather than the specific contents of the Subincision film, and their response indicates lack of autonomic selectivity in reaction. Their level of autonomic disturbance was as high during benign scenes and during the control film as during the operation scenes. It only dropped when the subject was told that nothing would happen for 5 minutes while he relaxed.

But what of the self-reports of affective distress which appeared entirely appropriate to the film contents and comparable to those of American populations? Several alternative explanations are possible. One is that the ups and downs of reported distress had nothing to do with the actual affective experience of the subjects, but reflected cognitions about what is appropriate during the various phases of the experiment. This, of course, assumes that the skin conductance more truly reflected arousal than the self-reports. On the other hand, it may be that in turning their attention to the specific content of the film, the Japanese could indeed discriminate the variations in their affective state caused by the film, without reference to concurrent affect with respect to the situation of being experimented on. The skin cannot choose to attend to one aspect of experience while ignoring another; hence, the overall level of arousal as reflected in skin conductance was so high as to overwhelm the smaller variations within the total experience. This is the explanation we favor. Moreover, skin conductance may become less sensitive as an indicator of variations in arousal when the overall level is very high. These and other alternatives can only be evaluated by further experiments. One is currently being conducted to test the assumption that generally apprehensive individuals will be insensitive to variations in threats induced during the experiment.

Further analyses of the Japanese data remain to be done, but the present indications are that some surprising and unexpected differences between the Japanese and American subjects have been found, differences which, *post hoc,* make great sense to the Japanese professionals and to our own reading of other experimental findings on the role of chronic anxiety in promoting generalized apprehension to the total experimental situation.

Concluding Statement

We have focused this essentially empirical report on the development of the motion-picture-film analogue of real-life psychological stress and on its application to methodological and substantive issues. We think that our findings on the appraisal of threat have pointed up the fruitfulness of a cognitive concept of psychological stress. There remain in the theory of psychological stress many difficult issues that we have not yet attacked.

The problem of individual differences is one such issue. Threat is produced when cues are interpreted by the individual as warnings of anticipated harm. We have defined harm in motivational terms as the thwarting of important goals. It is likely, therefore, that individual differences in motivational patterns are very important sources of variation in threat appraisal. Moreover, the stress-reaction patterns to the same stress situations vary greatly from individual to individual. Patterns of reaction to stress are undoubtedly determined by characteristics of personality, but we have given comparatively little attention to the personality determinants of coping processes. In this research we have only touched on some of these personality dispositions, in particular the defensive dispositions of the subjects as measured through questionnaire methods. Much more systematic work needs to be done.

With respect to motivational variables and the content of the threat (e.g., rejection, failure, bodily harm), it is likely that, in the context of human experience, frustrations of interpersonal and intrapersonal goals are as important as threats related to bodily harm, if not more so. Meaningful research on psychological stress requires that at some point we deal with the former, as well as the ecologically more rare threats such as electric shock, impalement by a piece of lumber, or the mutilation of the genitals as depicted in the esoteric Subincision film. Furthermore, it is our opinion that the identification of personality determinants of threat and coping will be favored by the utilization of interpersonal and intrapersonal threat themes. Thus, we must extend our film stimuli to these contents and attempt to evaluate the extent to which stress relations are consistent in given individuals over varying threat contents or are specific to particular types of threat.

Another exciting and pressing problem on which our research has barely touched is the divergence among the various types of stress-reaction indicators, that is, the fact that the inference derived from self-report or motor-behavioral indicators is often different from the inference derived from physiological indicators. Even within a single level of analysis, the physiological-autonomic, different response measures may yield different pictures of the intervening state of the individual. As we have stated earlier, we regard this lack of agreement not so much as a defect of the measures (although there are indeed multiple sources of error in each), but the result of particular intervening psychological processes which lead to different kinds of transactions with the situation, or different forms of coping which have their own specific response effects. Research must be designed to relate the different patterns of observable responses to the antecedent processes and conditions responsible for them. In our estimation, this is where increasing sophistication makes exciting advances most likely and where our particular laboratory analogue of psychological stress is most potent in making important contributions. The motion-picture-film approach makes it possible to record different levels and types of stress reaction simultaneously and to juxtapose them with normative data on the impact of the stressful stimulus. The places and conditions where the reactions diverge and converge can be readily monitored. It then becomes possible to evaluate theoretical conceptions of the intervening psychological processes of threat and coping that would account for the divergence or convergence.

For example, if we assume that three forms of attack as a form of coping with threat can occur—anger with behavioral expression, anger with its behavioral expression inhibited, or attack without anger—then we can make different predictions about the pattern of reactions among different indicators. In the first, when anger is experienced along with its behavioral expression in some aggressive act, we should find convergence among the behavioral, self-report, and physiological indicators. The individual will report anger, will show gestural-expressive signs of anger, and physiological changes, (e.g., hormonal secretions or autonomic patterns) compatible with this inference. If anger is experienced, but as a result of situational constraints it is inhibited from expression and denied, the self-report indicator will contradict the physiological reaction pattern, and there may or may not be expressive signs of anger, depending on the individual's ability to control such expresssive acts. Finally, if attack occurs without anger, only the motor-behavioral signs will necessarily reflect the instrumental act since the individual may experience and report no anger; the physiological pattern of reaction should relate to general mobilization rather than to a specific kind of emotion such as anger, since anger is not being experienced.

In any event, however we conceptualize psychological stress processes, the most exciting task is to evolve rules that relate these processes to a complex of antecedent conditions and consequences. We see clearly that at both ends of this analysis, cause and effect, the interplay of variables is complex and not readily subject to simple generalizations. Our perspective is to keep the laboratory study of psychological stress as close in form to the natural event as is consistent with the need to control and measure the most important variables. To this end, the simultaneous use of several response variables at different levels of analysis, behavioral and physiological, seems to offer the best chance of clarifying the relationships that exist in life stress.

In looking back over the work accomplished during the past 5 years, we think that the motion-picture analogue of psychological stress has been shown to be extremely promising for the study of many problems that are rather refractory to other methods. It now seems possible that this method will allow us to come to terms with issues that are of central importance in clinical and field research, but which have seldom been tackled in controlled, laboratory experimentation.

REFERENCES

Äas, A. *Mutilation fantasies and autonomic response.* Oslo: Olso Univer. Press, 1958.

Alfert, Elizabeth. Reactions to a vicariously experienced and a direct threat. Unpublished doctoral dissertation, Univer. of California, Berkeley, 1964.

Birnbaum, R. M. Autonomic reaction to threat and confrontation conditions of psychological stress. Unpublished doctoral dissertation, Univer. of California, Berkeley, 1964.

Davison, L. A. Adaptation to a threatening stimulus. Unpublished doctoral dissertation, Univer. of California, Berkeley, 1963.

Glickstein, M., Chevalier, J. A., Korchin, S. J., Basowitz, H., Sabshin, M., Hamburg, D. A., & Grinker, R. R., Sr. Temporal heart-rate patterns in anxious patients. *A.M.A. arch. neurol. Psychiat.,* 1957, **78**, 101-106.

Goldstein, M. J., Jones, R. B., Clemens, T. L., Flagg, G. W., & Alexander, F. G. Coping style as a factor in psychophysiological response to a tension-arousing film. *J. pers. soc. Psychol.,* 1965, **1**, 290-302.

Jones, C. A., Jr. The effects of intellectualization and identification upon psychological reaction to stress. Unpublished doctoral dissertation, Univer. of California, Berkeley, 1963.

Krause, M. S. The measurement of transitory anxiety. *Psychol. Rev.,* 1961, **68**, 178-189.

Lacey, J. I. Psychophysiological approaches to the evaluation of psychotherapeutic process and outcome. In E. A. Rubinstein and M. B. Parloff (Eds.), *Research in psychotherapy.* Washington, D. C.: Amer. Psychol. Ass., 1959. Pp. 160-208.

Lazarus, R. S. A program of research in psychological stress. In J. G. Peatman and E. L. Hartley (Eds.), *Festschrift for Gardner Murphy.* New York: Harper, 1960. Pp. 313-329.

Lazarus, R. S. A laboratory approach to the dynamics of psychological stress. *Amer. Psychol.,* 1964, **19**, 400-411.

Lazarus, R. S. Psychophysiological reactions during emotional stress. Unpublished paper delivered at Sympos. held at the Karolinska Hospital, Stockholm, 1965. (a)

Lazarus, R. S. The dynamics of emotions: Autonomic and behavioral effects. Unpublished paper delivered at Western Psychol. Ass. meeting, Honolulu, June, 1965. (b)

Lazarus, R. S. *Psychological stress and the coping process.* New York: McGraw-Hill, 1966.

Lazarus, R. S., & Alfert, Elizabeth. The short-circuiting of threat by experimentally altering cognitive appraisal. *J. abnorm. soc. Psychol.,* 1964, **69**, 195-205.

Lazarus, R. S., Opton, E. M., Jr., Nomikos, M. S., & Rankin, N. O. The principle of short-circuiting of threat: Further evidence. *J. Pers.,* 1965, **33**, 622-635.

Lazarus, R. S., & Speisman, J. C. A research case-history dealing with psychological stress. *J. Psychol. Stud.,* 1960, **11**, 167-194.

Lazarus, R. S., Speisman, J. C., & Mordkoff, A. M. The relationship between autonomic indicators of psychological stress: Heart rate and skin conductance. *Psychosom. Med.,* 1963, **25**, 19-30.

Lazarus, R. S., Speisman, J. C., Mordkoff, A. M., & Davison, L. A. A laboratory study of psychological stress produced by a motion picture film. *Psychol. Monogr.,* 1962, **76**, No. 34 (Whole No. 553).

Malmstrom, E. J. The role of expectation in the production of threat. Unpublished master's thesis, Univer. of California, Berkeley, 1963.

Malmstrom, E. J., Opton, E. M., Jr., & Lazarus, R. S. Heart rate measurement and the correlation of indices of arousal. *Psychosom. Med.,* 1965, **27**, 546-556.

Martin, B. The assessment of anxiety by physiological behavioral measures. *Psychol. Bull.,* 1961, **58**, 234-255.

Mordkoff, A. M. The relationship between psychological and physiological responses to stress. *Psychosom. Med.,* 1964, **26**, 135-150.

Opton, E. M., Jr., Rankin, N. O., & Lazarus, R. S. A simplified method of heart rate measurement. *Psychophysiology,* 1966, **2**, 87-97.

Persky, H., Korchin, S. J., Basowitz, H., Board, F. A., Sabshin, M., Hamburg, D. A., & Grinker, R. R., Sr. Effect of two psychological stresses on adrenocortical function. *A.M.A. arch. neurol. Psychiat.,* 1959, **81**, 219-226.

Rankin, N. O., Nomikos, M. S., Opton, E. M., Jr., & Lazarus, R. S. The roles of surprise and suspense in stress reaction. Unpublished paper delivered at Western Psychol. Ass. meeting, Honolulu, June, 1965.

Riess, W. F. The effect of psychotherapy-like interviews upon adaptation to psychological stress. Unpublished doctoral dissertation, Univer. of California, Berkeley, 1964.

Schwartz, B. J. An empirical test of two Freudian hypotheses concerning castration anxiety. *J. Pers.,* 1956, **24**, 318-327.

Speisman, J. C., Lazarus, R. S., Davison, L. A., & Mordkoff, A. M. Experimental analysis of a film used as a threatening stimulus. *J. consult. Psychol.,* 1964, **28**, 23-33. (a)

Speisman, J. C., Lazarus, R. S., Mordkoff, A. M., & Davison, L. A. Experimental reduction of stress based on ego-defense theory. *J. abnorm. soc. Psychol.,* 1964, **68**, 367-380. (b)

Speisman, J. C., Osborn, Janet, & Lazarus, R. S. Cluster analysis of skin resistance and heart rate at rest and under stress. *Psychosom. Med.,* 1961, **23**, 323-343.

Weinstein, J., Lazarus, R. S., & Opton, E. M., Jr. The influences of degree of identification on vicariously experienced stress. Unpublished paper delivered at Western Psychol. Ass. meeting, Honolulu, June, 1965.

Wundt, W. M. *Outlines of psychology.* (3rd ed.) London: Williams & Norgate, 1907.

CHAPTER 11

Anxiety and the Interruption of Behavior[1]

George Mandler and David L. Watson

DEPARTMENT OF PSYCHOLOGY,
UNIVERSITY OF CALIFORNIA,
SAN DIEGO, CALIFORNIA

AND

PSYCHOLOGY DEPARTMENT,
UNIVERSITY OF TORONTO,
TORONTO, CANADA

Psychologists have long been concerned with the necessary and sufficient conditions that produce the anxiety state. We shall deal here with one such antecedent condition—the interruption of behavior. While we will deal with the effects of interruption upon behavior, it is not our aim to present a general theory of interruption, but to deal specifically with the relationship between interruption and anxiety. The argument to be developed is that the interruption of an organized behavioral sequence will, under certain specifiable conditions, serve as a condition sufficient to evoke anxiety.

---

[1] The research reported in this chapter was supported by grant no. HD 00912 from the U.S. Public Health Service to George Mandler, and by grant no. 67 from the Ontario Mental Health Foundation to David L. Watson. The first study reported was designed and supervised by Mandler, the second by Watson. The preparation of this paper was the joint responsibility of the two authors. We gratefully acknowledge the aid of our experimental assistants, Donna Scott, Luby Prytulak, and Andrew Solandt.

Interruption Theory

ORGANIZATION AND INTERRUPTION

In this section we shall review briefly the general arguments advanced for the importance and function of organization and interruption. The position has been discussed in detail elsewhere (Mandler, 1964), but a review of its basic assumptions is necessary for a development of our major theme.

In the first instance, interruption theory deals with organized behavior. In the present paper we shall extend it also to the development and organization of cognitive sequences, what Miller, Galanter, and Pribram (1960) have called plans. Organized behavior has one major characteristic, namely its unitary nature. Previous work on response organization and integration (Mandler, 1954; Mandler, 1962a; Mandler, 1964) has suggested that when discrete units of behavior are organized, the new unit behaves in the same unitary fashion as its previous constituents. Once initiated, organized responses run off smoothly and without pause; they have an inevitability of completion which is just as determined in long sequences as it is in such short sequences as speaking a word, pressing a button, or swallowing food. It has been suggested that these organized responses are centrally represented in the forms of analogic structures (Mandler, 1962a). These structures and their novel combinations are analogous to plans and also have sequential, unitary properties.

The initiation of a plan functions like a template, laying out the course of a sequence of overt behavior. Thus expectations are not conceived as a looking toward some desired goal, but rather as the laying down of a plan which involves the whole sequence of behavior or anticipated behavior from its initiation to its completion. Organized response sequences, or plans, are not means leading to an end; on the contrary, it seems impossible to speak of pure goals. Rather than consider end states to be desired or anticipated, it is more useful to look at response sequences to be performed by the organism. Such plans, sequences, and goal paths function as units and include both the means and the ends, not differentiable goals and paths to them. It is the interruption of such plans and goal paths that will concern us here.

All that is implied by the idea of interruption is that an organized sequence which has been initiated cannot be completed, or that a plan cannot be executed. Interruption necessarily implies that the blocking of the sequence has not been anticipated by the organism, since if the blocking is anticipated, it will necessarily become part of the plan. A drive into the country is not interrupted by a broken bridge if one knows beforehand that the bridge has in fact been washed out.

The general proposition on the effects of interruption has been stated by Mandler (1964): the interruption of an integrated response sequence produces a state of arousal which will be followed by emotional behavior.

Before dealing with the problem of arousal, three other consequences of interruption should be mentioned. In the first instance, it is assumed that a tendency to completion exists as long as the situation remains essentially unchanged. The interrupted organism will often persist in its efforts to complete the sequence. Another apparent and frequent consequence is the increased vigor with which the interrupted sequence is pursued. Either repetition or increased vigor might produce completion. If such a course is successful, the sequence is not appreciably altered. The third reaction, and frequently the more adaptive of the three, is the tendency to response substitution. Substitution of an alternate segment for the one that interruption or blocking prevent from execution leads to the completion of a substitute sequence. The assumption is that whenever the organism is prevented from completing any one organized sequence, he will, whenever possible, complete the sequence by substituting some other, even only tangentially relevant, organized response.

EMOTIONAL CONSEQUENCES OF INTERRUPTION

Interruption leads to a state of arousal. Following the two-factor theory of emotion developed by Schachter (Mandler, 1962b; Schachter & Singer, 1962) such (visceral) arousal sets the stage for a wide variety of different emotions, the specific character of which is determined by environmental and cognitive factors. Thus interruption in the absence of completion or substitution leads to the visceral precondition for emotional behavior, the exact nature of which will be determined by the specific occasions that accompany the interruption. While the emotional consequences of interruption need not be noxious or aversive, the present discussion will be mainly concerned with the distressing, unpleasant consequences of interruption.

What are the occasions that turn the arousal engendered by interruption into distress or anxiety? Mandler (1962b) has previously hypothesized that the emotion of choice is anxiety when the onset or offset of the visceral arousal is not under control of the organism. Thus, when no response is available whereby the arousal initiated by the interruption can be terminated, the emotion to be expected would be anxiety, distress, or fear. In other words, anxiety should appear when the organism, interrupted in the midst of well-organized behavior sequences or in the execution of a well-developed plan, has no alternate behavior available. The inability to complete a sequence and the unavailability of alternate completion sequences produce helplessness, a behavior sequence that has been initiated but which cannot be completed; the organism does not "know" what to do. The lack of adequate sequences and the absence of what, in another language, might be called purposeful behavior define the disorganized organism. Helplessness and disorganization *are* anxiety.

The major consequences of interruption and the absence of relevant or suitable behavioral strategies will be continuing visceral arousal and disruption of any other ongoing behavior sequences. One reason for the disorganized aspect of anxiety-dominated behavior is that with interruption and arousal a search for relevant substitutable behaviors is initiated. As long as such a search—seen often as inefficient attempts at initiating a variety of different behaviors—is unsuccessful, as long as the sequence is incomplete, further arousal will continue, more disorganization will result, and the typical picture of interference due to anxiety will emerge. We have already pointed out how the discovery of some apparently satisfactory substitute acts may control the arousal. Such acts, when nonadaptive, are called neurotic symptoms (Mandler, 1964).

The general function of organized behavior as an inhibitor of distress has been discussed by Kessen and Mandler (1961). These authors have discussed the origin of the distress or anxiety reaction and have suggested that organized behavior, starting in the newborn, controls or inhibits distress. Conversely, the interruption of organized behavior disinhibits the distress reaction.

In the following sections, two effects, changes in arousal and disruption of performance, will be discussed in the light of two sets of experiments. The first set will recapitulate some findings on the effects of interruption; the second will deal with the effect of behavior substitution on the anxiety produced by interruption.

Previous Studies on the Effects of Interruption

Mandler (1964) has reported studies on the effects of interruption on the behavior of rats and humans.

ANIMAL STUDIES

The inability to complete a well-learned response sequence should, as we have pointed out, produce distress or anxiety in the organism. Mandler (1964) has illustrated the relation between this notion and other approaches to the problem of anxiety (e.g., Hebb, 1946) and the concept of nonreward (e.g., Amsel, 1962). Amsel's development of the concept of frustration relates its appearance to the absence of reward in a situation in which the organism has been consistently rewarded. The most obvious method that produces such a contingency is, of course, the typical extinction procedure. There is nothing novel about a prediction that extinction, i.e., nonreward, produces excitement or frustration. What is of further interest is the behavior available to an animal during extinction. Presumably a hungry animal who fails to find food where food had previously been provided will then search for food in the maze or in the general vicinity of the goal box. Food searching is an alternate, previously practiced sequence of behavior available to the animal. What happens, however, when food searching behavior is not available in the animal's repertory? Presumably the degree of excitement should be much greater. Not only has the animal's previously practiced sequence been interrupted, but he also has no substitute readily available to control his state of distress.

The first study addressed itself to this question. The availability of food-searching behavior was removed by running animals during extinction under deprived as well as satiated conditions. An animal who has organized a running-to-food sequence should continue such behavior to some extent even when satiated. However, the probability of food-searching behavior is extremely low under conditions of satiation. Thus, extinction procedures for satiated animals should produce greater distress or excitement than for deprived animals. In this early study, animals in a Y-maze learned a brightness discrimination while hungry with a large food pellet as a reward. They were then given extinction trials under two conditions: *deprived,* i.e., the previous maintenance schedule was continued and the animals were 24-hours hungry when introduced to the maze; *satiated,* i.e., animals were put on an ad-lib regimen as well as fed just prior to their introduction to the maze. Under these conditions, a rather novel and interesting finding emerged. Satiated animals exhibited extremely excited behavior during extinction which increased with successive trials. The behavioral manifestation of this excitement was the presence of jerky or convulsive movement. While this behavior is relatively rare in the usual learning experiment, it was observed in this study with high frequency and reliability. It usually involved sudden jerks of the body and legs which sometimes developed into convulsions that immobilized the animal for several seconds. This disorganized behavior occurred in animals who not only had been interrupted in the completion of an organized sequence, but who also, through the introduction of satiation, were deprived of any other situationally relevant behavior. Distress, if that is what we want to call this disorganized behavior, is related to the unavailability of alternative responses.

HUMAN STUDIES

In the extinction study it was shown that interruption of a well-organized sequence will, in the absence of available substitute behavior, lead to marked distress. In another series of studies reported by Mandler (1964) the interruption of verbal sequences in human subjects was studied.

The method of choice consisted of serial learning of verbal sequences, primarily sentences. Subjects heard the words of a sentence at 3-second intervals and were instructed to anticipate the next word in the interval. After they had mastered this sequence of hearing a word, saying the next word, and so forth, they were interrupted, i.e., they heard a word other than the one they had anticipated. The sequence of saying a word and hearing it was interrupted. When the sequences had been overlearned the interruption produced greater arousal, as measured by the subjects' GSR, than when the sequence had been learned to mastery only. Similarly, when a sequence was easily learned, i.e., was easily organized, the interruption also produced greater arousal than when the sequence was more difficult to integrate. Parenthetically, it might be noted that word sequences, which are based on extensive prior overlearning of syntax and other verbal habits, produce greater arousal when interrupted than do sequences of digits.

Other experiments investigated the effect of the relevance or irrelevance of the interruption and of the locus of interruption on behavioral disorganization. Relevant interruptions were those in which the word substituted in the sequence fit the syntactic and semantic requirements of the position they occupied; irrelevant words did not. Change of locus varied the position in the sentence where the interruption occurred. It was found that relevant interruptions produce less behavioral disorganization than irrelevant ones; they are more easily fitted into the organized sequence. Interruption at the beginning of a sentence was generally more disrupting than interruption later when the sequence had been nearly completed.

In general these data support the general notion that interruption does produce emotional behavior and that it is related to the organization of the interrupted behavior.

We shall now turn to two other experiments, both concerned with the problem of substitution and the availability of substitute or alternate responses under conditions of interruption.

An Experiment on Substitute Behavior during Extinction

PROBLEM

In the animal experiment reported by Mandler (1964) satiated animals showed signs of distress under extinction conditions. The question to be raised here is whether the disorganization of the satiated animals can be controlled by providing them with alternate response sequences. The attempt to do so was based on training the animals to complete another response sequence during extinction.

METHOD

All animals were raised with littermates of the same sex. Two weeks prior to the start of training they were put on a 24-hour maintenance schedule. Acquisition consisted of 10 trials per day on a brightness (black-white) discrimination in a Y-maze. Four to 5 days before acquisition started and throughout acquisition the animals were given substitute behavior training. After the completion of the 10 daily acquisition trials, each animal was placed in a goal box the same color as the nonreinforced (S-) box, e.g., a white goal box if reinforcement followed entering the black door to a black goal box. This goal box contained a littermate of the same sex, and the two animals were separated by a wire mesh. The two animals remained in these S- like goal boxes for 20 to 30 minutes and were then returned to their individual cages. Animals were run on alternate days and for each pair one animal would be running while the other would serve as a companion, with the reverse being the case on the following day.

In this fashion it was expected that an association between the S- goal box and the presence of a known animal would develop, so that the experience of being in a known and familiar situation could substitute for the absent food.

All animals were given identical acquisition training to a criterion of 90% correct on 2 successive days plus 2 additional days (20 trials). At the conclusion of acquisition training the 48 animals were divided into six groups and given extinction trials. Half of the animals were continued on a deprivation schedule, while the other half were satiated as in the previous experiment. Each of these two groups was again divided into three subgroups:

(a) *Animal-present.* The companion animals were present in the S- goal box during extinction. They were again kept behind a wire mesh, but an animal could open the door to the S- box, enter the S- goal box, and then either stay there or retrace his steps.

(b) *Animal-absent.* These animals were treated in the same fashion as the previous groups except that no companion was present in the S- box.

(c) *Control.* The animals were run as in the previous experiment with the S- door locked.

All animals continued to receive companion training during extinction.

RESULTS

The only data to be presented here concern the manifestation of the jerky and convulsive movements during extinction. Figure 1 shows these data for 7 days (70 trials) of extinction. The first obvious finding is that the difference between satiated and deprived animals has been replicated, $F(1,36) = 22.99$, $p < .001$. The highly significant difference indicates that satiated animals show more of the jerky and convulsive behavior than do the deprived animals. In addition there is a significant interaction of trials

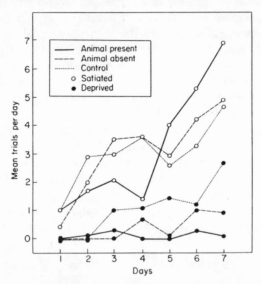

FIG. 1.   Mean trials per day (out of 10 trials) on which the jerky and convulsive behavior appeared for the six experimental groups. $N = 8$ per group.

by deprivation condition by substitute condition, $F(12,216) = 3.16$, $p < .001$. The significant part of this variance is taken up by the comparison between the *animal-present–satiated* group, and the other two satiated groups. There is a significant depression in jerky and convulsive behavior for the satiated animal-present group which dissipates after 40 trials. Thereafter, these animals recover their agitation over and above the other two groups. The presence and availability of the S- box alone produces no difference in agitation from the control group. It might be added that all animals entered or attempted to enter the S- box.

The experiment clearly produces the predicted inhibition or control of extreme excitation when an alternate response sequence is provided for the animals. The therapeutic effect of alternative behavior available to the distressed animals is, however, transitory. At first the alternate behavior suppresses distress but later it apparently loses its effectiveness; the satiated animals show even higher levels of agitation. This adaptation effect to the alternate behavior deserves further attention.

An Experiment on Choice and Anxiety

INTRODUCTION

Mowrer and Viek (1948, p. 193) have stated that ". . . a painful stimulus never seems so objectionable if one knows how to terminate it as it does if one has no control over it." In the Mowrer and Viek study, two groups of rats were trained to approach a certain place to feed. Following mastery of this task, both groups were shocked at the place where they had been fed. One group had available an instrumental response, jumping, which terminated the shock, but the other group of animals had no such instrumental response available to turn off the shock. The second group was yoked to the first, however, so that the amount and duration of the shock was identical for the two groups. Mowrer and Viek found that the group which had an instrumental response available showed much less disruption of the previously learned approach behavior than did the group which had no escape response available. Haggard (1943) demonstrated that human subjects who could administer a standard electric shock to themselves, compared to subjects who had the shock administered by the experimenter, showed less anxiety—as measured by GSR deflection. Stotland and Blumenthal (1964) told two groups of subjects that they were going to take an IQ test which was composed of several subtests. One group was informed that they could take the various subtests in any order they wished, while the second group was informed that they must take the subtests in a prescribed order. The group which was offered a choice of the order of taking the subtests showed no increase in GSR during the instruction period, but the group which did not have a choice did show a significant increase in GSR.

These three studies all demonstrate that if the organism has some control over the onset and offset of potentially stressful stimuli, or even if it simply expects to have such control, there is likely to be less anxiety or arousal. The essential element of the independent variable in each of these studies is a variation in the amount of control which the subject has over interruption. Control, even if it is control of some unpleasant, potentially interrupting event, makes it possible for the organism to plan the sequence of events to occur. Interruption is an arousing or noxious event if the expected sequence of events, i.e., the sequence that has been initiated, fails to run off in the prescribed manner. When the organism exercises control, however, the potential "interruption" becomes part of the plan and thus is not an interruption any more. The sequence "response → shock" when planned and executed in this way does not produce interruption since shock is expected and made part of the sequence.[2] We expect therefore that any time the organism is given control or choice, which may even involve an unpleasant event, the absence of interruption of a planned sequence should produce less anxiety than the occurrence of shock or failure when it has not been made part of the planned behavior sequence.

Furthermore, if the subject has a choice between a stressful task and a nonstressful one, then the choice of the latter following stress or failure also offers an alternate response to complete a success-seeking or failure-avoiding sequence. It follows that subjects who are able to exercise some control over the sequential order of stressful and innocuous tasks will evince less disruption of performance than will those who have no such control, even though all subjects must eventually deal with the same tasks.

If the subject is placed in a situation in which he must perform two tasks, only one of which is potentially anxiety-producing (e.g., failing an IQ test), and if the subject can determine the temporal order in which he deals with the two tasks, his anxiety will be less than if he cannot control the order. Under these conditions, performance on the potentially stressful task will be better. The first purpose of this study was to investigate the effects of a control or no-control condition to test the above hypothesis. A second purpose was to examine possible interactions of certain personality differences with the control and no-control conditions.

METHOD

The study began by administering a Canadian form of the Test Anxiety Questionnaire (Mandler & Sarason, 1952) to 283 students in an introductory psychology class. Sixteen subjects were randomly selected, respectively, from the top and bottom 15% of the TAQ distribution. Within the resultant high and low anxiety groups, subjects were randomly assigned to a control or no-control condition. The 2 × 2 design—high or low anxiety and control or no-control—had eight subjects in each of the four cells. Half the subjects in each cell were male, and half female.

Two experimenters were used, and each served for half the subjects

[2] It should be noted that the interruption of a sequence containing an unpleasant event will also have emotional consequences, though not necessarily unpleasant or noxious ones. For example, extreme euphoria can often be found when a planned-for unpleasant (even dreaded) event, such as a shock, fails to materialize. Here arousal sets the stage for a pleasant emotion.

in each cell. The experimenters did not know whether their subjects were high or low anxious.

On entering the experimental room, subjects were given a sheet of mimeographed instructions. The gist of these was that the purpose of the study was to compare two IQ tests. One was very old and well established as a valid measure of intelligence—called the Standard Individual Intelligence Test (SIIT)—and the other was brand new and of unknown validity—called the Preliminary Experimental Group Form (PEGF). Actually, the two tests were the two forms of the Wechsler-Bellevue Digit Symbol Subtest. Their identification as the SIIT or PEGF was, of course, balanced between all conditions of the design. Subjects were instructed that they would take each test five times "so that we can get enough data to make a meaningful comparison between the two tests." Thus they had 10 trials, 5 on each test.

The subjects were led to believe that they should expect to finish the SIIT within the allotted time period. The instructions read, "The test is designed so that it should be fairly easy for the average university student to finish within the time period. You should have little difficulty in finishing it, at least by the second or third time." Concerning the PEGF, subjects were told, "We don't know whether this test is easy or hard. Therefore, you should not necessarily expect to finish it within the time period." It was further implied that, while performance on the SIIT would be a quite valid indicator of one's IQ, performance on the PEGF was meaningless because the test was still in a trial period. The subjects were not given sufficient time to complete either test, i.e., they were given only 50 seconds for each test.

Subjects in the control condition were given completely free choice to take the 5 trials on each test in any order they wished. Just before each of the 10 trials they told the experimenter which of the two tests they wanted to take on that trial. No-control subjects were told that "for administrative reasons" they had to take the tests in a particular sequence, and were informed which test they would take at the beginning of each trial. All subjects were instructed that the sequence in which they took the tests had previously been found not to affect a person's score. The order chosen by control subjects was recorded, and each subject in the no-control condition was yoked to one in the control condition. Hence, there were no differences between conditions in the sequential order of the two tests.

Each subject took each test five times. No subject had sufficient time to finish either test, and the number of items per line was varied from trial to trial for each test so that it would be difficult for a subject to tell whether or not he was improving. At the end of trials 1 and 3 on the SIIT the subject was reminded that he should be able to finish within the time limit, and at the end of trials 1 and 3 on the PEGF he was told that his failure to finish probably indicated that something was wrong with the test. After completing the 10 trials, the subjects were asked to complete additional material in the following order: (1) a sheet on which they were asked to recall as many of the symbols as they could; (2) parts of the Nowlis and Nowlis (1956) Adjective Check List; (3) a brief questionnaire.[3] Following this, the purpose of the experiment was explained and the subjects were reassured concerning their performance.

RESULTS

Figure 2 presents the performance data of subjects on the SIIT. The hypotheses were that low anxious subjects would perform at a higher level

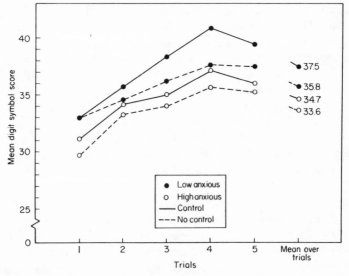

FIG. 2.   Mean digit symbol subtest performance on the SIIT over 5 trials. $N = 8$ per group.

than high anxious subjects, and that control subjects would show higher performance levels than no-control subjects. Analyses of variance were performed for each of the 5 trials, and for mean score over the 5 trials. The trial by trial analyses yielded no significant differences. It can be seen from the figure that the performance scores were in the predicted direction. On the mean performance on the SIIT over all 5 trials there were significant

---

[3] Not all of the analyses performed will be reported here.

differences between groups both for the anxiety condition, $F(1,28) =$ 18.61, $p < .001$, which replicates earlier studies (cf., Sarason, 1960), and for the control condition, $F(1,28) = 5.71$, $p < .025$. Thus, exercising choice over the order of taking the two tests, produces a significant increment in performance.

There were no significant differences or conspicuous trends between groups on performance on the PEGF. There were no significant interactions between anxiety and control conditions on either test.

Table I presents the mean combined number of symbols recalled for the SIIT and the PEGF. There was no difference between the low and high

TABLE I
MEAN NUMBER OF SYMBOLS RECALLED

Group	Control group	No-control group
Low anxiety	9.1	6.0
High anxiety	9.4	5.1

anxiety groups, but there was a significant difference between the control and no-control groups, $F(1,28) = 6.97$, $p < .025$. Out of a possible score of 18 symbols correctly recalled, the mean for the control groups was 9.25, and that of the no-control groups was 5.55.

These results were the major differences observed between the control and no-control conditions. We will report two other observations which are relevant to the low versus high anxiety dichotomy.

The pattern of choices made by the subjects in the control condition was analyzed. By noting whether a subject first completed the set of 5 trials on the SIIT or on the PEGF, an index of the subject's pattern of choices could be obtained. Six of the low anxious subjects completed the PEGF trials first, and two completed the SIIT trials first, while the ratio for the high anxious subjects was exactly reversed, χ^2 (1 df) $= 4.0$, $p < .05$. The high anxious subjects tended to persevere on the SIIT more than did the low anxious subjects.

Some theorists (Child, 1954; Mandler & Sarason, 1952) have hypothesized that the problem the high anxious subject faces is that, when confronted with a potentially stressful task, he makes responses which are irrelevant to task completion and which in fact can interfere with responses leading to task completion. One class of such responses would be obsessive or ruminative thoughts, and on the posttask questionnaire an attempt was made to determine what the subjects had been thinking during the experiment. Two questionnaire items are relevant. The first asked the subjects,

"How often during the testing did you find yourself thinking how well, or how badly, you seemed to be doing?" The subjects responded on a 10-point graphic scale labeled "Never" at one end and "Constantly" at the other. There was a significant difference between anxiety groups, $F(1,28) =$ 11.11, $p < .005$. Table II presents the mean frequency of these thoughts. Their occurrence was markedly greater in the high anxious groups.

TABLE II

MEAN SCALED FREQUENCY OF OBSESSIVE OR RUMINATIVE THOUGHTS

Responses	Control group	No-control group
Thinking how well or badly they were doing:		
Low anxiety group	4.9	4.9
High anxiety group	8.6	7.3
Wondering about other students:		
Low anxiety group	3.6	3.5
High anxiety group	6.6	4.4

A second questionnaire item asked, "How often during the testing did you find yourself thinking or wondering about how well other university students might perform?" These data are also presented in Table II. Again there was a significant difference between anxiety groups, $F(1,28) = 4.43$, $p < .05$. The high anxious subjects reported that they engaged more in this kind of social comparison than did the low anxious subjects.

DISCUSSION OF THE EFFECTS OF THE CONTROL CONDITION

As in the previous animal study, this study produced the predicted inhibition of disorganization by offering the subjects an alternate response following interruption, i.e., failure. The fact that both the anxiety and control conditions yield significant effects on performance on the SIIT, but not on the PEGF, is not surprising. This result suggests that, because of experiential and situational factors, the completion of certain organized sequences is more imperative than the completion of other sequences. A number of different theoretical phrases come to mind to label this phenomenon: self-esteem, expectancy, importance of the goal, ego involvement, etc. One could say, for example, that the SIIT was more "ego-involving" than the PEGF, but use of the term "skill" by Butterfield (1964) is more appropriate because of its behavioral emphasis. Butterfield writes that ". . . (skill) emphasizes the nature of the instructions rather than the subject's hypothetical reaction to the instructions" (p. 311). In the present study, the SIIT instructions clearly emphasized skill while the PEGF instructions did not. Again quoting Butterfield, ". . . skill instructions simply induce the subject to believe that he controls task completion" (p. 320). Obviously the subject has had experience in executing response sequences on which he is skilled, or believes himself to be skilled, which implies that the sequences include plans or possibilities for favorable outcomes, and thus their interruption, with no available alternate response, would disrupt performance more than interruption of a nonskilled sequence.

We do not wish to imply that the effect of skill instructions is to increase the "motivation" or drive level of the subject. Mandler has previously postulated that ". . . if—at the time of interruption—the goal path of the organized sequence has been laid down centrally, then the uncompleted part of the sequence will persist at the cognitive level as a plan. . . ." (1964, p. 173). Skill instructions increase the tendency of the subject to treat the response sequence as one including final success, and the plan for success is also included in the parallel, cognitive sequence or plan which is activated by the information that the task is one on which the subject is skilled. The interruption of such cognitive sequences, with no available alternate response, would produce anxiety.

Interruption of the SIIT, in other words, not only served to interrupt the overt response sequence which the subject was executing at the time the experimenter said "Stop," but also served to interrupt parallel cognitive sequences leading to previously learned outcomes, such as doing well on a test. Interruption on the PEGF, on the other hand, would not have the parallel function of interrupting such cognitive sequences, for the PEGF was administered under nonskill instructions. Thus, to interrupt a test before completion may produce a certain amount of emotional behavior, but such interruption can also interrupt long-term, easily activated, well-organized, cognitive sequences such as a goal path or plan to success, and this latter interruption can produce emotional behavior or disrupt performance.

We are assuming here not only the existence of specific plans relevant to circumscribed behavior sequences, but also the existence of more abstract plans, organized out of the multitude of specific plans. Such higher-order cognitive sequences toward success, in the abstract or nonspecific sense, presumably develop out of repeated specific plans including the notion of successful completion, just as primary cognitive sequences develop out of overt behavior sequences.

It should be noted that once interruption has occurred on the SIIT, anxiety will have been conditioned to the test; in other words, the SIIT, completely apart from interruptive effects and the sequences and plans involved in it, becomes a signal for visceral arousal. With no alternate responses available while the subject is taking the test, such arousal should produce distress or anxiety. Few such sequences should take place with the PEGF. Thus, on the PEGF there should be no arousal, no interruption, and therefore no differential performance under choice and no-choice conditions. Similarly, previous data have suggested that individual differences in anxiety produce performance differences only if the task is one which involves skill instructions. No such instructions were involved in the PEGF and differences in anxiety level did not affect performance on this test.

We had expected that recall should be better under the control condition on the simple assumption that anxiety engendered by the no-control condition would produce interference and therefore lessened attention and worse recall of the symbols. The data clearly bear out this prediction.

DISCUSSION OF THE EFFECTS OF THE ANXIETY CONDITION

The superiority of performance of the low anxious subjects on the SIIT is a replication of several previous studies. With some consistency, low anxious subjects have been shown to perform at a higher level under conditions where success or failure is possible (cf., Sarason, 1960), and it has been suggested (Child, 1954; Mandler & Sarason, 1952) that the inferior performance of the high anxious subjects is due to the relatively large number of task-irrelevant responses which they make. The data from the two questionnaire items support the notion that the high anxious subject does spend more time making responses irrelevant to task solution. They report worrying more and engaging in social comparison more. Such ruminative or obsessive thoughts are, of course, irrelevant to task solution and perhaps inimical to it. It should be noted, however, that the performance data for the two anxiety groups are confounded by the difference in their choice of behavior, i.e., the two anxiety groups did not work on the same sequence of tasks. This difference may also account for the fact that we did not obtain the expected difference in recall between the high and low anxiety groups.

It is possible to assess the general, abstract plan to do well and to achieve success in a situation. Presumably, presence of such a general cognitive structure would lead subjects to articulate the existence of such a plan. If somebody says that he wants to do well on a task, we assume the existence of a plan; if he says that doing well is not important, such a plan is either absent or not well-organized.

On the posttask questionnaire, the subjects in this study were asked, "How important personally was it for you to do well on the two tests?" and they responded on a 10-point scale labeled, at its extremes, "Not important" and "Very important." The mean scaled responses of the low anxious subjects was 3.45 and that of the high anxious subjects was 6.45. This difference was significant, $F(1,28) = 9.93$, $p < .005$. The conclusion seems clear: the implications of interruption are not the same for the two groups of subjects; high anxiety subjects exhibit more success-related plans.

We have seen that the anxiety groups differed in their performance, the frequency of ruminative or obsessive thoughts, and the expressed planning for success. If we consider these results in conjunction with those on patterns of choice between the two tests, a clearer picture of the differences between low and high anxious subjects emerges.

It should be noted, first, that 14 out of 16 subjects in the control condition chose the SIIT on the first trial. Thus, continuing to choose the SIIT following the first trial, and particularly completing it before the PEGF was completed, indicates persistence in the face of failure. The high anxious subject was more likely to persist, in spite of his failures, on the skill task. Furthermore, the questionnaire suggests that high-anxiety subjects more frequently show evidence of a plan to succeed, which is of course exactly the sequence that is interrupted by failure.

It might be suggested that high anxiety subjects suffer more from the effect of interruption. Their arousal might have been greater since the success sequence was more highly organized. They respond to interruption first with the production of ruminative, obsessive thoughts and second with persistence rather than with choice of the less threatening task. However, the expected interaction between anxiety level and control did not materialize. The indications from the questionnaire data suggest further investigation in this direction.

These data offer little support for the notion of Atkinson (Atkinson, 1964; Atkinson & Litwin, 1960) that high anxiety subjects are concerned with the avoidance of failure. The sequences of choice contradict such a position. However, Atkinson has also hypothesized that high anxiety subjects seek to avoid uncertainty, and this position is quite consistent both with our data and the notions presented here. High anxiety subjects will choose any situation which is "certatin," i.e., a situation which does not produce interruption. Thus, the certainty of failing would be chosen over an uncertain situation.

The persistence of the high anxiety subjects on the test described herein when alternate behavior was available suggests that their previous history has favored this essentially maladaptive mode of response. This also fits in with notions about the lack of flexibility of the anxious person. Failure, i.e., interruption, produces blind persistence, partly induced by the strong cognitive plan to do well. But the high level of interfering responses further precludes success. The learning experiences of high and low anxious subjects with respect to the handling of interruption should provide further evidence for this pattern. Davitz (1952) has demonstrated that preinterruption training influences the response to interruption. The question now remains how persistence versus a search for alternatives is developed.

The Two Determinants of Anxiety

Our argument has been that the emotional states of anxiety and distress can be deduced from the arousal following interruption coupled with the unavailability of alternate responses. These are two determinants of anxiety which occurs when the organism is helpless. It is of course also possible for the organism to "anticipate" helplessness. If a situation occurs in which no adequate plans can be formulated, a preliminary scanning of the available plans will bring the search up against the point where no further plans, no further alternatives, are available. Such a sequence of events is also an interruption of a plan and should also produce anxiety, often prior to the point at which no alternatives are in fact available. Mandler (1966) has pointed out that the notion of helplessness as the prototype of anxiety is present in psychoanalytic and existentialist theory as well as in experimentally oriented statements. The advantage of the present formulation is that it specifies more clearly the situation in which helplessness is produced. If helplessness, with attendant anxiety, occurs when a response sequence has been interrupted and no alternate response is available, a number of consequences emerge for the field of psychopathology and for personality theory.

ENVIRONMENTAL DETERMINANTS OF ANXIETY

Any situation which interrupts, or threatens the interruption of organized response sequences, and which does not offer alternate responses to the organism, will be anxiety-producing. We have shown a few ways in which laboratory situations may be manipulated to produce these conditions.[4] It may be more interesting to examine real-life sources of interruption. In this section we will discuss two such instances: guilt and social factors in anxiety production.

Anxious guilt may be seen as an instance of the effects of interruption. The guilty person is one who feels anxious about some past action, real or imagined. Usually, of course, he cannot undo what he has done. Attempts to begin a sequence leading to the undoing of the previously com-

---

[4] There is some evidence that some plans and cognitive structures may be temporally quite flexible, i.e., that the organism plans for *what* will happen relatively independently of *when* it will occur (Elliott, 1966).

mitted act are invariably interrupted by the situational fact that the consequences of the act are in the past. One can atone, but one cannot undo. The cognitive sequence which would lead to the undoing of some act is, in reality-oriented persons, inevitably interrupted by the knowledge that the act is in the past and cannot be undone.

We often teach our children two things: that they should always be good and that there is no substitute for being good. Certain cognitive sequences, in other words, such as the plan to right the wrongs that one has committed, will be well-organized. Furthermore, such sequences will be organized so that there are very few substitute sequences which can be performed if the original sequence is interrupted. The knowledge of having committed some wrong, therefore, should activate the sequence to right the wrong, but if the act is in the past and cannot be righted, then the cognitive sequence will be interrupted. Yet there may be no substitute for righting a wrong. Thus, the guilty person is one who is continually instigating a sequence to undo what cannot be undone and is therefore continually interrupted in this sequence, yet has no alternate response available following interruption. This is the prototypical situation for anxiety.

The only difference between the emotions of anxiety and guilt may be the situational variables which lead us to label the two situations differently (cf., Mandler, 1962b). Such an analysis would explain two of the aspects of guilt. The guilty person ruminates on his guilt, which we would describe as persistent attempts to complete a sequence of undoing, and the guilty person may feel better after confession, which we would describe as a response substitute for undoing. There are social variables which determine the degree to which confession is available and the degree of its accepted relevancy as an alternate response. A Catholic child, for example, is likely to be taught that confession is a socially acceptable substitute response for the interrupted cognitive sequence leading to undoing. The point of confession is that it enables the guilty person to complete a substitute sequence.

The consequence of confession may seem to be paradoxical, for while it enables guilty individuals to complete at least some cognitive sequences, it leads to punishment as often as it leads to forgiveness. The paradox does not persist, however, if one views the punishment which may follow confession as the completion of a sequence, rather than as a peculiar, even masochistic, goal. Confession feels good, whether it leads to punishment or forgiveness, because it leads somewhere: it enables the human to complete organized sequences. The assumption that men seek goals often leads one to posit situations in which the goals which are sought are distinctly unpleasant. By not making this assumption, but rather by postulating that men seek to complete organized sequences, the paradox is resolved.

The mention of social variables raises the general question of the relationship between social factors and anxiety or psychopathology. This issue has been of increasing concern to social scientists and psychiatrists (cf., Scott, 1958). In considering the influence of social or cultural factors on psychopathology, a number of different problems have been noted. One of these is the question: how do social or cultural factors influence the production of anxiety or other symptoms? Mandler (1964) has pointed out that symptom formation might occur when some objectively inappropriate response systems are used in the completion of an interrupted sequence. We will make the common assumption that symptoms follow the appearance of anxiety and will discuss how social variables can produce anxiety.

Social and cultural variables can influence the anxiety of the members of the society by (a) inculcating organized sequences which have a high probabilty of interruption, (b) interrupting organized sequences for various reasons, (c) not providing alternate responses to follow such interruption, and (d) providing only inappropriate alternate sequences.

A society inculcates organized sequences with a high probability of interruption when, for example, it teaches a high degree of "achievement motivation" to a large number of the members of the society but offers only a limited number of social positions which are sufficient to gratify the achievement motive. In other words, a number of the members of the society develop well-organized plans leading to success, but the society does not provide a relatively equal number of social positions through which the organized sequence can be completed. Obviously, social pressures, to be optimal, would provide for almost continuous interruption of organized sequences to success for all but the fortunate few.

Societies or groups often interrupt the organized sequences of their members for a number of reasons. For example, it may be efficient from the group's point of view for most of its members to possess organized sequences leading to positions of social power in that it guarantees sufficient competition so that the most promising gain power. However, once any given group has arranged itself into some power structure, it is inefficient for the group to allow its members to continue to attempt to exercise power unless they are in a socially institutionalized position of power. Thus, the group would interrupt the organized sequences leading to power which were attempted by some group member who held no social right to exercise it.

A group or society, then, can inculcate organized sequences and at the same time provide for their interruption. Furthermore, the society may not provide substitute behavior to follow the interruption. There may be, for example, no socially acceptable substitute for success even though not all members of a society have an opportunity to achieve success. The range of acceptable substitute responses may be fixed by membership in certain social groups. The American Negro is exposed to a large number of communications which would lead to the development of organized sequences leading to the achievement of social power. At the same time he is denied access to social positions through which he could complete the necessary sequences and is provided with few socially acceptable substitute sequences.

Last, a society, group, or culture may provide substitute responses which are either inappropriate to whatever organized sequences are interrupted or serve to interrupt other organized sequences. Becoming the town's best garbage collector is probably at best only a partial substitute for an interrupted sequence leading to social recognition. Becoming a juvenile delinquent may enable a youngster to complete certain sequences but is likely to lead to the interruption of others.

Zander and Quinn (1962) have summarized a number of studies of social structure which also bear on the question we are discussing. For example, Raven and Rietsema (1957) demonstrated that membership in groups which had unclear goals, or unclear paths to attain the goals, produced unpleasant emotional states among the group members. Unclear communication procedures, inefficient work flow, and vague power channels produce a type of social disorganization maximally designed to interrupt response sequences and not to offer alternate responses following the interruption.

In short, social or cultural variables can determine both the degree of control a person has over potential interruption and what he can do if interruption occurs. If an individual has a good deal of control over situations, he is much less likely to be interrupted. Further, his "control" implies that he has relevant alternate responses available to him. We would like to suggest that any social system can be analyzed in terms of (a) the degree to which it inculcates or presses for completion of sequences which are, in fact, often interrupted, (b) the degree of control which it allows over potential interruption, and (c) the range and availability of alternate responses which it offers. Such an analysis would enable one to make predictions concerning the anxiety- or symptom-producing characteristics of the social system.

THE RESPONSES OF THE INDIVIDUAL TO INTERRUPTION

We have been speaking of certain situational determinants of anxiety. Obviously, any dichotomy between situational and personal or individual determinants of anxiety is a false one, but one may vary the emphasis. In this section we want to pay more attention to the individual. A number of theorists have spoken of the anxiety of schizophrenics, and among the several theories of schizophrenia one seems particularly relevant to the notions we have advanced here. That is the idea of the double-bind communication (Bateson, Jackson, Haley, & Weakland, 1956; Weakland, 1960) to which schizophrenics are supposedly subjected. Briefly, the idea is that the communications from important others, such as the mother, which are directed to schizophrenics are within themselves contradictory. If one views the intent of certain communications as setting the recipient into action, the communication can be seen as activating some organized sequence on the part of the recipient. A double-bind communication, however, would be one which, as soon as it has activated some organized sequence, interrupts it. Completion is not allowed. To the degree that schizophrenics are subjected to such communications, it is not surprising that they develop a great deal of anxiety, for the organized sequences which they could execute are almost continuously being activated and then interrupted. Any conflictful situation, of course, can be seen as one which both activates and interrupts response sequences.

Given that socially induced acts, produced by the double-bind communications, are anxiety producing, it is also not surprising that the individual will develop idiosyncratic, often socially irrelevant, acts which can be completed. Schizophrenic behavior then becomes an admirable substitute for the acts demanded and interrupted by the social milieu.

Lazarus (1964) has spoken for the necessity of evaluating an individual's cognitive appraisal of a situation in order to determine the threatening or stressful aspects of the situation. Lazarus and his colleagues (Lazarus & Alfert, 1964; Lazarus, Speisman, Mordkoff, & Davison, 1962) have shown that by altering a subject's cognitive appraisal of a situation—for example, viewing a disturbing movie of a subincision rite from the stance of anthropological detachment or as a simple spectator—it is possible to alter the subjects' emotional responses to produce less anxiety. From our point of view, Lazarus is providing his subjects with an alternate response which they can execute when confronted with the anxiety-provoking movie. Lazarus has suggested that the subjects identify with the people in the film, and identification can be seen as a shared set of cognitions or plans. The subjects would like to escape from the situation which is potentially painful but the sequence of escape is interrupted by the constraints of the psychological experiment. The various sets or sound tracks which Lazarus has used do provide the subject with alternate responses, i.e., psychological escape, and thus his anxiety is lowered.

Janis (1958), working with surgical patients, demonstrated that the expectation of a future threatening event—postoperative pain—lowered its anxiety-producing characteristics. The data of Janis indicate that, at least at the cognitive level, it is possible for the human organism to incorporate the expectation of pain into a plan.[5] In the study by Janis, those patients who expected postsurgical pain were not interrupted, while those who did not expect pain were interrupted. The patients who expected pain were not rendered helpless, for any distress could be a cue for the thought, "Things are going as planned." Hence there would be no experience of interruption and no arousal.

Lazarus and his colleagues and Janis, it seems, are studying phenomena very similar to those we have discussed. In the studies by both Janis and Lazarus certain subjects either had organized sequences which dealt with potential interruptions by incorporating them into the sequence or they were explicitly provided with alternate responses. The point is that in these studies the subjects were provided with some control over interruption. From our point of view, defense mechanisms can also be construed as attempts to control interruption. They are either responses which avoid interruption or alternate responses which follow interruption.

The idea of control over interruption is somewhat similar to the idea of competence discussed by White (1959). Competence as a personality variable is, from our point of view, the degree of control an individual can exercise over the environment. This concept includes the notion of control over the interruption of organized sequences. A sense of competence is presumably generated by the individual's appraised control in executing organized response sequences. White's term *competence,* we suggest, can be defined as the individual's ability to avoid interruption or, if he is interrupted, to provide· alternate responses which aid in completion of the interrupted sequence. Mandler has touched on this before (1964) in discussing the idea of frustration tolerance, which can be defined as the ability to delay responding following interruption until an appropriate substitute response can be found. It is quite obvious that individuals vary in their ability to delay, (cf., Mischel & Metzner, 1962) and also, because of either experiential or constitutional factors, in their ability to find or learn appropriate alternate responses.

One further variable which should be mentioned is the degree of control over the environment which the individual appraises himself to hold. Rotter, Seeman, and Liverant (1962) and their colleagues have recently

---

[5] Mandler (1964) has discussed elsewhere the conditions which might influence the flexibility of an organized sequence or the conditions under which such sequences might be modified.

been at work on this variable. A locus of control scale has been developed which differentiates individuals according to the degree to which they appraise themselves or the environment to control the occurrence of reinforcement. In terms appropriate to interruption theory: the degree to which a person considers himself to control reinforcing events should be highly correlated with his appraised degree of control over interruption. Since a high degree of appraised control over interruption is presumably based on the individual's history of successful attempts to cope with interruption, he would presumably be rendered less anxious by any present interruption, for he would have a repertory of available alternate responses and would also be more likely to search for substitute responses when confronted with interruption.

There is not yet available a large body of data to support interruption theory, though the preliminary results have been encouraging. What remains is a number of unanswered questions. On what continua do the relevancy of alternate responses vary? What is the relationship between the relevancy of the alternate response and the interrupted sequence? Do organized sequences vary in their imperative quality of completion? If so, is it possible that what has been called the strength of a learned or social motive is a function of the degree of overlearning of certain sequences? What happens when, for various reasons, an individual interrupts his own organized sequences?

A start has been made toward exploring these and other problems. What is most encouraging is the ease with which various aspects of human functioning fit into the formulations of these first attempts toward a theory of organization and interruption.

REFERENCES

Amsel, A. Frustrative nonreward in partial reinforcement and discrimination learning. *Psychol. Rev.,* 1962, **69**, 306-328.

Atkinson, J. W. *An introduction to motivation.* Princeton, N.J.: Van Nostrand, 1964.

Atkinson, J. W., & Litwin, G. H. Achievement motive and test anxiety conceived as motive to approach success and motive to avoid failure. *J. abnorm. soc. Psychol.,* 1960, **60**, 52-63.

Bateson, G., Jackson, D. D., Haley, J., & Weakland, J. Toward a theory of schizophrenia. *Behavioral Sci.,* 1956, **1**, 251-264.

Butterfield, E. C. The interruption of tasks: Methodological, factual, and theoretical issues. *Psychol. Bull.,* 1964, **62**, 309-322.

Child, I. L. Personality. *Annu. Rev. Psychol.,* 1954, **5**, 149-170.

Davitz, J. R. The effects of previous training on postfrustration behavior. *J. abnorm. soc. Psychol.,* 1952, **47**, 309-315.

Elliott, R. Effects of uncertainty about the nature and advent of a noxious stimulus (shock) upon distress. *J. pers. soc. Psychol.,* 1966, in press.

Haggard, E. Some conditions determining adjustment during and readjustment following experimentally induced stress. In S. Tomkins (Ed.), *Contemporary psychopathology.* Cambridge, Mass.: Harvard Univer. Press, 1943. Pp. 529-544.

Hebb, D. O. On the nature of fear. *Psychol. Rev.,* 1946, **53**, 259-276.

Janis, I. L. *Psychological stress.* New York: Wiley, 1958.

Kessen, W., & Mandler, G. Anxiety, pain, and the inhibition of distress. *Psychol. Rev.,* 1961, **68**, 396-404.

Lazarus, R. S. A laboratory approach to the dynamics of psychological stress. *Amer. Psychologist,* 1964, **19**, 400-411.

Lazarus, R. S., & Alfert, Elizabeth. Short-circuiting of threat by experimentally altering cognitive appraisal. *J. abnorm. soc. Psychol.,* 1964, **69**, 195-205.

Lazarus, R. S., Speisman, J. C., Mordkoff, A. M., & Davison, L. A. A laboratory study of psychological stress produced by a motion picture film. *Psychol. Monogr.,* 1962, **76**, No. 34 (Whole no. 553).

Mandler, G. Response factors in human learning. *Psychol. Rev.,* 1954, **61**, 235-244.

Mandler, G. From association to structure. *Psychol. Rev.,* 1962, **69**, 415-427. (a)

Mandler, G. Emotion. In R. W. Brown *et al.* (Eds.), *New directions in psychology.* New York: Holt, 1962. Pp. 267-343. (b)

Mandler, G. The interruption of behavior. In D. Levine (Ed.), *Nebraska symposium on motivation: 1964.* Lincoln, Nebr.: Univer. of Nebraska Press, 1964. Pp. 163-219.

Mandler, G. Anxiety. In D. L. Sills (Ed.), *International encyclopedia of the social sciences.* New York: Crowell, 1966, in press.

Mandler, G., & Sarason, S. B. A study of anxiety and learning. *J. abnorm. soc. Psychol.,* 1952, **47**, 561-565.

Miller, G. A., Galanter, E., & Pribram, K. H. *Plans and the structure of behavior.* New York: Holt, 1960.

Mischel, W., & Metzner, R. Preference for delayed reward as a function of age, intelligence, and length of delay interval. *J. abnorm. soc. Psychol.,* 1962, **64**, 425-431.

Mowrer, O. H., & Viek, P. An experimental analogue of fear from a sense of helplessness. *J. abnorm. soc. Psychol.,* 1948, **43**, 193-200.

Nowlis, V., & Nowlis, Helen H. The description and analysis of mood. *Ann. N.Y. Acad. Sci.,* 1956, **65**, 345-355.

Raven, B. H., & Rietsema, J. The effects of varied clarity of group goal and group path upon the individual and his relation to his group. *Human Relat.,* 1957, **10**, 29-45.

Rotter, J. B., Seeman, M. R., & Liverant, S. Internal versus external control of reinforcement: a major variable in behavior theory. In N. F. Washburne (Ed.), *Decisions, values and groups.* Vol. 2. London: Pergamon Press, 1962. Pp. 473-516.

Sarason, I. G. Empirical findings and theoretical problems in the use of anxiety scales. *Psychol. Bull.,* 1960, **57**, 403-415.

Schachter, S., & Singer, J. E. Cognitive, social, and physiological determinants of emotional state. *Psychol. Rev.,* 1962, **69**, 379-399.

Scott, W. A. Social psychological correlates of mental illness and mental health. *Psychol. Bull.,* 1958, **55**, 65-87.

Stotland, E., & Blumenthal, A. The reduction of anxiety as a result of the expectation of making a choice. *Canad. J. Psychol.,* 1964, **18**, 139-145.

Weakland, J. H. The "double-bind" hypothesis of schizophrenia and three-party interaction. In D. Jackson (Ed.), *The etiology of schizophrenia.* New York: Basic
Books, 1960. Pp. 373-388.

White, R. W. Motivation reconsidered: The concept of competence. *Psychol. Rev.,*
1959, **66,** 297-333.

Zander, A., & Quinn, R. The social environment and mental health. *J. soc. Issues,*
1962, **18,** 48-66.

Part V

THE EFFECTS OF ANXIETY ON BEHAVIOR

CHAPTER 12

The Motivational Components of Manifest Anxiety: Drive and Drive Stimuli[1]

Janet Taylor Spence and Kenneth W. Spence
DEPARTMENT OF EDUCATIONAL PSYCHOLOGY,
UNIVERSITY OF TEXAS,
AUSTIN, TEXAS

AND

DEPARTMENT OF PSYCHOLOGY,
UNIVERSITY OF TEXAS,
AUSTIN, TEXAS

The central role assigned to anxiety in many personality theories and the interest that anxiety as a personality phenomenon has for psychologists are nowhere better reflected than in the volume of research utilizing the Manifest Anxiety Scale (MAS). The majority of those who have employed the scale have had anxiety as a personality variable as their primary concern, in spite of the fact that the research program for which the scale was devised has not been centrally concerned with anxious individuals. Rather, the interests of those of us who developed and first used the scale can be described as being both broader and narrower than anxiety as a personality characteristic, the studies growing out of a series of investigations that have been concerned with the role of aversive motivational or drive factors in learning situations, primarily classical conditioning, within the framework of Hull-Spence behavior theory (Spence, 1956; Spence, 1958).

[1] Preparation of this chapter was facilitated, in part, by the Hogg Foundation for Mental Health, University of Texas (J.T.S.) and Contract Nonr 375 (18) between the Office of Naval Research and The University of Texas (K.W.S.).

Drive level (D) has been manipulated or defined in many of these studies by such traditional methods as varying the intensity of noxious stimulation. Attempts have also been made to identify individuals who differ in emotional responsiveness and hence in drive level, including the selection of subjects on the basis of a response measure, scores on the MAS, obtained independently of the experimental situation. The assumption, then, in constructing the MAS and in employing it as a selective device has been that the drive level of high-scoring Ss, as a group, will be higher in such situations than that for low-scoring Ss. Thus, our concern with these "anxious" subjects has been narrower than an attempt to develop a personality theory about such individuals but has gone far beyond the personality area in investigating drive per se.

Although our purpose in studying individuals scoring at the extremes of the MAS has primarily been to investigate hypotheses concerning emotionally based drive, we have always recognized that such high and low anxiety groups undoubtedly differ in a number of characteristics and that all performance differences that occur between anxiety groups cannot be explained in terms of drive level. Development of a theory of anxiety as a personality phenomenon would thus appear to demand that these additional factors and the conditions under which they are evoked be identified and the manner in which they influence performance be determined.

The purpose of the present chapter is twofold. The first is to outline briefly the theory of emotionally based drive (D) out of which the work on the MAS developed and to describe our attempts to extend this theory about classical conditioning phenomena to investigations of the effects of anxiety (drive) level on the performance of more complex learning tasks. The second purpose is to present hypotheses concerning an additional set of characteristics that may differentiate between high and low anxiety groups by considering another aspect of the Hullian motivational complex, drive stimuli (S_D) and the responses they elicit. The role of S_D, it will be suggested, is particularly important to consider when the effects of experimentally manipulated stress on the performance of complex learning tasks are being investigated. More precisely, these latter hypotheses might be described as being a theory about individuals receiving scores on the MAS since the investigations using this scale as a selective device will be considered almost exclusively. Whether their results can be generalized to other measures of manifest anxiety, e.g., clinical judgments, will require empirical demonstration. Investigations using such clinical criteria have found results parallel to our findings with the MAS in several instances (e.g., Beam, 1955; Bitterman & Holtzman, 1952; Korchin & Levine, 1957; Welch & Kubis, 1947). In addition, studies relating MAS scores to clinical ratings of anxiety have at least found statistically significant relationships, albeit modest in absolute magnitude (e.g., Gleser & Ulett, 1952; Lauterbach, 1958).

A Theory of Emotionally Based Drive (D) and Its Relation to Performance in Classical Aversive Conditioning

OUTLINE OF THE THEORY

The origins of the research involving the MAS, as was stated earlier, are to be found in a series of studies concerning the role of aversive motivational factors in simple learning situations, particularly classical aversive conditioning. The basic theoretical notions underlying these conditioning studies are shown in Fig. 1. Several of the independent variables that have been manipulated in these investigations are shown at the top of the

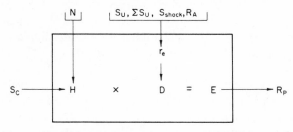

FIG. 1. Diagram representing the portion of theoretical schema relevant to data from classical aversive conditioning. (See text for explanation of symbols.)

diagram: N, the number of paired conditioning trials; S_U, the unconditioned stimulus; ΣS_U, the number of prior presentations of S_U; S_{shock}, shock unpaired with the conditioned stimulus (S_c) or with S_U; and R_A, scores on the MAS or some other measure of S's emotional responsiveness. The dependent variable, the frequency of a conditioned response (R_P) is shown at the lower right. The major theoretical concepts and the interrelations between them are represented inside the rectangle, with the arrows indicating the relations of the independent variables and of the dependent variables to the theoretical concepts.

The theory assumes that a learning factor (H) combines multiplicatively with a generalized drive factor (D) to determine excitatory potential (E). Thus $E = f (H \times D)$. It has further been assumed that in the conditioning situation, the level of drive (D) is a function of the magnitude of a hypothetical mechanism, r_e, a persistent emotional response aroused by aversive stimuli. This mechanism, it will be recognized, is similar to that proposed by Miller (1951) and Mowrer (1939) in connection with their work on the acquired drive of fear.

On the assumption that the same properties could be assigned to r_e as have been found with overt responses to noxious stimulation, a number of implications can be drawn from this theoretical schema. For example, since the magnitude or strength of reflexive responses to noxious stimulation has been found to vary with the intensity of that stimulation, it follows that the magnitude of the hypothetical emotional response, r_e, and hence the level of drive, D, should be a positive function of the intensity of the S_U in classical aversive conditioning. This assumption, in conjunction with the remaining portions of the theory, leads to the expectation that performance, as reflected in frequency of CR's, will vary positively with the intensity of the S_U.

A review of the evidence supporting this expectation, as well as a discussion of further implications of the theory and the experimental data relevant to them, may be found elsewhere (Spence, 1958). Most germane to the present chapter are the deductions that follow from the well-established observation that individuals differ in the magnitude of their reflex responses to a given intensity of noxious stimulation. Again assigning by analogy the same properties to the hypothetical mechanism r_e as are observed with overt responses, it was assumed that individuals would vary characteristically in the magnitude of r_e and therefore in level of D under a given set of experimental conditions. Again it follows from this assumption that more emotionally responsive individuals would exhibit higher performance levels in classical aversive conditioning than the less responsive.

The Manifest Anxiety Scale (MAS) was devised as one method of selecting subjects differing in emotional responsiveness so that this aspect of the theory could be tested. The rationale underlying the development of the scale was based, first, on the experimental evidence (e.g., Miller, 1951) concerning acquired fear or anxiety which provides firm support for the hypothesis that conditioned, anxiety-provoking stimuli evoke internal emotional responses which, in turn, increase drive level. Second, it was based on the observation that many of the symptoms exhibited or reported by individuals diagnosed clinically as suffering from anxiety reactions are similar to the overt behaviors elicited by the conditioned, as well as the unconditioned, stimulus in experimental studies of acquired fear. Thus it seemed reasonable to assume that acquired anxiety or fear as it is described by the experimentalist had properties in common with overtly observable or manifest anxiety as it is described by the clinical psychologist or psychiatrist. In order to obtain a convenient and objective device for rating subjects, a series of items judged by clinical psychologists to describe both the physiological reactions reported by individuals suffering from anxiety reactions and the accompanying subjective reports of worry, self-doubt, anxiety, etc., were chosen from the Minnesota Multiphasic Inventory (MMPI) to form the Manifest Anxiety Scale (Taylor, 1951; Taylor, 1953). Thus it was assumed that the degree to which an individual admitted to characteristically exhibiting manifest symptoms of anxiety, as described by items on the scale, would be related to the magnitude of his emotional responsiveness and therefore to level of D in a conditioning situation.

EXPERIMENTAL EVIDENCE

A recent survey of the eyelid-conditioning literature (Spence, 1964) reveals that in some 25 independent comparisons the implications of these assumptions, namely that MAS scores should be positively related to level of performance, were confirmed in all but four instances. Representative sets of data from two of our conditioning studies (Spence & Haggard, 1954; Spence & Taylor, 1951) are presented in Fig. 2. The studies employed two levels of puff intensity (.6 and 2.0 psi) as well as two levels of anxiety (upper and lower 20% of the subjects on the MAS distribution). As predicted by the theory, the high anxiety groups were clearly superior in performance to the low anxiety groups under both puff strengths. It will further be noted that, as expected, performance was also positively related to the intensity of S_U.

Confirmation of a more detailed implication of the theory can also be observed in Fig. 2. The assumption that the learning or habit factor (H) combines multiplicatively with drive (D) leads to the expectation that frequency curves of conditioning for the two anxiety levels, as well as for the two levels of S_U intensity, will gradually diverge over trials. Inspection of the sets of curves in Fig. 2 indicates that this indeed occurred.

Several studies involving GSR conditioning and the MAS have also been reported. Using groups of college students drawn from the extremes of the MAS distribution, M. T. Mednick (1957) found that conditioning performance was significantly related in the predicted direction to anxiety level. Gilberstadt and Davenport (1960), testing 19 neuropsychiatric patients unselected with respect to the MAS, and Bitterman and Holtzman (1952), testing 37 unselected students, also demonstrated a positive relationship between conditioning performance and the MAS. In neither study, however, was the relationship statistically significant, perhaps because of the small numbers of Ss involved, particularly those falling at the extremes of the MAS distribution.

Although the evidence from these conditioning studies has quite uniformly been positive, the magnitude of the correlations that have been obtained between the MAS and conditioning measures for unselected groups of Ss or the degree of overlap in the performance of groups selected from the extremes of the MAS distribution suggests that variations in MAS scores account for a relatively small portion of the intersubject variance in conditioning performance. The implications of this finding are many, the most obvious being the necessity of testing relatively large samples if adequate tests of this aspect of the theory are to be made.

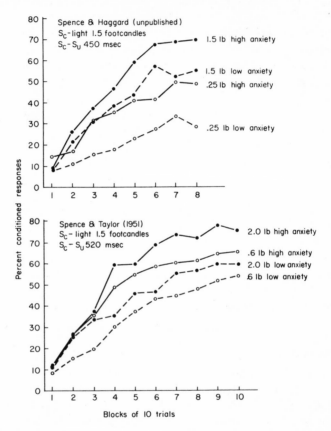

FIG. 2. Performance in eyelid conditioning as a function of anxiety (MAS) level and intensity of S_U.

In addition to using scores on the MAS obtained outside of the experimental situation as a method of identifying individuals differing in emotional responsiveness, we have used several intraexperimental methods of manipulating or identifying emotional level. One such method was used in the original eyelid-conditioning study involving the MAS (Taylor, 1951). In this investigation, an attempt was made to raise or lower the intensity of the Ss' emotional responsiveness by instructing half of them after the twentieth conditioning trial that the strength of the air puff would be increased on subsequent trials and instructing the remainder that it would be lowered (although, in fact, S_U remained constant). There was some evidence of a change in performance level following these instructions but the effect was small and temporary. However, in a subsequent study (Spence & Goldstein, 1961) in which Ss were instructed to expect an increase in the strength of the S_U but the trial on which this would occur was not specified, a significant increase in performance in comparison to a control condition was found to occur. In several other investigations in which Ss were given strong extra stimulation in the form of electric shock between conditioning trials or merely threatened with shock after receiving shock just prior to the conditioning trials, experimental groups have also exhibited higher levels of conditioning performance than nonshocked, nonthreatened control groups (Spence, 1958; Spence, Farber, & Taylor, 1954).

Still another intraexperimental method we have employed is differentiation of subjects on the basis of physiological measures purportedly reflecting emotionality. The results of several eyelid-conditioning studies in which pulse rate changes, skin conductance, and muscle-action potentials were recorded in the experimental situation were also consistent with the dual assumption that these measures were related to level of D and hence to performance (Runquist & Ross, 1959; Runquist & Spence, 1959).

Since there has been an increasing interest in relating physiological indexes of this type to performance in a number of kinds of situations, some general comments about their relation to the drive concept might be made at this point. A number of investigators have suggested that physiological indexes such as those mentioned above provide more "direct" measures of drive level than paper-and-pencil tests like the MAS and might therefore be used to greater advantage in investigations of the effects of drive. Still others, asserting that the MAS should be demonstrated to have validity as a measure of drive in some manner that is independent of experimental tests of its capacity to affect performance as predicted by our theory, have suggested that it is necessary to show that MAS scores are correlated with these physiological indexes or that the drive interpretation of the findings obtained with the MAS would be verified if the same experimental relationships found with the latter were also demonstrated to occur with a physiological measure.

Such suggestions seem to be based on a rather serious confusion between the drive concept as it is employed in the quantitative Hull-Spence behavior theory and as it is employed in the physiological theories of such individuals as Duffy (e.g., 1957) or Malmo (e.g., 1957; 1959). In these physiological theories, the term drive or such alternate expressions as motivation or arousal appear to be used to refer to an assumed physiological state of the organism, thus making it legitimate to seek methods of measuring this state and to compare proposed methods of measurement on the basis of directness, purity, etc. In the Hull-Spence system, on the other hand, the drive concept is purely mathematical in nature, being defined in terms of observable manipulations and related mathematically to other similarly defined concepts, deductions from the entire theoretical network permitting predictions to be made about behavior. Since the concepts in this behavioral system are convenient mathematical fictions rather than speculations about physiological facts, it is totally inappropriate to refer, literally, to "measuring" drive and thus to compare the directness, purity, or whatever of various methods of defining the concept. In short, it is by definition impossible to inquire about, as Cronbach and Meehl (1955) put it, the *concurrent* validity of the MAS or any other proposed definition of the Hullian drive concept. The *construct* validity of alternate definitions of a concept, again to use a term of Cronbach and Meehl, may of course vary, i.e., differ in the degree to which they are related to performance in the manner demanded by the total theoretical network of which the proposed concept is a part. However, the usefulness of any given definition may be determined only by this kind of experimental test and not on *a priori* grounds.

In view of the fact that physiological measures have been used infrequently to define drive level by investigators utilizing Hull-Spence behavior theory and certainly have not been accepted by Hullians as a reference set of measures of drive against which all other measures are to be compared and judged, it is also inappropriate to suggest that such indexes be used to "verify" the drive interpretation of our data; the physiological measures employed in the conditioning studies described above were as much on trial as useful devices for identifying individuals differing in level of the hypothetical r_e mechanism and therefore drive level as was the MAS when it was first introduced. Relationships with performance consistent with the emotionality hypothesis were, of course, found, but it is interesting to note that in spite of the fact that the physiological measures were obtained in the experimental situation itself, the magnitude of the relationships was no greater than that typically found with MAS scores obtained outside of the situation.

This finding was not too surprising; in fact, it would not have been unexpected had one or more of these physiological measures failed to be related to conditioning performance at all. A number of investigations of the various indexes said to reflect level of motivation or arousal by physiological theorists have shown that intercorrelations among the indexes are extremely low, individuals varying considerably from measure to measure in their position with respect to other individuals (e.g., Lacey & Lacey, 1958; Schnore, 1959). Furthermore, the relationships of various measures to performance on a given type of task have not been found to be consistent (e.g., Burgess & Hokanson, 1964) or equally responsive to the introduction into an experimental situation of stimuli purportedly raising level of arousal (e.g., Schnore, 1959). Thus, as physiological theorists have freely admitted, it is obvious that, whatever process or processes these indexes are measuring, they are not identical, and the relation of each of them to the physiological concept of drive or arousal is therefore ambiguous. It is to be hoped that as physiological knowledge develops it will be possible to provide a coordinating equation between the notion of drive or arousal as used by physiological theorists and the concept of drive as used by Hullian behavior theorists to their mutual advantage. At the present time, however, it is apparent on both theoretical and empirical grounds that whatever the deficiencies of a paper-and-pencil test like the MAS as a selective device for testing hypotheses about the Hullian drive concept, or whatever the problems in interpreting the data obtained with the MAS, they cannot be overcome simply by substituting some physiological measure in its place.

Extensions of the Theory of Emotionally Based Drive to Complex Learning Phenomena

THEORETICAL PREDICTIONS

In contrast to classical conditioning phenomena for which fairly detailed and satisfactory theoretical schema have been devised, theories of complex learning in humans are, at best, in very early stages of development. In attempting to extend our notions concerning the effects of drive (MAS) level on performance to more complex learning phenomena, it has therefore been necessary to develop hypotheses about these learning situations that are quite independent of the drive factor. As a result, there has been some degree of trial-and-error in our attempts to arrange for task conditions that would meet the boundary conditions of our theory. Furthermore, our theorizing has had to be limited to a circumscribed set of learning tasks and even within these it has sometimes been necessary to confine our predictions to restricted portions of the learning curve.

In discussing our theorizing about the effects of drive (MAS) level on the performance of complex learning tasks, attention should first be called to the fact that in classical conditioning a single response to a simple stimulus is being acquired. Complex, selective learning tasks, in contrast, typically employ a series of stimulus items, each of which may evoke a number of competing responses with varying habit (H) strengths. If, in the case of a single item, the initial habit strength of the correct response is stronger than the strength of competing responses, the multiplicative relationship between H and D in determining excitatory potential, E, implies that the higher the level of D, the greater is the difference between the E values of the correct and the incorrect competing responses. Assuming that only the magnitude of the difference in E values needs to be taken into account in predicting the effects of drive level on performance, it follows that in instances in which the correct responses are initially strong, performance should be positively related to drive level,[2] just as it is in classical conditioning.

The same set of assumptions leads to the expectation that if the correct to-be-learned response is instead initially *weaker* than one or more of the competing response tendencies, then the higher the drive level, the poorer will be the performance during the early stages of learning. However, as learning of the correct responses increases over trials, the habit strength of these responses would be expected to equal and then exceed those of competing responses. Thus, while the performance of a high drive group would be expected to be inferior to that of a low drive group in early stages of learning, it should become superior in later stages.

EXPERIMENTAL EVIDENCE

Our initial studies employed serial verbal or spatial mazes, two response alternatives (right or left) being presented at each choice point. On the assumption that anticipatory and perseverative tendencies would be present to such a degree that the incorrect choice would be stronger at many choice points than the correct one, it was expected that high drive (MAS) groups would exhibit a greater number of errors over the learning trials

---

[2] As was noted, only the magnitude of the difference between E's was taken into account in deducing the performance differences that would be predicted to occur between groups varying in drive level. As one of the writers has discussed in detail elsewhere (Spence, 1958), more elaborate models have been developed to account for data obtained in selective learning situations with animal Ss, models which take into consideration other portions of the theory (e.g., the absolute level of competing E's above the threshold L) to describe the manner in which competing response tendencies interact with each other and which may lead to different predictions about behavior under varying drive levels than those described above. The relative lack of knowledge that exists about complex human learning led us to choose, from a number of possible alternative conceptions, the simplest set of assumptions in deriving implications about the effects of drive on performance in these learning situations.

than a low drive group. On the further assumption that errors would be largely due to the interfering effects of these anticipatory and perseverative tendencies, it was also expected that a significant correlation would be found between the rank order of the "difficulty" of the choice points (total number of errors made by the Ss on each) and the magnitude of the difference between the errors made by the high and low anxiety groups. With but one exception (Hughes, Sprague, & Bendig, 1954) one or both of these predictions have been tested and confirmed in both our own studies (Farber & Spence, 1953; Taylor & Spence, 1952) and those of other investigators (Axelrod, Cowen, & Heilizer, 1956[3]; Matarazzo, Ulett, & Saslow, 1955). One negative aspect of our results should, however, be mentioned. The small number of errors made at the "easiest" choice points suggested that competing response tendencies at these points were minimal and that the high anxiety group should therefore have been superior in performance to the low anxiety group. This superiority did not, however, occur, suggesting that the theoretical model was incorrect in some respect; but whether the fault lay in our assumptions about the effects of drive or in our analysis of the task was not clear.

In addition to these serial maze experiments, several other early studies (Lucas, 1952; Montague, 1953) employed more traditional serial learning tasks in which Ss were presented with each successive item and required to anticipate the next item on the list. These investigators were able to demonstrate that the differences between the overall performance of high and low anxiety groups increased in favor of the latter as did intralist similarity and hence, presumably, degree of intralist competition.

Despite the generally positive results of these studies, the serial learning arrangement, as we began to recognize, has serious deficiencies as a method of testing the implications of our theory. Most prominent among these is the fact that intralist interference due to such factors as remote associations is an inherent part of serial learning, and it is difficult to specify the number and strength of the response tendencies elicited by each stimulus. The paired-associate arrangement, with its use of discrete S-R pairs, permits

---

[3] Axelrod et al. (1956) reported a significant correlation between choice-point "difficulty" and magnitude of the differences between groups in number of errors but did not find a similar relationship when differences between groups in *percent* of total errors per choice point were used instead of number. The latter results led them to conclude that their results did not support our predictions. When total number of errors is not the same for each group, the number and percent measures are, of course, not necessarily isomorphic. Since our theory clearly makes predictions about number of errors and not percent, their data must be considered as confirming the theory.

more precise control of the relative strengths of the competing responses in each hierarchy, and we therefore turned in subsequent investigations to the use of this type of list.

In one type of study we have attempted to develop noncompetitive lists in which the formation of each S-R association is isolated as much as possible from the others by minimizing the degree of formal and meaning-ful similarity among the stimulus and response terms as well as the degree of associative connection between each stimulus and the nonpaired response terms. In several experiments the initial associative connection between the paired words was also at a minimum. In this instance our theory would predict that although there would be little or no difference between the groups in the early stages of learning, the high anxiety group would grad-ually become superior in performance as learning progressed. Three studies (Spence, 1958; Taylor, 1958; Taylor & Chapman, 1955) using this type of list have confirmed our prediction and two have not (Kamin & Fedor-chak, 1957; Lovaas, 1960). The negative results of the Lovaas study (1960) are difficult to evaluate, however, since not only were high and low anxiety Ss chosen on the basis of an abbreviated 20-item version of the MAS (Bendig, 1956) rather than the full 50-item scale but also Ss who received more than a certain minimum score on the MMPI K scale, a scale which has consistently been found to have a high negative correla-tion with the MAS, were eliminated.

We have also employed a second type of noncompetitive list in which there was an initial associative connection between each S and R term, acquired as a result of extraexperimental experience. In this instance it was expected that performance would be well above zero on the first anticipation trial for both groups and that the performance curve for the high anxiety group would be consistently above that of the low anxiety group. Our findings have also supported these predictions (Besch, 1959; Spence, Farber, & McFann, 1956a; Spence, Taylor, & Ketchel, 1956b) although the differences between the anxiety groups were statistically sig-nificant only in the studies by Spence *et al.* (1956a; 1956b). Positive findings were also reported by Standish and Champion (1960) who used a list of highly associated pairs and compared the performance of anxiety groups on a latency measure during an advanced stage of practice in which Ss had ceased to give incorrect responses.

Paired-associate lists have also been devised to test the prediction that high anxiety (D) groups will be poorer in performance than low anxiety groups when the initial habit strength of the response term paired with a given stimulus is weaker than the strength of one or more competing response tendencies. In these lists, the members of some of the S-R pairs have a high initial associative connection (e.g., Tranquil-Placid) while others have a minimal associative connection. In these low association pairs, stimulus terms are employed that are similar in meaning to the stimulus word in one of the highly associated pairs (e.g., Serene-Head-strong). In the case of the latter type of pairs it was assumed that the presence of a highly associated response term elsewhere in the list would evoke a competing response tendency, one that was stronger in the initial stages of learning than the response word actually paired with the stimulus. It was expected, then, that *on the initial trials* the performance of high anxiety Ss would be inferior to that of low anxiety Ss on these competitive items, an expectation that was confirmed in several studies employing this type of list (Spence *et al.,* 1956a; Spence *et al.,* 1956b) or a variation of it (Ramond, 1953). As was discussed earlier, predictions about later trials are difficult to make since the initially weak habit strength of the correct response is gradually increasing. If training were carried on long enough, it is possible that the correct responses would become sufficiently dominant over competing responses so that the latter would not interfere, thus result-ing in the high anxiety group overcoming its initial performance inferiority and ultimately becoming superior to the low anxiety Ss. Evidence support-ing this implication was found in an investigation by Standish and Champion (1960) that involved a type of negative transfer design rather than an intralist method of evoking competing responses. Giving Ss a number of trials on a list of highly associated pairs and then a second list consisting of the same stimuli and new responses of low initial associative connection, these investigators found that although the response latencies of the high anxiety group were slower (and number of errors greater) than those of the low anxiety group early in learning, the latency curves of the groups were reversed in a series of final, overlearning trials.

Confirmation of our hypotheses concerning the interaction between drive level and degree of intratask competition has also been found in a series of investigations of motor learning in children by Castaneda and his colleagues in which Ss were classified into high and low drive groups by means of a children's version of the MAS (Castaneda, 1961; Castaneda, Palermo, & McCandless, 1956) or in which drive was manipulated by means of time stress (Castaneda, 1956; Castaneda & Lipsitt, 1959). A similar interaction between time stress and competition in determining performance on a motor learning task has also been demonstrated in adults by Clark (1962).

As was pointed out earlier, theories about the types of complex learn-ing phenomena investigated in these studies are, at best, in a primitive stage of development. The assumptions we have made about them in conducting this anxiety research have not only been limited in scope but undoubtedly incomplete in many ways. This state of affairs has made it particularly difficult to evaluate the significance of negative findings with respect to the relations between the MAS and performance since the deficiency may be in any part of the theoretical network. Assessing the results of studies designed to test the implications of our drive hypotheses becomes even more difficult when the investigators have employed very different types of learning materials than have been involved in our studies and those of our associates. In a number of instances we have been forced to conclude that supposed tests of our theory—whether the results are interpreted as confirming or disconfirming its implications—are actually irrelevant since the task materials are such that they do not meet the boundary conditions of the theory and thus do not permit derivations about the effects of drive (MAS) level on performance to be made. There can be no objections, of course, to attempts to extend our analyses to other types of situations or to include other types of variables than we have considered, and a number of investigators have explicitly tried to do so (e.g., Maltzman, Fox, & Morrisett, 1953). But the credit or the blame for the success or failure of these ventures clearly rests with the investigators who have suggested these additional hypotheses.

There has also been an unfortunate number of occasions on which we have had to reject the findings of a particular study as bearing on our theory because the investigator has misunderstood the task variables specified by the theory and has therefore selected inappropriate task materials. One of the most common misunderstandings has involved the translation of our notions concerning degree of intratask competition between correct and incorrect response tendencies into level of task "complexity," with an accompanying statement that the evidence shows that as complexity increases, high anxiety (D) groups become increasingly inferior in performance to low anxiety Ss. It is true, of course, that *other things being equal,* tasks of increasing degrees of intratask competition could also be described as becoming increasingly complex. However, varying competition is not the only way to vary complexity. For example, paired-associate lists would probably be considered to be less complex than many conceptual or problem-solving tasks. In the absence of analyses of the latter in terms of intratask competition, it is obviously impossible for us to derive any implications from our theory about the effects of drive level on the performance of such problem-solving tasks. As still another example, it might be pointed out that classical conditioning, involving the acquisition of only one response, is less complex than paired-associate learning. But, as we have seen, our predictions about paired-associate performance—which have received substantial empirical confirmation—are dependent on degree of competition within the list; according to our theory, the results can either be similar to those of conditioning (high anxious superior to low anxious) or the reverse (low anxious superior to high). Thus, not only our theoretical predictions but also the empirical data do not support the statements that have been made about the interaction between task complexity per se and level of drive or anxiety.

Even more frequent, perhaps, have been statements that the theory predicts that the direction of the performance difference between high and low anxiety groups is a function of task "difficulty." However, just as in the case of the complexity variable, there are a number of ways to vary task difficulty that do not involve manipulating intralist competition and about which our theory makes no differential predictions.

Still other investigators have clearly recognized the task variables specified by our theory but have suggested the difficulty hypothesis as an alternate explanation of our results with complex learning tasks—that difficulty per se is the relevant task characteristic contributing to the inter-action between anxiety level and type of task, and not, specifically, degree of intralist competition. Since this difficulty hypothesis has continued to be mentioned by many investigators in one guise or another, a more detailed version of it might be described at this point. According to this conception, Ss become more emotionally tense and upset as task difficulty increases, the effect of this emotionality being the disruption of perform-ance. Since high anxiety Ss are assumed to be more easily threatened than low anxiety Ss, differences in performance between the two groups are expected to become more pronounced as task difficulty increases. These hypotheses have always struck the writers as having several inherent diffi-culties. First, these notions lead to the expectation that high anxiety Ss will show varying degrees of *inferiority* to low anxiety Ss, but they fail to ac-count for the *superiority* of these Ss on "easy" tasks. Second, the demon-stration of interactions between degree of competition ("difficulty") and anxiety level in studies in which both competitive and noncompetitive items were included *within a single task* would seem to demand that it be as-sumed that S's emotionality shoots up and down within very brief intervals of time from item to item, an assumption which does not appear to be too tenable. Even more broadly, the difficulty hypothesis would seem to require Ss either to have some absolute standard against which to judge the diffi-culty of any given task or some absolute expectation as to how quickly they should be able to master a task, an expectation which remains constant whatever its difficulty. Undoubtedly there are extremely difficult, confusing tasks on which progress is so slow or so irregular that the Ss become frustrated, discouraged, or otherwise emotionally disturbed. But with the limited range of task difficulty that has been used in the studies reported above, Ss being able to progress rapidly toward complete mastery on even the most difficult of them, it is hard to conceive of any marked differences between the "easy" and "difficult" tasks in the magnitude of the emotional responses they elicited.

The empirical issue of difficulty versus competition can be settled, however, only by the experimental evidence. Only one study (Saltz & Hoehn, 1957) was specifically designed to test these rival interpretations, but the task materials were such that conclusions could not be reached from the data about the two hypotheses (Taylor, 1958). When the data from our various studies are considered together, however, it is clear that the assumed relationship between task difficulty and anxiety level is not confirmed. For example, several of our studies (Taylor, 1958; Taylor & Chapman, 1955) have employed noncompetitional lists of nonsense syllables that, despite being shorter, were more difficult (as inferred from mean number of correct responses on a given trial) than were competitional lists of meaningful words given in other studies under similar experimental conditions (e.g., Spence et al., 1956a). Considering the nature of the materials employed, nonsense syllables versus words, this difference in difficulty is not unexpected. But it will be recalled that the performance of high anxiety Ss was better than that of the low anxious in the studies employing the noncompetitional nonsense syllable lists and worse in the studies employing the easier but competitional lists of words, results that were predicted from our theory but opposite to what would be expected by the difficulty hypothesis.

Still another problem that arises in assessing the results of studies comparing high and low anxiety groups is concerned with specification of the conditions under which the groups can be expected to differ in degree of emotional responsiveness and hence to differ in performance in the manner predicted by our theory. In this connection we have considered two alternative possibilities. One of these is that the intensity of the emotional responses (r_e) of high anxiety Ss tends to be greater than that of the low anxious in any and all types of experimental situations, due perhaps to the former tending to be chronically more anxious and emotionally aroused. The second possibility is that high anxiety Ss differ from the low primarily in their lower threshold for emotional arousal in response to situations perceived as having some degree of threat. If the second of these hypotheses were correct, then differences in performance due to differences in drive level would be expected to occur only in situations involving some element of stress. The evidence clearly indicates that it is not necessary to introduce stress stimuli into the situation (e.g., a noxious event or instructions designed to elicit fear of failure or some other type of psychological threat) to obtain performance differences between anxiety groups. For example, the results of the studies of complex learning just described were all obtained under neutral, task-oriented instructional conditions and did not involve the use of noxious stimulation. These findings do not necessarily confirm the chronic hypothesis, however, since it could be argued that Ss perceive psychological experiments as being threatening, particularly when the tasks they are asked to perform appear to reveal something about their personality or intelligence.

Although the evidence is not unambiguous, we are inclined, because of a number of considerations, to accept the situational hypothesis rather than the chronic one. For example, a study by S. A. Mednick (1957) indicated that while experimentally naive high anxiety Ss differed from low anxiety Ss in performance on a stimulus generalization task, no differences between anxiety groups were found for Ss who had served in several prior psychological experiments. Since Ss are likely to lose their initial apprehensiveness about participating in such experiments and become quite blasé after several such experiences, these findings suggested that, in the absence of experimental conditions designed to be stressful, anxiety groups differ in emotional responsiveness only when the experimental situation is novel and thus more likely to be perceived as potentially threatening. Still other evidence favoring the situational hypothesis may be found in the results of conditioning studies. In contrast to classical aversive conditioning, no differences have been found between anxiety groups in classical reward (salivary) conditioning (Bindra, Paterson, & Strzelecki, 1955), a situation which involves neither noxious stimulation nor performance on a task which reflects some valued characteristic. Even within eyelid conditioning there is some evidence (Spence, 1964) that more satisfactory results are obtained when experimentally naive Ss are used and physical arrangements are such that they make the Ss somewhat fearful and uneasy (e.g., placement of Ss in a dimly lit room, isolation of S from E, etc.).

In view of these data, it might appear that in designing experiments to test implications of our theory about the effects of drive level on performance, it would be wise to deliberately include stressful stimulation (in the form of noxious stimuli, ego-involving or failure instructions, etc.) in order to increase the probability that anxiety groups will differ in emotionality in the experimental situation. The results of a number of investigations, however, suggest that these stress conditions have effects in addition to increasing drive (D) level which differentiate high and low anxiety Ss and that in the case of complex learning situations of the type described above, performance differences between anxiety groups are in part a function of these nondrive factors. Thus, the inclusion of stress stimuli in situations involving complex learning tasks may be inappropriate if hypotheses concerning the effects of drive level on performance are to be investigated. However, if the nature of these additional factors that differentiate anxiety groups and the manner in which they influence performance could be determined, the resultant knowledge would be of interest in itself and extend our understanding of anxiety as a personality phenomenon. It is to this topic that we now turn.

Manifest Anxiety and the Response Interference Hypothesis

DRIVE STIMULUS (S_D) AND TASK-IRRELEVANT RESPONSES IN COMPLEX LEARNING

The extension of our notions concerning drive and anxiety involves what might be called the "response interference hypothesis," the hypothesis that states that task-irrelevant responses which in some situations may interfere with efficient performance are more easily elicited in high than in low anxiety Ss (Spence, 1956; Taylor, 1956; Taylor, 1959). The hypothesis may be said to emphasize, not general drive or D with its "energizing" (multiplicative) properties, but another aspect of the Hullian motivational complex: drive stimulus or S_D with its capacity to evoke responses both learned and unlearned, covert and overt (Hull, 1943). Like D, the intensity of S_D and therefore the number and strength of the response tendencies it evokes is postulated to be a function of the hypothetical response, r_e. As has been demonstrated in animal studies (e.g., Amsel, 1950; Amsel & Maltzman, 1950), whether an increase in D and S_D facilitates or deters performance depends, in part, on whether the response tendencies elicited by S_D are compatible or incompatible with the response being acquired or performed.

Among the responses aroused by the S_D associated with r_e in human Ss, we hypothesize, are those that may be described as task-irrelevant, e.g., heightened autonomic reactions or covert verbalizations reflecting self-depreciation, anger, desire to escape, etc. To the extent that the situation is one in which irrelevant responses are elicited and the task is one in which the particular irrelevant tendencies elicited by S_D interfere with correct responding, a hypothesis that states that such tendencies are more easily aroused in high anxiety Ss than in low leads to the prediction that the performance of high anxiety Ss will be inferior. This hypothesis was also suggested by Child in 1954 but as an alternative to the drive interpretation of the results of our early studies showing the performance inferiority of high anxiety Ss on serial learning tasks, a possibility we also recognized (e.g., Montague, 1953).

According to Child's hypotheses, high anxiety Ss tend to react emotionally to many experimental situations, even those in which stress stimulation is not explicitly employed, and consequently are higher in both D and S_D than are low anxiety Ss. The superior performance of high anxiety Ss in eyelid conditioning, Child suggested, is due to the facilitating effects of D, as we originally hypothesized, the reflexive eyeblink response being relatively invulnerable to interference from the task-irrelevant responses elicited by S_D. In more complex learning tasks, on the other hand, efficient performance *is* capable of being disrupted by these extra-task responses. Thus, on the assumption that these tendencies deter performance to a greater degree than D facilitates it, it would be expected that high anxiety Ss would exhibit poorer performance on such tasks than the low anxious.

In subsequent studies, however, we were able to demonstrate that high anxiety groups were not consistently inferior in performance to the low anxiety Ss on complex learning tasks, as demanded by Child's hypotheses, but rather, as we have already indicated, varied from being inferior to superior from task to task or even from one type of item to another within a task, depending on the degree of intratask response competition.

The results of these studies of complex learning thus have several implications for the response-interference hypothesis. First, an appeal to irrelevant response tendencies does not adequately account for these data from complex learning situations since the superiority of high anxiety Ss on low competition items or tasks cannot be explained. Second, if high anxiety Ss do differ from the low anxious with respect to the ease with which task-irrelevant responses are elicited, these responses are typically not aroused with sufficient frequency or intensity in the affectively neutral conditions under which these experiments were conducted to affect the performance of the group differentially.

Their findings, however, do not preclude the possibility that in situations in which stress is deliberately introduced, differences in performance between anxiety groups which support the implications of a response interference hypothesis might appear. This expectation gains some support from the investigations of Mandler, S. B. Sarason, and their colleagues (e.g., Mandler & Sarason, 1952; Mandler & Sarason, 1953; S. B. Sarason, Mandler, & Craighill, 1952) who developed a questionnaire concerning "test anxiety," a scale which is moderately correlated with the MAS (e.g., Mandler & Cohen, 1958). Also utilizing a version of the response interference hypothesis, they have stated that when the predicted differences in performance between their anxiety groups appear, they tend to occur in situations into which some element of stress has been introduced. Similar results with Ss selected by means of a version of the Test Anxiety Questionnaire have also been obtained in a series of investigations conducted by I. G. Sarason and his co-workers (e.g., I. G. Sarason, 1960).

In reviewing the data bearing on the interaction between MAS scores and stress in determining performance on complex learning tasks, studies employing three major types of stress conditions, singly or in combination, will be considered: ego-involving instructions, induced failure experience on a prior task, and application of noxious stimulation such as electric shock. In evaluating the results of these studies it is first necessary to acknowledge that despite extensive investigations of these experimental conditions, independent of their possible interaction with individual difference variables, our understanding of their effects is woefully deficient. The empirical findings have demonstrated all varieties of relationships, suggesting that these stress conditions are complex in their effects and interact with a number of variables to determine performance (Farber, 1955; Lazarus, Deese, & Osler, 1952). In presenting the data from high and low anxiety groups, the following assumptions will tentatively be made, with the recognition that neither is too well supported. First, the major effect of each of these experimental manipulations is to increase D and S_D, with the latter, in turn, eliciting task-irrelevant responses. Second, the tasks used in these investigations are of such a type that performance is deterred by these task-irrelevant tendencies.

EXPERIMENTAL EVIDENCE

Effects of Psychological Stress

Ego-Involving Instructions. Turning now to consideration of the empirical evidence concerning the effect of ego-involving instructions, all of the relevant studies have represented the experimental task to the Ss (college students) as being related to IQ or to success in college and have contrasted the performance of these ego-involved Ss with task-oriented controls. Three studies (Nicholson, 1958; I. G. Sarason, 1956; I. G. Sarason, 1957a) employing serial or paired-associate lists all found that the introduction of ego-involving instructions impaired performance in a high anxiety group, such Ss being poorer than their task-oriented controls. Low anxiety groups, in contrast, tended to improve in performance with ego involvement. One of these investigations (Nicholson, 1958) is of particular interest since degree of intratask competition was also manipulated in the experimental design. Using the low and high competition lists devised by Montague (1953), Nicholson found an interaction between list and MAS group of the kind predicted by our drive theory for Ss tested under task-oriented conditions. Under ego-involved conditions, however, the high anxiety groups were inferior to the low anxious even on the low competition list. If the major effects of ego-involving instructions were merely to raise drive level, we would expect that performance on such low competition tasks would improve with the introduction of such instructions, the relative increase in high anxiety Ss perhaps being greater than in low anxiety Ss due to their greater responsiveness to them. The fact that the opposite occurred, a decrease in the performance of high anxiety Ss under ego-involvement, confirms our hypotheses concerning S_D and the competing irrelevant responses it may elicit.

In addition to these verbal learning studies, several other investigations have used speed tasks, typically involving some type of symbol substitution. Katchmar, Ross, and Andrews (1958), studying performance on a complex verbal coding task in which the importance of both speed and accuracy were stressed, also reported a significant interaction between anxiety and ego involvement on an error measure. Similar results were obtained by I. G. Sarason (1961b) in a study employing a "difficult" anagrams task and by I. G. Sarason and Palola (1960) in two experiments employing a Wechsler-type digit-symbol substitution task in which highly similar symbols were employed. Although the interaction was not statistically significant, the number of correct completions within the time limit was greater for low anxiety Ss given ego-involving instructions than for their controls, the opposite relationship being found for the high anxiety groups. Furthermore, under both experimental conditions, the performance of the high anxiety Ss was poorer than that of the low anxiety Ss. In both of the Sarason-Palola experiments, additional groups of Ss were tested on versions of the digit-symbol task in which the symbols were minimally rather than highly similar to each other. On these "easy" tasks an interaction was also found between anxiety level and experimental condition, but it was of a different nature than was found with the difficult task in that high anxiety Ss not only were *better* in performance under ego involvement than under the neutral condition but the magnitude of their superiority was greater than that of the low anxiety groups. Also unlike the results obtained with the "difficult" task, a between-groups comparison showed that the high anxiety Ss were better in performance than the low anxiety Ss under both experimental conditions.

It might also be noted that in these Sarason studies Ss were classified into high and low anxiety groups on the basis of scores on the Test Anxiety Questionnaire (TAQ) as well as on the basis of MAS scores. The relationships found between the experimental variables and the extreme MAS groups were even more pronounced for the TAQ groups. While the more satisfactory results obtained with the TAQ may in part be due to the use of a 20-item form of the MAS scale (Bendig, 1956) rather than the full scale, to classify Ss into high and low anxiety groups, it is also quite possible, as I. G. Sarason (e.g., 1960) has suggested, that the difference was due to the fact that while the MAS is quite general in content, the TAQ was specifically designed to reflect Ss' characteristic anxiety reactions to situations testing intellectual ability or achievement[4] and thus was more successful in classifying Ss according to the amount of anxiety they experienced in the experimental situation.

The same phenomenon—more marked differences between anxiety groups when Ss were classified by means of TAQ rather than MAS scores—was also found in a third experiment reported in the I. G. Sarason-Palola study (1960) in which "easy" and "difficult" arithmetic tasks were used. In this experiment, however, there was no interaction between anxiety level and instructional condition on either task, the high anxiety groups differing from the low only in that their performance was poorer on the "difficult" task under both ego-involved and neutral conditions.

Failure Experience. Studies investigating the effects of failure on performance have compared the performance of groups informed that their performance on a prior task had been substandard with groups either given no evaluation or led to believe that their performance had been above average. I. G. Sarason (1956), in a study of serial learning, found that although failure groups were poorer in performance than nonfailure Ss, the decrement was equal in low and high anxiety groups. Opposed to these negative results are several verbal learning studies (Gordon & Berlyne, 1954; Lucas, 1952; I. G. Sarason, 1957b; Walker, 1961), and one study employing a complex speed task (Katchmar et al., 1958) in which interactions were found between anxiety level and failure, the performance of high anxiety Ss uniformly being inferior under failure as compared to the nonfailure condition with the performance of low anxiety Ss experiencing failure varying from being inferior to slightly superior to the parallel nonfailure groups. One additional verbal learning study (Taylor, 1958) found

---

[4] On the basis of data obtained in a study of word association, I. G. Sarason (1961a) has also suggested that the TAQ may be *less* highly related to performance than the MAS when task instructions stress that personality factors rather than intellectual ones are being tested. Assuming that similar results would be obtained with learning tasks, it would be interesting to compare high and low MAS groups under the two types of ego-involving instructions to determine whether the differences between extreme MAS groups are more marked if the instructions emphasize personality rather than intelligence. Such results would suggest that high anxiety Ss are relatively more vulnerable to certain kinds of stress than to others.

a similar but nonsignificant interaction between anxiety and failure, with both high and low anxiety groups given failure instructions being significantly inferior to their controls. In the latter study, noncompetitive paired-associate lists were employed and the high anxiety Ss performed better than the low anxiety Ss under neutral conditions, as predicted by our theory about drive. The performance decrement resulting from failure instructions that was found in both groups thus adds additional confirmation to the suggestion that stress may arouse interfering task-irrelevant responses rather than merely raising drive level.

Evaluation of the Evidence Concerning Psychological Stress. Considering the ego-involvement and failure studies as a whole, we might elaborate our initial suggestions concerning the effects of these conditions on performance and their interaction with the anxiety variable. Assuming that ego-involving and failure instructions fall at two points along a continuum of "psychological stress," we suggest that, in addition to raising the level of D, an increase in stress has two major effects. The first might be described as changes in task-attending behavior. In tasks requiring some degree of voluntary effort, Ss must be "cooperative" in that they must pay attention to E's instructions and attempt to follow them by attending to the appropriate stimuli and making an effort to perform the required response. In conducting any experiment, at least those employing normal adult Ss, we typically take for granted that Ss will exhibit appropriate task-oriented behavior; on those rare occasions on which we note a gross deviation from an acceptable minimum, we exclude the offending S from further consideration.

Instructions that stress the importance of doing well or state that performance reflects a valued characteristic, such as intelligence for the college-student subject, may be expected to lead most individuals to increased effort and attention and hence to better performance. However, emphasis on doing well may also arouse anxiety (fear of failure) and negative evaluations of performance (failure reports) to intensify it. As anxiety, with its D and S_D components, increases in intensity, so do the frequency and intensity of task-irrelevant responses. To the extent that the responses to be acquired can be adversely affected by them, these irrelevant tendencies will lead to performance decrement. Thus, as externally manipulated psychological stress increases, performance might first be expected to increase due to an increase in task-oriented behaviors and then to decrease as irrelevant responses are aroused and begin to be predominant in their influence. The initial rise in performance might be greater and more prolonged when tasks of a low degree of intratask competition are employed since the increase in drive (D) produced by the addition of stress would also be expected to facilitate performance rather than, as would be expected in the case of competitive tasks, deter it.

Adding the MAS variable to this conception, we might describe high anxiety Ss as having a lower threshold for the arousal of anxiety than the low anxious, tending to react even to mild ego-involving instructions with fear of failure. Thus, while the performance of low anxiety groups would be expected to rise and then decline as stress increases, the period of initial rise in high anxiety groups, if it appears at all, would be expected to be attentuated and their decline in performance appear not only earlier on the stress continuum but be, at any given point, more pronounced.

These hypotheses account quite well for the data from studies employing verbal learning tasks and certain complex speed tasks but not for the results obtained with simpler speed tasks (I. G. Sarason & Palola, 1960). On the latter, it will be recalled, both anxiety groups were found to *improve* in performance under stress, the high anxiety Ss to a greater degree than the low. While Sarason and Palola suggested that task difficulty was the variable determining the direction of the effect of stress on performance and hence the nature of the interaction between stress and anxiety level, the writers would like to suggest that the results found in their experiments may be specific to speed tasks since the type of interaction between anxiety and stress found in verbal learning studies has been the same for both "easy" and "difficult" (i.e., noncompetitive and competitive) lists (e.g., Nicholson, 1958). We further suggest that even within speed tasks the relevant variable contributing to the kind of results reported by Sarason and Palola is what loosely might be called task complexity rather than difficulty per se.

As is well-known, Ss given motivating instructions in situations involving timed tasks attempt to respond faster. On tasks in which Ss are required to make fine discriminations among stimulus items or to execute a series of complicated motor patterns, increases in speed are typically made at the expense of accuracy, and may thus lead to overall performance decrement. In contrast, attempts to go faster on simpler tasks interfere to a lesser degree with accurate responding and may thus result in a greater absolute number of correct responses. The differences in the nature of the interaction between anxiety level and stress condition that were found by I. G. Sarason and Palola (1960) in simple versus complex speed tasks would be explained simply by postulating that high anxiety Ss, being more responsive to the stress instructions, exhibit greater increases in speed of responding than low anxiety Ss, without any reference being made to task-irrelevant responses. Whether or not the latter play any role in speed tasks and therefore contribute to performance differences between anxiety groups is not clear. It could be argued that the performance of complex speed tasks is not only more likely to be disrupted by task-irrelevant responses than the performance of simpler tasks but also, by placing Ss in greater conflict about speed versus accuracy, are more likely to *elicit* irrelevant tendencies in the form of irritation and self-disgust with speed-induced errors, etc.

Before leaving this series of speculations about the effects of psychological stress on the performance of complex learning tasks, an alternative hypothesis whose simplicity gives it an attractive appeal might be considered. Instead of assuming that stress has complex effects, not only raising Ss' drive level but also eliciting task-relevant and task-irrelevant responses, would it not be more parsimonious merely to assume that there is a nonmonotonic relationship between performance and drive level (D)? According to this conception, any set of conditions that increases drive level will at first lead to an increased level of performance and then, as drive level continues to rise, to a decrease in performance. Many psychologists, citing such data as that in the well-known study of the effects of degree of induced muscular tension by Courts (1942), have suggested an inverted U-shaped function as describing the relationship between motivation (i.e., drive level) and performance. Malmo (e.g., 1957; 1958; 1959) has been particularly articulate in proposing that this is the function holding between performance and drive or arousal level. By appealing to the notion that "difficult" tasks elicit more emotionality (and hence drive) than "easy" ones, particularly in high anxiety Ss, Malmo (e.g., 1957) has also suggested that all of the data obtained with the MAS that have been reviewed here, including the interaction between anxiety and degree of intratask competition, can be satisfactorily explained by assuming that the relationship between drive and performance takes the form of an inverted-U.

Following Malmo's lead, a number of investigators have attempted to test the inverted-U hypothesis in studies employing the MAS as an indicator of drive or arousal level. Included among these are studies in which the design consisted of comparing the performance of high and low anxiety groups under two levels of stress, the assumption being that by considering the values of the two variables jointly, a drive continuum with at least three points could legitimately be constructed. Thus, demonstrations that Ss who were low in both anxiety score and experimentally manipulated stress and those who were high in both were poorer in performance than members of the other two groups have been regarded as "confirming" the inverted-U hypothesis. While such an interpretation might be offered as one of a number of possible *post hoc* hypotheses to explain data already obtained, experiments whose purpose it is to *test* the inverted-U notion ought to be designed so that the shape of the empirical function could be determined for each empirical variable separately. Thus, at least three widely separated points on the MAS or the stress continuum, or both, should be employed. (The same remarks hold true if the writers' speculations about degree of psychological stress are to be tested, more than two levels of stress having to be used.)

Although there have been few investigations in which both stress condition and MAS scores have been varied over more than two levels, there have been a number of studies in which Ss were unselected with respect to the MAS so that correlations could be obtained between performance and the full range of MAS scores, or in which a middle-scoring group was tested as well as groups falling at the extremes of the MAS distribution. Considering only the studies employing tasks falling within the purview of this chapter, monotonic (although not necessarily linear) relationships have quite consistently been found between performance and the full range of MAS scores, although, if the entire body of literature involving the MAS is surveyed, studies can be found in which the results suggest the presence of a nonmonotonic function.

It should be clearly understood, however, that the relationship revealed in these latter MAS studies, or in any of the studies that have been cited as supporting the nonmonotonic hypothesis, is a purely empirical one holding between performance on the one hand and experimentally manipulated variables on the other. To infer from a set of empirical findings taking the form of an inverted-U that there is a nonmonotonic relationship between performance and drive is an *assumption* or hypothesis and only one of a number of alternative possibilities. Thus, one might assume instead that the relationship between drive level *and the experimental variables determining it* is nonmonotonic, the relationship between performance and drive being a positive, monotonic one. Or one may hold, as does the Hull-Spence behavior theory from which our predictions concerning the MAS have been derived, that both of these relations are positive functions (or, more precisely, that there is a positive, monotonic relationship between the experimental variables and D, between D and excitatory potential (E), and between the latter and the dependent response variables) but that performance in different behavioral situations depends not only on the drive factor but also on the nature of the interactions of this factor with other determining variables in the different situations. Predictions from the theory are thus derived from the total network of constructs together with the special boundary conditions holding for a given situation.

Such a theoretical network may lead to a variety of implications as to the empirical relations holding between performance and motivational variables, including positive, negative, and nonmonotonic (inverted-U) functions. Examination of the data in this area reveals that all of these different functions have actually been obtained, each in a wide variety of situations. For example, in contrast to studies demonstrating a nonmonotonic function between performance and induced muscular tension (e.g., Courts, 1942; Wood & Hokanson, 1965) are the studies of classical eyelid conditioning in which, as already indicated, performance has uniformly been found to be a positive, monotonic function of the intensity of the noxious S_U. The maximum levels of puff intensity used in these studies, incidentally, have been quite high. The correlations between conditioning performance and MAS scores have also been found to be positive and monotonic (e.g., Spence & Spence, 1964). Monotonic correlations have also been found between the MAS and performance in studies employing competitive tasks which were *negative* rather than positive in sign (e.g., Taylor & Rechtschaffen, 1959). These MAS findings, we might remind ourselves, have not been "explained" *post hoc* but have been predicted by a theory specifying the interaction between drive (D) and learning or habit (H) variables in determining performance in the different experimental situations.

Still another example that might be cited is a study by Pinneo (1961), done under Malmo's direction, in which Ss were required to perform a tracking task under five levels of induced muscular tension. Instead of the inverted-U function that had been found in several previous studies of induced tension and that was anticipated in this one, no initial performance facilitation was found, performance being negatively related throughout to degree of tension. As an incidental note, it might be mentioned that in attempting to explain these unexpected results, Pinneo discussed the possibility that Ss had had to divide their attention between attempting to perform the experimental task and maintaining the required degree of muscular tension, thus resulting in interference with tracing performance, and advised that the kind of task selected for tests of the inverted-U hypothesis is important to consider—suggestions with which we have a great deal of sympathy.

As is quite apparent from this brief series of examples, there is no single empirical function that describes the relationship between performance and any given set of independent variables defining drive level. Whether or not some version of the inverted-U hypothesis ultimately turns out to be more useful than the assumption that the various functions involving D are uniformly positive and monotonic, any theory in this area that pretends to be at all comprehensive must be able to account for all the varieties of empirical relationships that have been obtained. A theory which assumes a nonmonotonic function between performance and drive level is therefore not as parsimonious as one might think. Each of the very frequent exceptions to the empirical, nonmonotonic function between performance and motivational variables necessitates, in the absence of a more comprehensive theoretical network, the introduction of a number of *ad hoc* factors.

If the more detailed account of the interaction of psychological stress and anxiety (MAS) in complex learning situations that has just been proposed has any value, it is because it appears to be related to a broader set of theoretical notions and to permit the integration of a larger set of empirical data than the results of these stress studies alone. For example, our notions concerning the interaction of drive level and *intratask* competition, which in turn were drawn from Hullian behavior theory and the large body of experimental literature relevant to it, are included in the total set of hypotheses. The results of the studies testing our hypotheses concerning intratask competition could not, however, be encompassed by appealing to some simple, consistent relationship between motivational variables and performance. Furthermore, the present suggestions concerning task-behavior and the interfering role of task-irrelevant responses can be extended into areas of investigation other than stress and anxiety as a personality variable. As an example, the work of McClelland, Atkinson, and their colleagues with the achievement motive might be cited (e.g., McClelland, Atkinson, Clark, & Lowell, 1953). These investigators have reported that Ss scoring high on their measure of need achievement exhibit better performance on a variety of tasks than low scoring Ss, due presumably to their high level of "motivation." The latter is said to include directive as well as "energizing" (D) properties. Among these directive properties are those that we have called "task-attending behavior" whose major effect, at least in those situations in which a high degree of attention and voluntary effort is required, is an increase in the efficiency of performance. If one were to assume that "drive," as we have defined it, were equivalent to their "motivation," the results of our MAS studies and the McClelland-Atkinson need achievement studies would be contradictory. That is, it would be necessary from their hypotheses to predict that our high anxiety subjects, due to a higher motivational level, would be consistently better in performance than the low anxious, a prediction, of course, which is contrary to fact. The distinction between task-attending behavior and drive not only avoids the apparent inconsistency but also reconciles the two sets of data.

Such kinds of evidence suggest, then, not the unnecessary complications created by postulating the diversity of effects that psychological stress may have on performance, but rather that our previous failures to find a consistent relationship between stress and performance (independent of personality factors) may be due in part to the oversimplified assumption that stimulus-defined stress has only a single, simple effect (e.g., raising drive level) and that stress has a uniform relationship to performance in all types of situations.

Effects of Noxious Stimulation

The hypotheses just proposed and the experimental evidence relevant to them concern *psychological* stress. Still another group of studies must be examined, those that have introduced some form of noxious stimulation, typically electric shock, into the situation and have studied its effect on the performance of high and low anxiety groups on complex learning tasks.

Three of these studies (Besch, 1959; Chiles, 1958; Lee, 1961) employed paired-associate lists which contained both competitive and noncompetitive pairs. In all three studies, comparison of the performance of high and low anxiety groups tested under the neutral, nonshock condition revealed interactions between anxiety level and type of pair which, although not in all cases statistically significant, were in accord with our theoretical predictions concerning *D*. However, their results were more variable with respect to the effects of shock and the interaction between shock and the other two experimental variables. Both Lee (1961) and Besch (1959) found that shock had little or no effect on performance when low competition pairs were considered but impaired performance on high competition pairs. No significant interaction between shock and anxiety (MAS) level was found by Lee, but Besch reported that on the competitive items the *low* anxiety Ss (particularly the males) exhibited more decrement under the shock condition than the high anxiety Ss. In contrast to these results, Chiles (1958) found that there was *no* interaction between shock and degree of intratask competition and that shock *facilitated* performance on both types of pairs. Furthermore, this facilitation was significantly greater in the high anxiety group.

In part, the differences in results among these studies may have been the result of procedural variations. For example, although shock was administered in all three studies during predetermined intertrial intervals, the studies differed in the explanation of the shock given to Ss, Besch (1959) stating that it was given when too many errors occurred on a given trial, Lee (1961) instructing her Ss that the appearance of shock was unrelated to their performance, and Chiles (1958) allowing Ss to terminate the shock by pressing a switch, explaining that their reaction time was being studied. The investigations also differed in the number of shocks given and in the method used to determine shock intensity, Chiles using a standard value for each S and the others adjusting shock level to each S's reported threshold of pain or unpleasantness.

Still another method of introducing the noxious stimulation was used in a study of serial learning by Deese, Lazarus, and Keenan (1953) who shocked Ss each time they failed to anticipate correctly. High anxiety Ss improved in performance in comparison to their nonshocked controls while the low anxiety Ss deteriorated. These investigators also found that in another shock condition in which Ss were shocked after randomly selected responses and thus could not avoid it, both groups were poorer than their controls, the low anxiety Ss to a greater degree than the high anxiety Ss. In a repetition of this study (Lazarus, Deese, & Hamilton, 1954), in which a much more difficult list was employed, there was no significant interaction between anxiety and shock or any effect of shock per se in either the avoidable or unavoidable condition. However, the amount of learning that took place in the standard number of trials given to each S was so low that the groups had little opportunity to differ.

To add further confusion to an already inconsistent picture, Silverman and Blitz (1956) investigated the effects of threat of shock on the performance of a serial learning task, finding that low anxiety Ss told they *might* be shocked were better than their nonthreatened controls while those told they *would* be shocked were poorer; on the other hand, high anxiety Ss were similar in performance to their controls under both threat conditions. Finally, Davidson, Andrews, and Ross (1956) obtained results indicating that shock deterred performance on a high-speed color-naming task in both high and low anxiety groups, but particularly in high anxiety Ss. In this latter study, as in the investigation by Besch (1959), shock was interpreted to the Ss as indicating that their performance had been below expectation.

It is quite clear that with respect to the effects of shock per se the data from these studies are not adequately explained by either a hypothesis that assumes that shock acts primarily to raise Ss' drive level or a hypothesis that states its major effect is to elicit competing response tendencies that interfere with performance. The data suggest instead that no simple empirical or theoretical statement about the influence of shock can be made and that in predicting its effect on performance, account must be taken of such variables as the nature of the task materials, the manner in which shock or anticipation of shock is introduced into the situation, the instructions Ss are given about its significance, the number and intensity of the shocks, etc. As yet, such variables have not been systematically investigated and the interactions that exist among them are little understood, if at all.

The difficulties that may be encountered in attempting to explain the effects that shock may have on the performance of complex tasks, even when it is administered to all Ss under the same conditions, is further illustrated by the results of an investigation reported by Bardach (1960). In this study, Ss who were shocked on a single occasion during the course of learning a serial list showed no difference in performance, as a group, from Ss tested under neutral conditions. On the basis of responses to a postexperimental interview, Ss in the experimental group were classified as to whether their attitude towards the shock had been primarily compatible or incompatible with effective task performance. (Ss who claimed to be undisturbed by the shock, who believed, despite the instructions, that they would be shocked for errors or could avoid future shock by trying harder, or who did not expect additional shocks, were all considered to have compatible attitudes.) Those with incompatible attitudes were found to be *poorer* in performance than the nonshocked control group while those with compatible attitudes were better, particularly if shock had been given early in learning.

Turning to a consideration of the anxiety variable, the results of these studies as a whole provide little support for the hypothesis that noxious stimulation elicits more irrelevant, competing responses in high anxiety Ss than in low and that their performance will therefore show more decrement, even when this hypothesis is broadened to include "less facilitation" of performance as well as, literally, "more decrement." While this type of interaction was found in several instances, the opposite pattern (if any interaction was demonstrated at all) occurred even more frequently, the high anxiety Ss exhibiting *more* facilitation or *less* decrement than the low. Explanations of the several kinds of interactions between anxiety level and shock that have occurred in these studies will have to await the accumulation of more empirical data and the development of more detailed theoretical analyses than are currently available.

Conclusions

As can easily be recognized, the theorizing offered in this chapter about anxiety as a personality characteristic has been extremely narrow in scope, being confined to a consideration of a circumscribed set of properties that may differentiate between individuals scoring at the extremes of the MAS within limited types of experimental settings. In part this restriction reflects the fact that in our work involving the MAS we have been primarily concerned with the role of aversive motivational factors in relatively simple types of learning situations, and not with anxious individuals per se. But it also reflects the fact that, in the present state of psychological knowledge, it is unlikely that a useful theory of anxiety—or of any other personality characteristic—that is both comprehensive in the phenomena it encompasses and detailed enough to permit precise predictions about behavior can be developed.

In formulating such a theory, it would not be enough merely to describe the various properties that differentiate individuals of varying anxiety levels. In addition, one must specify the kinds of situations in which each of these properties or set of properties are expected to operate and the precise manner in which they are expected to influence the overt behaviors being measured or observed. To the extent that hypotheses about different personality groups are to be tested in situations which are themselves not too well understood, as is frequently the case, it is necessary also to have developed a theory about the experimental situation itself. As has been amply illustrated by the present chapter, psychological phenomena tend to be extremely complex, performance even in relatively simple situations being determined by a host of interacting stimulus and individual difference variables. Thus, attempts to develop hypotheses about the behavior of anxiety groups even within a limited type of experimental setting is a major undertaking.

In this connection, it is interesting to note that disagreements that arise in personality research about the interpretation to be given to sets of empirical data are often concerned with the hypotheses proposed about the experimental situation per se and not with those concerning the personality variable itself. For example, the proponents of the "difficulty hypothesis" which we have described above appear to agree with our contentions that high anxiety Ss are more reactive to psychological stress than are low anxiety Ss and that the competing responses evoked by this emotionality may result in the former being inferior in performance on complex learning tasks. We disagree, however, about the role of task difficulty in *eliciting* these competing responses and hence about the appropriateness of a response-interference hypothesis in explaining certain of the MAS data.

The search for more satisfactory experimental arrangements in which to test hypotheses about personality variables has always been a major part of personality research and probably will continue to be so for some time. To repeat an earlier statement, the development of even limited theories is a difficut undertaking in which progress is likely to be slow.

REFERENCES

Amsel, A. The effect upon level of consummatory response of the addition of anxiety to a motivational complex. *J. exp. Psychol.,* 1950, **40**, 709-715.

Amsel, A., & Maltzman, I. The effect upon generalized drive strength of emotionality as inferred from the level of consummatory response. *J. exp. Psychol.,* 1950, **40**, 563-569.

Axelrod, H. S., Cowen, E. L., & Heilizer, F. The correlates of manifest anxiety in stylus maze learning. *J. exp. Psychol.,* 1956, **51**, 131-138.

Bardach, Joan L. Effects of situational anxiety at different stages of practice. *J. exp. Psychol.,* 1960, **59**, 420-424.

Beam, J. C. Serial learning and conditioning under real life stress. *J. abnorm. soc. Psychol.,* 1955, **51**, 543-551.

Bendig, A. W. The development of a short form of the Manifest Anxiety Scale. *J. consult. Psychol.,* 1956, **20**, 384.

Besch, Norma F. Paired-associates learning as a function of anxiety level and shock. *J. Pers.,* 1959, **27**, 116-124.

Bindra, D., Paterson, A. L., & Strzelecki, Joanna. On the relation between anxiety and conditioning. *Canad. J. Psychol.,* 1955, **9**, 1-6.

Bitterman, M. E., & Holtzman, W. H. Conditioning and extinction of the galvanic skin response as a function of anxiety. *J. abnorm. soc. Psychol.,* 1952, **47**, 615-623.

Burgess, M., & Hokanson, J. E. Effects of increased heart rate on intellectual performance. *J. abnorm. soc. Psychol.,* 1964, **68**, 85-91.

Castaneda, A. Effects of stress on complex learning and performance. *J. exp. Psychol.,* 1956, **52**, 9-12.

Castaneda, A. Supplementary report: Differential position habits and anxiety in children as determinants of performance in learning. *J. exp. Psychol.,* 1961, **61**, 257-258.

Castaneda, A., & Lipsitt, L. P. Relation of stress and differential position habits to performance in motor learning. *J. exp. Psychol.,* 1959, **57**, 25-30.

Castaneda, A., Palermo, D. S., & McCandless, B. R. Complex learning and performance as a function of anxiety in children and task difficulty. *Child Develpm.,* 1956, **27**, 327-332.

Child, I. L. Personality. *Annu. Rev. Psychol.,* 1954, **5**, 149-170.

Chiles, W. D. Effects of shock-induced stress on verbal performance. *J. exp. Psychol.,* 1958, **56**, 159-165.

Clark, R. E. The role of drive (time stress) in complex learning: An emphasis on prelearning phenomena. *J. exp. Psychol.,* 1962, **63**, 57-61.

Courts, F. A. The influence of practice on the dynamogenic effect of muscular tension. *J. exp. Psychol.,* 1942, **30**, 504-511.

Cronbach, L. J., & Meehl, P. E. Construct validity in psychological tests. *Psychol. Bull.,* 1955, **52**, 281-302.

Davidson, W. Z., Andrews, T. G., & Ross, S. Effects of stress and anxiety on continuous high-speed color naming. *J. exp. Psychol.,* 1956, **52**, 13-17.

Deese, J., Lazarus, R. S., & Keenan, J. Anxiety, anxiety reduction, and stress in learning. *J. exp. Psychol.,* 1953, **46**, 55-60.

Duffy, Elizabeth. The psychological significance of the concept of "arousal" or "activation." *Psychol. Rev.,* 1957, **64**, 265-275.

Farber, I. E. The role of motivation in verbal learning and performance. *Psychol. Bull.*, 1955, **52**, 311-327.

Farber, I. E., & Spence, K. W. Complex learning and conditioning as a function of anxiety. *J. exp. Psychol.*, 1953, **45**, 120-125.

Gilberstadt, H., & Davenport, G. Some relationships between GSR conditioning and judgments of anxiety. *J. abnorm. soc. Psychol.*, 1960, **60**, 441-443.

Gleser, Goldine, & Ulett, G. The Saslow Screening Test as a measure of anxiety-proneness. *J. clin. Psychol.*, 1952, **8**, 279-283.

Gordon, W. M., & Berlyne, D. B. Drive-level and flexibility in paired-associate nonsense syllable learning. *Quart. J. exp. Psychol.*, 1954, **6**, 181-185.

Hughes, J. B., II, Sprague, J. L., & Bendig, A. W. Anxiety level, response alternation, and performance in serial learning. *J. Psychol.*, 1954, **38**, 421-426.

Hull, C. L. *Principles of behavior.* New York: Appleton, 1943.

Kamin, L. J., & Fedorchak, Olga. The Taylor scale, hunger, and verbal learning. *Canad. J. Psychol.*, 1957, **11**, 212-218.

Katchmar, L. T., Ross, S., & Andrews, T. G. Effects of stress and anxiety on performance of a complex verbal-coding task. *J. exp. Psychol.*, 1958, **55**, 559-564.

Korchin, S. J., & Levine, S. Anxiety and verbal learning. *J. abnorm. soc. Psychol.*, 1957, **54**, 234-240.

Lacey, J. I., & Lacey, Beatrice C. Verification and extension of the principle of autonomic response-stereotypy. *Amer. J. Psychol.*, 1958, **71**, 50-73.

Lauterbach, C. G. The Taylor A scale and clinical measures of anxiety. *J. consult. Psychol.*, 1958, **22**, 314.

Lazarus, R. S., Deese, J., & Hamilton, R. Anxiety and stress in learning: the role of intraserial duplication. *J. exp. Psychol.*, 1954, **47**, 111-114.

Lazarus, R. S., Deese, J., & Osler, Sonia F. The effects of psychological stress upon performance. *Psychol. Bull.*, 1952, **49**, 293-317.

Lee, Lee Charlotte. The effects of anxiety level and shock on a paired-associate verbal task. *J. exp. Psychol.*, 1961, **61**, 213-217.

Lovaas, O. I. The relationship of induced muscular tension, tension level, and manifest anxiety in learning. *J. exp. Psychol.*, 1960, **59**, 145-152.

Lucas, J. D. The interactive effects of anxiety, failure, and intra-serial duplication. *Amer. J. Psychol.*, 1952, **65**, 59-66.

McClelland, D. C., Atkinson, J. W., Clark, R. A., & Lowell, E. L. *The achievement motive.* New York: Appleton, 1953.

Malmo, R. B. Anxiety and behavioral arousal. *Psychol. Rev.*, 1957, **64**, 276-287.

Malmo, R. B. Measurement of drive: An unsolved problem in psychology. In M. R. Jones (Ed.), *Nebraska symposium on motivation.* Lincoln, Nebr.: Univer. of Nebraska Press, 1958. Pp. 229-265.

Malmo, R. B. Activation: A neuropsychological dimension. *Psychol. Rev.*, 1959, **66**, 367-386.

Maltzman, I., Fox, J., & Morrisett, L., Jr. Some effects of manifest anxiety on mental set. *J. exp. Psychol.*, 1953, **46**, 50-54.

Mandler, G., & Cohen, Judith E. Test anxiety questionnaires. *J. consult. Psychol.*, 1958, **22**, 228-229.

Mandler, G., & Sarason, S. B. A study of anxiety and learning. *J. abnorm. soc. Psychol.*, 1952, **47**, 166-173.

Mandler, G., & Sarason, S. B. The effect of prior experience and subjective failure on the evocation of test anxiety. *J. Pers.*, 1953, **21**, 336-341.

Matarazzo, J. D., Ulett, G. A., & Saslow, G. Human maze performance as a function of increasing levels of anxiety. *J. gen. Psychol.,* 1955, **43**, 79-95.

Mednick, Martha T. Mediated generalization and the incubation effect as a function of manifest anxiety. *J. abnorm. soc. Psychol.,* 1957, **55**, 315-321.

Mednick, S. A. Generalization as a function of manifest anxiety and adaptation to psychological experiments. *J. consult. Psychol.,* 1957, **21**, 491-494.

Miller, N. E. Learnable drives and rewards. In S. S. Stevens (Ed.), *Handbook of experimental psychology.* New York: Wiley, 1951, Pp. 435-472.

Montague, E. K. The role of anxiety in serial rote learning. *J. exp. Psychol.,* 1953, **45**, 91-96.

Mowrer, O. H. A stimulus response analysis of anxiety and its role as a reinforcing agent. *Psychol. Rev.,* 1939, **46**, 553-565.

Nicholson, W. M. The influence of anxiety upon learning: Interference or drive increment? *J. Pers.,* 1958, **26**, 303-319.

Pinneo, L. R. The effects of induced muscular tension during tracking on level of activation and on performance. *J. exp. Psychol.,* 1961, **62**, 523-531.

Ramond, C. K. Anxiety and task as determiners of verbal performance. *J. exp. Psychol.,* 1953, **46**, 120-124.

Runquist, W. N., & Ross, L. E. The relation between physiological measures of emotionality and performance in eyelid conditioning. *J. exp. Psychol.,* 1959, **57**, 329-332.

Runquist, W. N., & Spence, K. W. Performance in eyelid conditioning related to changes in muscular tension and physiological measures of emotionality. *J. exp. Psychol.,* 1959, **58**, 417-422.

Saltz, E., & Hoehn, A. J. A test of the Taylor-Spence theory of anxiety. *J. abnorm. soc. Psychol.,* 1957, **54**, 114-117.

Sarason, I. G. Effect of anxiety, motivational instructions, and failure on serial learning. *J. exp. Psychol.,* 1956, **51**, 253-260.

Sarason, I. G. Effect of anxiety and two kinds of motivating instructions on verbal learning. *J. abnorm. soc. Psychol.,* 1957, **54**, 166-171. (a)

Sarason, I. G. The effect of anxiety and two kinds of failure on serial learning. *J. Pers.,* 1957, **25**, 383-391. (b)

Sarason, I. G. Empirical findings and theoretical problems in the use of anxiety scales. *Psychol. Bull.,* 1960, **57**, 403-415.

Sarason, I. G. A note on anxiety, instructions, and word association performance. *J. abnorm. soc. Psychol.,* 1961, **62**, 153-154. (a)

Sarason, I. G. The effects of anxiety and threat on the solution of a difficult task. *J. abnorm. soc. Psychol.,* 1961, **62**, 165-168. (b)

Sarason, I. G., & Palola, E. G. The relationship of test and general anxiety, difficulty of task, and experimental instructions to performance. *J. exp. Psychol.,* 1960, **59**, 185-191.

Sarason, S. B., Mandler, G., & Craighill, P. G. The effect of differential instructions on anxiety and learning. *J. abnorm. soc. Psychol.,* 1952, **47**, 561-565.

Schnore, M. M. Individual patterns of physiological activity as a function of task differences and degree of arousal. *J. exp. Psychol.,* 1959, **58**, 117-128.

Silverman, R. E., & Blitz, B. Learning and two kinds of anxiety. *J. abnorm. soc. Psychol.,* 1956, **52**, 301-303.

Spence, K. W. *Behavior theory and conditioning.* New Haven, Conn.: Yale Univer. Press, 1956.

Spence, K. W. A theory of emotionally based drive (D) and its relation to performance in simple learning situations. *Amer. Psychologist,* 1958, **13**, 131-141.

Spence, K. W. Anxiety (drive) level and performance in eyelid conditioning. *Psychol. Bull.,* 1964, **61**, 129-139.

Spence, K. W., Farber, I. E., & McFann, H. H. The relation of anxiety (drive) level to performance in competitional and noncompetitional paired-associates learning. *J. exp. Psychol.,* 1956, **52**, 296-305. (a)

Spence, K. W., Farber, I. E., & Taylor, Elaine. The relation of electric shock and anxiety to level of performance in eyelid conditioning. *J. exp. Psychol.,* 1954, **48**, 404-408.

Spence, K. W., & Goldstein, H. Eyelid conditioning as a function of emotion-producing instructions. *J. exp. Psychol.,* 1961, **62**, 291-294.

Spence, K. W., & Haggard, D. Upublished data, 1954.

Spence, K. W., & Spence, Janet T. Relation of eyelid conditioning to manifest anxiety, extraversion, and rigidity. *J. abnorm. soc. Psychol.,* 1964, **68**, 144-149.

Spence, K. W., & Taylor, Janet A. Anxiety and strength of UCS as determiners of amount of eyelid conditioning. *J. exp. Psychol.,* 1951, **42**, 183-188.

Spence, K. W., Taylor, J., & Ketchel, Rhoda. Anxiety (drive) level and degree of competition in paired-associates learning. *J. exp. Psychol.,* 1956, **52**, 306-310. (b)

Standish, R. R., & Champion, R. A. Task difficulty and drive in verbal learning. *J. exp. Psychol.,* 1960, **59**, 361-365.

Taylor, Janet A. The relationship of anxiety to the conditioned eyelid response. *J. exp. Psychol.,* 1951, **41**, 81-92.

Taylor, Janet A. A personality scale of manifest anxiety. *J. abnorm. soc. Psychol.,* 1953, **48**, 285-290.

Taylor, Janet A. Drive theory and manifest anxiety. *Psychol. Bull.,* 1956, **53**, 303-320.

Taylor, Janet A. The effects of anxiety level and psychological stress on verbal learning. *J. abnorm. soc. Psychol.,* 1958, **57**, 55-60.

Taylor, Janet A. Manifest anxiety, response interference and repression. Paper given at symposium, Experimental Foundations of Clinical Psychology, Univer. of Virginia Med. School, April, 1959.

Taylor, Janet A., & Chapman, Jean P. Anxiety and the learning of paired-associates. *Amer. J. Psychol.,* 1955, **68**, 671.

Taylor, Janet A., & Rechtschaffen, A. Manifest anxiety and reversed alphabet printing. *J. abnorm. soc. Psychol.,* 1959, **58**, 221-224.

Taylor, Janet A., & Spence, K. W. The relationship of anxiety level to performance in serial learning. *J. exp. Psychol.,* 1952, **44**, 61-64.

Walker, R. E. The interaction between failure, manifest anxiety, and task-irrelevant responses in paired-associate learning. Unpublished doctoral dissertation, Northwestern Univer., Ill., 1961.

Welch, L., & Kubis, J. The effect of anxiety on the conditioning rate and stability of the PGR. *J. Psychol.,* 1947, **23**, 83-91.

Wood, C. G. Jr., & Hokanson, J. E. Effects of induced muscular tension on performance and the inverted-U function. *J. pers. soc. Psychol.,* 1965, **1**, 506-510.

CHAPTER 13

Cognitive Responses to Internally Cued Anxiety[1]

Charles W. Eriksen

DEPARTMENT OF PSYCHOLOGY,
UNIVERSITY OF ILLINOIS,
URBANA, ILLINOIS

The laboratory rat can be conditioned to show fear or anxiety in response to a buzzer or other external stimulation but only man has the extensive capacity to carry within himself numerous anxiety-evoking cues in the forms of thoughts, memories, and other mediational processes. Due to his time-binding characteristics he can relive in the present anxiety experiences of the past or anticipate disasters and dangers in the future. With plenty to eat, good health, lack of pain, and an opportunity for enjoyment of a variety of pursuits, man still can be miserably ill with anxiety through preoccupation with memories of an event that occurred weeks ago or with anticipation of a stressful situation weeks in the future.

The responses to this internally aroused anxiety might be expected to be different from behavior elicited by externally presented threats or dangers. Since the cue is internally (self) elicited, anxiety can be reduced or avoided by the elimination or avoidance of the cue. Thus, anxiety evoked by memories or thoughts about future dangers can be eliminated by the avoidance of the relevant memories or thoughts. This is distinguished from external threat where the nature of the situation and the kind of threat determines what responses or behaviors, if any, will be effective.

[1] Much of the research reported in this chapter was supported by research grant No. M-1206 from the National Institutes of Health, Public Health Service. The preparation of the chapter has been facilitated by Research Career Award No. K6 MH-22014.

Responses to these internally cued anxieties have traditionally been studied under the rubric of defensive mechanisms. An extensive list of behaviors labeled repression, denial, projection, reaction formation, etc., have been catalogued. All represent responses by which the human alleviates or avoids internally elicited anxiety. Although an extensive research literature deals with defensive mechanisms, this type of behavior is still not fully understood, and in fact, the existence of some of the responses is questioned.

This is in a large part attributable to the fact that defensive mechanisms and attendant research have been heavily enmeshed with Freudian theory. All too often experiments have been designed solely to demonstrate the existence of Freudian-type repression. Experiments are singularly unproductive when they are used as demonstrations rather than as posing questions of nature. As a result of this preoccupation with psychoanalytic theory, scientifically meaningless controversies arise as to whether a given experiment meets or does not meet all the nebulous criteria for *Freudian* (1925) repression. Actually, to the extent that a given experiment is successful in evoking anxiety from internal cues, it provides us with valid information as to how the person cognitively responds.

The Freudian mechanism of repression (cognitive avoidance) has received the most experimental attention. This is partly due to its dramatic nature as characterized by psychoanalytic theory and in part to the traditional interest of psychology in learning and memory phenomena. Experimental investigation of repression as well as other defenses has been severely limited by the lack of simple efficient techniques for producing the phenomena in laboratory settings. The essential requirements for studying repression are first of all a set of stimuli or cues that are effective in arousing moderate or severe anxiety in the individual subjects. Second, an arrangement or stimulus situation is required that tends to evoke these cues as covert responses in the form of thoughts, memories, or perceptions in the individual subject. Third, this experimental arrangement must be such that it doesn't absolutely require the occurrence of the covert cue. Stated otherwise, the experimental situation must be such as to give the subject an opportunity cognitively to avoid the cue and thus escape the anxiety. The degree of structure of this experimental arrangement required before the covert response occurs can be the dependent variable as in experiments where the number of learning trials required or the duration of exposure of the stimulus before the subject elicits the particular anxiety-evoking response is used to infer the amount of cognitive avoidance that is occurring. Since in all cases the occurrence or nonoccurrence of a covert response is inferred from the subject's verbalized responses, the experimental situation finally must be such that there is no anxiety reduction by inhibiting the verbalization of the cue once the cue has occurred at the covert level.

Research has varied markedly in the adequacy with which these different requirements have been satisfied. The earliest as well as the most numerous studies on repression have depended upon traditional learning, relearning, and memory measures. The assumption is made that stimuli which lead to anxiety and therefore cognitive avoidance will require more learning trials to achieve a given criterion of mastery or will be forgotten more readily than will neutral stimuli or cues. Many of these studies have been markedly deficient in the selection of anxiety-evoking stimuli. All too frequently the assumption has been made that words reflecting sexual or aggressive ideation will lead to a cognitive avoidance. Paired associates in which a member of the pair contains a sexual or an aggressive word are expected to be learned less readily than those consisting of neutral word pairs, but no independent experimental operations are employed to demonstrate that the chosen stimuli are indeed effective anxiety evokers for the individual subjects in the experiment.

An important improvement in methodology is obtained when experiments use tests or procedures to determine anxiety-evoking material for the individual subjects in the experiment. Here subjects are pretested using most typically a word association test. Stimulus words that elicit indications of anxiety (defined as long association times, blocking of associations or large GSRs) are selected for the individual subject and later used as the stimulus material in a learning and memory experiment. A serious limitation of this method is that the experimenter must demonstrate convincingly that the particular stimulus material chosen does not differ from the neutral material with which it is compared on other relevant variables determining learning such as familiarity, reluctance to verbalize, and competing response tendencies.

The most satisfactory method for equating neutral and experimental stimuli on relevant variables is to use a methodology in which the anxiety is experimentally conditioned to stimuli. Thus, the neutral and experimental stimuli can be matched on other relevant variables. Experimenters have attempted to condition anxiety to specific stimuli in various ways. Association of certain words or cues with severe failure experience has been employed (Caron & Wallach, 1957; Eriksen & Browne, 1956; Glixman, 1949) as well as association with undesirable personality traits (D'Zurilla, 1965) or even with electric shock (Lazarus & Longo, 1953).

Inconsistency in the results of experiments using experimentally conditioned anxiety is most likely attributable to failure to allow for individual differences in response to covertly aroused anxiety. Preoccupation with attempts to demonstrate the Freudian concept of repression have led experimenters to overlook individual differences in the way subjects are responding. As has been pointed out elsewhere (Eriksen, 1951a), even Freudian theory allows for types of defenses other than repression, and the memory and perceptual consequences of variation in defense mechanisms is expected to be different. Even though the stimuli when they occur covertly in the subject are effective in arousing anxiety, not all subjects will respond by a cognitive avoidance. Some will use rationalization techniques and others projection. Both of these mechanisms might be expected to lead to awareness of the covert cue, but the anxiety is handled when it occurs by some other means.

An impetus was given to research on defense mechanisms when clinical and personality psychologists discovered the tachistoscope. By means of a tachistoscope stimuli can be presented at very short durations, and the length of exposure duration required for a subject to recognize a given stimulus provided a new dependent variable. Instead of trials to a learning criterion or number of items remembered, the exposure duration necessary for recognizing anxiety as opposed to neutral stimuli could be used to detect cognitive avoidance mechanisms. The logic of the methodology, however, remained the same. Instead of the subject having to think of the anxiety-evoking stimulus as the response member in paired associate learning or remember it on a memory task, he now had to think of it as a possible response to the fragmentary perception he received from the tachistoscopic exposure.

As might be expected, due to the identity of the logic, all the designs that have been used in the learning and memory studies have been repeated using perceptual recognition as the dependent variable. And of course all the defects in these methodologies were transferred intact. Thus, experimenters attempted to demonstrate perceptual defense by showing that college sophomores had higher recognition thresholds for words like "bitch" and "belly" than for words like "flower" and "house" even though only the most naive would expect the average college sophomore to be made anxious by perceiving the word "belly." Also, many experiments failed to control for individual differences in cognitive responses to the covertly elicited anxiety even when they were sophisticated enough to insure that the stimuli were anxiety arousing for the individual subjects by pretesting or through experimental conditioning of the anxiety. This was the case despite the fact that quite early in the need and perception experimentation individual differences in the form of defense and sensitization for anxiety-arousing stimuli had been shown (Bruner & Postman, 1947; Lazarus, Eriksen, & Fonda, 1951).

My own research interests in defensive mechanisms began in the late 1940's through the then-current interest in projective techniques. From tests such as the Rorschach and the TAT, clinicians were making personality interpretations not only on the basis of what the patient saw in the ambiguous stimuli, but also on the basis of what he failed to see. Thus, a patient who failed to give sexual or aggressive responses or interpretations to any of the Rorschach inkblots might be inferred to have repression in these areas, for while the blots are ambiguous enough so as not to demand a sexual or aggressive interpretation, they also are ambiguous enough to yield such concepts with fairly high frequencies in the normal person. A person failing to give such concepts at least occasionally might be suspected of having some kind of inhibition to this ideation.

In order to test this assumption it was necessary to vary experimentally the ambiguity of neutral and anxiety-evoking stimuli from a level where a number of interpretations were reasonable to a degree of definiteness that permitted only one reasonable interpretation. The work of Douglas (1947) on the tachistoscopic presentation of Rorschach inkblots and other stimuli suggested a method for achieving this systematic variation in ambiguity.

A series of cartoon drawings depicting aggressive, dependent, and homosexual activities were constructed along with cartoons of neutral content (Eriksen, 1951a). These were presented at systematically varied exposure durations until a duration long enough for the subject to identify the activity of the cartoon was achieved.

The subjects were selected from a population of mental-hospital patients in order to maximize the likelihood of disturbances in the three need areas and the use of avoidant-type defensive mechanisms. Prior to the perceptual recognition tasks all patients were individually administered a specially constructed word association test containing, along with a number of neutral words, eight aggressive, eight dependent, and eight homosexual stimulus words. For each subject three disturbance scores corresponding to the three need areas were computed based upon association disturbances to the words in the respective need area. These word association disturbance indicators were then correlated with the subject's perceptual recognition performance for the corresponding need scenes, first correcting these latter scores for perceptual acuity on the neutral scenes. For all three need areas significant relationships were found between the number of anxiety indicators for a need area obtained on the word association test and the exposure duration necessary to recognize cartoons depicting material related to the need area. The greater the amount of association disturbances, the longer was the durations required for reaching the criteria of recognition of the need scenes relative to the neutral scenes.

In a follow-up study (Eriksen, 1951b) performance on the TAT was correlated with perceptual recognition for neutral and aggressive cartoons. Four TAT cards that tend to elicit stories with aggressive themes with high frequency were used to predict patients' recognition accuracy for the aggressive cartoons. The TAT stories were scored on the degree of overt aggression expressed in the story content. It was found that patients who expressed considerable overt aggression freely and easily in their TAT stories had, in general, lower recognition durations for the aggressive cartoons relative to the neutral, whereas patients who avoided aggressive themes in their stories and actually tended to distort the stimulus content of the picture away from aggression tended to have much higher recognition durations for the aggressive cartoons.

The results of these two studies had shown that there was a relationship between a person's perceptual recognition behavior and clinically accepted criteria of anxiety and avoidance on two different diagnostic tests. The next step in research seemed to be a further refinement of the individual differences noted in the perceptual recognition performance. The study using the TAT had indicated that subjects who freely expressed aggressive ideation with a minimal amount of cueing in the TAT showed facilitation or sensitization for aggressive cartoons. The subjects on the other hand who blocked or distorted aggressive implications in the TAT material were the ones indicating a defensive response to the perceptual task. Bruner and Postman (1947) previously had reported that for some of their subjects there was a monotonic relation between reaction time to a word on an association test and the duration of exposure necessary for the word's visual recognition. But for other subjects the relationship was curvilinear with both short and long reaction-time words requiring shorter exposure durations for recognition than did words with medium reaction times. They had characterized the first of these patterns of recognition behavior as perceptual defense and the second as perceptual vigilance. In their study, however, the interpretation was *post hoc* since the experiment did not contain operations or procedures for differentially predicting defense or vigilance reaction prior to the fact.

In an experiment carried out with Lazarus and Fonda (Lazarus *et al.,* 1951) an attempt was made to relate more explicitly perceptual defense and sensitization pattern to clinically defined defensive mechanisms. The subjects were out-patients in a mental hygiene clinic. Instead of a visual perceptual task, an auditory perceptual recognition measure was used.

Sexual and aggressive sentences were played against a white noise background at an average intelligibility level of 50%. Disturbances in the sexual and aggressive areas were individually assessed in the subjects by means of a sentence-completion test which contained a number of aggressive and sexual stems as well as an intermixture of neutral ones. Performance on this sentence-completion test was scored in terms of the ease or freedom with which the subject completed the sexual and aggressive sentences. A repressivelike performance was characterized by those subjects who distorted and/or by other means avoided the aggressive or sexual implication of the stem. The sensitizing reaction on the other hand was characterized by the subjects whose reaction times to these sentence stems was short

TABLE I

The Intercorrelations of Sentence-Completion Test Scores and Auditory Perception by Need Areas[a]

Tests	Sentence-completion		Auditory perception		
	Sex	Hostility	Sex	Hostility	Neutral
Sentence-completion:					
Sex	—	.521	.643	.310	.477
Hostility	—	—	.410	.514	.151
Auditory perception:					
Sex	—	—	—	.609	.125
Hostility	—	—	—	—	−.088

[a] Evaluated via Fisher's z transformation, r's of .336 and .430 are significant at the .05 and the .01 levels, respectively.

and whose completions freely expressed the aggressive or sexual idea implied in the stems. Performance on the auditory perceptual tasks was scored separately for each subject for the two need areas, and the score was corrected for overall perceptual performance on the neutral sentences.

In Table I the intercorrelations of the sentence-completion test scores and the sense-perceived scores for the auditory perceptual task are shown. As can be seen, significant and appreciable correlations were obtained for each of the two need areas. Furthermore, the specific content of the area, whether sex or aggression, was important in determining the relationship as is shown by the finding of a significant partial correlation between the disturbance scores for sex on the sentence-completion task and auditory perceptual task, holding constant the hostility scores on these two measures. Also, the corresponding partial correlation for hostility, holding constant the sex scores, was significant.

From case history and therapy interview material it was possible to classify 25 of the subjects into those who predominantly used intellectualizing approaches to their problem areas and those who characteristically used repressive-avoidant defenses. It was anticipated that the patients using the intellectualizing, ruminating approach to their problems would most likely be characterized by a sensitization to areas of conflict or anxiety whereas those using the repressive-avoidant response would show the perceptual defensive reaction. In Table II the 12 subjects characterized as repressors and the 13 characterized as intellectualizers are compared on their performance on both the sentence-completion test and the auditory perceptual recognition test. In this table negative scores indicate that on the auditory perceptual task the group did less well on the respective content area than they did on the neutral sentences, and on the sentence-com-

TABLE II

COMPARISON OF REPRESSORS AND INTELLECTUALIZERS ON PERCEPTUAL RECOGNITION AND THE SENTENCE-COMPLETION TEST

Tests	Repressors ($N = 12$)		Intellectualizers ($N = 13$)		
	Mean	S.D.	Mean	S.D.	t
Auditory perceptual recognition:					
Sex[a]	− .25	1.18	+1.60	1.48	3.32
Hostility[a]	−1.10	1.32	+ .30	1.25	2.67
Neutral	5.27	1.59	6.17	1.59	1.36
Sentence-completion:					
Sex	6.20	1.39	9.10	4.52	2.02
Hostility	5.50	1.70	8.00	4.31	1.77

[a] For a one-tailed test, t values of 1.71 and 2.50 are significant at the .05 and the .01 levels, respectively.

pletion test low scores represent a high incidence of blocking or distortion of the need sentences into an innocuous form.

These results provided confirmation of our expectations. They supported the generally accepted clinical interpretation of sentence-completion test performance and more importantly revealed different perceptual recognition concomitants associated with different defense mechanisms in logically expected directions. The patient using a characteristic repressive-avoidant defense to conflict and anxiety manifested a similar kind of behavior in the perception of anxiety-evoking stimuli. On the other hand, the patient who dealt with conflict by intellectualizing and ruminating on the problem showed little or no defensive avoidance on the perceptual recognition task but rather a heightened sensitivity.

The next steps in the research program were to further substantiate the differences between the sensitizers and the repressors by independent criteria and to relate the perceptual recognition phenomena to the more traditional learning and memory work on repression. Several investigators (Glixman, 1949; Rosenzweig, 1943) had reported that when a series of tasks were administered under the guise of an intelligence test, and failure to complete a task was defined as failure, subjects as a group tended to remember more of the completed (successful tasks) than the incompleted tasks relative to a control group. This differential recall had been interpreted as supporting the repression concept since it was assumed that failure on an intelligence test would be highly threatening to the subjects employed. While the groups as a whole tended under these ego-involved conditions to remember successes as opposed to failures, Rosenzweig noted that there were marked individual exceptions to this tendency. The question posed in our next experiment (Eriksen, 1952a) was whether the subjects who were predominantly success recallers were the ones who showed perceptual defense while those who tended to show a preference for recall of their failures would be the sensitizers on perceptual recognition.

The subjects were college freshmen, predominantly premedical students, nearly all of whom could be assumed to be made anxious by information indicating they were not as bright as their fellow classmates. The experimental material consisted of 14 sentences divided into two- and three-word phrases. The phrases for each sentence were presented in a jumbled order and it was the subject's task to rearrange the phrases to obtain a meaningful sentence. Half of the sentences were unsolvable due to their construction. The sentences were administered to the experimental group under the pretext that it was an intelligence test. They were told that the experimenter was engaged in research on abstract thinking and concept formation and he needed subjects for this research. The intelligence test was being given as a means of selecting students who were intelligent enough to participate in the abstraction experiment. The subjects were further told that anyone with an IQ of 115 or better should be able to complete all or practically all of the sentences within the time limits provided. To increase the experimental group's feelings of failure, classmate stooges were scattered throughout the group. These stooges pretended to complete successfully all of the sentences.

A control group was administered the sentences under the impression that it was some material invented for the purpose of keeping subjects in a learning experiment from rehearsing during a rest interval. They were also told that many of the sentences could not be solved within the time provided. Outside of this difference in set and the absence of stooges, the experimental and control groups were treated identically.

After completion of the sentences test several other pseudointelligence-test items were given before a recall of the sentences was requested under the guise of a memory test.

In Table III the experimental and control subjects are compared on the differences in recall of completed and incompleted sentences. The two groups did not differ in total sentences recalled, but as can be seen from the table, the experimental group favored successful completions in their recall relative to the control subjects. The biggest difference between the groups, however, was in the variance of the difference scores between successful and unsuccessful sentences recalled.

In the second phase of the study the 7 subjects in the experimental group who showed the most tendency to recall their successes relative to their failures and the 7 who showed the reverse tendency were selected for the perceptual recognition task. Each of these 14 subjects was individually

TABLE III

COMPARISON OF EXPERIMENTAL AND CONTROL GROUPS ON INCOMPLETED
MINUS COMPLETED SENTENCES RECALLED

Score	Experimental ($N = 39$)	Control ($N = 22$)	t	F	p^a
Range	+5 to −5	+3 to −2	—	—	—
Mean	−.86	+.41	1.87	—	<.05
S^2	14.13	2.18	—	6.47	<.001

a The probabilities are for a one-tailed test.

administered a word-association test and for each subject 25 words were selected representing the range of shortest to longest association time. In a second individually administered session the subjects' recognition durations were obtained for each of the 25 words.

In Table IV the 7 success-recalling subjects and the 7 failure-recalling subjects are compared on the correlation between association time and recognition duration for the respective words. For the 7 success-recalling subjects the correlations between association time and recognition duration for words were all positive and of appreciable magnitudes. For the failure-recalling subjects on the other hand, three of the correlations were negative and the others of low magnitude. The difference in average correlation between the groups was highly significant.

This experiment was successful, then, in demonstrating a consistency of individual defensive behavior across memory and perceptual tasks. In doing so it indicated the continuity between the perceptual recognition approach and the more traditional learning and memory approaches to the study of defensive behavior. Perhaps most important, however, was the substantiation of the differences between the repressor-like behavior of some subjects and the sensitization behavior of others.

The next experiment carried out (Eriksen, 1952b) was designed to substantiate further the differences that had been found so far between the sensitizer and the repressor and to ascertain whether these differences in defensive reaction could also be obtained in paired associate learning. The completed and incompleted task procedure, under the guise of an intelligence test, was again used to select subjects showing the sensitizing and the repressing reaction to recall of failures. After ascertaining that the ex-

TABLE IV

CORRELATIONS BETWEEN ASSOCIATION TIME AND RECOGNITION THRESHOLDS FOR THE SUCCESS-RECALL AND FAILURE-RECALL GROUPS[a, b]

Subject	Success-recall (product-moment correlation)	z^c	Subject	Failure-recall (product-moment correlation)	z^d
A	.76	1.00	a	.37	.39
B	.74	.95	b	.37	.39
C	.64	.76	c	.31	.32
D	.60	.69	d	.27	.28
E	.58	.66	e	−.01	−.01
F	.56	.63	f	−.22	−.22
G	.50	.55	g	−.35	−.37

[a] $N = 25$ for each subject. For a one-tailed test, z values of .36 and .50 are significant at the .05 and the .01 levels, respectively.
[b] Combined variance estimate: .062; $t = 4.77$; $p < .001$.
[c] Mean = .75.
[d] Mean = .11.

perimental manipulation had been successful through comparison with a control group, the 10 subjects having the strongest tendency to recall successful items relative to failures and the 10 showing the strongest opposite tendency were selected for the paired associate learning procedure. Each of the 20 subjects was individually administered a word-association list, and 8 words with long, 8 with medium, and 8 with short association times were selected for each subject. Paired associates were formed by using nonsense syllables as the stimulus members of the pairs and the 24 selected words as the response members.

In Table V the failure recall and success recall groups are compared on the number of trials required to learn and relearn paired associates formed from long, medium, and short association-time words. The subjects who showed evidence of defensive forgetting in the completed and incompleted task situation were found to require more trials both to learn and

TABLE V

Differences in Learning and Relearning Rates for Long, Medium, and Short Association-Time Words for the Success- and Failure-Recall Groups

Association times	Failure-recall group						Success-recall group						t (group difference)	
	Learning			Relearning			Learning			Relearning				
	Mean difference	S.D. difference	t	Mean difference	S.D. difference	t	Mean difference	S.D. difference	t	Mean difference	S.D. difference	t	Learning	Relearning
Long-short	.24	.79	.96	−.01	.97	.00	2.47	2.37	3.29	2.26	2.19	3.26	2.82	3.01
Long-medium	−.05	1.63	.10	.13	.93	.44	2.30	1.48	4.91	1.51	1.71	2.79	3.37	2.24
Medium-short	−.15	1.51	.31	−.29	.95	.96	.17	1.59	.34	.75	1.49	1.59	.46	1.86

to relearn affective words (long association time) than were required for neutral words. On the other hand, the subjects who showed little or no evidence of defensive forgetting in the completed-incompleted task test learned the affective words at least as easily as they did the neutral. These results are quite consistent with the findings from the two preceding experiments and suggest at the very least that there are certain individuals who are highly consistent in showing cognitive avoidance to anxiety-evoking stimuli across different experimental situations.

At this point the question arose as to whether there are measurable personality correlates of the repressor-sensitizer reaction to anxiety-evoking stimuli. A relationship between differences in defensive behavior and personality variables had been suggested by Rosenzweig (1943) when he found that children rated high on pride were more apt to recall completed tasks when the tasks had been administered under orientation involving self-esteem. Subsequently Rosenzweig and Sarason (1942) found a relation between successs recall and impunitiveness and suggestibility. Also, Alper (1948) related differences in success and failure recall under two differing degrees of stress to personality differences on a small group of subjects upon whom extensive clinical evaluations existed. She reported that subjects characterized as strong egos tended to remember proportionately more successful items as the stress increased whereas subjects characterized as weak egos tended to show a reverse pattern. The traits of suggestibility and impunitiveness are suggestive of the hysterical personality, and considerable clinical theory and lore support the expectation that repressive avoidant defenses tend to be associated with the hysterias and the extroversive personality. In the experiment by Lazarus *et al.* (1951) patients clinically characterized as psychasthenics had been found to show the sensitizing reaction on the auditory perceptual recognition task.

Also, Eysenck (1947) in his factor analysis of neurotic populations had arrived at two higher-order factors, one corresponding to a general trait of neuroticism and the other an introversion-extroversion dimension. The hysterias characterized the extroversive pole and the psychasthenic neurotics the introversive pole. The general neuroticism factor might be considered as having a good deal in common with Alper's variable of ego strength.

From these suggestive leads it was decided to attempt to correlate completed-incompleted task recall under anxiety-evoking circumstances to the personality variables of hysteria, psychasthenia, and general neuroticism (Eriksen, 1954). To measure these personality variables the hysteria and psychasthenia scales from the MMPI were employed, and the McReynolds Concept Choice Test was used as a measure of general neuroticism or ego strength. This latter measure was quite similar to one used by Eysenck and found to be highly saturated on the neuroticism factor. In addition, the rationale bears a strong relationship to the clinical conception of ego strength.

College freshmen were again administered the pseudointelligence test under circumstances identical to those previously described. A control group was again employed to evaluate whether the ruse had been successful.

For each subject in both the experimental and control groups a recall score was computed by subtracting the number of successful tasks recalled from the number of unsuccessful tasks recalled and dividing by the total tasks recalled. In Table VI the correlations of this recall index with the neuroticism measure for both the experimental and control groups are

TABLE VI
CORRELATIONS BETWEEN THE NEUROTICISM SCORE AND COMPLETED-INCOMPLETED
TASK RECALL SCORE FOR THE EXPERIMENTAL AND CONTROL GROUPS

Group	N	r^a	p
Experimental	43	—.60	.001
Control	19	.38	.055

a The significance of r is evaluated via Fisher's z transformation. The probabilities are for a one-tailed test.

given. For the control group a positive correlation of borderline significance was obtained, indicating that subjects high on neuroticism tended to recall relatively more successful tasks under a condition of little or no objective threat to self-esteem. For the experimental group the direction of the relationship was reversed. The experimental subjects who are high on neuroticism tended to favor incompleted tasks in their recall while those low on neuroticism showed a tendency to favor successful tasks. These results supported Alper's previous finding.

In Table VII are shown the correlations of the MMPI scales for hysteria and psychasthenia with the recall index for the subjects in the experimental group. Subjects scoring high on hysteria showed a tendency to favor successful tasks in their recall whereas subjects scoring high on psychasthenia tended to favor the incompleted tasks. Again the finding was in agreement with the previous research and in the direction to be anticipated from general clinical thinking. However, the correlation of the hysteria and psychasthenia scales with the recall index might have been mediated by the fact that both of these scales are correlated with the neuroticism measure. To determine whether a relationship between recall index and the traits of hysteria and psychasthenia existed independently of a joint correlation with neuroticism, partial correlations were computed between recall index and the hysteria scale holding constant the measure of neuroticism. The partial correlation was found to be —.53. The corresponding partial correlation for psychasthenia and recall score was .14. The size of the partial correlation between the hysteria scale and the recall score was large enough to suggest that the hysteria scale is related to recall score independently of the correlation with neuroticism. However, the small partial correlation between recall and psychasthenia suggests that the correlation between these two variables is not larger than can be accounted for by the respective correlations with the neuroticism measure. Thus, the evidence supports the conclusion that hysteria and neuroticism are independent variables related to success-failure recall ratio but is inconclusive with respect to the relation of task recall and psychasthenia.

TABLE VII

CORRELATION BETWEEN COMPLETED-INCOMPLETED TASK RECALL SCORE AND THE
HYSTERIA AND PSYCHASTHENIA SCALES FOR THE EXPERIMENTAL GROUP

Scale	N	r^a	p
Hysteria	40	—.27	.05
Psychasthenia	40	.28	.05

a The significance of r is evaluated via Fisher's z transformation. The probabilities are for a one-tailed test.

An opportunity was provided to clarify further the meaning of the hysteria and psychasthenia scales. Harry Murray made available to us (Eriksen & Davids, 1955) the data on 20 Harvard undergraduates who had been intensively studied in the Harvard psychological clinic and for whom extensive personality data and clinical evaluations existed. These 20 subjects were administered the hysteria and psychasthenia scales of the MMPI along with the Taylor Manifest Anxiety Scale. Scores on these scales were then correlated with clinical rankings of the subjects on tendency to use repression and on an optimism-pessimism variable. Table VIII summarizes the results.

The results were as expected. Psychasthenia was significantly and negatively correlated with tendency to use repression and negatively correlated with optimism. Also, the correlation between the psychasthenia scale and the MAS was about as high as the respective reliabilities of the two scales would permit, suggesting that they are measuring essentially the same variables. In order to eliminate in part a general neuroticism component from the hysteria and psychasthenia scales, a composite scale was formed by subtracting a subject's score on the psychasthenia scale from his score on the hysteria scale. Thus, high scores on the composite scale would indicate hysteria and low scores psychasthenia. As is seen in Table VIII this composite scale correlated in a positive direction with the tendency to use repression and with optimism. However, the correlation of the composite scale with the psychasthenia sale was so high as to suggest there is little gain in using the composite or the hysteria scale alone. Most, if not all, of the variance can be accounted for in terms of psychasthenia-scale scores.

In general the results from this study suggested that the hysteria and psychasthenia scales of the MMPI were distinguishing between persons on the same behavioral variables that are clinically observed to be associated with differences in defensive mechanisms. This is congruent with

TABLE VIII

RANK-ORDER CORRELATIONS BETWEEN MMPI SCALES AND CLINICAL RANKINGS ON REPRESSION AND OPTIMISM-PESSIMISM[a, b]

	Psychasthenia	Hysteria-psychasthenia	Anxiety (Taylor Scale)	Repression	Optimism-pessimism
Psychasthenia	—	—.89	.92	—.47	—.90
Hysteria-psychasthenia		—	—.78	.42	.78
Anxiety (Taylor Scale)			—	—.41	—.87
Repression				—	.51

[a] Rank-order coefficients of .38 and .52 are significant at approximately the .05 and the .01 levels for a one-tailed test.

[b] $N = 20$.

our previously found relationships of these scales to differential recall of successes and failures. Also, the intercorrelation of the psychasthenia scale with the MAS suggests that the variable or variables involved in response to covertly elicited anxiety may be related to differential performance under the variety of anxiety situations that have been studied using the MAS.

One final experiment was carried out on the relation of personality variables and responses to covertly stimulated anxiety (Eriksen & Browne, 1956). The relationship of the MMPI scales as predictors of differential perceptual recognition performance had not yet been shown although the pattern of evidence from the other studies strongly suggested that such a relationship would exist.

Two groups, one composed of subjects scoring high and the other of subjects scoring low on the psychasthenia scale, were administered an anagrams test in an intellectually competitive situation designed to produce moderate to severe failure. Upon completion of the anagrams test both groups were told the correct solution to each of the anagrams and required to write these solutions on the back of the test booklet. Following this, the perceptual recognition thresholds for the anagrams solutions were obtained along with the recognition thresholds for the same number of comparable control words. It was anticipated that the recency of experience with the anagram words would tend to lower their recognition durations relative to the control words for both groups of subjects. In addition, however, it was expected that the high psychasthenia subjects would show a greater difference in recognition thresholds between the anagram and the control words than would the low group. Since the anagram solutions had been experienced in a context of failure it was anticipated that their occurrence as responses would lead to self-devaluing thoughts which in keeping with previous findings would evoke cognitive avoidant behavior; since high psychasthenia scores in past research had tended to be associated

TABLE IX

MEAN TRIALS FOR RECOGNITION OF THE ANAGRAM AND CONTROL WORDS
BY THE HIGH AND LOW GROUPS

| Groups | Words | | Combined mean |
	Anagram	Control	
High	8.26	11.69	9.98
Low	10.77	12.73	11.75
Combined mean	9.39	12.16	

with the sensitizing reaction, the subjects in the high group would show a greater gain from the recency effect since less avoidant responses would be elicited by the words associated with failure.

The results are presented in Table IX and commensurate with the expectations the anagram words for both groups showed lower recognition thresholds than did the control words. Again, commensurate with expectations from prior research, the high psychasthenia subjects showed lower thresholds for the failure-associated words relative to control words than did the low-scoring psychasthenia subjects.

When the results of this series of experiments, extending over a period of 6 years, are considered *in toto,* three general conclusions seem well established. First, there is individual consistency in defensive behavior that extends across memory tasks and across memory and perceptual tasks. Individuals who show cognitive avoidance through poorer recall of failure associated tasks also take longer to learn anxiety-related words and require longer exposure durations for perceptual recognition of these words. Second, there is a relationship of this experimentally observed defensive behavior to clinically observed defensive mechanisms. Subjects who are classified clinically as using repressive-avoidant defenses show cognitive avoidance in the experimental tasks. Those characterized clinically as using sensitizing or intellectualizing defensive mechanisms show little or no cognitive avoidance to anxiety-evoking material in laboratory situations. And third, in addition to establishing a repressor-sensitizer variable, this research has shown the relation of this variable to psychometric measures of hysteria, psychasthenia, and also to a general neuroticism.

These conclusions are considerably substantiated by the fact that independent investigators in other laboratories have widely confirmed the findings. Individual consistency in defense responses has been confirmed, for example, by Lazarus and Longo (1953) and Caron and Wallach (1957; 1959). The former experimenters had their subjects learn paired associates composed of nonsense syllables, but on half of the pairs a severe electric shock was administered one-third of the time irrespective of whether the subject correctly anticipated the correct response. On a recall test 24 hours later, subjects who in a previous experiment had shown a preponderant tendency to remember successful rather than failed tasks showed an appreciable recall deficit for the nonsense syllable pairs that had been shocked. However, subjects who had been predominantly failure recallers, showed a significant reverse tendency. No differences between these groups of subjects were found on the learning trials.

Caron and Wallach studied the recall of completed and incompleted items administered under the guise of an intelligence test and followed this with a determination of the perceptual recognition of neutral words and words related to an intelligence-testing experience. Subjects who had a low recall of failed items from the pseudointelligence-test experience were found to have much higher recognition thresholds for words related to intelligence testing whereas subjects who had shown a preponderant tendency to recall failed items showed significantly less decrement in their recognition thresholds for intelligence-testing related words.[2]

The relation of clinically described defensive mechanisms to this laboratory-observed defensive behavior has also been confirmed by various in-

---

[2] In a subsequent paper Caron and Wallach (1959) reported the results of a factor analysis of a number of personality measures and completed-incompleted success-failure recalls and recognition thresholds. They failed to find significant relationships between recall tendency and recognition threshold with the hysteria and psychasthenia scales. However, there is reason to suspect that these negative findings may have been attributable to a biased sample resulting from the use of volunteer subjects. The correlation of these personality scales with laboratory-observed defensive behavior is not large, accounting typically for between 10 and 20% of the variance. A bias in the populations sampled could well reduce the relationships to a magnitude that would not be detected with small samples.

vestigators. Carpenter, Weiner, and Carpenter (1956) conducted an experiment very similar to that of Lazarus *et al.* (1951). Sentence completions were judged by four clinical psychologists for indications of conflict and for the particular type of defense, repressive or sensitizing, used by the subject. Subjects characterized as using repressive defenses were found to have higher perceptual recognition thresholds for conflict relative to neutral material whereas those characterized as sensitizers showed the opposite reaction.

An extensive investigation of the relation between clinical assessments of defensive mechanisms and perceptual recognition was carried out by Shannon (1962). Case-history and rating data were used to classify psychiatric patients into three groups: those using externalization defenses, those acting out defenses, and those using internalization defenses. As predicted, externalizers and actor-outers had lower perceptual recognition thresholds for conflict-relevant stimuli than for matched controlled stimuli. Internalizers on the other hand had significantly higher recognition thresholds for the conflict-related pictures.

Most widely confirmed has been the existence of the repressor-sensitizer dimension and its relation to a number of established personality variables. Truax (1957) selected extreme scoring groups from a composite of the hysteria-psychasthenia scales and found that subjects high on the hysteria end of this dimension required appreciably longer to relearn paired associates in which the stimulus member was a word that had been associated with experimentally produced failure. Subjects on the psychasthenia end of the scale learned the paired associates with the failure words actually quicker than neutral pairs. Mathews and Wertheimer (1958) confirmed the finding of Eriksen and Browne (1956) of a relation between psychasthenia-scale scores and perceptual recognition of anxiety-related words. Mathews and Wertheimer found that subjects scoring high on the psychasthenia scale from the MMPI had lower recognition thresholds for conflict words detected by word-association tests than did low-scoring subjects. More recently Gossett (1964) related the repressor-sensitizer personality scale to differential recall of successful and failed tasks administered under the guise of an intelligence or personality test, and Tempone (1962) related an improved repressor-sensitizer scale to perceptual vigilance and perceptual defense. In Tempone's study 40 repressors and 40 sensitizers were selected on the basis of an improved measure of the hysteria-psychasthenia dimension. A pseudointelligence test consisting of anagrams was administered with stooges employed to increase the plausibility of the situation and to increase the stress. Half of both extreme groups were administered the anagrams under success conditions and the other half under failure. The correct solution to each anagram was given to the subjects after each trial. Following this phase of the experiment perceptual recognition was determined for the anagram solutions and comparable control words. The repressors and sensitizers who had experienced the success treatment did not differ in their perceptual recognition behavior, but, for the groups who had undergone the failure experience, the repressors in the group showed significantly higher thresholds for the anagram solutions than the sensitizing subjects. There was no difference in perceptual recognition for neutral words as a function of experimental treatment or personality classification.

Still other investigators have used different personality scales (Osler & Lewinsohn, 1954; Van de Castle, 1960) and found relationships between the repressing and sensitizing response to anxiety. Since these other scales have been shown to be highly correlated with the hysteria and particularly the psychasthenia scales, the results of these investigators must also be considered confirmatory.

In addition to defensive behavior, the repressor-sensitizer dimension has been related to various other personality characteristics. Altrocchi, Parsons, and Dickoff (1960) developed a repression-sensitization index based upon various MMPI scales including the hysteria and psychasthenia. From this index they found that repressors differed from sensitizers on self-ideal discrepancies, primarily due to the more negative self-concept that sensitizers had. Furthermore, Altrocchi (1961) found differences in interpersonal perception associated with scores in the repressor-sensitizer index which were shown to be due to differences in self-concepts between these two groups. Important psychometric refinements in the repressor-sensitizer index have been made by Byrne (1961), and an independent attempt to develop a measure of the repressor-sensitizer variable was undertaken by Ullmann (1958). Originally his scale was applicable only to neuropsychiatric patients since it was based on ratings of case history material using essentially the criterion that Shannon (1962) had employed in detecting his perceptual externalizers and internalizers. Ullmann later undertook to construct a scale derived from MMPI items (1962) to measure this dimension that he termed facilitation-inhibition.

Research employing one or the other of these repressor-sensitizer scales has shown an interesting pattern of relationships with personality variables and performances that most clinical theorizing would expect to be related to a repressor-sensitizer difference. Ullmann and Lim (1962) found that sensitizers (facilitators) showed greater appreciation for sexual and aggressive humor than did repressors. Numerous other correlations of the repressor-sensitizer scale and the facilitator-inhibitor index with various personality adjustment and task performance measures are summarized by Byrne (in press).

Explanatory Accounts of Defensive Behavior

The existence of a class of cognitive avoidance responses to internally cued anxiety seems to be sufficiently established to require attempts to relate this behavior to our general knowledge and concepts of learning, memory, and perceptual functioning. It is to be noted that such explanatory attempts must not only be an account of the experimental findings on memory and perceptual recognition tasks but must also be a general explanatory attempt at the clinical concept of defenses, specifically repression. While the clinical concept of repression might be different in degree, it seems most unlikely that it is qualitatively different.

One of the oldest and most obvious explanations for the experimental results on defensive behavior is that of deliberate response suppression. Sears (1936) has applied this criticism to many of the learning and memory studies and Howes and Solomon (1950) and Zajonc (1962) have applied it to some of the perceptual recognition experiments. Response suppression is a very effective explanation of the results from the naively designed experiments as Howes and Solomon have so well illustrated in their analysis of the McGinnies experiment (1950). In these naively designed studies, the experimenters have used dirty or taboo words with the gratuitous assumption that they are anxiety-arousing for all or nearly all of their subjects; no provision is made for individual differences in response. Response suppression due to social embarrassment arising from verbalization of vulgar words would appear to be a real factor in such experiments. However, a response-suppression explanation becomes strained at explaining the results of better-designed studies where independent operations are employed to insure that specific stimuli are anxiety-evoking for the individual subjects in the experiment. The response-suppression explanation becomes completely inappropriate for those studies where the anxiety is conditioned in the experiment itself to previously neutral stimuli (Caron & Wallach, 1957; Eriksen & Browne, 1956; Lazarus & Longo, 1953; Tempone, 1962). Also, the response-suppression explanation provides no rationale for why subjects scoring high on the hysteria scale should be expected to show response suppression whereas those scoring high on the psychasthenia scale should not.

Differences in familiarity for neutral and emotional stimuli have been used as an explanation for the differential learning and retention of these two classes of stimuli and also for differential perceptual recognition. Howes and Solomon (1951) have supplied the most sophisticated and complete statement of this explanation. They assume that the more frequently a subject has experienced a stimulus in the past, the more familiar he will be with it and the more readily he will learn and remember it or the fewer cues he will require in order to recognize it when presented in a tachistoscope.

There can be little argument that stimulus familiarity is a factor in learning and memory as well as in perceptual recognition, but the role of this variable has most likely been overextended (Eriksen, 1963). Like the response-suppression explanation, it is an effective account of the naively designed studies on repression and defensive behavior, but it is seriously inadequate when extended to account for the results of the more adequately designed studies. A familiarity explanation does not account for, or have its proponents attempted to extend it to, those experiments where anxiety is conditioned in the experimental situation to previously neutral stimuli or where personality correlates are observed for individual differences in response to anxiety-evoking stimuli, whether on memory or perceptual recognition tasks.

The explanation for defensive behavior with which most psychologists are familiar is in terms of psychoanalytic concepts. Though psychoanalytic theory has a lot to say about defensive mechanisms, it is of little help in understanding how they operate. The theory is formulated at a primitive naturalistic level and as such does not concern itself with the details of the learning, memory, and perceptual processes underlying the operation of repression and other defenses. Our knowledge and theories of behavior have advanced much beyond the rather crude formulations of psychoanalysis, and an adequate explanation in psychology now requires description of phenomena in terms of extant knowledge and current concepts.

A key concept in the Freudian or analytic treatment of defensive mechanisms is the unconscious mind which is portrayed as having many of the characteristics that we subjectively note as characteristic of the conscious mind except in a more mischievous, irresponsible version. This unconscious mind is assumed to have a greater perceptual sensitivity and a greater memory reserve than the conscious mind and, therefore, the ability to prescreen perceptual inputs that might be anxiety-arousing (Blum, 1955; Lazarus & McCleary, 1951) or to inhibit the occurrence of memories from reaching the conscious mind. In one respect repression is analogous in the unconscious mind to suppression in the conscious mind. Thus, the unconscious mind suppresses a memory or a perception much as the conscious mind might do, but when this suppression occurs at the unconscious level it is a repression.

In a series of experiments we have attempted to define the meaning of the unconscious mind and to determine its characteristics experimentally. The results of our many experiments are too numerous to be summarized here (see Eriksen, 1960), but suffice it to say that the Freudian concept of the unconscious mind is not substantiated. The phenomena that can be substantiated do not form a unified concept of the unconscious but rather are explainable in terms or as instances of a variety of other concepts and known processes. Experimental evidence that has been introduced in support of a Freudian concept of the unconscious is found upon examination to be due to several factors such as misunderstanding of psychophysical thresholds and indicator methodology (Bernstein & Eriksen, 1965; Eriksen, 1958; Goldiamond, 1958), artifacts due to uncontrolled variables (Chatterjee & Eriksen, 1960; Fuhrer & Eriksen, 1960; Johnson & Eriksen, 1961), or uncorrelated error in independent but concurrent response systems (Eriksen, 1956a; Eriksen, 1956b). One conclusion that seems most clear is that no level of discrimination in the human nervous system has been found to be more sensitive than verbal report (Dulany & Eriksen, 1959).

The existence of the perceptual defense phenomena has been considered by many as an example of the discriminating powers of the unconscious mind. The mechanism assumed to underlie perceptual defense is that of a discrimination at an unconscious level as to the nature of the threatening stimulus. This unconscious discrimination then activates defenses preventing the recognition of the stimulus at the conscious level. It has been shown, however, that the perceptual defense phenomena can be genuine without requiring a concept of unconscious discrimination (Eriksen & Browne, 1956). Perceptual defense is consistent with the well-known data of the effects of punishment upon the probability of occurrence of responses. A mystery to the phenomena arises only when there is a failure to distinguish between perception and the responses from which perception is inferred.

The preoccupation in the 1930's of psychology with operationism and operational definitions led to the adopting of an excessively rigid conception of operational definitions. Although every psychologist knew subjectively that his responses were not the same as his perceptual experiences, nonetheless the idea became generally accepted that perception could not be distinguished from the responses that defined it. Fortunately our theoretical sophistication has increased since then. Experiments in which operational methods of separating response variables from the perceptual process (Eriksen & Hake, 1957; Eriksen & Wechsler, 1955) were successful in showing that many characteristics that had been attributed to the concept of perception could be relegated to response variables. A systematic treatment of the distinction between perception and response has been offered by Garner, Hake, and Eriksen (1956). Perception is treated as a concept or construct of what intervenes between stimulation and response and the concept becomes clearer and more exact as we are increasingly successful in eliminating stimulus and response variables from it. At the present time the distinction between perception and the responses from which it is inferred is well-recognized and a significant portion of current research in perception has received its impetus from this distinction. The theory of signal detection applied to psychophysical and perceptual problems (Swets, Tanner, & Birdsall, 1961) and Blackwell's (1953) work on forced choice indicators have made tremendously important contributions in providing methodology for separating response effects from perceptual phenomena.

When the tachistoscopic recognition procedure is examined from a viewpoint that distinguishes between perception and response, it is seen that the procedure is essentially a guessing experiment. What the subject perceives in the typical tachistoscopic exposure are some fragmentary parts of a word or the stimulus to which he tries to fit a response that is commensurate with the impoverished cues he perceives. If subjects are asked to describe exactly what they perceive in a tachistoscopic exposure of a word stimulus, they typically give responses such as, "It looked like a short word. There may have been a c at the beginning and it looked like a tall letter at the end." However, in the typical recognition experiment the subject is not asked to describe exactly what he perceives but is either implicitly or explicitly asked to respond in terms of whole English words or whole units, depending upon the stimulus material employed. If we consider the subject's perception to be most adequately described under the conditions where he is given the freedom of the English language to describe what he perceives, then the usual recognition experiment is essentially asking the subject to guess what word might fit the vague cues he receives in perception. What he is required to do is to associate or find a word that fits the fragmentary letters or impressions of letters and word length that correspond with his actual perception.

Viewed as essentially a guessing task for the subject, the perceptual recognition experiment becomes a way of measuring associative strength of responses to partial indefinite cues. The stronger the association or the response, the higher will be the probability that it will be elicited by fewer cues or perceptual fragments. If we consider the prior history of positive and negative reinforcement as determining the response strength, then words or other responses that have received high positive reinforcement should be elicited with more impoverished or restricted cues than responses that had been punished or been followed by anxiety. If the word *shot* leads to anxiety in a subjected due to its associations with anxiety-arousing experiences and thoughts, it would be expected that a fragmentary perception described by the subject as, "a short word beginning with s and having a tall letter toward the front," would be less apt to elicit the association or response of shot than it would other neutral or positively reinforced alternatives to these cues such as shad, sham, shut. The exposure duration necessary for recognition of this word would have to be increased until the perceptual cues received were much more definite before the subject would have a high probability of giving the word *shot* as his response. The operation of this process over a population of words would lead to the statistical finding that words associated with anxiety have higher recognition thresholds than words associated with positive reinforcement.

In responding to these fragmentary perceptual cues the subject does not necessarily have to feel subjectively that he is searching for words to fit the partial cues. The association of a response to the cue can be as immediate and automatic as the association *white* is to *black*.

Dollard and Miller (1950), in their extensive treatment of defensive mechanisms, have viewed covert responses such as thoughts, memories, and images as similar to overt responses and subject to the same laws of learning and reinforcement. This is probably a fairly general assumption among psychologists. Empirically we know that responses that are punished have a reduced probability of occurrence whereas those that are rewarded increase in probability. How the mechanisms of reward and punishment act to change probability of occurrence of either covert or overt responses is not our primary concern. It is sufficient to integrate the phenomena of defensive mechanisms with the general problems of learning.

Experimental support for the belief that covert responses and associations can be modified by punishment was found in an experiment carried out by Eriksen and Kuethe (1956). We presented subjects with a 15-item word-association list under the guise that they were taking part in an experiment to determine the limit of speed of associations. The subjects were instructed to respond with the first word that came to mind as quickly as possible after the stimulus word was presented. During the first trial on the list a strong electric shock was administered immediately after 5 arbitrarily selected response words. The subjects were then given a number of trials on the same 15 stimulus words, and every time a subject responded with 1 of the 5 first-trial punished responses he received another electric shock.

On the basis of postexperimental questioning the subjects were classified into insightful and noninsightful groups, depending upon their ability to verbalize the basis for the electric shocks and what they had done to avoid receiving them. However, both groups were found to have shown a rapid learning of avoidance behavior by changing their responses to stimulus words that had elicited punished responses. For the 10 stimulus words that had not had punished responses, the subjects continued to give their first trial responses throughout the experiment at a high level.

An analysis of the reaction times to stimuli having punished responses showed some interesting differences between the subjects in the two insight classifications. For subjects classified as insightful, reaction times to stimuli having had punished responses showed an increase for the first three trials through the list but then reaction time began to decrease and by the final trial had reached a level that was not significantly or appreciably different from that to the 10 stimulus words that had not had shocked responses. The noninsightful subjects on the other hand, showed a progressive decrease in reaction time for both classes of stimuli throughout the experimental trials. These differences in reaction time corresponded with the subjects' verbalizations of what they had tried to do in the experiment. The insightful subjects reported that they had quickly learned not to give the punished response but had to pause when the stimulus occurred to think of a new response. They further reported that after several trials through the list the new association came to mind automatically and there was no longer the subjective feeling of having to inhibit the punished response. The noninsightful subjects were unable to state how they avoided shock, and the progressive decrease in their reaction time would appear to have occurred by an automatic nonaware substitution of a new response for the punished one.

The results of this experiment would seem to demonstrate that associative connections can be modified by punishment in the same manner as overt responses. In other words, the stimulus elicits a thought or association that is followed by punishment, and the punished association would appear to be inhibited or replaced by a new association. Even in the insightful subjects where the change in response was accompanied by awareness of the mediational process, the subjects' verbal reports, substantiated by reaction time data, indicate that the new association becomes automatic within a few trials.

When covert behavior is viewed in terms of stimulus and response elements, modified and effected by the variables that influence learning and elicitation of overt behavior, defensive behavior becomes less mysterious and is seen to be part and parcel of the general phenomena of learning and response modification. The various techniques and methodologies employed in studying defensive behavior have in common the manipulation or investigation of strength of associative connections. This is true whether we're dealing with perceptual recognition experiments, the word association test, or learning and retention methodologies. Even the clinical concept of repression or cognitive avoidance is manifested most clearly through associative procedures. One of the defining operations for the detection of repression comes from the psychoanalytic free association procedure. Here the analyst detects or suspects the operation of a repressive mechanism when the patient's associations show peculiar gaps or blockages or deviate from what the analyst considers to be a reasonable type of associative chain. Humans have considerable latitude in the associative connections or trains of thought they experience. As a result of its private nature there is room for considerable idiosyncrasy without it becoming too conspicuous to one's fellows. In other words, there is room for considerable avoidance behavior at the covert level. By learning to change directions of association the person can effectively prevent the occurrence of covertly stimulated anxiety, and it is only under the relatively controlled condition of the clinician's couch or the structured administration of a word-association test that these peculiarities or deviations in associative connections become evident.

The question arises as to whether this cognitive avoidance in associative connections or in covert behavior is a conscious or unconscious process. If conscious, it corresponds to what Dollard and Miller (1950) call suppression, but in order to meet the usual criteria of repression this cognitive avoidance would have to occur at the unconscious level. Like unconscious discrimination, the evidence that human adults learn without awareness of the mediational steps has become increasingly negative. Dulany (1962) has shown that in the verbal conditioning experiments it is not only necessary that the subject be able to verbalize the relationship between the correct response and the reinforcement for learning to occur, but also the subject must be able to verbalize the intention to perform in this manner. Spielberger (1962) has presented other evidence that the subject's performance in verbal learning or conditioning experiments corresponds quite closely with his verbalizable statements concerning relationships between stimuli, responses, and reinforcement. Negative evidence for perceptual learning without awareness has also been reported (Eriksen & Dorosz, 1963). And Chatterjee and Eriksen (1960; 1962) and Branca (1957) have seriously questioned whether conditioning occurs in human subjects without concomitant verbalizable mediational steps. In view of this negative evidence of unconscious learning in humans, it is reasonable to question not only whether such a process occurs in cognitive avoidance but also whether the attribution of such a process is even necessary to explain the data.

In the Eriksen and Kuethe experiment the noninsightful subjects appeared to have learned avoidance of the punished association uncon-sciously, corresponding to a typically conceived repression process. How-ever, Martin and Dean (1965), in an extensive series of replications of the Eriksen and Kuethe study, have raised serious doubts as to whether the noninsightful subjects can be described as having learned avoidance with-out awareness. By extensive and careful postexperimental questioning of their subjects, Martin and Dean found that unless a subject verbalized some hypothesis related to changing his response there was no evidence of learn-ing. When they applied their more stringent criteria of unawareness, no evidence was found that unaware subjects successfully avoided. Martin and Dean were successful in reproducing the differences in reaction time in certain of their replications, but more extensive analyses, suggested that the differences observed in the reaction time data for the insightful and nonin-sightful subjects in the Eriksen and Kuethe study may have had a complex relationship to the familiarity of the stimulus words to which shock was applied during the learning phase of the experiment.

If a subject is aware that he is avoiding thinking of certain anxiety-arousing or unpleasant topics, then it can be argued that we are dealing only with a response suppression and not repression in the Freudian sense. This may be a valid argument but it is also quite possible that the phenom-enon observed clinically does not require the assumption of an unconscious automatic process, at least in the acquisition phase. In view of the extreme difficulty experimenters have had in producing convincing demonstrations of learning without awareness in the laboratory, the possibility must be seriously entertained that the clinical concept of repression is only a very well-learned or overlearned response suppression.

The clinical observations on repression in patients are obtained many years after the original repression has occurred. It may well be that at the time of the traumatic experience the patient went through a period of several days of engaging in a deliberate response suppression which after enough rehearsal became automatic. While human adults may not learn without awareness, each of us can attest to the knowledge that responses that have been well overlearned seem capable of running off without our being aware of them. Many of our mannerisms, patterns of speaking, and even complex motor skills seem capable of smooth execution for appre-ciable periods of time without our devoting subjective awareness to the specific task. Just as we can walk by a hot radiator and automatically avoid touching it, so perhaps, we can automatically avoid thinking certain thoughts that lead to anxiety when the original avoidance learning has been well established.

Unresolved Issues

There is still much to be learned about cognitive responses to internally cued anxiety, but to me there are three major questions that seem to be the next steps in the development of our knowledge in this area. First, is there an active inhibitory process that prevents the occurrence of the anxiety cue in cognitive avoidance or can the phenomenon be accounted for in terms of an interference theory of forgetting, differential learning, and learning of new competing responses? Second, what is the nature of the repressor-sensitizer dimension? And third, how is the sensitizing response acquired and what reinforces a subject for ruminating over his failures and inadequacies?

Central to the Freudian conception is the idea that repression is an active inhibitory process requiring the expenditure of psychic energy. Laboratory studies of cognitive avoidance have not been clear in demonstrating the need for a concept of active inhibition. If the memory loss or the recognition impairment that is observed in the laboratory is attributable to inhibition, then removal of the inhibition ought to reinstate memory and remove differential recognition effects. Several studies have attempted to demonstrate this "return of the repressed" but with little success. Experiments by Zeller (1950) and Merrill (1954) found a recall improvement following removal of the anxiety, but due to weaknesses in their experimental designs neither experiment is very convincing that this recall increment was due to the removal of inhibition. In neither experiment was the material to be remembered in any way associated with anxiety. Suppressing or repressing the learned material served no adaptive function for the subject since no anxiety was engendered by its conscious recall. The initial recall decrement in both studies is most parsimoniously attributed to an increase in drive level, to the distraction of competing responses, or loss of motivation on the part of the subject for participation in the experimental situation. Consequently, when the anxiety was reduced, recall would be expected to improve since the subject can devote himself more single-mindedly to the recall and relearning task.

The previously discussed experiment by Caron and Wallach (1957) is the best designed experiment that has addressed itself to the removal of inhibition. Caron and Wallach employed several subgroups in their experiment who had the pseudonature of the intelligence test explained to them before recall was asked for the items in the pseudointelligence test. They found that the explanation with resulting catharsis and relief did not change significantly the pattern of recall for failed and succeeded items over that of subjects who recalled while still under the impression they had failed miserably on the intelligence test. From this finding Caron and Wallach concluded that the decrement in failed item recall by the repressor group and the decrement in successful items shown by the sensitizer group were attributable to differences in the learning process rather than to differences in repression or inhibition of these respective items.

Their conclusion seems less certain when the performance of these subjects on the perceptual recognition measures is considered. Even the subjects who had the ruse explained to them had differences in perceptual recognition for words pertaining to a testing situation relative to neutral words. If the experimenter's explanation of the pseudonature of the intelligence test and the group cathartic experience had been successful in removing all anxiety associated with the experimental stress, then patterns of defensive response to perceptual recognition of words not previously experienced in the experimental context but remindful of this stress experience would no longer be anticipated. The finding of such differences, however, makes it questionable as to whether the experimental removal of the stress was effective.

There are other experiments not directly classified as research on defense mechanisms that suggest the presence of some type of internal inhibition. Experiments such as those of Berkowitz and Holmes (1960) and Thibaut and Riecken (1955) that have experimentally instigated anger and aggression have characteristically found that when the instigator of aggression is an authority figure the aggressive responses of the subject do not occur or are displaced to less potent objects. In this situation the internal cues of the aggressive response in the subject are also cues for anxiety that has been learned from the consequences of overt expression of aggression. As a result of the anxiety associated with these cues it would appear that the aggressive behavior is inhibited or displaced to less threatening external objects. Similarly, Murray (1959) has shown that apparent inhibition of drive-related ideation occurs in subjects undergoing prolonged sleep deprivation. Sleep-deprived subjects in response to projective material showed fewer sleep-related themes and ideas than control subjects. Similar findings are reported by Lazarus, Yousem, and Arenberg (1953) with respect to food ideation in food-deprived subjects.

These experiments are not traditionally considered as studies on defensive behavior, but the type of thought inhibition and thought direction they seem to reflect has a strong resemblance to the type of thought inhibition and control that would occur for anxiety-arousing memories or cues in the more traditional defensive mechanism experiments.

An extensive program of research on the repressor-sensitizer dimension has been undertaken by Byrne and his associates (in press). Already an interesting pattern of relationships of this dimension with other personality measures has been established. In addition to a relationship with social desirability, several findings have indicated that at the overt level the repressors appear less anxious and better adjusted. A pressing question concerns whether the appearance of the repressor subjects as free of anxiety is actually due to their avoidance mechanisms or whether it reflects a genuine greater freedom of conflict. Some suggestive indications have been obtained that the better adjustment revealed in personality inventories of the repressor groups is superficial and perhaps part of their cognitive avoidance pattern (Lazarus & Alfert, 1963). Also relevant to the repressor-sensitizer dimension is the question of differences in child-rearing experiences.

One of the more intriguing questions from both the theoretical and the clinical point of view concerns the sensitizer. We all have among our acquaintances people who are the chronic worriers, who dwell inordinately upon their unpleasant experiences and failures, as contrasted with others who seem to have a remarkable facility for placing these out of their minds. The interesting question is what reinforces those who seem to preoccupy themselves with picking their psychological scabs? It may be that the constant dwelling on anxiety experiences in thought and memory somehow reduces the anxiety associated with them in much the same manner that familiarity with original anxiety experiences at the overt level results in lessening the anxiety on repeated exposures. If so, the type of learning experiences that the child or the adult has engaged in that turn him toward this approach to anxiety reduction needs to be determined. Perhaps it's an interaction of innate dispositions and environmental experiences that results in this sensitizer personality.

REFERENCES

Alper, Thelma G. Memory for completed and incompleted tasks as a function of personality: Correlation between experimental and personality data. *J. Pers.,* 1948, **17**, 104-137.

Altrocchi, J. Interpersonal perceptions of repressors and sensitizers in component analysis of assumed dissimilarity scores. *J. abnorm. soc. Psychol.,* 1961, **62**, 528-534.

Altrocchi, J., Parsons, O. A., & Dickoff, Hilda. Changes in self-ideal discrepancy in repressors and sensitizers. *J. abnorm. soc. Psychol.,* 1960, **61**, 67-72.

Berkowitz, L., & Holmes, D. S. A further investigation of hostility generalization to disliked objects. *J. Pers.,* 1960, **28**, 427-442.

Bernstein, I. H., & Eriksen, C. W. Effects of "subliminal" prompting on paired-associate learning. *J. exp. Res. Pers.,* 1965, **1**, 33-38.

Blackwell, H. R. Psychophysical thresholds: Experimental studies of methods of measurement. *Bull. Engng. Res. Inst., Univer. Mich.,* 1953, Bull. No. 36.

Blum, G. S. Perceptual defense revisited. *J. abnorm. soc. Psychol.*, 1955, **51**, 24-29.

Branca, A. A. Semantic generalization at the level of the conditioning experiment. *Amer. J. Psychol.*, 1957, **70**, 541-549.

Bruner, J. S., & Postman, L. Emotional selectivity in perception and reaction. *J. Pers.*, 1947, **16**, 69-77.

Byrne, D. The repression-sensitization scale: Rationale, reliability, and validity. *J. Pers.*, 1961, **29**, 334-349.

Bryne, D. Repression-sensitization as a dimension of personality. In B. Maher (Ed.), *Progress in Experimental Personality Research.* New York: Academic Press, 1965.

Caron, A. J., & Wallach, M. A. Recall of interrupted tasks under stress: A phenomenon of memory or of learning? *J. abnorm. soc. Psychol.*, 1957, **55**, 372-381.

Caron, A. J., & Wallach, M. A. Personality determinants of repressive and obsessive reactions to failure stress. *J. abnorm. soc. Psychol.*, 1959, **59**, 236-245.

Carpenter, B., Wiener, M., & Carpenter, Janeth T. Predictability of perceptual defense behavior. *J. abnorm. soc. Psychol.*, 1956, **52**, 380-383.

Chatterjee, B. B., & Eriksen, C. W. Conditioning and generalization as a function of awareness. *J. abnorm. soc. Psychol.*, 1960, **60**, 396-403.

Chatterjee, B. B., & Eriksen, C. W. Cognitive factors in heart rate conditioning. *J. exp. Psychol.*, 1962, **64**, 272-279.

Dollard, J., & Miller, N. E. *Personality and psychotherapy.* New York: McGraw-Hill, 1950.

Douglas, Anna G. A tachistoscopic study of the order of emergence in the process of perception. *Psychol. Monogr.*, 1947, **61**, (Whole No. 287).

Dulany, D. E., Jr. The place of hypotheses and intentions: An analysis of verbal control in verbal conditioning. In C. W. Eriksen (Ed.), *Behavior and awareness.* Durham, N.C.: Duke Univer. Press, 1962. Pp. 102-129.

Dulany, D. E., Jr., & Eriksen, C. W. Accuracy of brightness discrimination as measured by concurrent verbal responses and GSRs. *J. abnorm. soc. Psychol.*, 1959, **59**, 418-423.

D'Zurilla, T. J. Recall efficiency and mediating cognitive events in "experimental repression." *J. pers. soc. Psychol.*, 1965, **1**, 253-257.

Eriksen, C. W. Perceptual defense as a function of unacceptable needs. *J. abnorm. soc. Psychol.*, 1951, **46**, 557-564. (a)

Eriksen, C. W. Some implications for TAT interpretation arising from need and perception experiments. *J. Pers.*, 1951, **19**, 282-288. (b)

Eriksen, C. W. Defense against ego-threat in memory and perception. *J. abnorm. soc. Psychol.*, 1952, **47**, 230-235. (a)

Eriksen, C. W. Individual differences in defensive forgetting. *J. exp. Psychol.*, 1952, **44**, 442-446. (b)

Eriksen, C. W. Psychological defenses and "ego strength" in the recall of completed and incompleted tasks. *J. abnorm. soc. Psychol.*, 1954, **49**, 45-50.

Eriksen, C. W. An experimental analysis of subception. *Amer. J. Psychol.*, 1956, **69**, 625-634. (a)

Eriksen, C. W. Subception: Fact or artifact? *Psychol. Rev.*, 1956, **1**, 74-80. (b)

Eriksen, C. W. Unconscious processes. In M. R. Jones (Ed.), *Nebraska symposium on motivation.* Lincoln, Nebr.: Univer. of Nebraska Press, 1958. Pp. 169-227.

Eriksen, C. W. Discrimination and learning without awareness: A methodological survey and evaluation. *Psychol. Rev.*, 1960, **67**, 279-300.

Eriksen, C. W. Perception and personality dynamics. In R. W. Heine & J. M. Wepman (Eds.), *Concepts of personality*. Chicago: Aldine, 1963. Pp. 31-62.

Eriksen, C. W., & Browne, C. T. An experimental and theoretical analysis of perceptual defense. *J. abnorm. soc. Psychol.*, 1956, **52**, 224-230.

Eriksen, C. W., & Davids, A. The meaning and clinical validity of the Taylor anxiety scale and the hysteria-psychasthenia scales from the MMPI. *J. abnorm. soc. Psychol.*, 1955, **50**, 135-137.

Eriksen, C. W., & Doroz, L. Role of awareness in learning and use of correlated extraneous cues on perceptual tasks. *J. exp. Psychol.*, 1963, **66**, 601-608.

Eriksen, C. W., & Hake, H. W. Anchor effects in absolute judgments. *J. exp. Psychol.*, 1957, **53**, 132-138.

Eriksen, C. W., & Kuethe, J. L. Avoidance conditioning of verbal behavior without awareness: A paradigm of repression. *J. abnorm. soc. Psychol.*, 1956, **53**, 203-209.

Eriksen, C. W., & Wechsler, H. Some effects of experimentally induced anxiety upon discrimination behavior. *J. abnorm. soc. Psychol.*, 1955, **51**, 458-463.

Eysenck, H. J. *Dimensions of personality*. London: Routledge & Kegan, 1947.

Freud, S. Repression. *Collected Papers*. London: Hogarth Press, 1925. Vol. 4, pp. 84-97.

Fuhrer, M. J., & Eriksen, C. W. The unconscious perception of the meaning of verbal stimuli. *J. abnorm. soc. Psychol.*, 1960, **61**, 432-439.

Garner, W. R., Hake, H. W., & Eriksen, C. W. Operationism and the concept of perception. *Psychol. Rev.*, 1956, **63**, 149-159.

Glixman, A. F. Recall of completed and incompleted activities under varying degrees of stress. *J. exp. Psychol.*, 1949, **39**, 281-295.

Goldiamond, I. Indicators of perception: I. Subliminal perception, subception, unconscious perception: An analysis in terms of psychophysical indicator methodology. *Psychol. Bull.*, 1958, **55**, 373-411.

Gossett, J. T. An experimental demonstration of Freudian repression proper. Unpublished doctoral dissertation, Univer. of Arkansas, 1964.

Howes, D. H., & Solomon, R. L. A note on McGinnies' "emotionality and perceptual defense." *Psychol. Rev.*, 1950, **57**, 229-234.

Howes, D. H., & Solomon, R. L. Visual duration threshold as a function of word-probability. *J. exp. Psychol.*, 1951, **41**, 401-410.

Johnson, H., & Eriksen, C. W. Preconscious perception: A re-examination of the Poetzl phenomenon. *J. abnorm. soc. Psychol.*, 1961, **62**, 497-503.

Lazarus, R. S., & Alfert, Elizabeth. The short circuiting of threat by experimentally altering cognitive appraisal. Unpublished manuscript, Univer. of California, 1963.

Lazarus, R. S., Eriksen, C. W., & Fonda, C. P. Personality dynamics and auditory perceptual recognition. *J. Pers.*, 1951, **19**, 471-482.

Lazarus, R. S., & Longo, N. The consistency of psychological defense against threat. *J. abnorm. soc. Psychol.*, 1953, **48**, 495-499.

Lazarus, R. S., & McCleary, R. A. Autonomic discrimination without awareness: A study of subception. *Psychol. Rev.*, 1951, **58**, 113-122.

Lazarus, R. S., Yousem, H., & Arenberg, D. Hunger and perception. *J. Pers.*, 1953, **21**, 312-328.

Martin, R. B., & Dean, S. J. Word familiarity and avoidance conditioning of verbal behavior. *J. pers. soc. Psychol.*, 1965, **1**, 496-499.

Mathews, Anne, & Wertheimer, M. A "pure" measure of perceptual defense uncontaminated by response suppression. *J. abnorm. soc. Psychol.,* 1958, **57**, 373-376.

Merrill, R. M. The effect of pre-experimental and experimental anxiety on recall efficiency. *J. exp. Psychol.,* 1954, **48**, 167-172.

Murray, E. J. Conflict and repression during sleep deprivation. *J. abnorm. soc. Psychol.,* 1959, **59**, 95-101.

Osler, S. F., & Lewinsohn, P. M. The relation between manifest anxiety in perceptual defense. *Amer. Psychologist,* 1954, **9**, 446. (Abstract)

Rosenzweig, S. An experimental study of "repression" with special reference to need-persistive and ego-defensive reactions to frustration. *J. exp. Psychol.,* 1943, **32**, 64-74.

Rosenzweig, S., & Sarason, S. B. An experimental study of the triadic hypothesis: Reaction to frustration, ego defense, and hypnotizability. I. Correlational approach. *Charact. & Pers.,* 1942, **11**, 1-19.

Sears, R. R. Experimental studies in projection: I. Attribution of traits. *J. soc. Psychol.,* 1936, **7**, 151-163.

Shannon, D. T. Clinical patterns of defense as revealed in visual recognition thresholds. *J. abnorm. soc. Psychol.,* 1962, **64**, 370-377.

Spielberger, C. D. Role of awareness in verbal conditioning. In C. W. Eriksen (Ed.), *Behavior and awareness.* Durham, N.C.: Duke Univer. Press, 1962. Pp. 73-101.

Swets, J. A., Tanner, W. P., Jr., & Birdsall, T. G. Decision processes in perception. *Psychol. Rev.,* 1961, **68**, 301-340.

Tempone, V. J. Differential thresholds of repressers and sensitizers as a function of a success and failure experience. Unpublished doctoral dissertation, Univer. of Texas, 1962.

Thibaut, J. W., & Riecken, H. W. Authoritarianism, status, and the communication of aggression. *Human Relat.,* 1955, **8**, 95-120.

Truax, C. B. The repression response to implied failure as a function of the hysteria-psychasthenia index. *J. abnorm. soc. Psychol.,* 1957, **55**, 188-193.

Ullmann, L. P. Clinical correlates of facilitation and inhibition of response to emotional stimuli. *J. proj. Tech.,* 1958, **22**, 341-347.

Ullmann, L. P. An empirically derived MMPI scale which measures facilitation-inhibition of recognition of threatening stimuli. *J. clin. Psychol.,* 1962, **18**, 127-132.

Ullmann, L. P., & Lim, D. T. Case history material as a source of the identification of patterns of response to emotional stimuli in a study of humor. *J. consult. Psychol.,* 1962, **26**, 221-225.

Van de Castle, R. L. Perceptual defense in a binocular-rivalry situation. *J. Pers.,* 1960, **28**, 448-462.

Zajonc, R. B. Response suppression in perceptual defense. *J. exp. Psychol.,* 1962, **64**, 206-214.

Zeller, A. F. An experimental analogue of repression. II. The effect of individual failure and success on memory measured by relearning. *J. exp. Psychol.,* 1950, **40**, 411-422.

CHAPTER 14

The Effects of Anxiety on Complex Learning and Academic Achievement

Charles D. Spielberger

DEPARTMENT OF PSYCHOLOGY,
VANDERBILT UNIVERSITY,
NASHVILLE, TENNESSEE

The research reported in this chapter was initiated in 1955 at which time the writer was associated with the Duke University Psychology Department and the Psychiatric Out-Patient Clinic of the Duke Medical Center.[1] Although the clinic served the general community, it was conveniently located on the Duke campus, and many students with emotional problems were referred for diagnostic evaluation and treatment. Others came seeking help of their own accord. The number of students seen in the clinic always seemed to increase during and immediately following university examination periods. At such times, anxiety concerning academic performance was, in most cases, either the salient symptom or an important background factor. This, of course, was not surprising.

Students who came to the clinic during examination periods complained that anxiety reduced effectiveness in studying and actively interfered with thought processes during examinations. Regarding the latter, many students reported that, although they "knew" the answers to test questions, they were often unable to reproduce them because they

[1] This research was supported in part by grants from the Duke University Research Council and the National Institutes of Mental Health (OM 362, MH 7446) and Child Health and Human Development (HD 947), United States Public Health Service.

"blocked" or "choked-up" in the test situation. As a result, the student's level of achievement was not commensurate with his intellectual aptitude, and his confidence in his own abilities was seriously undermined. It seemed unfortunate that the learning problems observed in the clinic, intensified by emotional turbulence resulting from the demanding pressures of the academic environment, were so remote from the research problems addressed by psychologists who investigated learning in the laboratory.

Two points of contact between the suffering student and the psychology of learning, *circa* 1955, were to be found in the Yale investigations of test anxiety (Mandler & Sarason, 1952; S. B. Sarason, Mandler, & Craighill, 1952) and the Iowa studies of the effects of individual differences in emotionally based drive (anxiety) on the learning process (e.g., Spence & Farber, 1953; Taylor & Spence, 1952). Did this research have heuristic value for the clinician called upon to assist emotionally disturbed college students with their learning problems? Could the theory which guided the research be extended to encompass the complex learning processes involved in academic achievement? Would clinical observations of the therapeutic interaction between anxious college students and their counselors suggest hypotheses for extending the theory? Within the general framework reflected by questions such as these, our research was begun.

In this chapter my principal aim is to describe the results of several related experiments in which the influence of anxiety on learning, concept formation, and academic achievement was investigated. These studies, carried out in collaboration with colleagues and graduate students, compared the performance of high anxiety (HA) and low anxiety (LA) college students in laboratory and real-life learning tasks. The chapter is organized into three sections. The first comments briefly on the working definition of anxiety employed in our research and then outlines in some detail the context of theoretical formulations and empirical findings within which the research was carried out. In the second section the results of the several experiments are reported. Since most of the findings in these experiments have been published piecemeal in individual journal articles, the emphasis here is on providing continuity between the separate studies and describing the interplay of clinical "hunches" and learning theory as these guided the research and were in turn influenced by it. In the final section some implications of our findings for anxiety theory and clinical practice are suggested.

Anxiety and Drive Theory

Freud viewed anxiety as ". . . an affective state . . . of most obviously unpleasurable character" (1936, p. 69), and ". . . as a signal indicating the presence of a danger-situation" (1933, p. 119). On the basis of his analysis of the properties of anxiety states, Freud listed three main attributes: "(1)

a specific unpleasurable quality, (2) efferent or discharge phenomena, and (3) the perception of these" (1936, p. 70). As a first step toward the development of a systematic conception of anxiety, we accepted Freud's description of the properties of anxiety states as providing a meaningful working definition of the phenomena in which we were interested.

THE CONCEPT OF ANXIETY

At the time our research was begun, we regarded "anxiety" as a complex hypothetical construct for which the most meaningful and unambiguous empirical referent was a particular state or condition of the human organism. We conceived of this hypothetical anxiety state as characterized by subjective, consciously perceived feelings of apprehension and tension which were accompanied by or associated with activation (arousal) of the autonomic nervous system. We also believed that the anxiety level of an individual fluctuated over time in response to both internal and external stimulation, and that there were stable individual differences in the degree to which anxiety would be manifested in any given situation.

In learning theory terminology (Dollard & Miller, 1950), the anxiety state may be viewed as a complex, largely internal (nonobservable) response or process that has both stimulus-cue and stimulus-drive properties. The cue properties may be regarded as providing the basis for Freud's conception of anxiety as a "danger signal." Our research, however, has been particularly concerned with the arousal or drive properties of anxiety and its effects on behavior. In this regard, the conception and design of our several experiments was strongly influenced by a theory of emotionally based drive (Spence, 1956; Spence, 1958; Taylor, 1956) in which it was assumed that there are important individual differences in emotional responsiveness that contribute to drive level, D, as this concept is defined by Hull (1943). This theory and its ramifications will be collectively referred to in the present context as Drive Theory.

Since a detailed, current statement of Drive Theory is presented elsewhere in this volume (see Spence & Spence, Ch. 12), only an overview is given here of those aspects of the theory which provide relevant background for the research reported in the following section. A brief summary of the empirical support enjoyed by Drive Theory at the time that our research was initiated is also presented.

DRIVE THEORY AND LEARNING

Drive Theory proceeds from the basic asumption of Hull (1943) that the excitatory potential, E, which determines the strength of a given response, R, is a multiplicative function of total effective drive state, D, and habit strength, H. Thus:

$$R = f(E) = f(D \times H)$$

Total effective drive state results from the summation of all individual need states existent at a given time, irrespective of their source. The number and strength of specific habits elicited in any situation is determined by the subjects' previous experience in the same or similar situations; all habit tendencies evoked in the subject are multiplied by the total effective drive then operating. Predictions from Hullian theory regarding the effects of variations in D on performance have been succinctly stated by Taylor (1956, p. 304):

> The implication of varying drive level in any situation in which a single habit is evoked is clear: the higher the drive, the greater the value of E and hence of response strength. Thus in simple noncompetitional experimental arrangements involving only a single habit tendency the performance level of high-drive Ss should be greater than that for low-drive groups. Higher drive levels should not, however, always lead to superior performance (i.e., greater probability of the appearance of the correct response). In situations in which a number of competing response tendencies are evoked, only one of which is correct, the relative performance of high and low drive groups will depend upon the number and comparative strengths of the various response tendencies.

Taylor also notes that, in tasks involving a number of competing response tendencies, predictions concerning the performance of HA and LA subjects may require consideration of the Hullian concepts of oscillatory inhibition (O) and response threshold (L). While these concepts have been occasionally called upon to account for experimental findings in tests of Drive Theory utilizing complex learning tasks, such explanations have generally been *post hoc*. Since neither O nor L have been given operational meaning in investigations guided by Drive Theory, these concepts will not be further considered here.

Our discussion thus far has focused upon the explication of deductions derived from Hull's learning theory concerning the effects of variations in D on behavior. Drive Theory proper begins with the assumption that noxious or aversive stimuli arouse a hypothetical emotional response, r_e, which contributes to drive level. The Taylor (1953) Manifest Anxiety Scale (MAS) was developed specifically as an operational measure of individual differences in r_e on the assumption that scores on the MAS would be positively related to degree of emotional responsiveness, and would thus reflect D. Two alternative hypotheses concerning the relationship between D and MAS scores have been proposed (Farber & Spence, 1956; Taylor, 1956): (1) the "chronic" hypothesis assumes that HA subjects manifest higher D than LA subjects in all situations, whether stressful or not; and (2) the "emotional reactivity" hypothesis posits that HA subjects react with higher D than LA subjects only in situations containing some degree of stress. According to Spence (1958, p. 137): "So far as the usual type of human learning experiment is concerned, the question as to whether High A subjects would be more emotional than Low A subjects, and hence have a higher D level, is a moot one." Research will be reported in the next section which provides evidence bearing on the question of whether chronic or reactive D is reflected in MAS scores.

In much of the research stimulated by or designed to test Drive Theory, the performance of individuals characterized by low and high levels of emotionally based drive, as this was measured by MAS scores, has been compared on a variety of learning tasks. The experimental evidence on which Drive Theory rested *circa* 1955 was reviewed by Taylor (1956) and is summarized below.

DRIVE THEORY AND THE SUPPORTING EXPERIMENTAL EVIDENCE

Laboratory investigations of classical conditioning, human maze learning, and serial and paired-associate verbal learning have provided empirical findings generally consistent with predictions from Drive Theory. Since a single response tendency is usually acquired in classical conditioning, Drive Theory would predict that HA subjects would give more conditioned responses than LA subjects. Superior conditioning for HA subjects was indeed found in six independent eyelid-conditioning studies reviewed by Taylor (1956). Moreover, in several of these studies in which data were available for subjects in the middle range of anxiety, the relationship between conditioning and MAS scores was found to be monotonic, as would be predicted by Drive Theory. Findings from differential eyelid-conditioning experiments also tended to support the theory, as did the results from a single study in which GSR responses were classically conditioned.

On the assumption that errors in complex learning are determined largely by erroneous responses evoked by an experimental task, it would be predicted from Drive Theory that high drive subjects would make more errors on complex tasks than low drive subjects, and take more trials to reach a learning criterion. Two experiments (Farber & Spence, 1953; Taylor & Spence, 1952) provided evidence consistent with these theoretical expectations. In these studies, the overall performance of HA subjects on complex serial maze tasks was inferior to that of LA subjects. Furthermore, the degree of inferiority of the HA groups at individual maze choice-points increased as a positive function of the number of errors (competing responses) for the choice-point.

In paired-associate learning, the use of discrete S-R pairs permits the experimenter to alter the number and strength of competing erroneous response tendencies elicited by each stimulus. For paired-associate lists in which each stimulus tended to evoke its own specific (correct) response, and the association between S and R in each S-R pair was initially strong, the performance of HA subjects was found to be superior to that of LA subjects (Taylor & Chapman, 1955). For lists in which each stimulus word presumably elicited a large number of strong competing response tendencies, because of a high degree of synonymity among stimuli, the performance of HA subjects was observed to be inferior to that of LA subjects (Spence, 1953).

Montague (1953) investigated the effects of anxiety in serial verbal learning and found that the performance of HA and LA subjects differed for lists of nonsense syllables which presumably varied in degree of intralist interference. The performance of HA subjects was superior to that of LA subjects on a low-interference list in which similarity between syllables was low and association value was high; the performance curves for the HA and LA groups were reversed on a high-interference list in which there was high similarity between syllables of relatively low association value. Results on a serial learning task with similar implications were reported by Lucas (1952). He manipulated intralist duplication in order to vary the degree of response competition and found that the amount recalled by HA subjects decreased as a function of the number of duplicated consonants within a list. The performance of LA subjects was not affected by intralist duplication.

In the studies reviewed thus far, expectations based on Drive Theory concerning the directional effects of anxiety on performance were generally confirmed. For simple learning tasks in which it could be assumed that relatively few competing response tendencies were elicited, HA facilitated performance. For complex tasks in which, presumably, a number of relatively strong competing response tendencies were elicited, HA resulted in performance decrements. Farber and Spence (1953) compared the *same* HA and LA subjects in *both* simple and complex learning tasks. As in the studies previously cited, they found that the performance of HA subjects was superior to that of LA subjects in eyelid conditioning and inferior in stylus maze learning. Indeed, on the maze-learning task, the performance of HA subjects tended to be inferior to that of LA subjects even for the very easiest choice-points on which relatively few errors were made.

Taylor (1956) has noted that failure to find performance facilitation for high drive subjects on elements of complex tasks for which there was little evidence of competing erroneous response tendencies could be interpreted as discrepant with expectations based on Drive Theory. In commenting on the effects of anxiety on performance for tasks of varying complexity, Child (1954, p. 154) called attention to such discrepancies and concluded:

At the present stage of knowledge, the reviewer is of the opinion that the most plausible general interpretation of these findings about task complexity is that the disruptive effects of various responses to anxiety vary with the nature of the task; that in simple conditioning, where a stable relationship is established between a single stimulus and a single response, what internal responses the subject is making at the time do not have any great effect, whereas the presence of high drive level does make for heightened performance; but that in complex situations, where the subject is already in conflict between various response tendencies relevant to the task, the presence of irrelevant responses made to anxiety heightens the conflict and interferes with performance to a greater extent than the increased drive improves it.

Thus, Child contends that HA subjects have stronger anxiety-produced, task-irrelevant, competing responses than LA subjects. In essence, Child's interpretation assumes that HA subjects are characterized by high drive, and by *two* different types of competing response tendencies—those associated with heightened anxiety and those elicited by the experimental task.

The disruptive interfering responses associated with the anxiety state itself are considered by Child, and by Mandler and Sarason (1952), as responsible for the performance decrements of HA subjects in complex tasks. While this view is not necessarily incompatible with Drive Theory, it clearly differs in its emphasis on anxiety-produced competing responses rather than the task-produced competing responses favored in Drive Theory explanations. The relative contributions of task-produced and anxiety-produced interferring response tendencies to the performance decrements of HA subjects in complex learning tasks are explored in the studies reported in the next section.

The Effects of Anxiety on Performance in Complex Learning Tasks

The studies described below are presented in the approximate chronological order in which they were carried out. This approach permits us to trace the development of our theoretical conceptions concerning the influence of anxiety on complex learning and to show the intimate linkage between theoretical ideas, clinical hunches, and empirical findings. The results from five related studies will be reported in detail, and supporting evidence from several additional experiments will be introduced.[2] In our

---

2 The collaboration and assistance of colleagues and students in these experiments is gratefully acknowledged. I am particularly indebted to Professors W. Grant Dahlstrom, Leonard D. Goodstein, and Henry Weitz, and to Larilee Baty, Edna Bissette, Dr. J. Peter Denny, Dr. James Brown Grier, Kay Howard, Dr. Edward S. Katkin, Dr. William G. Katzenmeyer, Lou Hicks Smith, and Ann Wescott.

first study we investigated the effects of anxiety on incidental learning and recall. In Study II, the relationship between anxiety and intelligence was examined. The combined influence of anxiety and intelligence on academic achievement was evaluated in Study III. The performance of HA and LA subjects in a serial learning task was compared in Study IV in which serial-position phenomena were also taken into account. Finally, in Study V, the effects of anxiety on concept formation for subjects who differed in intelligence was investigated.

The subjects in these studies were college students selected on the basis of extreme scores on the MAS. It was assumed that these students differed in anxiety level as previously defined. There were three major reasons which prompted us to use the MAS for selecting subjects.

1. The *content* validity (Cronbach, 1960) of the MAS was consistent with our working definition of anxiety. Individual MAS items, selected by clinical psychologists as consonant with Cameron's (1947) description of manifest anxiety in chronic anxiety reactions, inquire about feelings of apprehension (e.g., fears, worries, nervousness, tension); they also elicit subjective reports concerning the perception of symptoms reflecting heightened autonomic nervous system activity (e.g., sweating, heart pounding, blushing, nausea).

2. The *concurrent* validity of the MAS as a measure of anxiety was moderately well established in terms of the correlations of the scale with clinicians' ratings of anxiety in patients or clients (e.g., Gleser & Ulett, 1952; Hoyt & Magoon, 1954; Kendall, 1954; Taylor, 1953), especially when such ratings were based upon carefully defined behavioral criteria rather than global clinical impressions (Buss, Wiener, Durkee, & Baer, 1955).

3. The *construct* validity of the MAS as an index of the drive component of anxiety was empirically demonstrated by experimental findings such as those previously cited, although this conclusion was not unchallenged (Hill, 1957; Jessor & Hammond, 1957).

Thus, among the various operational measures of anxiety that were available at the time our research was initiated, the MAS had the most impressive credentials. Furthermore, the MAS had been used in more studies than all other anxiety measures combined and thereby permitted a broader basis for comparing our findings with those reported by other investigators. For these reasons we started with the MAS as our measure of anxiety, and we continued to use it because it appeared to get at the anxiety phenomena in which we were interested.

STUDY I. THE EFFECTS OF ANXIETY ON RECALL

Our first study grew out of Drive Theory and the clinical observation, previously described, that anxious students often choke-up or block in test situations. It will be recalled that such students report they are unable to reproduce answers to test questions which they feel reasonably certain they "know." Since examinations in college courses would seem to qualify as complex tasks, the observation that anxious students have difficulty on them is consistent with expectations from Drive Theory. But Drive Theory would also predict that anxious students should do better than non-anxious students on the simple or easy items of an otherwise complex test, assuming, of course, that the degree of original learning for the two groups was comparable. As previously noted, however, there was little objective evidence *circa* 1955 to support this prediction. Do HA subjects perform more poorly than LA subjects even on the simple elements of complex laboratory tasks because they block on these as they do on classroom tests? Can blocking on classroom examinations be considered an anxiety-produced, interfering response of the type described by Child and by Mandler and Sarason? In order to explore these questions, we decided to investigate the effects of anxiety on a laboratory task which embodied some of the important features of the classroom test.

Most classroom tests require the examinee to recall specific elements from a larger body of previously learned materials. Typically, the material to be learned for an examination varies in complexity, and the precise elements that will need to be recalled on the test are not generally known to the student. Furthermore, in preparing for tests, individual students invest differential amounts of practice in the various elements to be learned. Since we were interested primarily in the effects of anxiety on recall, we sought an experimental task for which practice, and hence original learning, could be controlled. It was also desirable to have a task that was comprised of a number of elements of graded levels of difficulty.

We first examined standard clinical tests of memory or recall, for example, the Digit Span Test and the Wechsler Memory Scale, but these did not seem suitable for our purpose. The subjects' attention in such tests is either directed to the specific materials to be recalled (immediate memory) or to highly overlearned information often dating back into childhood (remote memory). Classroom tests, especially those comprised of objective and/or short-answer items, generally require the recall of unspecified elements from a larger body of materials learned in the recent but not the immediate past. In terms of the material to be recalled, classroom tests would seem to fall somewhere in the middle of a continuum defined at its extremes by immediate and remote memories.

An experimental task, which we had helped to develop in an earlier study (Goodstein, Spielberger, Williams, & Dahlstrom, 1955) appeared to have many of the characteristics we were seeking. This task consisted of a series of nine geometric designs (Bender, 1938) which were presented one by one in the same order to each subject. The subject was required simply to copy each design within a 40-second time limit; he was not told that he would be asked to reproduce the designs later in the experiment. Following the completion of an unrelated 6-minute interpolated task (draw-a-person) utilized to control the time interval between original learn- and recall, the subject was told to reproduce as many of the designs as he could remember. Each design reproduced in the recall period was scored as correct or incorrect on the basis of an objective scoring system developed in the previous study.

In the earlier study it was demonstrated that recall of individual designs was influenced by *both* the intrinsic complexity of a design and the serial position in which it was presented during the copying phase of the task. In general, designs presented at the end of the series were more frequently recalled than those presented at the beginning. Therefore, in order to maximize the range of recall difficulty in the present study, which was carried out in collaboration with Dr. W. Grant Dahlstrom, the most difficult design (the design recalled least frequently in the earlier study) was presented first in the series, the next most difficult design was presented in the second position in the series, and so on for the nine designs, with the easiest design presented last. The individual designs were regarded as independent tasks for which the level of difficulty[3] decreased mono-tonically from position 1 to position 9. For these same designs presented in the same order, over 80% of the subjects in the previous study correctly reproduced the tasks presented at the end of the series, while fewer than 40% reproduced the tasks given at the beginning of the series.

The subjects in the present study were 24 HA and 24 LA students, equally divided as to sex. These students were selected from introductory psychology courses at Duke University and the University of North Carolina on the basis of extreme scores on the MAS: the HA group had scores of 19 or higher, the LA group scored 7 or lower. After a few moments of

---

[3] The "level of difficulty" of a task is assumed to be a positive function of the number and strength of competing erroneous response tendencies elicited by the task. Hence, task difficulty will depend on the intrinsic complexity of a task and other variables such as serial position which govern the number of competing responses elicited by the task in a specific experimental situation.

casual conversation to establish rapport, the experimental task as described above was given to each subject in an individual testing session.

Since there were no differences in the performance of men and women, the data for both sexes were combined. For the combined data the percent of HA and LA subjects who correctly reproduced each of the nine tasks is indicated in Fig. 1; the number of the task corresponds to its position in the series. It may be noted that the performance of HA subjects was inferior to that of LA subjects for the more difficult tasks (presented early in the series) and superior on the less difficult tasks (presented later in the series), as would be predicted from Drive Theory.[4] The Child-Mandler-

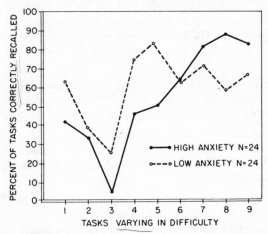

FIG. 1. Mean percent of high anxiety and low anxiety subjects who correctly recalled each of nine tasks of varying levels of difficulty. The number of the task corresponds to the order in which it was presented in the series during the copying phase of the experiment.

Sarason interpretation of performance decrements in "complex situations" as resulting from "irrelevant responses made to anxiety" would not seem to account for our results—*both* increments and decrements in performance were found for HA subjects in the *same* situation for different elements of a complex task. If anxiety-produced irrelevant responses were present

---

[4] Our assumption that probability of recall was an increasing monotonic function of serial position appeared to be in error, as may be noted in Fig. 1. The elevated performance observed for both LA and HA groups for designs presented in the first and second serial positions would seem to indicate that recall is facilitated for designs presented at the beginning of a series. The findings in this study were substantially replicated by Goodstein in an independent sample of 40 subjects at the University of Iowa; the data for the two studies were combined and published together (Spielberger, Goodstein, & Dahlstrom, 1958).

in the situation, they influenced performance in precisely the same manner as would be expected for task-produced competing responses.

Although our findings provided little or no clarification of the clinical observation that anxious students often block in test situations, they did suggest that the performance of HA subjects on classroom tests might vary as a function of the difficulty of individual test items. In subsequent discussions of test-taking problems with anxious students, it was apparent that HA students did relatively well on clearly worded test items but had considerable difficulty on ambiguous items ("trick questions"). For the latter, there were at least two identifiable processes which appeared to interfere with test performance. The first, which we have already described as blocking, is more frequently reported by students seen in the clinic than in the classroom. The second, which may be described as "misinterpretation" or "misreading" of the test items, was observed in going over examination papers with students enrolled in undergraduate courses; it, too, appeared to occur more frequently in anxious or nervous students. Answers for misinterpreted questions were often very detailed and specific, suggesting that the content of the answer consisted of an overlearned response given to an inappropriate stimulus. Thus, the misinterpretation difficulty on examinations appeared to reflect a dynamic process in which the effect of high drive on task-produced interfering response tendencies led to performance decrements for HA subjects.

Upon inquiring about the misinterpretation type of examination difficulty in interviews with anxious students seen in the clinic, many acknowledged they frequently experienced this but did not bring it up in therapy because they did not consider it important. One obvious reason that misinterpretation of a test question is considered less traumatic than blocking is that it is not generally discovered until sometime after the examination. In contrast, blocking occurs in the test situation itself, apparently as a response to anxiety, and often serves to intensify the student's anxiety level, sometimes almost to the point of panic. It is this intense experience of anxiety which is recounted by the student in the counselling session. Implicit in this line of reasoning is the assumption that anxiety-produced response tendencies, such as blocking, which interfere with performance on complex tasks, will be observed only at moderately intense levels of anxiety.

Since *both* performance facilitation and performance decrements for HA subjects relative to LA subjects were found in the present study, it may be concluded that task-produced interfering response tendencies interacted with high drive to bring about the observed effects. If the situation were made more stressful, however, it is conceivable that anxiety-produced irrelevant response tendencies would have been evoked in HA subjects, and that these would have interfered with performance in the manner suggested by Child (1954) and noted earlier. Under these circumstances, inferior performance for HA subjects relative to that of LA subjects might be expected, even for the least difficult elements of an experimental task.

STUDY II. ANXIETY AND INTELLIGENCE

While our first study was in progress, Grice (1955) and Kerrick (1955) reported that the MAS scores of Air Force basic trainees were negatively and significantly correlated with a number of different measures of intelligence. Moreover, Grice demonstrated that the inferior performance of HA subjects relative to LA subjects on a complex reaction-time task could be attributed as readily to lower intelligence as to the effects of higher drive. On the other hand, Farber and Spence (1955) noted that, over a period of years, they had not found any relation between the MAS scores of college students and conventional measures of intellectual ability such as entrance tests and grade point averages. Others have also reported the failure to find a relation between various measures of anxiety and intelligence (Dana, 1957; Klugh & Bendig, 1955; Mayzner, Sersen, & Tresselt, 1955; I. G. Sarason, 1956). Since measures of anxiety and intelligence were available to us for a large number of college students, we decided to take a closer look at the relationship between these variables (Spielberger, 1958).

The MAS had been given to students enrolled in introductory psychology courses at Duke during six consecutive semesters from the fall of 1954 to the spring of 1957. The ACE Psychological Examination, a measure of scholastic aptitude generally regarded as a valid index of intelligence in college students, had been administered routinely to entering freshmen as part of a battery of placement tests. Pearson product-moment correlations between MAS and ACE scores were computed for the total sample of 1142 students, for men and women separately, and for each sex in each of the six semester-samples. The correlation between the MAS and ACE for the total sample was —.02; the correlations for males and females were —.06 and .01, respectively. These results would seem to indicate unequivocally that anxiety and intelligence as measured by the MAS and ACE were unrelated in our population of college students.

But when the data for the individual semester-samples were examined, an interesting trend in the correlations for male subjects was revealed. As mean ACE *increased,* the size of the negative correlation between MAS and ACE *decreased* monotonically from —.34 to .04, with only one minor inversion. The standard deviations for ACE scores in the semester-samples were approximately equal, suggesting that the magnitude of the negative

TABLE I

Means and Correlations for MAS and ACE, and Distribution of ACE Scores for Semester-Samples

Group	N	Mean ACE	Mean MAS	Pearson r	ACE national norms (percentiles)				
					0–20 (%)	21–40 (%)	41–60 (%)	61–80 (%)	81–100 (%)
Spring, 1955	72	111.4	13.1	−.34[a]	14	25	14	24	24
Spring, 1956	79	116.8	11.3	−.21	9	18	20	19	34
Spring, 1957	101	120.5	15.5	−.16	4	12	24	27	33
Fall, 1954	140	120.3	12.4	−.13	7	8	21	26	38
Fall, 1955	122	124.2	12.0	−.08	3	10	14	32	41
Fall, 1956	160	124.6	14.8	.04	2	10	15	34	39

[a] $p < .01$.

correlation between MAS and ACE scores was determined by the proportion of subjects in each sample with low intelligence. This is confirmed in Table I in which mean ACE scores, distributions of ACE scores, and MAS-ACE correlations for males in each of the six semester-samples are presented. The rank-difference (rho) between ACE means and magnitude of the MAS-ACE correlation was —.94; the rho between the percentage of subjects with scores below the fortieth percentile on ACE national norms and magnitude of the MAS-ACE correlation was —1.00. Examination of individual semester-samples for women, however, revealed no evidence of any systematic relation between MAS and ACE scores.

In pondering these findings, we concluded that two different selection factors apparently determined the proportion of male students with low ACE scores who were included in the particular semester-samples of this study: (1) As university standards were raised, fewer male students with low intelligence were accepted (Weitz, 1955), resulting in higher mean ACE scores for successive years. (2) Peculiarities in the elective system at the university resulted in a larger proportion of low-ability students taking introductory psychology in the spring because they had failed the first semester of a two-semester science sequence the previous fall (fall mean ACE = 123; spring mean ACE = 117; F = 11.1, p < .001). These factors did not appear to operate for our female subjects whose ACE scores were, in general, substantially higher and more homogeneous than our males.

A hypothetical model for explaining the obtained correlations between MAS and ACE scores is depicted graphically in Fig. 2. The proposed model suggests that a small negative correlation between anxiety and intelligence may be found for male subjects if one samples a wide range of intelligence and if the sample contains a sizeable proportion of subjects from the lower part of the range. As the proportion of subjects with low ability decreases, the anxiety-intelligence correlation will be correspondingly attenuated. Thus, in the present study, as the proportion of subjects with lower ability declined in the individual semester-samples (see Table I), through the operation of the aforementioned selection factors, the correlation between MAS and ACE scores became less negative (approached zero).

The model predicts that negative correlations between measures of anxiety and intelligence will be observed empirically only for samples that contain a sizeable proportion of subjects with low ability. This would seem to account for the significant negative correlations obtained between MAS scores and measures of intelligence by Grice (1955) and by Kerrick (1955). It will be recalled that the subjects in these studies were basic trainees in the Air Force, a population which would be expected to contain a larger proportion of individuals of lower ability than would be the case for college students. A major implication of the empirical findings, and of the hypothetical interpretation of them provided by the model, is that it is important to control for intelligence in experiments that select subjects on the basis of extreme MAS scores, especially when studying heterogeneous populations of low average ability.

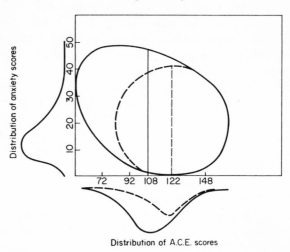

FIG. 2. An explanation of the effects of selection factors on the relationship between empirical measures of anxiety and intelligence. The solid lines represent the hypothetical sampling distributions of MAS and ACE scores in an unselected population of male subjects. The dotted line represents the effects of the operation of selection factors which curtailed the range of ACE scores obtained for males in the semester-samples of this study (see Table I). From Spielberger (1958).

In this study we have pursued, essentially, a methodological tangent which drew us away from our primary concern with the effects of anxiety on complex learning. However, as we worked with intelligence as a variable, we began to realize that task difficulty was in part a function of intelligence and that individual differences in intelligence should be taken into account in deriving predictions from Drive Theory concerning performance on complex learning tasks. In the studies which follow, intelligence was either controlled or utilized as an independent variable.

STUDY III. THE EFFECTS OF ANXIETY ON ACADEMIC ACHIEVEMENT

In Study I we found that the performance of HA subjects was inferior to that of LA subjects for the more difficult elements, and superior for the less difficult elements, of a complex laboratory task which embodied some of the characteristics of a classroom test. These findings suggested that the effects of anxiety on classroom tests would vary as a function of the level of complexity of individual test items. On the assumption that the average test in college courses is relatively difficult for the average student, i.e., many erroneous responses are elicited which compete with correct responses, Drive Theory would lead us to expect that the net effect of anxiety on test performance would be detrimental and that HA students would earn lower grades than LA students.

When we speak of difficulty, we usually mean "average difficulty" for a given population of subjects such as college students. But materials of average difficulty may actually be quite easy for bright students; for less able students such materials might be extremely difficult and, in some cases, beyond the student's learning capacity. Thus, task difficulty would seem to depend on *both* the intrinsic complexity of the materials to be learned and the intellectual ability of the student. In this study, we examined the effects of anxiety on academic achievement for college students who differed in intellectual ability.

Anxiety and Grade Point Average

The subjects in this study (Spielberger & Katzenmeyer, 1959) were the same male college students for whom we found no overall relationship between MAS and ACE scores in Study II. The data for the six semester-samples were pooled, and male students scoring in approximately the upper and lower 20% of the MAS distribution (raw scores of 19 and above and 7 and below) were designated as the HA and LA groups, respectively. Grade point averages (GPAs) were obtained for each student for the *single* semester during which he took the MAS, and these served as the principal criterion of academic achievement. The student's GPA was defined as the weighted average of his academic performance in individual courses where 4 points were credited for each hour of A, 3 points for B, 2 points for C, 1 point for D, and 0 for F. It should be noted that MAS scores were obtained at the *beginning* of the semester, and GPAs were based on performance *during* the semester.

After students who obtained scores of 7 or higher on the Lie Scale of the MMPI were eliminated, MAS scores, ACE scores, and GPAs were available for 140 HA and 144 LA students. The HA and LA students were subdivided into five levels of scholastic aptitude (intelligence) on the basis of their ACE scores, each level consisting of approximately 20% of the total sample. The lowest level of aptitude was designated I; the highest was designated V. The ACE score ranges for level I through level V were: 62-102, 103-116, 117-126, 127-137, and 138-174, respectively. Mean GPAs for the HA and LA students at each of these levels of ability were then determined.

The relationship between anxiety and grades for students at different levels of intellectual aptitude is depicted in Fig. 3. It may be noted that the HA students obtained poorer grades than did the LA students in the broad middle range of ability, a finding consistent with predictions from Drive Theory. However, the grades of low aptitude students were uniformly low, irrespective of their anxiety level; poor academic performance presumably resulted from limited ability. Failure to find a difference between HA and LA students at the lowest level of ability was contrary to expec-

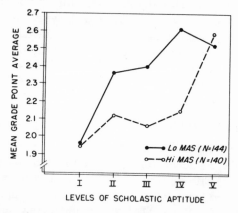

Fig. 3.   Mean grade point averages for high and low anxiety college students at five levels of scholastic aptitude (intelligence). From Spielberger (1962).

tations based on Drive Theory and seemed to be due to a floor effect which made it unlikely for students to obtain GPAs of less than 2.0. This floor effect resulted from grading practices in many upper-class courses which made grades below C relatively infrequent; there were proportionally more juniors and seniors among our low ability students (see Table I).

For superior students (those at level V) grades were high and apparently independent of anxiety level. It would seem reasonable to assume that college work was relatively easy for most of these students, and that their superior intellectual endowment made it possible for them to obtain good grades irrespective of their anxiety level. But if course work were easy, then Drive Theory would predict that high anxiety should facilitate the performance of the most able students. In order to examine this possibility, a more detailed analysis of the performance of students who scored at the highest level of academic aptitude was undertaken. The median

ACE score for level V was determined to be 150, and mean GPAs were calculated for the students at level V whose ACE scores were above and below the median for this group. These mean GPAs are presented in Fig. 4 in which it may be noted that the performance of the very brightest HA students (96-99+ percentile on ACE national norms) was superior to that of LA students of comparable ability, as would be predicted by Drive Theory. However, with the small *N* and the marked variability of the data, the interaction reflected in Fig. 4 did not reach a satisfactory level of statistical significance when evaluated by analysis of variance. The com-

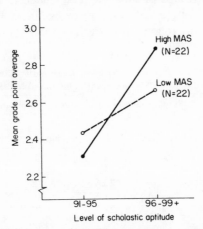

FIG. 4.   Mean grade point averages for high anxiety and low anxiety students in the level V aptitude group whose ACE scores were above and below the median for this group. Compared to national ACE norms, the range of percentile ranks for students below the median was 91–95; the percentile range for students above the median was 96–99+.

bined influence of anxiety and intelligence on a complex learning task is further explored in Study V.

Anxiety and Academic Failure

Were the detrimental effects of anxiety on grades limited to the single semester for which GPAs were examined or did anxiety have persisting and cumulative effects on academic achievement? In order to evaluate the long-term effects of anxiety on academic performance, the graduation status of each of the HA and LA students was determined in a follow-up study conducted 3 years subsequent to the time the original data collection was completed (Spielberger, 1962). For students who had not graduated from the university, and who were no longer enrolled, the reasons for leaving and the cumulative GPAs at the time they departed were obtained from official university records.

For the purposes of this study, academic failure was defined as: (1) having been dismissed from the university because of unsatisfactory academic performance, and/or (2) having left the university with a GPA of 1.75 or lower (a GPA of 1.90 is required to graduate). Both criteria were deemed necessary because students who performed poorly were often allowed to leave school for "personal" reasons so that the stigma of academic failure would not deter their acceptance at other institutions.

Of the original groups of HA and LA students, 17 were either still enrolled in the university or left with averages above 1.75; these students were excluded from the follow-up study. The total number of HA and LA

TABLE II

High and Low Anxious Students at Five Levels of Scholastic Aptitude Who Dropped Out of School Classified as Academic Failures

Scholastic aptitude	High anxious students			Low anxious students		
	Number	Failures		Number	Failures	
		Number	%		Number	%
V	22	2	9.1	30	3	10.0
IV	21	5	23.8	37	0	0.0
III	31	7	22.6	23	1	4.4
II	22	3	13.6	26	1	3.8
I	33	9	27.3	22	3	13.6
Total	129	26	20.2	138	8	5.8

students at each level of scholastic aptitude, and the number and percentage at each level who dropped out of school because of academic failure, are presented in Table II. More than 20% of the HA students were classified as academic failures as compared to fewer than 6% of the LA students. Excluding students from the lowest aptitude group, whose failure might be due largely to lack of ability, the percentage of HA students who failed (17.7%) was nearly four times as great as the percentage of LA academic failures (4.5%). Considering only the lowest aptitude group (level I), it may be noted that there were more than twice as many academic failures among HA students as there were for LA students. Apparently, anxiety had a cumulative influence on the performance of low aptitude students, resulting in a higher proportion of failures even though no detrimental effects of anxiety were observed for the single semester in which GPAs were examined in this study.

On the basis of these findings, it seemed to us that the loss to society of the full contributions of potentially able students through underachievement and/or academic failure constituted an important mental health problem in education. But the findings also suggested that it was possible to identify members of the college population who, because of emotional problems, were not likely to function at levels commensurate with their intellectual potential. If identified early in their academic careers and offered appropriate therapeutic opportunities, could the academic mortality rate be reduced for able students whose emotional problems predisposed them to failure?

This question was explored in collaboration with Dr. Henry Weitz, Director of the Duke University Bureau of Testing and Guidance. Supported by a grant from the National Institute of Mental Health, we identified anxious freshmen at the beginning of their first academic semester and invited them to participate on a voluntary basis in an "Academic Orientation Program" designed to help them make a better adjustment to college life. We reasoned that anxiety might be expected to be even more detrimental to the academic performance of college freshmen than it was for the upper classmen in the present study. The freshman must adjust to demands for academic achievement under conditions of increased complexity of subject matter and heightened competition from his peers at the same time he is attempting to establish a new set of social relationships in a strange environment.

Freshmen who volunteered for the Academic Orientation Program were seen in weekly group-counseling sessions throughout their first semester at college, and they were given the opportunity to continue during the second semester if they wished to do so. The academic performance of the students who participated in the counseling groups was compared with the performance of a control group of nonparticipating volunteers and with nonvolunteers. Although the procedures and results of our approach to improving the academic adjustment of anxious college freshmen will not be discussed here, they are touched on later and described in detail elsewhere (Spielberger, Weitz, & Denny, 1962; Spielberger & Weitz, 1964).

STUDY IV. THE EFFECTS OF ANXIETY ON SERIAL ROTE LEARNING

It was demonstrated in Study III that the influence of anxiety on performance in a complex, real-life learning situation was quite similar in certain respects to the relation in Study I between anxiety and performance on a complex, laboratory learning-recall task. While the findings in both studies were generally supportive of Drive Theory, the variability and floor effects encountered in Study III pointed up the advantages of investigating the influence of anxiety on the learning process under the controlled conditions of the laboratory. In this study, we further explored the effects of individual differences in anxiety on complex learning by evaluating the performance of HA and LA subjects on a serial verbal learning task.

Predictions from Drive Theory

Drive Theory would predict that the performance of HA subjects would be superior to that of LA subjects in learning a serial word list in which correct responses were dominant relative to incorrect responses, and inferior for lists in which competing erroneous responses were stronger. Findings in serial verbal learning experiments, in which the relative strengths of correct and competing response tendencies were manipulated through intralist duplication, similarity, or association value, have been generally consistent with these rather gross theoretical predictions (Deese, Lazarus, & Keenan, 1953; Lazarus, Deese, & Hamilton, 1954; Lucas, 1952; Montague, 1953). But the relative strengths of correct and incorrect response tendencies change during learning as a function of practice, and the implication of these changes for Drive Theory have been given relatively little attention.

On tasks where the correct response was well established prior to the beginning of learning, as with strongly associated S-R pairs in paired-associate learning, it would be expected that the performance of HA subjects would be initially superior to that of LA subjects. On more difficult tasks, however, correct responses are likely to be relatively weak in the early stages of learning. As a function of practice, the strength of correct responses would be expected to increase over trials relative to that of incorrect response tendencies. Assuming that D remains constant throughout learning, it would be predicted from Drive Theory that the performance of HA subjects would be inferior to that of LA subjects early in learning, and that the difference between HA and LA subjects would gradually diminish as the correct responses gained in strength. If the habit strength for correct responses eventually exceeded that of competing responses, the performance of HA subjects should become superior to that of LA subjects. To the extent that these predictions from Drive Theory have been examined, they have received little empirical support. In most studies of anxiety and verbal learning which present performance curves, the results indicate essentially parallel performance for HA and LA groups after the first few trials (e.g., Spence, Farber, & McFann, 1956; Spence, Taylor, & Ketchell, 1956).

Another factor that has been largely ignored in investigations of the effects of anxiety on verbal learning concerns the influence of serial-position on performance. Since words in the middle of a serial list are learned more slowly than those at the extremes, it is reasonable to assume that the embedded words elicit more competing erroneous responses than words at the beginning and the end of the list. Accordingly, Drive Theory would predict that the high D associated with anxiety would begin to facilitate performance sooner for words at the extremes of a serial list than for embedded words. However, in two serial verbal learning studies, in which the effects of anxiety and serial position were evaluated, the findings did not support Drive Theory (Kalish, Garmezy, Rodnick, & Bleke, 1958; Malmo & Amsel, 1948).

Anxiety and Serial Learning

The purpose of the present study was to investigate the effects of word-position on serial rote learning for subjects who differed in anxiety level, using a serial list which produced a moderate amount of interference (competing responses). On the basis of Drive Theory, it was expected that the performance of HA subjects on this task would be inferior to that of LA subjects in the early stages of learning, and relatively better later in learning. Taking serial-position phenomena into account, it was further expected that the facilitative effects of high drive would occur earlier in learning for words at the extremes of the list than for words embedded in it.

The present study (Hicks, 1960) employed essentially the same procedures as those used by Montague (1953) in investigating the effects of anxiety on serial learning. The stimulus materials consisted of a practice list and a test list, typed in capital letters on endless white tapes and presented on two standard Hull-type memory drums. The practice list contained 8 CVC nonsense syllables of 90% Glaze (1928) association value and low intralist similarity; these syllables were selected from Montague's least difficult list (List III). The test list consisted of 12 CVC nonsense syllables of 42.7% association value and low intralist similarity. The words in the test list and the order in which they were presented corresponded exactly with Montague's list of an intermediate level of difficulty (List II), except that "MIP" was replaced with "MUQ"; pilot data showed the former to have a very high association value ("M.P.," "military police") for the population of male subjects in this study. It should be noted that Montague found no significant differences in the performance of HA and and LA subjects in learning this particular list.

The subjects in the present study were 24 undergraduate males enrolled in the introductory psychology course at Duke University who obtained extreme scores on the MAS; subjects with scores of 21 or higher and 9 or lower were designated the HA and LA groups, respectively. These scores defined, approximately, the upper and lower 20% of the MAS

distribution after subjects with MMPI Lie scores above 7 had been eliminated. The HA and LA groups were well matched in ability; the ACE
scores for these groups were 127.4 and 129.8, respectively, and not significantly different.

The subjects were given standard instructions for the serial anticipation
method of verbal learning, followed by 6 trials on the practice list. The
test list was then repeatedly presented until the subject either attained the
learning criterion of 2 succesive perfect trials or received a maximum
of 25 trials. Subjects who reached the learning criterion prior to the twenty-

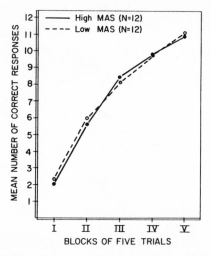

FIG. 5.   Mean number of correct responses given by high and low anxiety subjects on successive trial-blocks. From Spielberger & Smith (1966).

fifth trial were given credit for perfect performance on all trials subsequent
to the criterion trial.

The number of correct responses (anticipations) given by each subject
on each block of 5 trials served as the dependent variable in this study.
The mean number of correct responses for HA and LA subjects on successive trial-blocks are presented in Fig. 5. Since the curves for the HA and
LA groups did not differ over trials in any perceivable respect, further
analyses of the data taking serial position phenomena into account were
deemed unwarranted.

To say the least, these results were disappointing. Predictions from
Drive Theory, which had guided us so well in Study I and Study II, were
clearly *not* supported. Was the theory to be abandoned? Or could some
explanation of the predictive failure of the theory be found? Obviously,

the latter alternative needed to be explored. One reason for our failure to find drive differences for subjects who differed in anxiety immediately suggested itself, namely, that the anxiety measured by the MAS was *reactive* rather than *chronic*. If HA subjects react with higher D only to situations containing some degree of stress, perhaps there was insufficient stress in the present experiment for anxiety to be induced.

The findings in Study I and Study III could be interpreted equally well assuming either that MAS scores reflected a chronic level of anxiety or that factors were present in our experimental situations that induced differential amounts of anxiety in our HA and LA groups. In the present study, however, the experimenter was an undergraduate female honors student, regarded by her peers as pleasant, relaxed and nonthreatening. In reviewing the experiment with her, it became apparent that she was also exceedingly considerate of the needs of her subjects and did everything possible to make them feel comfortable while they participated in the experiment. Assuming that the anxiety measured by the MAS is reactive rather than chronic, it seemed quite possible that the stress produced by our experimental situation was not sufficient to induce differential levels of anxiety in HA and LA subjects. We decided, therefore, to repeat the experiment under more stressful conditions, using the same experimenter and exactly the same experimental task.

Anxiety, Stress, and Serial Learning

Since there is evidence accumulating that anxiety is differentially aroused in HA and LA subjects by "personal threat" (see review by I. G. Sarason, 1960), we attempted to threaten our subjects by making them believe that we were evaluating their intelligence. The subjects, 20 male students selected on essentially the same basis as in the previous unsuccessful experiment, were first given a brief concept-formation task. After they completed it, they were told: "The part of the experiment which you have just done is one measure of thinking and is related to one kind of intelligence. The rest of the experiment has to do with a somewhat different method of thinking in which your task is to memorize a list of nonsense syllables. We have done some research on the relationship between nonsense syllable learning and intelligence. Here is a graph of the relationship we found . . . . You see, speed of learning increases with intelligence." A graph, in which "Number of Correct Responses" increased rapidly and dramatically as a function of "IQ," was shown to the subjects who seemed duly impressed.

The practice and test lists were then presented exactly as they had been administered in the previous study. The mean number of correct responses given by HA and LA subjects over successive trial-blocks is shown in Fig. 6. These data were evaluated in an analysis of variance that yielded a significant anxiety $\times$ trial-blocks interaction. This interaction may be interpreted as indicating that the performance of HA subjects was inferior to that of LA subjects early in learning, and superior later in learning, as may be noted in Fig. 6.

To evaluate the joint effects of anxiety and serial position on performance, the mean number of errors for each word in the test list was determined for the total sample, and separately for HA and LA subjects

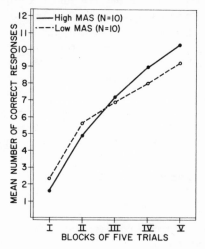

FIG. 6. Mean number of correct responses given by high and low anxiety subjects on successive trial-blocks under ego-stress conditions. From Spielberger & Smith (1966).

(these means are given in Spielberger & Smith, 1966). The data reflected the well-known bow-shaped, serial-position curve. For the combined data of HA and LA subjects, words in serial positions 1, 2, 3, and 12 individually elicited fewest errors, and words in serial positions 6, 7, 8, and 9 elicited the largest number of errors; the former were designated "easy" words, the latter "hard" words.

The mean numbers of correct responses for easy and hard words given by HA and LA subjects on successive trial-blocks are presented in Fig. 7. These data were evaluated in an analysis of variance in which the most important finding was the significant triple interaction involving anxiety, hard-easy words, and trial-blocks. This interaction indicated that the influence of anxiety on performance was different for hard and easy words at different stages of learning. On trial-block I, the performance of HA subjects was inferior to that of LA subjects for both easy and hard words; on trial-blocks II and III, the performance of HA subjects was superior to that of LA subjects for easy words, but inferior for hard words; by trial-block IV, the performance of the HA subjects was superior to that of LA subjects for both types of words, and this superiority was maintained on trial-block V.

These findings were strikingly different from the results obtained in the first part of this study. Since the two experiments differed only in the instructions given to the subjects, the findings would seem to indicate that

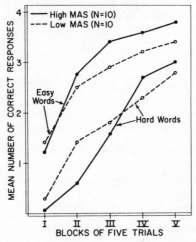

FIG. 7. Mean number of correct responses given by high and low anxiety subjects for easy and hard words on successive trial-blocks. From Spielberger & Smith (1966).

"ego-stress" instructions, i.e., informing subjects that they were participating in an intelligence-testing situation, induced differential levels of D in HA and LA subjects. Thus, empirical support is provided for the "emotional reactivity" hypothesis (Spence, 1958) which posits that HA subjects react with higher D than LA subjects in situations containing some degree of stress.

The demonstration in this study that the performance of HA subjects was inferior to that of LA subjects early in learning and superior later in learning was consistent with expectations derived from Drive Theory. Further support for the theory was observed when serial-position phenomena were taken into account. For words at the beginning and the end of the serial list (easy words), the performance of HA subjects exceeded that of LA subjects at an earlier stage of learning than was the case for the words in the middle of the list (hard words). The following interpretive conclusions are suggested by these findings: (1) The ego-stress instructions induced differential amounts of anxiety in HA and LA subjects. (2) The higher D of the HA subjects impaired their performance relative to LA subjects where strong error (competing) responses were elicited and facilitated performance where correct responses were dominant. (3) For all subjects the strength of correct responses relative to that of competing responses was a function of serial position and previous practice.

In examining the data for individual subjects in this study, it was observed that two HA subjects were performing almost perfectly at the end of the second trial block, whereas the performance of the majority of the HA subjects was well below the mean for LA subjects (see Figs. 6 and 7). In searching for an explanation of the superior performance of these deviant HA subjects, it was discovered that each had exceptionally high scores on the ACE, as well as on the College Entrance Examination Boards (CEEB). Was the superior performance of these subjects due entirely to their superior intelligence or did it reflect the interactive influence of high intelligence and high drive?

Evaluation of the joint influence of anxiety and intelligence for all subjects in this study revealed a tendency for high anxiety to facilitate the performance of high intelligence subjects (those above the ACE median) earlier in learning than was the case for low intelligence subjects (those below the ACE median), but these trends were not statistically significant. It should be noted, however, that our measure of intelligence was not highly correlated with performance on our verbal learning task, indicating that the task was not much easier for bright students than for less able students. The joint influence of anxiety and intelligence on the learning process is examined in Study V in which a more appropriate task is used.

STUDY V. THE EFFECTS OF ANXIETY ON CONCEPT FORMATION

Denny (1963) explored the effects of intelligence and anxiety upon proficiency in concept formation in his doctoral dissertation. This research was carried out within the general framework of Drive Theory, extended to encompass intelligence as a systematic variable. In deriving predictions from the theory, Denny (1963, p. 13) reasoned as follows:

A concept formation task of a certain degree of objectively specifiable complexity when presented to a more intelligent subject may call forth only the correct conclusion about the concept whereas when the same task is presented to a less intelligent subject it may call forth many erroneous conclusions. In other words, the relative difficulty of the task differs for the two subjects; it is easy for the bright subject and hard for the duller subject. Since both the objectively specifiable complexity of a task and the intellectual capacity of a subject may vary independently, *task difficulty* may be defined as a joint function of task complexity and the subject's intelligence.

Denny developed an ingenious task on which subjects were required to deduce the attributes which constituted a conjunctive concept from information given in separate "instances." Each instance consisted of a row of symbols (values), one symbol placed under each of eight lettered positions (columns) denoting potential attributes of the concept. Instances were presented to each subject one at a time in the same order. The instance was not seen by the subject until it was presented, but remained visible after that to reduce the subject's memory load. Each instance was marked with either a plus sign, indicating that it was a positive instance, or a minus sign, indicating that it was a negative instance. The attributes which formed the concept were contained in positive instances but not in negative instances.

The subject was presented successively with 13 instances, for each of which he reported eight conclusions, one for each potential attribute. After the subject had examined a particular instance, he was required to report his conclusions about the concept by recording, for each of the eight potential attributes, either that (1) the attribute was included in the concept, (2) the attribute was not included in the concept, or (3) he did not know whether or not it was included in the concept. The subjects' reports were scored as either correct or incorrect by comparing them to the conclusions that could be correctly deduced from the information given by the instances presented up to that point.

Denny's subjects were 56 male students from the introductory psychology course at Duke University who scored in the upper and lower quartiles of the MAS distribution for male students (raw scores of 20 and above and 8 and below) after students with scores of above 7 on the MMPI Lie Scale had been eliminated. The HA and LA groups were each divided into high and low intelligence groups by splitting them at the median CEEB score (V + M = 1156) for the *total* group.

The concept formation task was preceded by "ego-stress" instructions similar to those employed in Study IV. The subjects were told that the experiment was "an investigation of factors which affect college grades," and that "persons who are good at conceptual thinking should do better in college courses which involve abstractions and generalizations." Task complexity was held constant by running all subjects on the same concept formation task for which it had been determined in pilot work that there were minimal floor and ceiling effects, i.e., low intelligence subjects rarely achieved the worst possible score and high intelligence subjects rarely made the best possible score.

Denny found that high intelligence subjects gave significantly more correct conclusions on the concept formation task than low intelligence subjects, thereby demonstrating that the task was sensitive to the range of individual differences in intelligence represented in the sample. The mean number of correct conclusions given by HA and LA subjects of high and low intelligence is indicated in Fig. 8. For the low intelligence subjects, the performance of the HA group was impaired relative to that of the LA group. Conversely, for the high intelligence subjects, the performance of

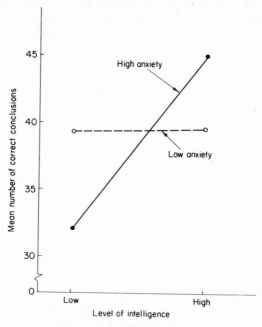

FIG. 8. Mean number of correct conclusions given by high and low anxiety subjects of high and low intelligence. From Denny (1963).

the HA group was facilitated relative to that of the LA group. On the assumption that task difficulty was inversely related to intelligence, i.e., the concept formation task was less difficult for the brighter subjects and more difficult for the less able subjects, the findings were consistent with expectations based on Drive Theory.

In examining the errors made by his subjects, Denny found that the interactive effect of anxiety and intelligence on correct conclusions was determined by a particular class of errors which he labeled "commission errors with information given," and which we shall refer to simply as commission errors. This type of error resulted when there was sufficient information to deduce either that an attribute was, or was not, included in the concept, and the subject reported the wrong conclusion. Such errors are analogous to giving an erroneous response to a stimulus in verbal learning (as contrasted with errors resulting from failure to respond). Commission errors are also roughly analogous to the misinterpretation type of difficulty, described earlier, which was observed in going over test papers with anxious undergraduates.

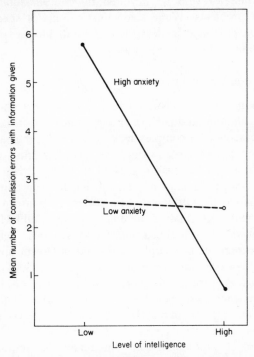

FIG. 9.   Mean number of commission errors with information given for high and low anxiety subjects of low and high intelligence. From Denny (1963).

The mean number of commission errors given by each of Denny's four experimental groups is indicated in Fig. 9. The HA subjects of low intelligence made more commission errors than the LA–low intelligence subjects. Conversely, HA–high intelligence subjects made fewer commission errors than LA–high intelligence subjects. On the assumption that the concept formation task elicited a large number of competing response tendencies for the low intelligence groups, and relatively few competing responses for the high intelligence groups for whom correct conclusions became dominant earlier in the task, these findings were quite consistent with expectations derived from Drive Theory.

Implications for Drive Theory and Clinical Practice

The findings in the studies reported in the previous section were generally supportive of Drive Theory and suggested meaningful ways in which the theory needs to be extended and refined if it is to be useful in accounting for behavior exhibited in complex learning situations. Our data would also appear to have potential significance for the practicing clinician, especially the counselor who is consulted by college students concerning their academic problems. While some implications of specific aspects of our results were suggested in describing the individual experiments, these may now be summarized and elaborated.

IMPLICATIONS FOR DRIVE THEORY

In Study I it was demonstrated that high anxiety can lead to *both* performance facilitation and performance decrements for the same subjects on different elements of a complex task. The finding that anxiety had opposite effects on performance within the relatively short period of time required to respond to this task suggested that high drive interacted with task-produced competing response tendencies to determine performance decrements, whereas high drive acted on correct responses when they were dominant to yield performance increments. The Child-Mandler-Sarason hypothesis that anxiety-produced interfering response tendencies cause performance decrements in complex tasks did not seem applicable to our data. However, blocking was frequently reported by anxious college students seen in the clinic, suggesting that there may be a threshold level of anxiety at which anxiety-produced responses begin to interfere with performance. Apparently the anxiety level of our HA subjects did not exceed this threshold.

The findings in Study II suggested that there is a slight negative relationship between anxiety and intelligence. This finding has important methodological implications for experimenters who select subjects with extreme anxiety scores from heterogeneous populations of low average ability. The findings in this study also showed that institutional selection factors can lead to systematic changes in subject populations with consequent modification of the relationship observed between anxiety and intelligence.

Perhaps the most important implication of the results obtained in Study III was that Drive Theory could be successfully generalized to real-life learning situations if the theory were extended to incorporate individual differences in intelligence. The anxiety-intelligence-GPA relationship obtained in this study should be interpreted with a note of caution, however, because subsequent efforts to reproduce these findings were only partially successful (Spielberger & Weitz, 1964, see Fig. 2 and discussion on pp.

15-17). While field studies such as this one are urgently needed, the investigator must be alert to the requirement of large samples and to the possibility that the characteristics of subject populations change over time. Moreover, there may be important systematic differences between students enrolled in the same course in a university at different times of the year.

The results in Study IV strongly suggested that "what is measured" by the MAS is a reactive disposition to respond with anxiety to experimental situations containing some degree of stress. The triple interaction obtained in this study between anxiety, hard-easy words, and trial-blocks indicated that the effects of high drive on performance depended on the position of a word in a serial list and the particular stage of learning that was observed. This highly complex state of affairs clearly affirmed Spence's contention that "In order to derive implications concerning the effects of drive variation in any type of complex learning task, it is necessary to have, in addition to the drive theory, a further theoretical network concerning the variables and their interaction that are involved in the particular learning activity" (Spence, 1958, p. 137).

The importance of extending Drive Theory to incorporate individual differences in intelligence, which was suggested by the findings in Study III and Study IV, was clearly demonstrated in Study V. On a challenging concept-formation task, anxiety impaired the performance of low intelligence subjects and facilitated the performance of high intelligence subjects. If it may be assumed that (1) the number of erroneous competing response tendencies elicited in a given situation is a function of task difficulty and (2) the level of difficulty of a complex task for an individual subject will be inversely related to the subject's intelligence, the findings in Study V were consistent with Drive Theory. The further finding in Study V that number of correct conclusions was determined largely by commission errors would seem to indicate that the process through which high anxiety leads to performance decrements involves the energizing of erroneous response tendencies.

IMPLICATIONS FOR CLINICAL PRACTICE

While our findings substantiated the clinical observation that high anxiety interferes with academic achievement, they also indicated that, for the very brightest students, anxiety tended to have facilitative effects on course grades. The anxiety–task difficulty interactions, obtained directly in Studies I and IV, and indirectly in Study V as a function of intelligence, suggested that task-produced competing responses were important determiners of the performance decrements of HA subjects. Concrete explorations of this possibility with anxious students seen in the clinic and in the

classroom revealed that they frequently misinterpreted complex or ambiguous test questions. The counselor who is called upon to assist anxious
students would be well advised to consider such test-taking difficulties in
working with them.

It was previously mentioned that our anxiety-intelligence-GPA findings
led us to develop a program designed to prevent underachievement in
anxious college freshmen by offering group counseling to such students
early in their first academic semester. We fully expected that a significant
portion of the counseling sessions would be devoted to discussions of experiences which had induced anxiety in these students prior to their entering college. We found instead that the students were concerned almost
exclusively with anxiety-arousing aspects of their present circumstances,
and with finding effective ways to cope with the stresses encountered in
their new environments. It should be noted that there was abundant evidence of high anxiety in the behavior of the students who participated in
the counseling groups, and in their descriptions of their reactions to environmental stresses. But in their comments in the counseling sessions, this
anxiety was related to immediate problems and situations and not to past
experiences, despite the counselors' interest in helping them to deal with
the underlying sources of their anxiety.

The topics of greatest concern in our counseling groups included:
methods of study, individual academic difficulties, relations with professors
in class and on the campus, dormitory life, vocational goals, etc. The
students wanted to know how to study, how to prepare for examinations,
how to figure out what instructors expected of them, how to budget their
time, and how to get work done in dormitories amid the distraction of noise,
interruptions, and incessant social demands. Thus, although as counselors
we anticipated and were prepared to deal with expressions of more basic
personal and emotional difficulties, these did not play a central role in
group sessions.

These clinical observations of anxious students in group counseling
were in agreement with the empirical findings of our laboratory studies in
at least one important respect. The data obtained in both the clinic and
the laboratory pointed to the centrality and significance of situational or
stimulus factors in arousing anxiety and in determining the effects of
anxiety on behavior. For the clinician who works with anxious college
students, it would seem especially important to deal with the students'
reactions to stressful environmental stimuli. We have found that providing
students with factual information about the environment and helping them
to deal with real and present stresses often alleviates anxiety or reduces
it to manageable levels. Furthermore, analysis of the immediate stresses

to which a student reacts with anxiety frequently leads to the discussion of significant past experiences which have made the student vulnerable and disposed to respond with anxiety in the present.

Summary

In this chapter the results of five related experiments concerned with the influence of anxiety on learning, concept formation, and academic achievement have been described along with observations of anxious college students in the clinic and in the classroom. The experiments were concerned primarily with the arousal or drive aspect of anxiety and its influence on complex learning, and were carried out within the context of a theory of emotionally based drive developed by Spence and his colleagues. This theory assumes that there are important individual differences in emotional responsiveness (anxiety) which contribute to drive level, and that habit strength and drive combine multiplicatively to determine performance in learning tasks. According to Drive Theory, high anxiety should facilitate performance when correct responses are dominant and should lead to performance decrements when competing erroneous response tendencies are numerous and/or stronger than correct responses.

In Study I the effects of anxiety on a laboratory learning-recall task which embodied some of the characteristics of a classroom test were investigated. The performance of high anxiety subjects was found to be superior to that of low anxiety subjects for task elements which evoked relatively few errors and inferior for task elements which elicited a larger number of errors. The correlation between measures of anxiety and intelligence was examined in Study II and found to be essentially zero for a large sample of males and females. However, a more detailed analysis of the data for males suggested that a small negative correlation between these variables might be observed in heterogeneous populations of low average ability.

The relation between anxiety, intelligence, and academic achievement was evaluated in Study III. For students in the broad middle range of academic aptitude, performance decrements were observed for those with high anxiety as compared to students with low anxiety; high anxiety had no demonstrable effect on the performance of low ability students whose grades were uniformly low and tended to facilitate the performance of the very brightest students. A follow-up study, designed to evaluate the long-term effects of anxiety on academic performance, indicated that the percentage of academic failures was nearly four times as great for able students with high anxiety as it was for low anxiety students of comparable ability.

The effects of anxiety on serial rote learning were investigated in Study IV. It was found that the performance of high anxiety subjects was inferior to that of low anxiety subjects early in learning and superior later in learning. When serial-position phenomena were taken into account, it was observed that high anxiety began to facilitate performance earlier in learning for words at the extremes of the serial list than for words embedded in the list.

In the final study, the effects of anxiety and intelligence on concept formation were investigated. The performance of high anxiety subjects with low intelligence was inferior to that of low anxiety–low intelligence subjects, whereas the performance of high anxiety–high intelligence subjects was superior to that of low anxiety–high intelligence subjects. The basis for these findings was traced to a particular type of erroneous response which was apparently energized by high anxiety in low intelligence subjects. This type of error was not strongly represented in the performance of high intelligence subjects for whom correct responses became dominant relatively early in learning.

The findings in these studies, while generally supportive of Drive Theory, suggested that the theory was applicable only to situations involving some degree of stress, and that it required extension and refinement. In order to explain behavior in complex learning situations, the theory must take individual differences in intelligence into account along with detailed information about factors that influence the relative strengths of correct and competing responses in the particular learning situation.

REFERENCES

Bender, Lauretta. *A visual motor gestalt test and its clinical use.* New York: Amer. Orthopsychiat. Ass., 1938.

Buss, A. H., Wiener, M., Durkee, A., & Baer, M. The measurement of anxiety in clinical situations. *J. consult. Psychol.,* 1955, **19**, 125-129.

Cameron, N. *The psychology of behavior disorders: a bio-social interpretation.* Boston: Houghton, 1947.

Child, I. L. Personality. *Annu. Rev. Psychol.,* 1954, **5**, 149-170.

Cronbach, L. J. *Essentials of psychological testing.* New York: Harper, 1960.

Dana, R. H. Manifest anxiety, intelligence, and psychopathology. *J. consult. Psychol.,* 1957, **21**, 38-40.

Deese, J., Lazarus, R. S., & Keenan, J. Anxiety, anxiety-reduction, and stress in learning. *J. exp. Psychol.,* 1953, **46**, 55-60.

Denny, J. P. The effects of anxiety and intelligence on concept formation. Doctoral dissertation, Duke Univer.; *Dissertation Abstr.,* 1963, **24**, 2132-2133. Order No.: 63-7013.

Dollard, J., & Miller, N. E. *Personality and psychotherapy.* New York: McGraw-Hill, 1950.

Farber, I. E., & Spence, K. W. Complex learning and conditioning as a function of anxiety. *J. exp. Psychol.*, 1953, **45**, 120-125.

Farber, I. E., & Spence, K. W. Main and interactive effects of several variables on reaction time. *U. S. Naval Res. Lab.*, 1955, Tech. Rep. No. 3. (Contract N9 onr-93802, State Univer. of Iowa).

Farber, I. E., & Spence, K. W. Effects of anxiety, stress and task variables on reaction time. *J. Pers.*, 1956, **25**, 1-18.

Freud, S. *New introductory lectures in psychoanalysis.* New York: Norton, 1933.

Freud, S. *The problem of anxiety.* New York: Norton, 1936.

Gleser, Goldine, & Ulett, G. The Saslow Screening Test as a measure of anxiety-proneness. *J. clin. Psychol.*, 1952, **8**, 279-283.

Glaze, J. A. The association value of nonsense syllables. *J. genet. Psychol.*, 1928, **35**, 255-267.

Goodstein, L. D., Spielberger, C. D., Williams, J. E., & Dahlstrom, W. G. The effects of serial position and design difficulty on recall of the Bender-Gestalt Test designs. *J. consult. Psychol.*, 1955, **19**, 230-234.

Grice, G. R. Discrimination reaction time as a function of anxiety and intelligence. *J. abnorm. soc. Psychol.*, 1955, **50**, 71-74.

Hicks, Lou Ella. Effects of anxiety and stress on serial rote learning. Unpublished honors thesis, Duke Univer., 1960.

Hill, W. F. Comments on Taylor's "Drive theory and manifest anxiety." *Psychol. Bull.*, 1957, **54**, 490-493.

Hoyt, D. P., & Magoon, T. M. A validation study of the Taylor Manifest Anxiety Scale. *J. clin. Psychol.*, 1954, **10**, 357-361.

Hull, C. L. *Principles of behavior.* New York: Appleton, 1943.

Jessor, R., & Hamond, K. R. Construct validity and the Taylor anxiety scale. *Psychol. Bull.*, 1957, **54**, 161-170.

Kalish, H. I., Garmezy, N., Rodnick, E. H., & Bleke, R. C. The effects of anxiety and experimentally-induced stress on verbal learning. *J. gen. Psychol.*, 1958, **59**, 87-95.

Kendall, E. The validity of Taylor's Manifest Anxiety Scale. *J. consult. Psychol.*, 1954, **18**, 429-432.

Kerrick, Jean S. Some correlates of the Taylor Manifest Anxiety Scale. *J. abnorm. soc. Psychol.*, 1955, **50**, 75-77.

Klugh, H. E., & Bendig, A. W. The Manifest Anxiety and ACE scales and college achievement. *J. consult. Psychol.*, 1955, **19**, 487.

Lazarus, R. S., Deese, J., & Hamilton, R. Anxiety and stress in learning: the role of intraserial duplication. *J. exp. Psychol.*, 1954, **47**, 111-114.

Lucas, J. D. The interactive effects of anxiety, failure, and intra-serial duplication. *Amer. J. Psychol.*, 1952, **65**, 59-66.

Malmo, R. B., & Amsel, A. Anxiety-produced interference in serial rote learning with observations on rote learning after partial frontal lobectomy. *J. exp. Psychol.*, 1948, **38**, 440-454.

Mandler, G., & Sarason, S. B. A study of anxiety and learning. *J. abnorm. soc. Psychol.*, 1952, **47**, 166-173.

Mayzner, M. S., Sersen, E., & Tresselt, M. E. The Taylor Manifest Anxiety Scale and intelligence. *J. consult. Psychol.*, 1955, **19**, 401-404.

Montague, E. K. The role of anxiety in serial rote learning. *J. exp. Psychol.*, 1953, **45**, 91-96.

Sarason, I. G. The relationship of anxiety and "lack of defensiveness" to intellectual performance. *J. consult. Psychol.*, 1956, **20**, 220-222.

Sarason, I. G. Empirical findings and theoretical problems in the use of anxiety scales. *Psychol. Bull.*, 1960, **57**, 403-415.

Sarason, S. B., Mandler, G., & Craighill, P. G. The effect of differential instructions on anxiety and learning. *J. abnorm. soc. Psychol.*, 1952, **47**, 561-565.

Spence, K. W. Current interpretations of learning data and some recent developments in stimulus-response theory. In *Learning theory, personality theory, and clinical research. The Kentucky symposium*. New York: Wiley, 1953.

Spence, K. W. *Behavior theory and conditioning*. New Haven, Conn.: Yale Univer. Press, 1956.

Spence, K. W. A theory of emotionally based drive (D) and its relation to performance in simple learning situations. *Amer. Psychologist*, 1958, **13**, 131-141.

Spence, K. W., & Farber, I. E. Conditioning and extinction as a function of anxiety. *J. exp. Psychol.*, 1953, **45**, 116-119.

Spence, K. W., Farber, I. E., & McFann, H. H. The relation of anxiety (drive) level to performance in competitional and noncompetitional paired-associates learning. *J. exp. Psychol.*, 1956, **52**, 296-305.

Spence, K. W., Taylor, J., & Ketchel, Rhoda. Anxiety (drive) level and degree of competition in paired-associates learning. *J. exp. Psychol.*, 1956, **52**, 306-310.

Spielberger, C. D. On the relationship between anxiety and intelligence. *J. consult. Psychol.*, 1958, **22**, 220-224.

Spielberger, C. D. The effects of manifest anxiety on the academic achievement of college students. *Ment. Hyg.*, 1962, **46**, 420-426.

Spielberger, C. D., Goodstein, L. D., & Dahlstrom, W. G. Complex incidental learning as a function of anxiety and task difficulty. *J. exp. Psychol.*, 1958, **56**, 58-61.

Spielberger, C. D., & Katzenmeyer, W. G. Manifest anxiety, intelligence, and college grades. *J. consult. Psychol.*, 1959, **23**, 278.

Spielberger, C. D., & Smith, L. H. Anxiety (drive), stress, and serial-position effects in serial-verbal learning. *J. exp. Psychol.*, 1966, in press.

Spielberger, C. D., & Weitz, H. Improving the academic performance of anxious college freshmen: a group-counseling approach to the prevention of underachievement. *Psychol. Monogr.*, 1964, **78**, No. 13 (Whole No. 590).

Spielberger, C. D., Weitz, H., & Denny, J. P. Group counseling and the academic performance of anxious college freshmen. *J. counsel. Psychol.*, 1962, **9**, 195-204.

Taylor, J. A. A personality scale of manifest anxiety. *J. abnorm. soc. Psychol.*, 1953, **48**, 285-290.

Taylor, J. A. Drive theory and manifest anxiety. *Psychol. Bull.*, 1956, **53**, 303-320.

Taylor, J. A., & Chapman, J. P. Paired-associate learning as related to anxiety. *Amer. J. Psychol.*, 1955, **68**, 671.

Taylor, J. A., & Spence, K. W. The relationship of anxiety level to performance in serial learning. *J. exp. Psychol.*, 1952, **44**, 61-64.

Weitz, H. Placement test performance of Duke University freshmen—a five year summary. Duke Univer., Bur. of Testing and Guidance, Staff Res. Rep. No. 14, Nov. 15, 1955.

AUTHOR INDEX

Numbers in italics refer to pages on which the complete references are listed.

A

Äas, A., 227, *261*
Alexander, F., 139, *140*
Alexander, F. G., 243, *261*
Alfert, Elizabeth, 235, 239, 243, 245, 246, *261*, 284, *287*, 357, *359*
Alper, Thelma, 339, *357*
Altrocchi, J., 346, *357*
Amber, E., 215, *223*
Amsel, A., 162, 163, 164, 165, *177*, 266, *286*, 308, *323*, 383, *397*
Andrews, H. L., 175, *176*
Andrews, T. G., 311, 312, 320, *323, 324*
Antunes-Rodrigues, J., 174, *176*
Arenberg, D., 356, *359*
Arnold, M. B., 107, *124*
Atkinson, J. W., 16, 19, *19*, 279, *286*, 318, *324*
Ax, A. F., 214, *223*
Axelrod, H. S., 301, *323*

B

Baker, R., 25, *59*
Bardach, Joan L., 321, *323*
Barnard, J. W., 66, 67, *79*
Basowitz, H., 8, 13, 14, *19*, 134, 135, 136, 137, 138, *140, 141, 142*, 256, *261, 262*
Bateson, G., 284, *286*
Beam, J. C., 292, *323*
Bear, M., 368, *396*
Becker, H. S., 221, *223*
Bélanger, D., 161, 169, *176, 177*
Beloff, J. R., 36, *60*
Bender, Lauretta, 370, *396*
Bendig, A. W., 301, 302, *323, 324*, 373, *397*
Bennett, E. L., 33, *59*

Berkowitz, L., 356, *357*
Berlyne, D. B., 312, *324*
Bernstein, I. H., 349, *357*
Besch, Norma, 302, 319, 320, *323*
Bindra, D., 307, *323*
Birdsall, T. G., 350, *360*
Birnbaum, R. M., 246, *261*
Bitterman, M. E., 292, 295, *323*
Blackwell, H. R., 350, *357*
Bleke, R. C., 383, *397*
Blewett, D. B., 36, *60*
Blitz, B., 320, *325*
Blum, G. S., 348, *358*
Blumenthal, A., 271, *287*
Board, F. A., 132, 135, 136, *140, 141, 142*, 256, *262*
Bradley, A. D., 130, *141*
Branca, A. A., 353, *358*
Britton, S. W., 216, *224*
Brody, M. W., 189, *189*
Browne, C. T., 329, 341, 345, 347, 349, *359*
Bruch, H., 223, *224*
Bruner, J. S., 331, 332, *358*
Bull, Nina, 104, 107, 108, *124*
Bunnell, B. N., 216, *224*
Bunney, W. E., Jr., 132, *140*
Burgess, M., 299, *323*
Buss, A. H., 368, *396*
Butcher, J., 45, *60*
Butterfield, E. C., 276, *286*
Byrd, E., 43, *59*
Byrne, D., 346, *358*

C

Cameron, N., 368, *396*
Campbell, D., 183, 188, *189*
Campbell, D. T., 16, *19*

Cannon, W. B., 194, 197, 214, 216, *224*
Cantril, H., 195, *224*
Caron, A. J., 329, 344, 347, 355, *358*
Carpenter, B., 345, *358*
Carpenter, Janeth T., 345, *358*
Castaneda, A., 7, *19*, 303, *323*
Cattell, R. B., 7, 8, 13, 15, *19*, 24, 25, 27, 28, 29, 30, 31, 32, 33, 34, 35, 36, 37, 38, 40, 41, 43, 44, 45, 46, 47, 49, 50, 51, 52, 53, 54, 55, 57, 58, *59, 60, 61, 62*
Champion, R. A., 302, 303, *326*
Chapman, Jean P., 302, 306, *326*, 366, *398*
Chatterjee, B. B., 349, 353, *358*
Chevalier, J. A., 135, 136, 137, *140, 141, 142*, 256, *261*
Child, I. L., 275, 278, *286*, 308, *323*, 367, 373, *396*
Chiles, W. D., 319, *323*
Clark, R. A., 318, *324*
Clark, R. E., 303, *323*
Cleghorn, R. A., 175, *177*
Clemens, T. L., 243, *261*
Coan, R. C., 25, *59*
Cohen, Judith E., 309, *324*
Cole, M. W., 194, 196, *224*
Connor, D., 45, 47, *60*
Courts, F. A., 315, 317, *323*
Covian, M. R., 174, *176*
Cowen, E. L., 301, *323*
Craighill, P. G., 309, *325*, 362, *398*
Cronbach, L. J., 298, *323*, 368, *396*

D

Dahlstrom, W. G., 370, 371, *397, 398*
Dana, C. L., 216, *224*
Dana, R. H., 373, *396*
Das, R. S., 53, *61*
Davenport, G., 295, *324*
Davids, A., 341, *359*
Davidson, K. S., 8, *20*, 64, 67, 70, 74, *79*
Davidson, W. Z., 320, *323*
Davis, J. F., 157, 166, 167, 175, *176, 177*
Davison, L. A., 231, 232, 238, 240, 242, 243, 244, 246, 252, 255, 257, *261, 262*, 284, *287*
Davitz, J. R., 280, *286*
Dean, S. J., 354, *359*

Deese, J., 8, *20*, 310, 320, *323, 324*, 382, *396, 397*
Denny, J. P., 381, 388, 390, 391, *396, 398*
Diamond, M. C., 33, *59*
Dickoff, Hilda, 346, *357*
Digman, J. M., 25, 28, 31, *60, 61*
Dollard, J., 8, *19*, 351, 353, *358*, 363, *396*
Doroz, L., 353, *359*
Douglas, Anna G., 331, *358*
Duffy, Elizabeth, 158, 160, 162, 174, *176*, 297, *323*
Dulany, D. E., Jr., 149, *155*, 349, 353, *358*
Durkee, A., 368, *396*
D'Zurilla, T. J., 329, *358*

E

Eber, H. J., 54, *60*
Elliott, R., 280, *286*
Engel, B. T., 139, *140*
Eriksen, C. W., 329, 330, 331, 332, 335, 337, 339, 341, 342, 345, 347, 348, 349, 350, 351, 353, *357, 358, 359*
Eriksen, E. H., 149, *155*
Ewing, T. N., 43, *61*
Eysenck, H. J., 8, *19*, 29, 41, *61*, 188, *189, 190*, 339, *359*

F

Farber, I. E., 188, *189*, 297, 301, 302, 303, 306, 310, *324, 326*, 362, 364, 366, 373, 382, *397, 398*
Fastovsky, A. A., 130, *141*
Fedorchak, Olga, 302, *324*
Feldman, S. M., 157, 158, 160, 161, *176*
Festinger, L., 196, 220, *224*
Flagg, G. W., 243, *261*
Fonda, C. P., 331, 332, 339, 345, *359*
Fox, J., 82, 88, *124*, 304, *324*
Franks, C. M., 175, 176, *176*
Freud, S., 9, 11, *19*, 24, 25, *60, 61*, 77, *79*, 328, *359*, 362, 363, *397*
Fuhrer, M. J., 349, *359*

G

Galanter, E., 149, *155*, 264, *287*
Gamm, S. R., 134, *142*

Gantt, W. H., 5, *19*, 180, *190*
Garmezy, N., 383, *397*
Garner, W. R., 350, *359*
Gilberstadt, H., 295, *324*
Gilbert, W. M., 43, *61*
Gilman, A., 221, *224*
Glasser, W., 146, 150, *155*
Glaze, J. A., 383, *397*
Gleser, Goldine, 293, *324*, 368, *397*
Glickstein, M., 135, *140*, 256, *261*
Glixman, A. F., 329, 335, *359*
Goldiamond, I., 349, *359*
Goldstein, H., 297, *326*
Goldstein, I. B., 138, *140, 141, 142*
Goldstein, M. J., 243, *261*
Goldstein, M. S., 138, *140*
Goodman, A. Joan, 175, *177*
Goodman, L. S., 221, *224*
Goodstein, L. D., 370, 371, *397, 398*
Gordon, W. M., 312, *324*
Gorsuch, R. L., 25, 53, *61*
Gossett, J. T., 345, *359*
Graham, B. F., 175, *177*
Grice, G. R., 373, 375, *397*
Grinker, R. R., Jr., 135, *140*
Grinker, R. R., Sr., 8, 13, 14, *19*, 32, 33,
   61, 62, 129, 130, 131, 132, 133, 134,
   135, 136, 137, 138, 139, 140, *140, 141,*
   142, 256, *261, 262*
Gussack, H., 138, *140*

H

Haggard, D., 295, *326*
Haggard, E. A., 8, *19*, 271, *287*
Hake, H. W., 349, 350, *359*
Haley, J., 284, *286*
Hamburg, D. A., 132, 135, 136, 137,
   140, 141, 142, 256, *261, 262*
Hamilton, R., 320, *324*, 382, *397*
Hamond, K. R., 368, *397*
Hanfmann, Eugenia, 8, *19*
Harlow, H. F., 101, *124*
Harris, C. W., 34, *61*
Harrower, M., 131, *141*
Heath, H. A., 135, 136, 137, 138, *141,*
   142
Hebb, D. O., 158, *176*, 266, *287*
Heilizer, F., 301, *323*
Herrick, C. J., 158, *176*

Herz, M., 135, 137, *142*
Heslam, R. M., 172, 174, *177*
Hicks, Lou Ella, 383, *397*
Hill, K., 64, 72, 75, *79*
Hill, W. F., 368, *397*
Hillman, J., 107, *124*
Hoagland, H. J., 33, *61*
Hoch, P. H., 4, 8, *19*
Hodges, W. F., 18, *19*
Hoehn, A. J., 306, *325*
Hohmann, G. W., 217, 219, 220, *224*
Hokanson, J. E., 299, 317, *323, 326*
Holmes, D. S., 356, *357*
Holtzman, W. H., 292, 295, *323*
Horn, J. L., 49, 52, 55, 58, *60, 61*
Hovland, C. I., 164, 165, *176*
Howes, D. H., 347, *359*
Hoyt, D. P., 368, *397*
Hughes, J. B., II, 301, *324*
Hull, C. L., 186, *190*, 308, *324, 363, 397*
Hundleby, J. D., 29, *61*
Hunt, J. McV., 43, *61*, 194, *224*
Hunt, W. A., 195, 196, *224*

I

Izard, C. E., 81, 82, 88, *124*

J

Jackson, D. D., 284, *286*
Jacobson, E., 185, *190*
James, W., 193, *224*
Janis, I. L., 8, *19*, 285, *287*
Jasper, H. H., 159, 160, 161, *176*
Jeans, R. F., 138, *142*
Jennings, J. R., 81, 82, 88, *124*
Jessor, R., 368, *397*
Johnson, H., 349, *359*
Jones, C. A., Jr., 250, 251, *261*
Jones, M. C., 183, *190*
Jones, R. B., 243, *261*
Jourard, S. M., 149, *155*

K

Kalish, H. I., 383, *397*
Kamin, L. J., 302, *324*
Karas, A. Y., 183, *190*
Karson, S., 25, 53, *60, 61*
Katchmar, L. T., 311, 312, *324*

Katkin, E. S., 18, *19*
Katzenmeyer, W. G., 377, *398*
Keenan, J., 320, *323,* 382, *396*
Kelly, R. F., 41, *62*
Kendall, E., 368, *397*
Kerrick, Jean S., 373, 375, *397*
Kessen, W., 266, *287*
Ketchel, Rhoda, 302, 303, *326,* 382, *398*
Kierkegaard, S., 122, *124*
Killam, E. K., 210, *224*
Kimble, J. P., 32, 37, *61*
Klugh, H. E., 373, *397*
Knapp, P., 107, *124*
Komlos, E., 41, *61*
Korchin, S. J., 8, 13, 14, *19*, 134, 135, 136, 137, 138, *140, 141, 142,* 256, *261, 262,* 292, *324*
Krause, M. S., 8, 13, 14, *19,* 235, *261*
Krech, D., 33, *59*
Krechevsky, I., 149, *155*
Kubis, J., 292, *326*
Kuethe, J. L., 351, *359*

L

Lacey, Beatrice C., 299, *324*
Lacey, J. I., 233, *261,* 299, *324*
Laforge, R., 43, *61*
Landis, C., 195, *224*
LaPiere, R., 144, *155*
Latané, B., 213, *224*
Lauterbach, C. G., 293, *324*
Laverty, S. C., 183, 188, *189*
Lazarus, A. A., 183, 189, *190*
Lazarus, R. S., 8, *20,* 226, 227, 228, 231, 232, 234, 235, 236, 238, 240, 241, 242, 244, 245, 246, 248, 251, 252, 253, 255, 257, *261, 262, 287,* 310, 320, *323, 324,.* 331, 332, 339, 344, 345, 347, 348, 356, 357, *359,* 382, *396, 397*
Lee, Lee Charlotte, 319, *324*
Levine, S., 134, *142,* 217, *224,* 292, *324*
Levy, L. H., 7, *20*
Lewinsohn, P. M., 346, *360*
Lewis, J. T., 216, *224*
Liddell, H. D., 180, *190*
Liddell, H. S., 5, *20*
Lighthall, F. F., 8, *20,* 64, 67, 70, 74, *79*
Lim, D. T., 346, *360*
Lindsley, D. B., 158, 159, *177*

Lipman, E., 131, *142*
Lipsitt, L. P., 303, *323*
Litwin, G. H., 279, *286*
Liverant, S., 285, *287*
Livsey, W., 81, 82, 88, *124*
Loeb, J., 148, *155*
Longo, N., 344, 347, *359*
Lorenz, K. F., 101, *125*
Lovaas, O. I., 302, *324*
Lowell, E. L., 318, *324*
Lucas, J. D., 301, 312, *324,* 366, 382, *397*

M

McCandless, B. R., 7, *19,* 303, *323*
McCleary, R. A., 348, *359*
McClelland, D., 85, 98, *125*
McClelland, D. C., 318, *324*
McFann, H. H., 302, 303, 306, *326,* 382, *398*
Magoon, T. M., 368, *397*
Magoun, H. W., 158, 159, *177*
Malmo, R. B., 8, 15, *20,* 157, 160, 161, 162, 163, 164, 165, 166, 167, 168, 169, 170, 171, 172, 173, 174, 175, *176, 177,* 297, 315, *324,* 383, *397*
Malmstrom, E. J., 234, 246, *261,* 262
Maltzman, I., 304, 308, *323, 324*
Mandler, G., 19, *20,* 40, 45, *62,* 217, *224,* 264, 265, 266, 268, 272, 275, 277, 278, 280, 281, 282, 285, *287,* 309, *324, 325,* 362, 367, *397, 398*
Marañon, G., 195, 214, *224*
Martin, B., 8, 14, *20,* 235, *262*
Martin, Irene, 162, *177*
Martin, R. B., 354, *359*
Mason, J. W., 132, *140*
Masserman, J. H., 5, *20,* 180, 183, *190*
Matarazzo, J. D., 301, *325*
Mathews, Anne, 345, *360*
May, R., 4, 5, 8, 9, 11, *20,* 107, *125*
Mayzner, M. S., 373, *397*
Mednick, Martha T., 295, *325*
Mednick, S. A., 307, *325*
Meehl, P. E., 153, *155,* 298, *323*
Mefferd, R. B., 32, 37, *61*
Meredith, G. M., 25, *60*
Merrill, R. M., 355, *360*
Metzner, R., 285, *287*
Miller, J., 132, *141*

Miller, J. G., 37, *62*
Miller, G. A., 149, *155*, 264, *287*
Miller, N. E., 5, 8, *19, 20*, 188, *190*, 293, 294, *325*, 351, 353, *358*, 363, *396*
Mirsky, I. A., 32, *62*, 131, 134, *142*
Mischel, W., 285, *287*
Mitchell, J. V., 25, *62*
Montague, E. K., 301, 309, 310, *325*, 366, 382, 383, *397*
Moran, L. J., 32, 37, *61*
Mordkoff, A. M., 231, 232, 234, 237, 238, 240, 242, 244, 246, 252, 255, 257, *261, 262*, 284, *287*
Morrisett, L., Jr., 304, *324*
Moruzzi, G., 158, *177*
Mowrer, O. H., 5, 8, 10, 11, *20*, 43, 54, *62*, 144, 147, 148, 149, 151, 152, 154, *155, 156*, 271, *287*, 293, *325*
Moyer, K. E., 216, *224*
Murray, E. J., 356, *360*

N

Nagler, S., 82, 88, *124*
Napalkov, A. V., 183, *190*
Nesselroade, J. R., 35, 36, *62*
Nicholson, W. M., 310, 314, *325*
Nomikos, M. S., 246, 248, 253, *261, 262*
Norman, W. T., 28, *62*
Nowlis, Helen H., 274, *287*
Nowlis, V., 274, *287*
Nunn, R., 132, *141*
Nunnally, J. C., 132, *141*
Nuttall, R., 25, *60*

O

O'Flaherty, J. J., 174, *176*
Oken, D., 137, 138, *140, 141, 142*
Opton, E. M., Jr., 234, 246, 248, 251, 252, 253, *261, 262*
Osborn, Janet, 232, *262*
Osgood, C. E., 149, *156*, 180, *190*
Osler, Sonia F., 8, *20*, 310, *324*, 346, *360*

P

Palermo, D. S., 7, *19*, 303, *323*
Palola, E. G., 311, 312, 314, *325*
Parsons, O. A., 346, *357*
Paterson, A. L., 307, *323*

Paul, G. L., 189, *190*
Pavlov, I. P., 5, *20*, 180, *190*
Pawlik, K., 29, *61*
Penfield, W., 158, *177*
Persky, H., 8, 13, 14, *19*, 32, *62*, 132, 134, 135, 136, 137, *140, 141, 142*, 256, 262
Pichot, P., 28, *60*
Pierson, G. R., 41, *62*
Pinneo, L. R., 317, *325*
Pool, K. B., 25, 53, *61*
Porter, R., 25, *62*
Postman, L., 331, 332, *358*
Pribram, K. H., 149, *155*, 264, *287*

Q

Quinn, R., 283, *288*

R

Radcliffe, J. A., 49, 55, 58, *60*
Ramond, C. K., 303, *325*
Randall, D., 82, 88, *124*
Rankin, N. O., 234, 246, 248, 253, *261*, 262
Rasmussen, T., 158, *177*
Raven, B. H., 283, *287*
Rechtschaffen, A., 317, *326*
Reis, E. C., 194, 196, *224*
Rennes, P., 28, *60*
Reymert, M. L., 107, *125*
Rickels, K., 32, 41, 43, *60, 61, 62*
Riecken, H. W., 356, *360*
Riess, W. F., 242, 243, *262*
Rietsema, J., 283, *287*
Robbins, F. B., 139, *141*
Rodnick, E. H., 383, *397*
Rosenzweig, M. R., 33, *59*
Rosenzweig, S., 335, 339, *360*
Ross, L. E., 297, *325*
Ross, S., 311, 312, 320, *324*
Rotter, J. B., 285, *287*
Royce, J. R., 37, *62*
Ruckmick, C. A., 194, *224*
Ruebush, B. K., 8, *20*, 64, 67, 70, 74, *79*
Runquist, W. H., 297, *325*

S

Sabshin, M. A., 132, 135, 136, 137, 138, *140, 141, 142*, 256, *261, 262*

Saltz, E., 306, *325*
Sanderson, R. E., 183, 188, *189*
Sarason, I. G., 8, *20*, 275, 278, *287*, 310, 311, 312, 314, *325*, 373, 385, *398*
Sarason, S. B., 8, 19, *20*, 40, 45, *62*, 64, 66, 67, 70, 72, 74, 75, *79*, 272, 275, 278, *287*, 309, *324*, 339, *360*, 362, 367, *397, 398*
Saslow, G., 301, *325*
Schachter, J., 214, *224*
Schachter, S., 14, *20*, 194, 196, 197, 200, 205, 209, 213, 221, *224*, 265, *287*
Schaie, K. W., 25, 28, *62*
Scheier, I. H., 7, 8, 13, 15, *19*, 24, 25, 32, 33, 35, 36, 37, 38, 40, 41, 43, 44, 45, 57, *61, 62*
Schlosberg, H., 194, *224*
Schnore, M. M., 299, *235*
Schoeck, H., 144, *156*
Schwartz, B. J., 227, *262*
Schwartz, N. B., 137, 138, *142*
Scott, W. A., *282, 287*
Sealy, A. P., 43, 45, 47, 52, 55, *61, 62*
Sears, R. R., 347, *360*
Seeman, M. R., 285, *287*
Seren, E., 373, *397*
Shagass, C., 157, 162, 166, 167, 168, 169, 170, 171, 172, 173, 174, 175, *176, 177*
Shannon, D. T., 345, 346, *360*
Sherrington, C. S., 216, *224*
Shipman, W. G., 138, *142*
Silverman, R. E., 320, *325*
Singer, J. E., 14, *20*, 198, 205, 212, 221, *224*, 265, *287*
Smart, R. G., 180, *190*
Smith, A. A., 169, 172, 173, *177*
Smith, L. H., 15, *20*, 384, 386, 387, *398*
Soliday, S., 217, *224*
Solomon, R. L., 217, 220, *224*, 347, *359*
Speisman, J. C., 227, 231, 232, 234, 238, 240, 241, 242, 244, 246, 252, 255, 257, *261, 262*, 284, *287*
Spence, Janet T., 317, *326*
Spence, K. W., 8, 15, 20, 45, *62*, 291, 294, 295, 297, 300, 301, 302, 303, 306, 307, 308, 317, *324, 325, 326*, 362, 363, 364, 365, 366, 373, 382, 383, 393, *397, 398*

Spiegel, J. P., 8, *19*, 32, 33, 61, 129, 135, *141, 142*
Spielberger, C. D., 15, 18, 19, *19, 20*, 353, *360*, 370, 371, 373, 376, 377, 378, 379, 381, 384, 386, 387, 392, *397, 398*
Sprague, J. L., 301, *324*
Standish, R. R., 302, 303, *326*
Stotland, E., 271, *287*
Strzelecki, Joanna, 307, *323*
Sullivan, H. S., 11, *20*
Sullivan, W. P., 41, *62*
Sweney, A. B., 45, 47, 49, 55, 58, *60, 62*
Swets, J. A., 350, *360*
Symonds, C. P., 182, *190*
Szasz, T. S., 150, *156*

T

Tanner, W. P., Jr., 350, *360*
Tatro, D., 41, *61*
Taylor, Elaine, 297, *326*
Taylor, Janet A., 7, 8, 15, *20*, 40, 45, *62*, 295, 296, 301, 302, 303, 306, 308, 312, 317, *326*, 362, 363, 364, 365, 366, 368, 382, *398*
Tempone, V. J., 345, 347, *360*
Thibaut, J. W., 356, *360*
Tinbergen, N., 103, *125*
Tollefson, D. L., 56, *62*
Toman, J. E. P., 138, *142*
Tomkins, S. S., 81, 85, 86, 87, 88, 93, 96, 97, 100, 102, 104, 105, 107, 109, 110, 111, 113, 117, 119, 120, 121, 122, *125*
Towne, J. C., 137, *141*
Tresselt, M. E., 373, *397*
Truax, C. B., 345, *360*
Tsujioka, B., 28, 45, 47, 54, *60, 62*
Tsushima, Y., 45, *62*

U

Uhr, L., 37, *62*
Ulett, G., 293, 301, *324, 325*, 368, *397*
Ullmann, L. P., 346, *360*

V

Van de Castle, R. L., 346, *360*
Viek, P., 271, *287*

W

Wadeson, R., 132, *140*
Waite, R. R., 8, *20,* 64, 67, 70, 74, *79*
Walker, R. E., 312, *326*
Wallach, M. A., 329, 344, 347, 355, *358*
Waller, H. J., 157, 158, 160, *176*
Warburton, F. W., 25, 28, *61*
Weakland, J., 284, *286, 288*
Wechsler, H., 349, *359*
Wehmer, G. M., 81, 82, 88, *124*
Weinstein, J., 251, 252, *262*
Weitz, H., 375, 381, 392, *398*
Welch, L., 292, *326*
Wenger, M. A., 37, *62,* 217, *224*
Wertheimer, M. A., 345, *360*
Wheeler, L., 209, *224*
White, R. W., 78, *79,* 84, *125,* 285, *288*
Wiener, M., 345, *358,* 368, *396*
Wiggins, J. W., 144, *156*
Willerman, B., 130, *141*
Williams, J. E., 370, *397*

Williams, R. J., 47, *62*
Wolf, S., 214, *224*
Wolff, H. G., 214, *224*
Wolpe, J., 183, 185, 186, 188, 189, *190*
Wood, C. G., 317, *326*
Woodworth, R. S., 194, *224*
Wrightsman, L. S., 200, *224*
Wurdt, W. M., 237, *262*
Wynne, L. C., 217, 220, *224*

Y

Yousem, H., 356, *359*

Z

Zajonic, R. B., 347, *360*
Zander, A., 283, *288*
Zeller, A. F., 355, *360*
Zimbardo, P. G., 64, 66, 67, *79*
Zimmermann, R. R., 101, *124*
Zubin, J., 4, 8, *19*

SUBJECT INDEX

A

Academic achievement, 361-362, 376-381
Acetylcholine, 33
Activation, *see also* Arousal
  definition, 157, 158
  stress reaction and, 234
Activation and performance, inverted U-function, 160
Activation theory, 157-161
Adaptation, 242-244
Adjective check lists, 236-237, *see also* Personality tests
Adrenal cortical hormones, 132, *see also* Epinephrine
Adrenal cortical steroids, 135-137
Adrenergic blocking, 210
Affective states, 9, 236-240
Affects, *see also* Anxiety, Fear, Drive, Motivation
  amplification, 90
  behavioral basis, 90-91
  characteristics, general, 88-89
  cognition and, 93-94
  density of, 95
  facial response and, 90-91
  freedom and, 96
  images and, 92-93
  intentions and, 92-93
  motivation and, 83-93
  neurological basis, 88-90
  personality and, 82-87
  primary, 116-123
    distress-anguish, 116-120
    enjoyment-joy, 114-115
    fear-terror, 116-117
    interest-excitement, 115-116
    shame-humiliation, 117-119
  relation to drives, 94-95
Affiliation, 193, 249
Aggression, *see* Anger, aggression

A.C.E. Psychological Examination, 373-381, 388
Anger, aggression, 137, 195, 219
  anxiety and, 356-357
  blood pressure and, 139
  experimental induction of, 201-202
  expression, factors affecting, 260
  fear and, 182
  self-ratings, 205
Anorexia nervosa, 95
Anxiety
  academic achievement and, 45-46, 361-362, 376-381
  adrenaline, induced by, 138
  age changes, 43-45, 64-69, 77-78
  as personality construct, 363
  breath holding and, 131
  characteristics and properties, 133-134
    acquired behavioral disposition, 16
    arousal, drive properties, 306, 363
    as affect, 99-104
    as negative affect, 81-125
    as signal, 131-133
    as unitary experience, 134
    obsessive thoughts, 279
    phenomenological qualitites, 9, 13
    psychiatric symptoms, 32, 40-42
  choice and, 271-280
  cognition and, 13-19, 47-49, 78, 327-357
  culture, relation to, 43-44
  defense and, 132, 138-139
  determinants, 263-286
    failure, 45, 278
    helplessness, 266
    novelty, 137, 307
    punishment, 10
    situational, 306-308, 394-395
    social and cultural, 282-283
    stimulus, 314-318
    stress, 14, 129-138

Freud's definition, 362-363
in everyday life, 3-4
in paratroop training, 134
intelligence and, 66-67, 75-76, 373-376
interruption of behavior, 263-286
learning, effects on
  aversive conditioning, 307
  classical conditioning, 45, 307
  complex learning, 367-396
  concept formation, 388-391
  salivary conditioning, 307
  serial position phenomena, 369-373,
    386-388
  serial rote learning, 162-165, 312-
    313, 381-388
measurement, 134-136, see also Anx-
    iety scales
  as second-order factor, 25-28
  introspective reports, 13-14
  quantitative ratings, 135-136
  questionnaires, 23-28
  self-ratings, 136
misbehavior and, 143-155
motivation and, 46
other personality variables and
  aggression, 18, 137
  dependency, 74
  depression, 132, 137
  emotion, 131, 307
  empathy, 11
  fear, 47, 132-133
  fear of failure, 19, 279, 307, 313
  persistance, 279
  social desirability, 31-32
physiological qualities and correlates,
    9, 13-14, 28-38, 130-131, 297-299
  as pattern of autonomic response,
    182
  defective regulatory mechanisms,
    165-174
  liver damage, 131
psychic nonbeing and, 149
psychosomatic aspects, 129-140
reduction of, 69
regression and, 30-31
research trends, 5-8
response interference and, 308-321
social comparison, 276, 278
success and, 278

task difficulty and, 304-306
task irrelevant responses and, 275-276
test performance
  anagrams, 311
  digit symbol substitution, 273-280,
    311
  in objective tests, 28-34
  misinterpretation of items, 372-373
  Rorschach, group responses, 131
  speed tasks, 314-315
  verbal coding, 311
threat and, 306-308
trait-state relation, 16-19, 34-38, 138
varieties of,
  bound, 12
  characterological, 13, 34
  chronic, 15, 132, 306-308
  free-floating, 12, 134
  moral, 11
  neurotic, 9-12, 134, 161
  objective, 9-11
  pathological, 157-176
  personality trait, 12, 15-19, 26, 133-
    134, 136
  source trait, 23-28
  transitory state, 12-19, 26, 34-38, 159
  unambiguous, 64-69
  unconscious, 12, 133
Anxiety theory
  Cattell, 46-58
  Freud, 9-11
  May, 11-12
  Mowrer, 11, 54
  Sullivan, 11
Anxiety-evoking cues, 327-357
Anxiety-inhibitors, 183-186
Anxiety neurosis, 5, 9, 12, 134, 167-171
Anxiety-proneness, 15-16, 133-134, 136
Anxiety and psychopathology, 38-43
Anxiety scales
  Children's Manifest Anxiety Scale, 7,
    303
  I.P.A.T. Anxiety Scale, 32, 36, 40-43
  limitations, 64-69
  Manifest Anxiety Scale, 7, 33, 291-322,
    364-393
  Test Anxiety Questionnaire, 272-280,
    311-312

Test Anxiety Scale for Children, 66, 71-72, 75-76
Welsh Anxiety Scale, 34
Arousal function, 158-160
Ascending reticular activating system (ARAS), 158
Assertive responses, 184
Atoxic sway suggestibility, 38
Autonomic blocking drugs, 209-212
Autonomic nervous system, 17, 36-38, see also Activation
    activation and, 234
    definition, 157-158
    drive stimuli and, 308
    emotion and, 194-198
    general factor, 37
    in Japanese subjects, 255-258
    interruption and, 280
    symptoms of discharge, 198
Autonomic nervous system reactions
    correspondence between measures, 233-234
    measurement of, 231-240

B

Basal metabolic rate, 33, 35, 37-38
Behavior therapy, 145-146, 148, 152, 182-189, see also Systematic desensitization
Bender Gestalt Designs, 370-373
Blood pressure, 13, 136, 139
    adrenaline, effects of, 198
    mirror-drawing test performance, 172-174
Brain-stem reticular system, 158-159
Breath holding, and anxiety, 131
Brightness discrimination, 267
Bulbar inhibitory system, 167

C

Capacity for choice, freedom, 147-152
Cardiac neurosis, 137
Castration anxiety, 105-107
Catharsis, 251
Cattell's dynamic structure, 23, 46-58
Child's Response Interference Hypothesis, 367
Children's Manifest Anxiety Scale, 7, 303
Chlorpromazine (Thorazine), 209-212

Classical conditioning, 45, 293-299, see also Eyelid conditioning
    aversive conditioning, 293-295
    Drive Theory and, 297
    GSR and, 295, 365
Classroom anxiety, 67
Claustrophobia, 182
Cognition
    affects and, 93-94
    anxiety and, 327-357
    emotion inducing, 200-208
    in labeling emotional states, 223
    marihuana, response to, 220-223
Cognitive appraisal, 18, 229
    defense mechanisms and, 244-254
Cognitive avoidance, see Repression
Cognitive processes, as activator of fear, 104-105
Cognitive sequences, see Plans
Cognitive style, 230
College Entrance Examination Boards, 388-391
Communication, and anxiety, 136
Competence, 285
Complex learning, 299-308, 363-393
Concept formation, 388-391
Conductance, see Galvanic skin responce, Palmer conductance
Conflict, 284
    experimental neurosis and, 180
    in sentence completion tests, 345
    interpersonal, 227
Conscience, 147
Coping processes, secondary appraisal, 229-231
Counseling, anxious college students, 381
Counterconditioning, to eliminate anxiety, 183-186
Creativity, and fear, 122-123
Cross-cultural research, and anxiety, 254-258
Cue function, 158

D

Deception experiments, 226
Deconditioning, neurotic anxiety, 182-189
Deep relaxation training, 185-186
Defense, concept of, 69-78
    against anxiety, 14-18, 138-139

against guilt, 152
aggression and, 331-334
in psychoanalytic theory, 328, 330
introspection and, 238
sexual responses and, 331-334
Defense mechanisms, 132, 347-357
cognitively constructed, 120-121
denial, 235, 238, 245, 253, 255-258
intellectualization, 238, 245, 250-258, 333-334
projection, 330
rating scales, 138
rationalization, 330
repression, 328
self-report-autonomic discrepancy, 237-240
Defensiveness Scale for Children (DSC), 70-71
Dejá vu experience, 195
Denial, 238, 253
in Japanese subjects, 255-258
MMPI measures, 235
stress reduction and, 245
Depression, 132, 137
Determinism, 148, 150
Distress
anxiety and, 266-267
as negative affect, 119-120
Drive (D), 49-50, 85-86, 363-365
as activator of fear, 103-104
emotionally based, 293-295
heart rate and, 161
intensity of noxious stimulation, 292-295
of Su, 294
learning and
maze learning, 300-301
paired-associate learning, 301-303
serial learning, 300-301
muscle potential and, 161
pain, relation to, 86
reduction, 84
task complexity (difficulty), 304-306
Drive stimuli (S_D), 292, 308-310

E

Effort-stress, 33-38
Ego-defense, 227, see also Defense mechanisms

Ego functions, and anxiety, 131
Ego-involving instructions, 310-312
Ego strength, 53
Electric shock
anticipation of pain and, 239-240
anxiety and, 18, 329
associative connections, effects on, 351-352
in experimental neurosis, 180-181
instrumental behavior and, 271
learning, effects on
paired-associate learning, 319-320, 344
serial verbal learning, 320-321
unconditioned stimulus, 297
Electroencephalograph (EEG), and ARAS discharge, 157-160
Electromyogram (EMG), 166-167
Emotion, 107, 131
bodily states and, 194
cognitive determinants, 194-223
in paraplegics and quadriplegics, 217-220
manipulated, during motion pictures, 210-212
physiological arousal, 208-212
physiological differences, 214-216
self-ratings, 203-208
situational determinants, 196-223
social determinants, 200-208
sympathectomy, effects on, 216-220
Emotional responsiveness (r_e)
drive (D) and, 293-295, 364
GSR and, 297
in rats, 212
manipulation by instructions, 296
muscle action potential and, 297
pulse rate and, 297
Emotional stability, 138
Empathy, 11
Eosinophils, 33
Ephedrine, 196
Epinephrine (adrenaline), 137
emotionality in humans, 195-223
in rats, 212-214
Euphoria, experimental induction, 200-201
Evaluative needs, 196

Excitatory potential (E)
  competing responses and, 300
  in Hull's learning theory, 293, 363-365
Existential vacuum, 149
Experimental neurosis, 5, 179-181
Eyelid conditioning, *see also* Classical
    conditioning
  anxiety and, 295-297, 309
  descending reticular system, 159
  GSR and, 175, 297
  muscle action potential, 297
  puff intensity, 295
  pulse rate and, 297

F

Failure
  effects of
    on memory, 335-337
    on perception, 335-337
    on performance, 312-313
    on recognition threshold, 342-343
    on serial learning, 312-313
  fear of, and anxiety, 279, 307, 313
  interruption, relation to, 276
Fear
  activation of, 102-107
  adrenaline injection, effects, 213-214
  anger and, 182, 214
  as acquired drive, 293
  cognition and, 108
  conflict and, 108
  creativity and, 122-123
  determinants, 99-107
  excitement and, 122
  hypnotically induced, 104, 107-108
  individuation and, 119
  innate releasors, 103
  of crowds, 182
  of public speaking, 182
  other affects, relation to, 119-123
  phenomenology, 107-108
  positive affects, relation to, 122-123
  shame and, 121
  socialization, 108-113
  trends in research, 6-7
Fear erg, 50-51, 56
Finger movements
  age and, 174
  response to pain stimulation, 175
    to thermal stimulation, 168-171

stress and, 174
Flicker fusion, 38
Frustration, 267
Frustration tolerance, 285

G

Galvanic skin response (GSR), 33, 35,
    37-38
  adjective check lists and, 237
  anxiety and choice, 271
  as measure of anxiety, 174-176, 329
  classical conditioning, 365
  emotionality and, 297
  eyelid conditioning and, 175
  motion picture films, response to, 231-
    234, 241-242, 247
  pain, reaction to, 175
Glucose concentration, 38
Grinker's EMB index, 138
Guilt, 144-152, 280-282

H

Habit strength (H), 293
Hardy-Wolff thermal pain apparatus, 168-
    171
Heart rate, 33, 35, 136
  adjective check lists, relation to, 237
  adrenaline, effects, 198
  age and, 174
  chlorpromazine, effects, 210
  in infants, 140
  mirror-drawing test, performance, 172-
    174
  motion picture films, response to, 231-
    234, 241-242, 247
  motivation (drive) and, 161
  "peak-rate" sampling, 234
  stress and, 174
Helplessness, and anxiety, 266-280
High School Personality Questionnaire
    (HSPQ), 25
Hippuric acid, 133-135
Histidine, 33
Homeostasis, 83-85
Hull-Spence behavior theory, 291, 362-
    364
Human maze learning, 365-367
Hypertension, 137-139
Hypothalamus, 159-160, 210
Hysterical personality, 339

I

Iatrogenic personality disorder, 144
Identification, 226, 250-254
Identity crisis, 147-152
Image, definition, 105
Incidental learning, 368-373
Inner fantasy, 138
Insight therapy, 189
IPAT Anxiety Scale, 32, 36, 40-43
Instrumental behavior, 148
Intellectualization, 238, 250-258, 333-334
  identification and, 250-251
  in Japanese subjects, 255-258
  stress reduction and, 245
Intelligence, and anxiety, 373-376
Interpersonal conflict, 227
Interpersonal threat, 250-254
Interruption of behavior
  arousal and, 265
  effects, 263-286
  failure and, 276
  substitute responses, availability, 268-271
  verbal sequences, 268
Introversion-extroversion, 25-27, 339

J

James-Lange Theory of Emotion, 91, 193-194, 197
  Cannon's critique, 194, 214-220
Joy, 114-115, 195

L

Law of initial values, 137
Lazarus' Theory of Psychological Stress, 228-231
Learning, 95, 291-322, 361-395, see also Paired-associate learning, Serial verbal learning
Learning theory, and psychopathology, 143-144
Learning without awareness, 353-354
Leaving field, 227
Lie Scale for Children, 70-71, 75-76
Limbic system, and cardiovascular activity, 174
Liver functions, and anxiety, 134
Locus of control, 286
Love, 154

M

McReynolds Concept Choice Test, 339-340
Macy Conference, 130
Mandler's Interruption Theory, 264-266
Manifest Anxiety Scale (MAS), 291-322, 364-393
  academic achievement and, 376-381
  chronic and reactive hypotheses, 364-365, 385-386, 393
  clinical anxiety, relation to, 292-294
  complex learning and, 299-308
  concept formation and, 388-391
  development, 294-295
  emotionally based drive and, 291-293, 368
  item selection, 294-295
  measure of emotional responsiveness, 293-295
  other anxiety scales, relation to, 7, 33
  state-anxiety threshold, 314
  validity, 298, 368
Marihauna, 220-223
Maze learning, and drive, 300-301
Mediating processes, 149
Memory, see also Recall
  effects of anxiety, 369-373
  tests
    Wechsler Digit Span Test, 369
    Wechsler Memory Scale, 369
Migraine, 139
Minnesota Multiphasic Personality Inventory (MMPI), 235, 295, 339-342, 346
Mood adjective check list, 236, see also Adjective check lists
Moral fear, see Guilt, Moral anxiety
Motion pictures, as sources of threat, 225-228
Motivation, see also Affect, Anxiety, Drive
  aversive, 291-293
  inverted U-function, 315-317
  performance, relation to, 315-319
Motivational subsystems, 85-87
Muscle potential
  emotionality and, 297
  motivation (drive) and, 161

Muscle tension
  defense and, 138-139
  tracking, relation to, 317

N

Negative transfer, 303
Neurasthenia, 5
Neurosis
  anticipation of fear, 121
  as learned behavior, 180-182
  conditioning and, 179-189
  defective regulatory control, 159
  in animals, 5, 179-181
  irresponsible behavior, 146-149
  personal responsibility and, 145-147
  repression and, 179
  sin and, 152-154
Neurotic anxiety, 134, 179-189, see also
    Anxiety, Guilt
  deconditioning, 182-189
  factors affecting, 186-188
Neuroticism, 29, 339
Neuroticism Scale Questionnaire, 40
Neutrophils, 33, 35
Norepinephrine, 137
Noxious stimulation, 319-321

O

Obesity, 223
Objective Analytic (O-A) Battery, 34, 42
Obsessive thoughts, and anxiety, 279
Oedipus complex, 105-107
Organized behavior, 264-265
Oscillatory inhibition (O), 364

P

Paired-associate learning
  drive and, 301-306
  ego-involving instructions, 310-311
  electric shock, 319-321, 344
  failure effects, 337
  repressor-sensitizer variable, 345
  response competition, 365-366
Palmer conductance, 174-176
Panic states, 134
Paranoid schizophrenia, 121, see also
    Schizophrenia
Penis envy, 106-107
Peptic ulcer, 139
Perception, 349-351

Perceptual defense
  unconscious discrimination and, 349
  vigilance and, 332-339
Persistence, 279
Personality tests, see also Anxiety scales
  adjective check lists, 236-237
  MMPI, 235, 295, 339-342, 346
  Neuroticism Scale Questionnaire, 40
  Objective-Analytic (O-A) Battery, 34,
    42
  Rorschach Inkblots, 331
  sentence completion tests, 345
  16 P.F. Test, 24-28, 38-41, 51-57
  Thematic Apperception Test, 331-333
  word association test, 331
Personality traits, 138
Phenylalanine, 33
Phenylhydracrylic acid, 33
Phobia
  generalization and, 182
  research trends, 6
  resistance to extinction, 183
  symptom of anxiety, 32
Physiological response patterns, 139-140
Plans
  behavior and, 264-265
  skill instructions and, 276-278
Pride, 339
Primal scene, 106-107
Projection, 330
Projective tests, see Personality tests
Psychasthenia
  recognition thresholds and, 345
  repressor-sensitizer variable, 339-342
Psychogalvanic response, see Galvanic
    skin response
Psychological defenses, see Defense, con-
    cept of, Defense mechanism
Psychological stress, see Stress, Stress re-
    actions
Psychomotor rigidity, 138-139
Psychoneurosis, see Neurosis, Psycho-
    somatic disorders
Psychopathology, see also Neurosis, Psy-
    chosis, Psychosomatic disorders
  basis of, 143-147
  learning theory and, 143-144
  misconduct (malbehavior) and, 144-
    147

Psychosis, 149, *see also* Schizophrenia
Psychosomatic disorders, *see also* specific disorders
  etiology of, 139-140
  research on, 139-140
Pulse pressure, 33, 35, *see also* Blood pressure
Pulse rate, and emotionality, 207, 297, *see also* Heart rate

Q

Questionnaires, *see* Anxiety scales, Personality tests

R

Rationalization, 330
Reactive inhibition, 188
Recall, 369-373, *see also* Memory
Reflexology, 148-149
Repression, 328-357
Repressors, 334-357
Respiration rate, 13, 33, 35
  adrenaline, effects, 198
  in motion picture films, 233
  thermal stimulation effects, 168, 171
Response Interference Hypothesis, 308-310
Response specificity, 139-140, 233
Response suppression, 347
Response threshold (L), 364
Reward, 97
Rheumatoid arthritis, 139
Rorschach Inkblots, 331

S

Schachter's Theory of Emotion, 197, 265
Schizophrenia
  anxiety and, 284
  catatonic states, 135
  paranoid schizophrenia, 121
Self-fear, 120
Self-report ratings, 236-237, *see also* Adjective check lists
Sensitizers, 334-357
Sentence completion tests, 345
Separation anxiety, 77-78
Serial position effects
  in serial verbal learning, 386-388
  on memory task, 369-373

Serial verbal (rote) learning
  anxiety and, 381-388
  competing response tendencies, 365-366
  drive (D) and, 300-301
  failure effects, 312-313
  "impact effect," 164
  intraserial interference, 164-165
  performance, anxious patients, 162-164
  serial position, 386-388
Serum cholinesterase, 33, 35, 37
17-OH ketosteroids, 33, 35
Sexual responses, 184-185
Shame
  as major affect, 91
  fear and, 121
Sin, 152-155
16 P.F. Test, 24-28, 38-41, 51-57
Skill instructions, 276-277
Social (interpersonal) threat, 227-228, *see also* Threat
Socialization, 98
Spence's Drive Theory
  classical conditioning and, 293-299
  complex learning and, 299-308; 363-393
    experimental evidence, 300-308
    theoretical predictions, 299-300
Startle reflex, 100-102, 165-167
Stimulus intensity, 317
S-R connectionism, 148
Stimulus specificity, 233
Stress
  ego involving instructions and, 310-312
  emotional responsiveness and, 306-308
  "end phenomenon," 130
  failure experience and, 312-313
  learning, effects on, 309-322
  manipulated experimentally, 292
  multidimensional concept, 235-236
  perceptual efficiency, 130
  performance and, 129-130
  produced by motion picture films, 225-260
  psychodynamics, 240-243
  psychophysiology, 231-240
  state anxiety and, 306-308
Stress reactions
  anticipation, effects, 254
  homosexual fantasies and, 241

individual differences, 140
physiological reactions, 226
Stress tolerance, 131
Sublimation, 97
Suicidal risk, 132
Symbolic experience, 98
Sympathectomy, 216-220
Sympathetic nervous system, 135, 198,
    see also Autonomic nervous system
Systematic desensitization, 185-189, see
    also Behavior therapy
therapeutic results, 189

T

Tachistoscopic recognition
    in study of repression, 330-337
    viewed as guessing task, 350
Task difficulty, 304-306
Taylor Scale, see Manifest Anxiety Scale
Test Anxiety Questionnaire (TAQ), 272-
    280, 311-312
Test Anxiety Scale for Children (TASC),
    66, 71-72, 75-76
Thematic Apperception Test (TAT), 331-
    333
Therapeutic results, 188-189
Threat
    as intervening variable, 229

autonomic arousal, level of, 247-249
deception and, 225-226
Trait anxiety, 15-19, see also Anxiety,
    Anxiety scales

U

Ulcerative colitis, 139
Unconditioned stimulus
    electric shock, 293, 297
    intensity, 294
Unconscious learning, 352-354
Unconscious mind, 348-349

V

Verbal coding, 311
Verbal conditioning, 353
Vicarious threat, 226

W

Wechsler-Bellevue subtests
    Digit Span, 369
    Digit Symbol, 273-280, 311
Wechsler Memory Scale, 369
Welsh Anxiety Scale, 34
Word association test, 331

Y

Y-Maze learning, 267-271

85
06\05 38
44095
BUI